# Migrating to Swift from Flash and ActionScript

Radoslava Leseva Adams
Hristo Lesev

Apress®

*Migrating to Swift from Flash and ActionScript*

Radoslava Leseva Adams
London, United Kingdom

Hristo Lesev
Kazanlak, Bulgaria

ISBN-13 (pbk): 978-1-4842-1667-5
DOI 10.1007/978-1-4842-1666-8

ISBN-13 (electronic): 978-1-4842-1666-8

Library of Congress Control Number: 2016955434

Managing Director: Welmoed Spahr
Acquisitions Editor: Louise Corrigan
Development Editor: Chris Nelson
Technical Reviewer: Robert Otani
Editorial Board: Steve Anglin, Pramila Balen, Aaron Black, Laura Berendson, Louise Corrigan, Jonathan Gennick, Todd Green, Robert Hutchinson, Celestin Suresh John, Nikhil Karkal, James Markham, Susan McDermott, Matthew Moodie, Natalie Pao, Gwenan Spearing
Coordinating Editor: Nancy Chen
Copy Editor: Lori Jacobs
Compositor: SPi Global
Indexer: SPi Global

Distributed to the book trade worldwide by Springer Science+Business Media New York, 233 Spring Street, 6th Floor, New York, NY 10013. Phone 1-800-SPRINGER, fax (201) 348-4505, e-mail orders-ny@springer-sbm.com, or visit www.springer.com. Apress Media, LLC is a California LLC and the sole member (owner) is Springer Science + Business Media Finance Inc (SSBM Finance Inc). SSBM Finance Inc is a Delaware corporation.

For information on translations, please e-mail rights@apress.com, or visit www.apress.com.

Apress and friends of ED books may be purchased in bulk for academic, corporate, or promotional use. eBook versions and licenses are also available for most titles. For more information, reference our Special Bulk Sales–eBook Licensing web page at www.apress.com/bulk-sales.

Any source code or other supplementary materials referenced by the author in this text is available to readers at www.apress.com. For detailed information about how to locate your book's source code, go to www.apress.com/source-code/.

Printed on acid-free paper

*Radoslava: To Sophia, who was born with the early chapters of this book, and to Steve for the many hats he wears.*

*Hristo: To Dani for her endless support, Radoslava for her patience when I was behind schedule, and the strong black coffee that kept my engine running . . . and to MS Word for the constant crashes, which taught me to make backups.*

*Hristo and Radoslava: In loving memory of our dad, Iliyan Lesev, who first sparked our interest in computers.*

# Contents at a Glance

# Contents

Contents

# About the Authors

**Radoslava Leseva Adams** is a software developer and programming book author. Her affair with programming languages began in the early 1990s, when her father handed her a book on Basic as a form of summer holiday entertainment. Since then she has built a career out of freely jumping between different languages and platforms, including C, C++, Delphi, Java, ActionScript, Objective-C, and most recently Swift. She passionately hates wordy manuals and having to click more than once to do a build. Radoslava and her brother Hristo run EasyNativeExtensions.com and DiaDraw.com, where they help ActionScript developers do cross-platform programming with AIR Native Extensions.

**Dr. Hristo Lesev** is a software developer at heart, passionate speaker, educator, and entrepreneur. Having had long experience with C++, C#, and ActionScript for desktop and mobile platforms, lately he can be heard more and more often advocating for Swift as the latest and greatest. When not busy developing mobile apps, Hristo enjoys teaching other developers as an assistant professor at Plovdiv University, Bulgaria. He is obsessed with computer graphics and can often be found coding 3D stuff late at night.

# About the Technical Reviewer

**Robert Otani** grew up in Los Angeles helping to repair cars in the family business, where got away with playing with welding torches and dangerous chemicals. He earned a B.S. in Physics from California State Polytechnic University and then entered the Ph.D. program at Arizona State University. He dropped out to pursue fortunes in the San Francisco Bay Area during the great Internet boom. Since then, he's worked as a designer and engineer for Sony Entertainment, Vitria, AvantGo (acquired by Sybase/SAP), Yahoo!, and virtual world startup IMVU. Most recently, he was iOS Lead at Mix.com (an Expa portfolio company) and is now an Engineering Lead for a yet-to-be named brand out of Silicon Valley. He's married to an amazing wife, with whom he's raising two children and a strange dog. He plans to update his site, otanistudio.com, sometime within the next decade.

# Acknowledgments

Deciding to write a book while running a business full time and with one of us eight months pregnant was what a lot of our friends politely called "adventurous." They were right; working on this book was an adventure. We are indebted to our families for their support throughout this project and especially to Radoslava's husband, Steve, for reading all chapter drafts and offering helpful advice while being on full-time dad duty every weekend.

This project would not have been possible without the hard work of the Apress editorial team. We would like to thank Steve Anglin for the idea for this book and Ben Renow Clarke and Nancy Chen for keeping us on track.

Special thanks go to Robert Otani and Chris Nelson. Robert's constructive input ensured technical accuracy and helped us stay ahead of changes in the rapidly evolving language that is Swift and Chris burned the midnight oil to help us improve the text.

Some of our most indispensable resources have been Apple's book *The Swift Programming Language* (`https://goo.gl/1GRVRM`) and the online project "Swift Programming Language Evolution" (`https://github.com/apple/swift-evolution`).

Last, but not least, we are grateful to all contributors on `stackoverflow.com` who tirelessly shine light in the darker corners of Swift and Xcode.

# Introduction

The Swift programming language has eased the learning curve for iOS development, compared with the early days when one had to become familiar with Objective-C. A lot of the Swift philosophy and syntax will be familiar to an ActionScript developer and will allow a rapid transition. This book offers the quickest way not just to learn a new programming language but also to migrate your whole workflow to a new platform.

## Who Is This Book For?

*Migrating to Swift from Flash and ActionScript* is for developers who are transitioning to Swift for iOS. In particular, it has been written with the Adobe AIR community in mind to help bridge the gap between ActionScript and Swift for mobile devices.

You do not need background in ActionScript in order to benefit from this book, however. Basic experience with any object-oriented language would ensure that you adapt to Swift in no time.

Personally we tend to learn much quicker by following screenshots and diagrams and getting our hands dirty with code, rather than from reading pages and pages of text. So we have prepared examples and tutorials for you to do the same.

## How to Use This Book

There is a lot to learn when you migrate your development process to a new platform: besides a new language, you have to become familiar with new tools and a new operating system, change your workflow, and learn what the best practices are in specific situations. This book is really four books in one, each part addressing an aspect of the migration process.

You don't need to read the material from cover to cover before you start coding with Swift. When you set your teeth into making native apps, we want this book to be your companion and provide guidance by walking you through a tutorial or two or by being a quick reference.

The book shows you how to make 16 different apps. Each chapter in the first three parts of the book offers a self-contained tutorial, so you are not dependent on having read and implemented the tutorials that come before it. The chapters on debugging and releasing your app are an exception and use code you have written in previous chapters.

Here is how the book is organized:

- **Part I: Tool Migration**. We recommend that you start here and go through the four chapters of **Part I** in order. We have intentionally kept this part brief. It will help you configure your environment and development devices, so that you are on your way to making your first app with Swift.

- **Part II: Workflow Migration**. This part walks you through the main parts of the programming workflow and shows you how to structure your user interface and use Xcode's help with layout, how to take advantage of concurrency, and how to use the debugger and automated testing tools. Apart from **Chapter 8**, which builds on the example of the preceding chapter to demonstrate debugging and testing techniques, each of the rest of the chapters comes with its own example. This means that you can go through this part in the order you find you need each topic as you migrate your workflow. Where there are new Swift concepts in the examples we have included pointers to the language reference part of this book, **Part IV**, so you can quickly find details on syntax or language idioms.

- **Part III: Making Apps with Swift—Applied Examples**. This is probably the most fun part of the book. It offers a series of tutorials that cover a lot of common scenarios you may want to include in your apps. Here you build 12 self-contained practical apps and learn how to

  - send e-mail, SMS, and make phone calls from your application.

  - post to social networks.

  - use the motion sensors and show a user's location on a map.

  - take photos, manipulate them, and communicate with the photo gallery.

  - work with local data and iCloud.

  - connect to and communicate with network services.

  - monetize your apps with advertisements and stay in touch with your users through push notifications.

  - build 2D and 3D games with iOS SDK's graphics frameworks.

- **Part IV: Language Migration**. This part was the most fun for us to write. In it we have tried to distill the main ideas that underpin the Swift programming language: it encourages you to be concise and at the same time forces you to be explicit and take maximum advantage of the compiler in order to ensure correct code. This is not meant to be a comprehensive Swift manual but to help you hit the ground running when it comes to language specifics. We recommend that you read the introductory **Chapter 17** first and then use the rest as a reference, which you can come back to whenever you need a Swift concept explained. There are no apps to build in this part of the book. Instead, we help you set up a Swift playground, where you can experiment with individual pieces of code. We have tried to make the explanations of the language concepts simple, so that our baba Ani can understand them too.[1]

---

[1]Baba (Bulgarian for "grandmother") Ani doesn't have ActionScript experience and is not even a programmer. She is one smart cookie, though.

- **Bonus Chapter: Publishing your app in the app store.** The point of making an app is to share it with the world and allow millions of users to enjoy your creation. Apple's process for releasing apps in the App Store, however, is far from intuitive. We thought that a book that that shows you how to create apps for iOS devices would not be complete without a walk through this process and some tips on how to keep it as smooth as possible.

# A Note on Swift Versions

To say that Swift evolves quickly would be an understatement. A lot has changed in the language itself and in the iOS SDK since the first version of Swift was released in 2014. The examples in this book are consistent with version 2.2, which is the state of the art as we are finishing the last chapter. However, with Swift 3 just around the corner, we want you to be ahead of the wave of changes, so we have added notes and extra examples where code will be affected.

Note that some of the application programming interfaces (APIs) in the iOS SDK may be renamed when Swift 3 is released. We maintain a list of changes and source code for download for each of the tutorials in this book at www.apress.com/9781484216675. If you would like to be notified when updates are made, we encourage you to join our mailing list at http://diadraw.com/migrating-swift-flash-actionscript/.

Now let us get on with some work, shall we? We will see you in **Chapter 1**.

**PART I**

# Tool Migration

# CHAPTER 1

■ ■ ■

# Setting Up Your Environment

Imagine a craftsman's workbench with tools nicely laid out and labeled, a cup of steaming coffee at one end … ideally the kind of image that gives you an itch to start a fresh project you can pour your heart into. This chapter is all about setting up that workbench by sourcing, installing, and configuring the tools that you will need for native iOS development.

In this chapter you will do the following:

- Learn about what Xcode can offer you as an iOS developer.

- Download and install Xcode.

- Set up Xcode for use with your Apple ID.

When you are done, you will have a fully set up IDE for developing iOS applications with Swift.

## What Is Xcode?

Xcode is an integrated development environment (IDE). It is free and is developed by Apple. With it comes the development toolset for making apps for Apple devices: Mac, iPhone, iPod, iPad, Apple Watch, Apple TV.

---

### FLASH ANALOGY

You have probably used one or more of the following IDEs to create Flash or AIR applications. They come with a source code editor, user interface editor, and integrated debugger and some even have a profiler, which you can use to measure your apps' performance.

- Adobe Flash Professional CC

- Adobe Flash Builder

- FlashDevelop

---

**Electronic supplementary material**  The online version of this chapter (doi:10.1007/978-1-4842-1666-8_1) contains supplementary material, which is available to authorized users.

Xcode provides the usual features you would expect from an IDE and more. If you have developed iOS applications with AIR, you will find that Xcode improves and speeds up your workflow considerably. It offers all the tools you will need along the way: from rapid prototyping using Swift Playgrounds, through managing devices and debugging your app on them, to automated testing and even submitting your finished app to Apple's App Store. Xcode's profiling instruments could have a whole new book dedicated to them and will leave no doubt about your apps' performance by measuring speed, memory, energy and network usage, GPU and CPU utilization, file activity and lots more.

## Before You Begin

To download, install, and run Xcode you will need the following:

- An **Apple ID**. If you don't have one, you can register at `https://appleid.apple.com/account`. This ID identifies you as an Apple user, just like an Adobe ID identifies you as an Adobe user. It will stand you in good stead for developing and testing simple apps and you won't need to enroll in any paid development program until you decide to use advanced SDK features or to publish your apps in the App Store— more on that in **Chapter 2**.

- A **Mac computer**. At the time of this writing Xcode 7.3 is the current release and requires that you run OS X 10.11 or later.

- At least **10 GB of free space** on your hard disk.

## Step 1: Download Xcode

You have several choices for how to get Xcode, depending on whether you want an official release or a pre-release version. When new versions of Apple software are made available, they typically go through three stages: beta, seed, and official release. The main differences between versions in different stages are how stable they are, who can use a given version, and whether it can be used to build apps for release in Apple's App Store.

- **Beta**. This is a pre-release version, which is still under development and is available for download to anyone who has an Apple ID. Using a beta version puts you ahead of changes, as it allows you to update and test your apps with the latest tools and SDKs before they are officially available. There are a couple of drawbacks, however. Although they are close to the final thing, beta versions are by definition not as polished as official releases, so you may encounter bugs or inconsistencies. Another drawback is that apps that were built using beta tools are not accepted in Apple's App Store: to be able to release your app in the store, you will need to use either an official Xcode and iOS SDK release or a GM seed (see the next bullet).

- **Seed**. A seed version also comes out before the official release but, unlike a beta, is available only to participants in Apple's testing and feedback program, *AppleSeed*. Taking part in the program is voluntary and by invitation only. As a participant you are in effect taking part in shaping Apple's software, so you are expected to give active feedback. In fact, failure to do so may get you excluded from the program. Similarly to betas, you cannot release an app built with a seed, unless it has been labeled Gold Master (GM).

- **Official release**. An official release is made after Apple's new or updated development tools have undergone rigorous testing and customer feedback as betas and as seeds, so you can expect it to be as stable and as polished as it gets. The release version is the one you are expected to build your apps with before you release them in Apple's App Store. Note that to publish your apps in the store you will need to be a member of the Apple Developer Program, which requires paid membership.

We will go through the steps for obtaining an official Xcode release and a beta.

## Option A: Get the Official Release

If you want to build apps for the app store, you will need the latest official version of Xcode and the iOS SDK. Open the **Store** app on your Mac and do a search for Xcode. Then click **Install** (Figure 1-1). This will take care of the download and the installation in one go.

*Figure 1-1.* *Option 1: Download Xcode from Apple's App Store*

## Option B: Get the Latest Beta

If the timeline for releasing your app is further in the future, you might prefer an even newer version of Xcode with the latest additions to Apple's SDKs, You can go for an early beta, usually available from Apple's web site at `https://developer.apple.com/xcode/download/` (Figure 1-2). This will download a `.dmg` file, which you can double-click to start the installation.

*Figure 1-2.* *Option 2: Download an Xcode beta from Apple's web site*

# Step 2: Run Xcode

Now that you have downloaded and installed Xcode, let us run it and see what it looks like out of the box. We will also lift the curtain a bit and have a look at where the SDK files are, as well as other locations that will come in handy when you start developing apps.

## Running Xcode for the First Time

The very first thing you see when you run Xcode after its installation is a **License Agreement**, which starts with the preemptive "Please scroll down and read all of the following terms and conditions carefully. . ." (Figure 1-3).

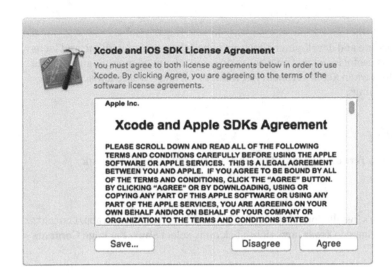

***Figure 1-3.*** *You need to agree with Xcode's License Agreement before you can use it*

After scrolling down, reading carefully for about a whole of five lines, then clicking **Agree** anyway, Xcode's welcome screen appears (Figure 1-4). If you are anxious to begin development, jump straight to **Chapter 2**, which shows you how to make and run your first iOS application.

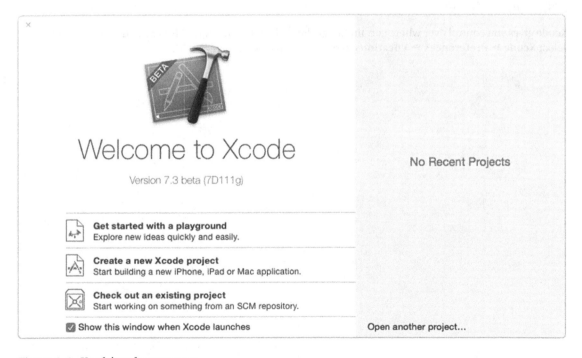

***Figure 1-4.*** *Xcode's welcome screen*

# Where Does It All Go?

If you like to be in control of your machine and development environment, take a detour with me and let us see where Xcode installs things. This is useful for when you want to do more advanced maintenance of your tools: check what's in the SDK, find logs when Xcode crashes (yes, it does . . .); know where it places your projects' temporary files among other things.

## The Xcode Installation Folder

To find where Xcode was installed, open **Terminal** on your Mac and run the following command:

```
xcode-select --print-path.
```

This will give you the path to Xcode's installation folder, typically /Applications/Xcode.app/Contents/Developer/. To explore it in **Finder**, navigate to **Xcode.app**, right-click on it, select **Show Package Contents** and open the **Contents** folder.

## The iOS SDK

You can find the iOS SDK that comes with Xcode in the Developer/Platforms/iPhoneOS.platform/Developer/SDKs folder inside the Xcode installation.

## Location Settings

Xcode gives you control over where certain things should be found or stored. From Xcode's main menu select **Xcode ➤ Preferences ➤ Locations** to see what you can set (Figure 1-5).

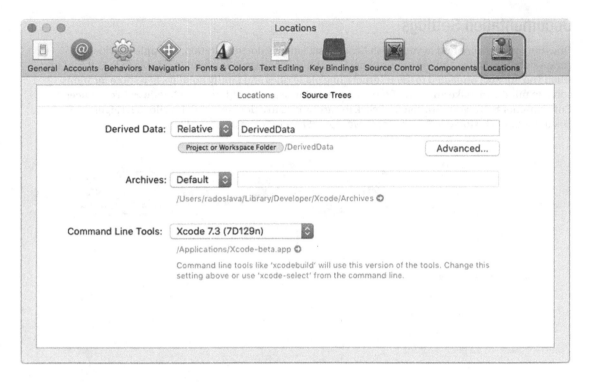

*Figure 1-5. Open Xcode ➤ Preferences ➤ Locations to see paths to important folders for your projects*

Following is a brief description of each of the locations you can control:

- **Derived Data.** Xcode uses two folders for putting temporary files when building a project: one is the **build** folder, which is always located in your project's directory; the other one is called **Derived Data** and you have a choice of where this goes: in the same location as the project or in the folder shared by all of your projects. It is good to know the location of this folder for dealing with compilation problems where a simple project clean doesn't seem to do the job. Deleting a project's **Derived Data** and **build** folders is equivalent to doing a manual clean.

- **Archives.** This is the location of the **.xcarchive** files Xcode creates for your projects: these contain your app executable and a .DSYM file—a file with debug information, which allows you to symbolicate a crash log, for example. You may have also used this to debug iOS native extensions for AIR.

- **Command-Line Tools.** Here you can choose the path to Xcode's command-line tools, in case you have more than one Xcode installation, thus more than one toolchain.

## Documentation Settings

One thing you will not find in your fresh Xcode installation is documentation, as Apple provides comprehensive guides and manuals online. Sometimes, however, it is useful to be able to look things up when you are not connected to the Internet (long plane rides and family holidays in remote locations come to mind). To make any part of the documentation available offline open **Xcode ➤ Preferences ➤ Components ➤ Documentation** and click the arrow next to a document to download it (Figure 1-6). Documentation is stored in ~/Library/Developer/Shared/Documentation/DocSets.

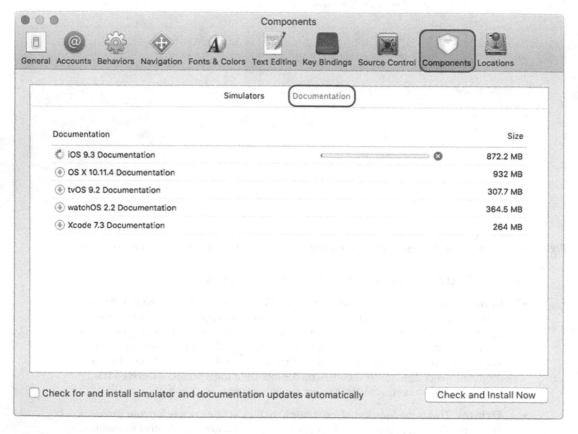

***Figure 1-6.*** *Make documentation available for offline reading from Xcode ➤ Preferences ➤ Components*

Use the same pane to keep your offline documentation up to date: click the **Check and Install Now** button to get an update if one is available.

# Step 3: Tell Xcode Who You Are

"Are we nearly there yet?" I can almost hear you say . . . I can't blame you: I am a coder at heart and to say that I don't enjoy following lengthy setup procedures would be putting it mildly. If you want to run applications on a physical device, there is one more thing left to do: Xcode needs to know about you. This section explains why and shows you how to finish the setup.

If, on the other hand, you would like to jump straight to creating your first native iOS app and see it run in a simulator, you can go to **Chapter 2** and come back to this step when you need to.

Before you can install and test your apps on physical devices the apps will need to be cryptographically signed. A code signature uses a *signing identity* to ascertain that an app was developed and built by you and a *certificate*, created specifically for that app or for a group of apps, which allows the group members to use particular services. A signing identity is based on your Apple ID: Xcode can create one for you and install it in **Keychain Access** automatically.

To help Xcode create a signing identity, you need to let it know your Apple ID: from Xcode's main menu select **Xcode ➤ Preferences** and in the dialog that appears open the **Accounts** tab (Figure 1-6). Click the + button to add a new account and enter your Apple ID and password.

After your account has been added and appears in the **Apple ID** column, select it, then select the relevant **Team** in the right part of the dialog shown in Figure 1-7—this could be a development team your Apple ID is part of or just your Apple ID. Then click the **View Details...** button. This will open another dialog with a list of signing identities (Figure 1-8).

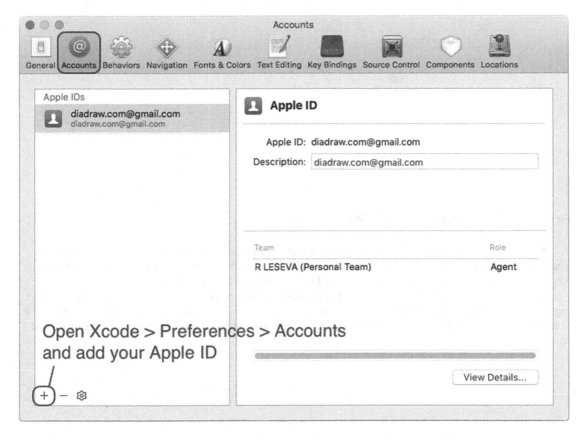

***Figure 1-7.*** *Let Xcode know who you are by adding your Apple ID in Xcode ➤ Preferences ➤ Accounts*

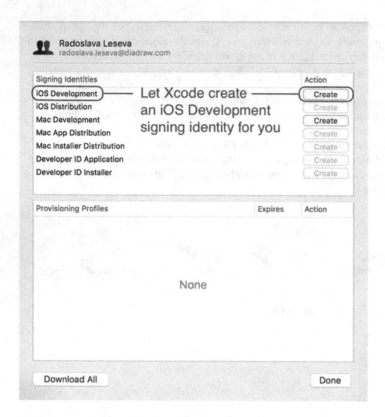

*Figure 1-8.* *Xcode 7 can create a signing identity for you*

A signing identity is effectively a certificate that will be installed in the keychain of your development machine and is used to sign the apps you build. For the purposes of the tutorials in this book we will need an iOS Development signing identity. Select it from the list and click the **Create** button.

To see what Xcode has created, launch the **Keychain Access** app on your Mac. Under **Keychains** select **login** and under **Category** select **My Certificates**. Your signing identity should appear in the list on the right as iPhone Developer: <The name you registered your Apple ID with> and should say certificate in the **Kind** column (Figure 1-9).

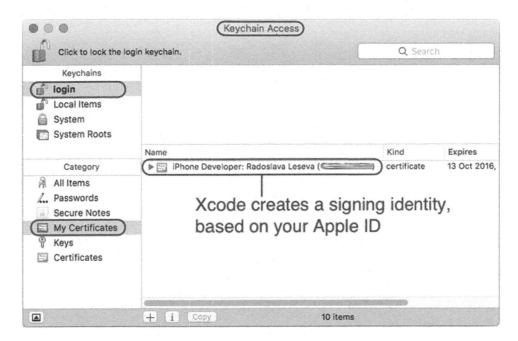

***Figure 1-9.*** *Check what Xcode has created in Keychain Access ➤ login ➤ My Certificates*

## Summary

Remember the workbench image, with which we opened this chapter? I hope that this is how your development machine looks and feels now: the tools for native iOS development laid out and ready to start crafting beautiful code. I'm afraid you will have to make the cup of coffee yourself, though.

With your choice of motivational drink ready, let us get on with making your first application in **Chapter 2**.

# CHAPTER 2

■ ■ ■

# Hello, Xcode!

We begin our journey into iOS development with Swift by making an app, for which you will not have to write a line of Swift code. . . . If you are a coder at heart, as I suspect you are, you probably can't wait to get your hands on Swift and start making applications, rather than allow an integrated development environment (IDE) to create them for you.

With that said, the purpose of this chapter is to show you the lay of the land and give you a map of where things are in the new IDE you downloaded and set up in **Chapter 1**. I promise to be brief and get you to **Part II**, where you can dip your hands in code sooner than you might expect.

In this chapter you will do the following:

- Set up an iOS app project.

- Explore Xcode's user interface.

- Run your first native iOS app in Xcode's simulator.

- Learn what provisioning is.

- Set up your iOS device for development and run the app on it.

When you are done, you will have a map of the Xcode IDE and a clear idea of its main tools and settings that will help you get started on app development.

## Creating an Xcode Project

Start Xcode. If the first thing you see is the **Welcome to Xcode** screen, select **Create a new Xcode project**. Or, create a new project by selecting **File ➤ New ➤ Project...** from Xcode's main menu. This starts a wizard, the first step in which is to choose an operating system and a product type for your project. We will start with something fairly simple: select **iOS ➤ Application ➤ Single View Application**, as shown in Figure 2-1.

© Radoslava Leseva Adams and Hristo Lesev 2016
R. L. Adams and H. Lesev, *Migrating to Swift from Flash and ActionScript*,
DOI 10.1007/978-1-4842-1666-8_2

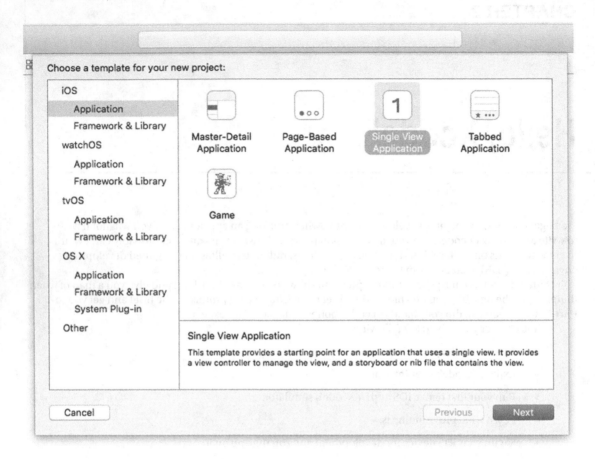

***Figure 2-1.*** *Start a new iOS Single View Application project in Xcode*

At the next step of the wizard name the project **HelloXcode**. Make sure that **Swift** is selected as the **Language** and **Devices** are set to **Universal,** and for this project don't tick any of the checkboxes for creating tests (see Figure 2-2).

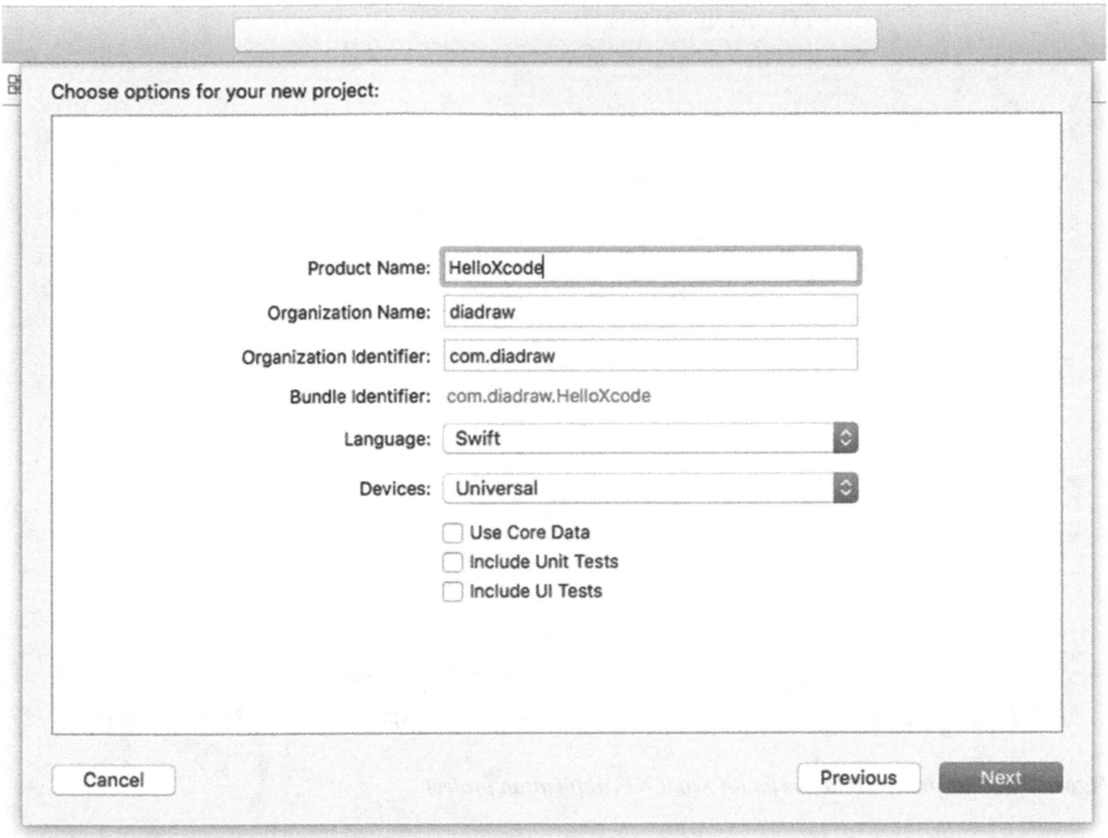

*Figure 2-2.* *Name your project and select Swift as the programming language*

Click **Next**, choose where to save the new project and let Xcode create it for you. Now let us see what's inside.

# The Xcode Interface

Our tour of Xcode starts with the big picture. If you set up your iOS Single View Application project following the steps above, your screen should look like Figure 2-3 when the project first appears.

Toolbar area

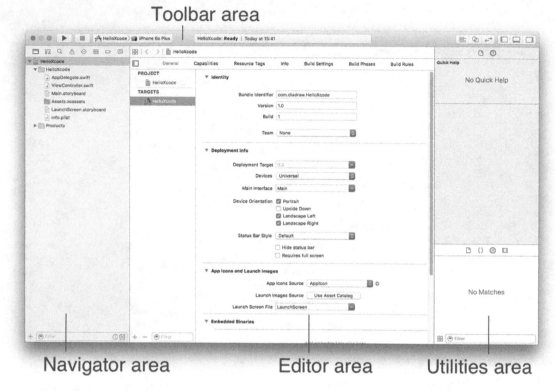

Figure 2-3. *The main IDE areas for an Xcode iOS appication project*

There are four main areas in the IDE (Figure 2-3):

- The toolbar area
- The editor area
- The navigator area
- The utilities area

## The Toolbar Area

On the left-hand side of the toolbar area you have controls for running your app and for choosing which device or simulator it should run on (see Figure 2-4).

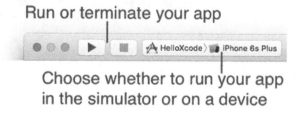

Figure 2-4. *Controls for running and quitting your app*

In the middle you can see a brief summary of your app's status (Figure 2-5). This answers questions like the following:

- Did the project compile?

- Were there any errors or warnings?

- Is the app running?

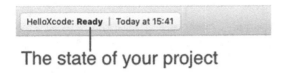

The state of your project

**Figure 2-5.** *The toolbar area is the place to get information about the state of your app at a glance*

At the right end of the toolbar area there are buttons for showing or hiding the other IDE areas and for toggling various views in them (Figure 2-6).

Switch between editors:
Standard, Assistant
and Version Editor

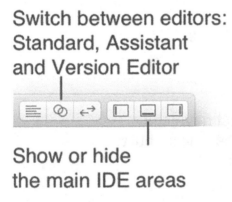

Show or hide
the main IDE areas

**Figure 2-6.** *You can show or hide the main areas of the IDE and choose how they are displayed*

## The Editor Area

This is where you will do most of your work: writing code, designing a user interface (UI), and controlling your project settings. Xcode has three editor modes:

- The *Standard editor* shows you one thing at a time: you can load a source file, a storyboard, assets, or project settings.

- The *Assistant editor* displays two files side by side. You can have two source files open, for example, if you want to have a glance at a function call in one and its definition in the other. Or, you can have a look together at a storyboard (UI file) and the source file, in which you implement the storyboard's actions—we will see how this works later, when we add a bit of UI to our app project.

- The *Version editor* is useful when your projects are under version control (as they should be): in this view you can see two revisions of the same file and compare what has changed.

19

If you select the main project in Project navigator, the project settings will appear in the editor area. Under **Targets** you can see the products that building the project should produce: at the moment we have one: the HeloXcode app. Across the top of the Editor area the project and target settings are distributed between several different tabs (Figure 2-7).

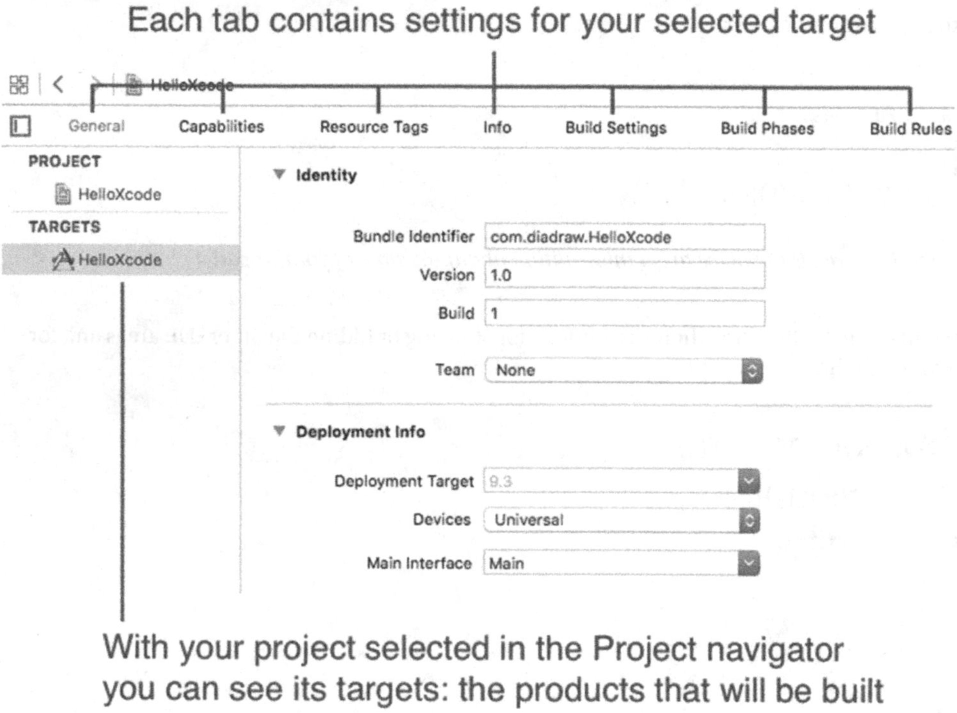

Each tab contains settings for your selected target

With your project selected in the Project navigator
you can see its targets: the products that will be built

**Figure 2-7.** *Project and target settings*

# The Navigator Area

Here you can switch between various navigators (Figure 2-8):

- *Project navigator*: shows the files in your project. You can organize files in groups that logically belong together. Note that the groups don't have to correspond to folders on disc.

- *Find navigator*: lets you search for strings in your project.

- *Symbol navigator*: shows the class hierarchies in your code.

- *Issue navigator*: has a list of errors and warnings if any appeared during a build. Clicking an issue takes you to the file it was found in.

- *Test navigator*: if you choose to include unit or UI tests in your project, you can browse them here.

- *Debug navigator*: this navigator is active during a debug session and lets you drill into stack traces for each thread that is running in your app, as well as see statistics about how your app is utilizing system resources.

- *Breakpoint navigator*: this is where you can see and manage all of the breakpoints you have put in your code.

- *Report navigator*: shows you a list of reports about builds, debug sessions, and tests.

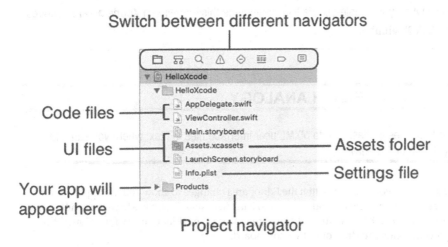

*Figure 2-8. Your app source files in Project navigator*

You can also switch between navigators from the main menu by choosing **View ➤ Navigators**.

If you open Project navigator, you will see the files Xcode has created for you: in the HelloXcode group there are two source files (AppDelegate.swift and ViewController.swift), two UI files (Main.storyboard and LaunchScreen.storyboard), an Assets folder, and a file called Info.plist, which contains the settings for your app. There is a second group, called Products, where the app executable file will appear when we build it.

## The Utilities Area

This area shows different types of tools and utilities, depending on what's in the Editor area. For example, if you are editing a storyboard, one of the things you will see in the Utility area is the Object library—use it to drag and drop UI elements onto the storyboard.

# Getting Your Fingertips Dirty

Even when you are not expected to write code for your first native app, it doesn't mean you can't customize the app. Adding something as simple as a label to the main view can be an excuse to explore one way of designing UI in Xcode 7. We will add a label and a date picker to our app and have Xcode generate code that will let us access them programmatically.

In Project navigator select the Main.storyboard file. In this context a *storyboard* is the visual representation of your app's interface and workflow. It shows you and lets you define not only what the screens of your app will look like but also how they will flow from one to the other: the flow is shown with arrows.

■ **Note** If you are used to IDEs like Flash Builder, your instinct will be to open a file by double-clicking its name in Project navigator. Xcode might surprise you by opening a new window every time you double-click a file. Its default behavior is to load a file in the main window the moment you select it in the navigator and to load the file in a new window when you double-click it. You can change this behavior in **Xcode ➤ Preferences ➤ Navigation ➤ Double Click Navigation**.

## FLASH ANALOGY

Storyboards are similar to scenes in Flash and to MXML user interface files in Flex, where you can add UI elements and partly define their behavior.

With Main.storyboard selected you will notice that the Editor area changes to show you the application's main screen. The gray arrow coming from the left and pointing to it in effect says, "Here is where the action starts."

Let us leave a little fingerprint on this app. In the Utility area locate the Object library (see Figure 2-9): it has a list of UI elements you can drag and drop onto the storyboard.

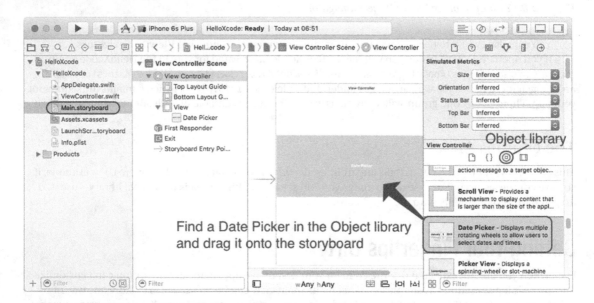

*Figure 2-9. Drag and drop a Date Picker onto Main.storyboard*

■ **Tip** You can also use the main menu to show the Object library: **View ➤ Utilities ➤ Show Object Library**.

Find a **Date Picker** controller in the Object library and add it to the storyboard by doing a drag-and-drop as shown in Figure 2-9. You should see the date picker appear both in the UI view and in the Document outline on the left. Select it and let's change it to show the date, but not the time: in the Attributes inspector on the right set **Mode** to **Date** and leave the rest of the properties as they are (Figure 2-10).

Document outline    Storyboard    Attributes inspector

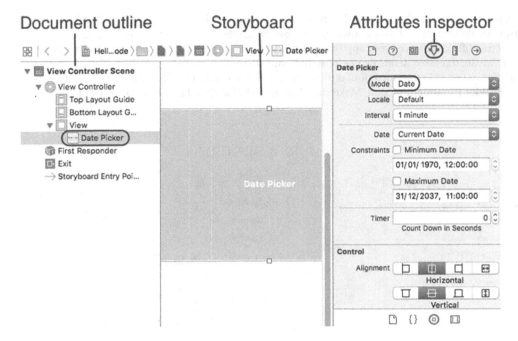

**Figure 2-10.** *Select the Date Picker to change its properties*

Add a Label from the Object library to the storyboard and place it above the date picker. Double-click the label to change its text to "Day of the week" (Figure 2-11).

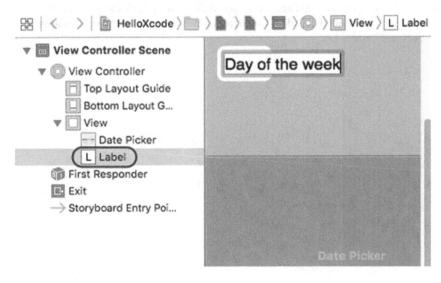

**Figure 2-11.** *Add a label to the storyboard*

You have probably noticed that the storyboard we are working with is square and doesn't match the size or the aspect ratio of any iOS device known to man. Before Xcode 7 you needed to provide separate storyboards for the different devices your app was expected to run on. Now we have one storyboard to work with, which has an abstract size. Xcode can help us make our UI adaptive: let us do that.

With the View selected in the Document outline, open File inspector in the Utility area and locate the **Interface Builder Document** section. Make sure that you tick **Use Auto Layout** and **Use Size Classes** (Figure 2-12).

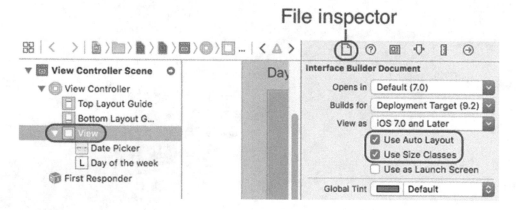

***Figure 2-12.*** *Set up the view to Use Auto Layout and Use Size Classes*

Now select the date picker and click the Pin button at the bottom right of the screen where the storyboard is. We will constrain the date picker to move and resize itself, so that there is always the same distance between it and its nearest neighbor: the label and the edges of the view in this case. Set **Spacing to nearest neighbor** to 10 pixels on each side and click **Add 4 Constraints**. You will see the constraints appear in the Document outline on the left (Figure 2-13).

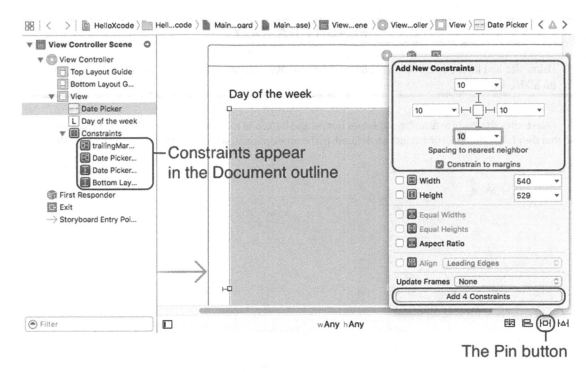

*Figure 2-13. Add constraints to the date picker*

Add the same constraints to the label (Figure 2-14).

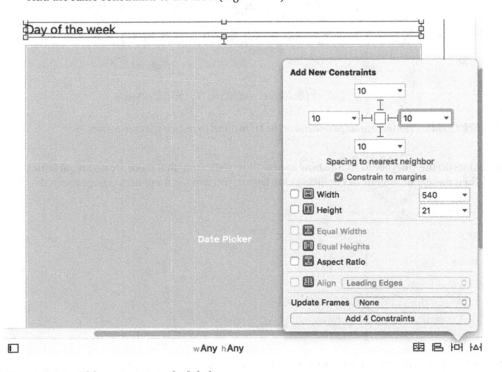

*Figure 2-14. Add constraints to the label*

## FLASH ANALOGY

Using size and layout constraints in Xcode is similar to how you would set up size rules and spacers in an MXML file.

Next, click the Resolve Auto Layout Issues button and let Xcode move the label and the date picker around, so that they fall within the constraints we defined: in the pop-up menu select **Update Frames** (Figure 2-15).

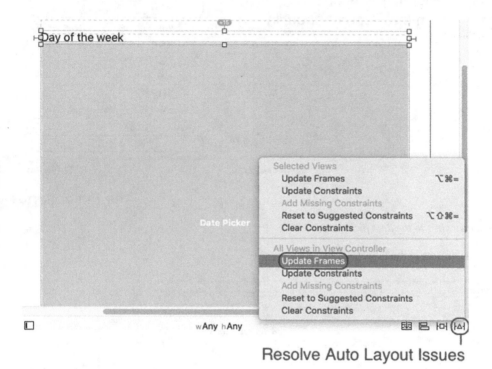

*Figure 2-15.* Click Update Frames and let Xcode move the UI around to match the constraints

The constraints on the storyboard should now appear blue, indicating that there are no layout issues (Figure 2-16). When there is ambiguity or conflicts in the layout, you will see them turn orange and red.

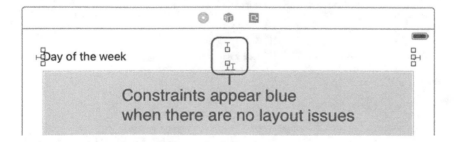

*Figure 2-16.* Make sure that constraints on the storyboard appear blue

The last thing we will do before running the app is to create *outlets* for the two UI elements we put on the storyboard. An outlet is defined as "a property of an object that references another object." In this case we will create properties in the ViewController class that will reference the date picker and the label. Correction: we will help Xcode create these properties. I made a promise that you will have an app without writing a line of code and I'm sticking with it.

With the storyboard still in the editor area, activate the Assistant editor. This will split the editor area in two: in one half you have the storyboard and in the other the ViewController.swift file. If a different file or no file appears in the second half, you can manually select ViewController.swift to be loaded there by clicking the strip above the file, which shows a file path (Figure 2-17).

***Figure 2-17.*** *Create properties in ViewController.swift that will reference the label and the date picker*

On the storyboard select the label, then Ctrl + drag it into ViewController.swift and drop it at the top of the ViewController class definition.

In the pop-up dialog that appears name the outlet dayOfTheWeek and click **Connect** (Figure 2-18). This creates a property in the ViewController class of type UILabel, which will let us access the label programmatically—we will do this in **Chapter 3**.

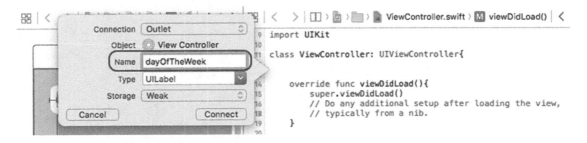

***Figure 2-18.*** *Name the outlet and let Xcode create a definition for it in the ViewController class*

Repeat the steps to create an outlet for the date picker and name it datePicker. The ViewController class should now look like Listing 2-1.

*Listing 2-1.* The ViewController Class After the Outlets Have Been Added

```swift
class ViewController: UIViewController{

    @IBOutlet weak var dayOfTheWeek: UILabel!
    @IBOutlet weak var datePicker: UIDatePicker!

    override func viewDidLoad(){
        super.viewDidLoad()
        // Do any additional setup after loading the view,
        // typically from a nib.
    }

    override func didReceiveMemoryWarning(){
        super.didReceiveMemoryWarning()
        // Dispose of any resources that can be recreated.
    }
}
```

# Running Your App in the Simulator

Time to see this app in action. Let us run it in Xcode's simulator first. Click the device drop-down next to your project's name on the Toolbar (Figure 2-4). If any of your iOS devices are plugged in your machine, their names will appear in the top part of the list under the **Device** category. The **iOS Simulators** category contains a number of options: select one, for example iPhone 6 (Figure 2-19).

*Figure 2-19.* *Select an iOS simulator from the list on the toolbar*

Click the Run button. This starts the simulator, which does a pretty convincing job of showing you (and making you wait for) the device booting up for the first time. Once the simulated iOS has booted, your app will start and you should be able to see the label you added to its main screen (Figure 2-20).

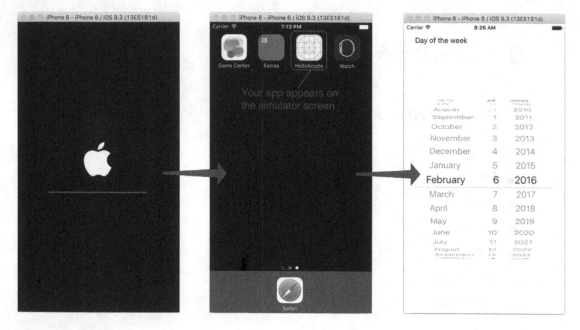

*Figure 2-20.  Your app in the iOS simulator*

# Running Your App on a Device, Using Free Provisioning

Now that we are satisfied that the app builds and runs on a simulator, let us have Xcode install and run it on an actual iOS device.

## Provisioning

If you have done iOS development with ActionScript, you know that an app needs to be provisioned in order to be run on a physical device and what that means and thus you can skip this section and move on to the practical part in "Running your app." But if you are new to programming for iOS, the following sections briefly describe how an app is prepared for installation and what you need to do.

## What Is Provisioning?

An app must match certain criteria in order to launch on an iOS device. *Provisioning* is Apple speak for what you need to do in order to prepare your app to match these criteria: the information about them is stored in a *provisioning profile*. A provisioning profile is an encrypted file, which is embedded in the app and is checked when the app tries to install itself on a device.

So, what criteria must be met?

- The app needs to have a unique identifier, *App ID*. The App ID can be specific to only one app, for example, **com.diadraw.ideadrawapp**. Alternatively, during development, the App ID can contain a wildcard in the place of the app name and be shared between several apps you are working on, for example: **com.diadraw.\***.

- Apple must know about you, the developer: this is where the Apple ID you registered before downloading Xcode comes in. Your Apple ID is used to create a *signing identity*—we helped Xcode create this for you at the end of **Chapter 1**. When Xcode builds your app it also cryptographically signs it using this identity and this serves to certify that the app was built by you and not modified by anyone else.

- Before your app is ready for distribution, it can run only on devices that are known to Xcode, are registered for development, and have been set to trust your code signing identity. A third kind of ID helps with that: each iOS device has its own unique device identifier (UDID) that Xcode can access when the device is plugged in your development machine.

- If your app uses special features like push notifications, for example, it must have permission for that: the respective feature *entitlements* must be enabled in its provisioning profile.

Figure 2-21 illustrates this.

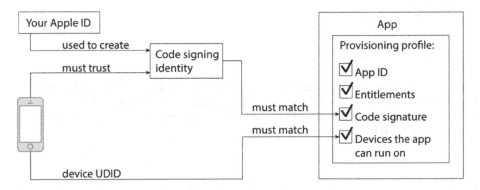

***Figure 2-21.*** *Criteria an app's provisioning profile must meet*

## Where Does Free Provisioning Come In?

Until recently provisioning an app for development involved a lot of steps: you needed to source the information for the provisioning profile, register your app and device in Apple's Developer Member Center, create and download the profile, then point Xcode to it. To be able to do all of this also required that you enroll and pay a yearly subscription for Apple's iOS Development Program.

In contrast to this, Xcode 7 comes as a breath of fresh air: provisioning an app during development has been automated for you and done by the IDE and for the most part you don't need a paid membership.

## Free Lunch?

Maybe. Did you notice in the previous section how I said, "for the most part you don't need a paid membership"? That's right: while you develop your apps you can provision and test them for free, as long as they use only the basic iOS features. You will have to purchase membership in the iOS Development Program when you need to include more advanced features, also known as entitlements, or when you want to release your apps on the market. Following is a list of the entitlements that at the moment require you to be a member of the program:

- Apple Pay

- App Sandbox

- Associated Domains
- Game Center
- iCloud
- In-App Purchase
- Personal VPN
- Push Notifications
- Wallet

You can keep up to date with changes and additions to this list on Apples' web site.

---

■ **Note**    The code in this book can be built and run using free provisioning. The two exceptions are the tutorials for using Push Notifications and iCloud in Part III: being able to implement these will need an iOS Development Program membership.

---

## Running Your App

Before you run your app on a device, ensure that Xcode knows your Apple ID: it should appear in **Xcode ➤ Preferences ➤ Accounts**. If your account is not there, see the end of **Chapter 1** for how to add it.

Now, select the main project in Project navigator. In the editor select the HelloXcode target, go to the **General** tab and choose your Apple ID from the **Team** drop-down (Figure 2-22).

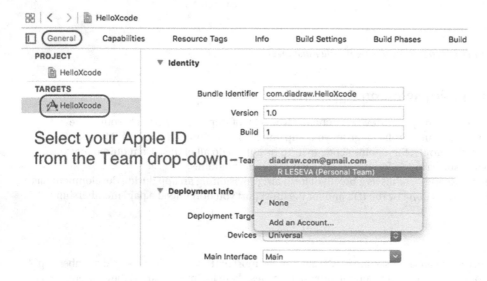

*Figure 2-22.*  *Select your Apple ID in the project settings: General ➤ Identity ➤ Team*

At this point you are likely to see a warning under the Team setting, saying "No code signing identities found." If this appears, click the **Fix Issue** button and let Xcode resolve the problem: it will create a signing identity for you (Figure 2-23).

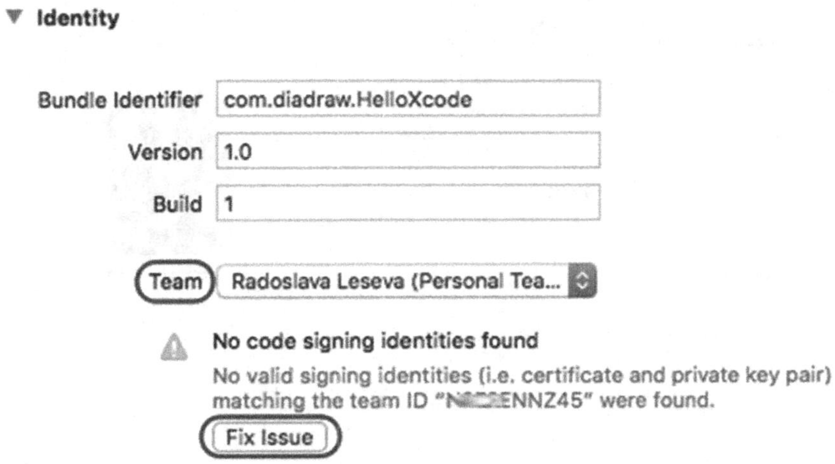

▼ **Identity**

Bundle Identifier  com.diadraw.HelloXcode

Version  1.0

Build  1

(Team)  Radoslava Leseva (Personal Tea... ↕)

⚠ **No code signing identities found**
No valid signing identities (i.e. certificate and private key pair)
matching the team ID "N░░ENNZ45" were found.
( Fix Issue )

***Figure 2-23.*** *Let Xcode create a signing identity for you by clicking Fix Issue*

## Connecting Your iOS Device

Now connect an iOS device to your Mac. The device's name should appear in the Scheme toolbar as shown in Figure 2-24.

***Figure 2-24.*** *Select your device on the toolbar*

### The device doesn't appear on the toolbar?

If this is the first time you are using this device for iOS development, you will need to do a bit of preparatory work. From Xcode's main menu select **Window ➤ Devices**. This opens Xcode's central point for managing devices, which we will take a more detailed look at in **Chapter 4**. Register your device for development by adding it to the list of devices known to Xcode: click the + button at the bottom of the window and follow the instructions (Figure 2-25).

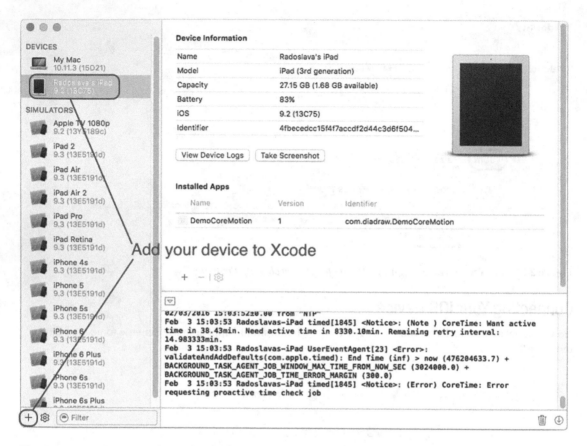

*Figure 2-25.* *Register your device for development*

## The device appears grayed out?

If you can see your device on the toolbar but it appears grayed out, it's likely that the iOS version that our HelloSwift project is built for is higher than the iOS on your device. When this is the case, Xcode 7 displays a friendly warning next to the device's name, saying "Unavailable Device" and "(OS version lower than deployment target)."

To fix that, open your app target settings (select the main project in Project navigator, then select the HelloSwift target in the editor), go to the **General** tab and in the **Deployment Info** section set **Deployment Target** to be the same or lower than the iOS version on your device (Figure 2-26).

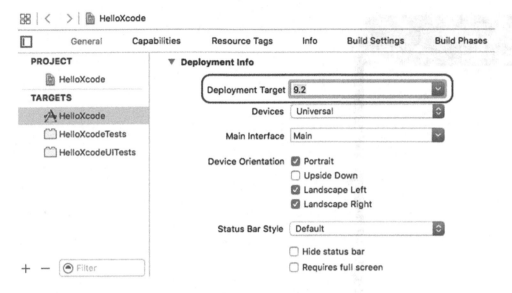

*Figure 2-26.* *Check if Deployment Target matches the iOS version on your device*

## Seeing Your App Running

Now, when you click the Run button, Xcode should automatically install and launch the app on your device (Figure 2-27).

*Figure 2-27. Your first native app running on an iOS device*

## App won't launch?

If this is the first time you have used the combination of this device and your Apple ID to do iOS development, there is yet another step you need to take.

If you see an error message like the one in Figure 2-28, open **Settings ➤ General ➤ Device Management** on your device. The signing identity Xcode created for you in **Chapter 1** should be listed there: tap it and then tap **Trust <Your Apple ID➤**.

*Figure 2-28. To fix this, get the device to trust your signing identity*

# Summary

In this chapter we created an app in Xcode and ran it in the simulator and on a physical device. This gave us an opportunity to explore the main parts of the Xcode IDE that you will use when you develop apps for iOS. Surprisingly, most of the work that needed to be done had nothing to do with coding but with what is necessary to prepare the app, your Apple account, and your development devices for testing.

With all of this in the bag, we can now move on to another development topic: debugging your apps, which is the subject of the next chapter.

# CHAPTER 3

■ ■ ■

# Introducing the Xcode Debugger

Having an integrated debugger is one of the best parts of using an integrated development environment (IDE). The easier and the more convenient a debugger is to use, the more regularly it will be put to work: without one you are shooting in the dark.

As you saw in the previous chapter, Xcode's debugger automatically installs and runs apps for you on devices or in a simulator. Here you will familiarize yourself with the basic things the debugger can help you with: stepping through your code and inspecting values.

In this chapter you will do the following:

- Extend the app you created in **Chapter 2** and add Swift code to it.

- Step through your code in the debugger.

- Inspect variables and change their values at runtime.

- Learn how to execute commands in Xcode's console for simple diagnostics.

- Have a peak at Xcode's Memory view.

When you are done, you will have an idea of the debugging tools available to you in Xcode to help you stay in control of your code. In **Chapter 8**, we will drill down into more advanced debugging topics.

## Preparation: Write Code to Debug

In **Chapter 2** we made a simple app that shows a date picker and a label. Let's breathe some life into it by getting these user interface (UI) elements to do something interesting and make the label say what day of the week the date shown by the date picker is.

### Starting Point: The HelloXcode App

If you followed the tutorial in **Chapter 2**, you have an Xcode project, called HelloXcode, which builds an iOS app. Open it and in Project navigator find the ViewController.swift file. It contains the definition of a class called ViewController, which is responsible for the app's main view and looks like Listing 3-1.

© Radoslava Leseva Adams and Hristo Lesev 2016

R. L. Adams and H. Lesev, *Migrating to Swift from Flash and ActionScript*,

DOI 10.1007/978-1-4842-1666-8_3

*Listing 3-1.* The ViewController Class with Outlets for a Label and a Date Picker

```
class ViewController: UIViewController {
    // Outlets for accessing the label and the date picker in Main.storyboard:
    @IBOutlet weak var dayOfTheWeek: UILabel!
    @IBOutlet weak var datePicker: UIDatePicker!

    override func viewDidLoad() {
        super.viewDidLoad()
        // Do any additional setup after loading the view,
        // typically from a nib.
    }

    override func didReceiveMemoryWarning() {
        super.didReceiveMemoryWarning()
        // Dispose of any resources that can be recreated.
    }
}
```

The two viewDidLoad and didReceiveMemoryWarning methods were put there by Xcode when it defined the ViewController class for us upon setting up the project. viewDidLoad is called when the view has been fully created and presented on the screen. didReceiveMemoryWarning will be executed in low-memory conditions, giving us a chance to release any unused memory.

In the course of **Chapter 2** we added two UI controls to the main view's storyboard: a date picker and a label. The IBOutlet members of the ViewController class give us access to these controls: dayOfTheWeek references the label and datePicker references the date picker. We had Xcode generate the IBOutlet definitions by dragging and dropping references from the storyboard into code.

## Adding Action

The first piece of code we will add is an event handler, also known as *action*. It will be called when the date picker's value changes. With Main.storyboard and ViewController.swift open in the Assistant editor side by side select and right-click the date picker on the storyboard. In the pop-up menu find the **Value Changed** event, then drag and drop the circle next to it into the ViewController class (Figure 3-1). This generates a method that will listen to and handle the **Value Changed** event for the date picker.

**Figure 3-1.** *Add a Value Changed event handler for the date picker*

Name the event handler dateChanged and add the code in Listing 3-2 to it.

**Listing 3-2.** Implement the dateChanged Event Handler

```
@IBAction func dateChanged(sender: AnyObject) {
    updateDayOfWeek()
}
```

## Updating the Label

At this point Xcode will complain that updateDayOfWeek is an "unresolved identifier." This is because updateDayOfWeek is a method we haven't implemented yet. Let us do that: add a new method to the ViewController class and have it update the label's text (Listing 3-3).

***Listing 3-3.*** Add a Method That Will Update the Label's Text

```
func updateDayOfWeek() {
    // Change the label's text
    // to show what day of the week the date in the picker is:
    dayOfTheWeek.text = getDayOfWeek(date: datePicker.date)
}
```

It would be good if our label is synchronized with the date picker and shows the correct day of the week when the app first launches, so let us add a call to updateDayOfWeek to ViewController's viewDidLoad method too (Listing 3-4).

***Listing 3-4.*** Update the Label When the View Is First Loaded

```
override func viewDidLoad() {
    super.viewDidLoad()

    // Update the label when the view is first loaded:
    updateDayOfWeek()
}
```

# Working Out the Day of the Week

getDayOfWeek (called in Listing 3-3) is another method that we need to implement: this is where we will work out the day of the week for the date shown by the picker. Listing 3-5 shows you the implementation of this method: it creates an instance of NSCalendar, which is part of the iOS SDK. The NSCalendar gives us access to the components (NSDateComponents) for a given date (NSDate) and these include the day of the week. Let us see how this works: implement the method as shown in Listing 3-5.

***Listing 3-5.*** Work Out the Weekday from a Given Date

```
func getDayOfWeek(date date: NSDate) -> String {
    // The NSCalendar instance can give us access to the date components,
    // which have the weekday information:
    let gregorianCalendar = ↵
        NSCalendar(calendarIdentifier: NSCalendarIdentifierGregorian)!

    // weekDay in an integer between 1 and 7:
    let weekDay = ↵
        gregorianCalendar.components ↵
            ( NSCalendarUnit.Weekday, fromDate: date ).weekday

    // Now turn the integer into a day's name.
    // Keep in mind that the week in our chosen calendar starts on Sunday.
    switch weekDay {
        case 1: return "Sunday"
        case 2: return "Monday"
        case 3: return "Tuesday"
        case 4: return "Wednesday"
        case 5: return "Thursday"
        case 6: return "Friday"
        case 7: return "Saturday"
```

```
        // This will print out an error message in Xcode's console:
        default: print("weekDay must be between 1 and 7")
    }

    // We haven't been able to work out the weekday for some reason:
    return "Unknown"
}
```

---

■ **Note**    You may have noticed the additional date in getDayOfWeek(date date: NSDate) -> String. This is a parameter label. Labels help you document your code, especially at the point where you call a function that takes parameters. For example, getDayOfWeek would be called like this: getDayOfWeek(date: someDate). Here the label date serves as a reminder for what the parameter is intended to do. You can find out more about labeling parameters in Chapter 17.

---

Now, if you run the app in the simulator or on a device, you should be able to see the label get updated when you flick the date picker (Figure 3-2).

*Figure 3-2.* *The app now shows the day of week for the date in the picker*

# Getting Debug Information

Let us go over a few simple ways of getting inside information on what's going on inside the app.

## Using Print to Output to the Console

The simplest way to output runtime information in Xcode's console is to call the print function.[1] Activate the Standard editor (Figure 3-3); in Project navigator find the **ViewController.swift** file and open it. Locate and change the updateDayOfWeek function to print out what it's doing (Listing 3-6).

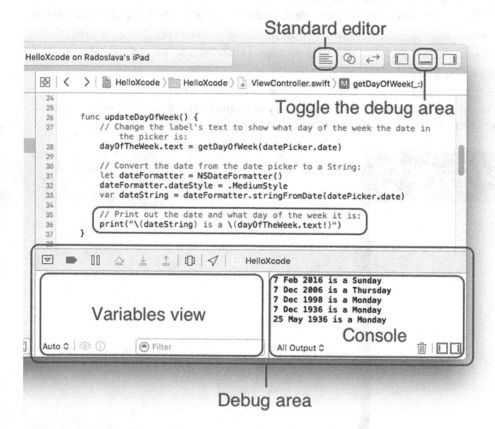

*Figure 3-3.* *Using print to output to the console*

*Listing 3-6.* Output Values to Xcode's Console Using Print

```
func updateDayOfWeek() {
    // Change the label's text to show
    // what day of the week the date in the picker is:
    dayOfTheWeek.text = getDayOfWeek(date: datePicker.date)
```

---

[1]We actually used it already (sneakily): have another look at Listing 3-5.

```
    // Construct a string for the date in the date picker:
    let dateFormatter = NSDateFormatter()
    dateFormatter.dateStyle = .MediumStyle
    let dateString = dateFormatter.stringFromDate(datePicker.date)

    // Print out the date and what day of the week it is in Xcode's console:
    print("\(dateString) is a \(dayOfTheWeek.text!)")
}
```

The first three lines that we added to this function take the current date value from the date picker and run it through an instance of the NSDateFormatter class (part of the iOS SDK), so that we can get a nicely formatted string from it.

The last line is the interesting one: here we call the print function and ask it to output a string in Xcode's console. This string is constructed from the value of the dateString variable and the label's text. To insert a given value in a string literal, you wrap the value's name in parentheses and prefix it with a backslash: \(variableOrConstant); this goes inside the string literal quotes.

Run the app on your device or in a simulator to see the effect of printing into Xcode's console. If the Debug area is not visible at the bottom of the screen, toggle it as shown on Figure 3-3.

The Debug area is split in two parts: the left part, called the **Variables view**, is where you can watch the values of variables: we will look at it later. The right part is Xcode's **console**, which shows you two types of information: anything you choose to print out with the print function and messages from iOS about any runtime issues in your app. With the app running flick through the date picker to see the print messages pouring into the console.

---

## FLASH ANALOGY

Using print in Swift is similar to using trace in ActionScript to output to Flash Builder's Console view (available in Debug Perspective) or to the Output window in Flash.

---

## Stepping Through Your Code

You can set a breakpoint in Xcode by single-clicking the gray strip to the left of a line of code. Clicking for a second time deactivates the breakpoint. If you want to delete a breakpoint, right-click it and select **Delete breakpoint** from the pop-up menu.

Let us set a breakpoint somewhere inside the getDayOfWeek function in ViewController.swift and run the app. As soon as the breakpoint is hit you can see several changes on the screen (Figure 3-4):

- The Debugger controls appear at the top of the Debug area: use these to step over or into code, pause the execution, simulate location on the device, or move up and down the stack trace.

- The Debug navigator is populated with information on the state of system resources, the state of the UI, and stack traces for each thread running in your app.

- The Variables view contains variables you can inspect: you can switch between monitoring all variables and registers or only local variables, or let Xcode automatically choose what is available for inspection at a given breakpoint.

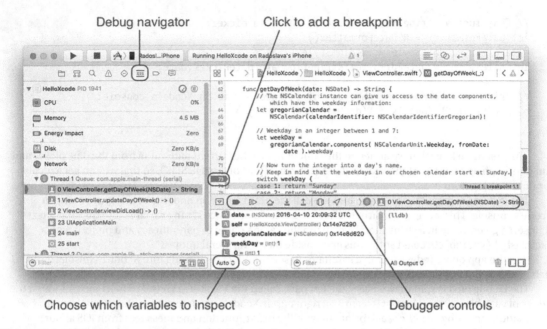

**Figure 3-4.** *Xcode's screen gets updated with debug information when a breakpoint is hit*

Click the **Step over** button in the Debugger controls strip or press F6 to step through your code. Use F8 to continue execution.

## Watching Variables

With the debugger still paused at the breakpoint, have a look at the Variables view (Figure 3-4) and switch between the filters to see different sets of variables and registers reported: **Auto**, **Local Variables,** and **All**. Use the Debugger controls to step through your code and see the values change.

If you right-click inside the Variables view, you will be given the option to add values for inspection by selecting **Add Expression...** from the pop-up menu.

## Executing Commands in the Console

The console allows you to type and execute commands at runtime. For example, you can manually output the value of a variable. Try this: type print weekDay in the console to get the value of the weekDay variable (Figure 3-5).

---

■ **Tip** We will look at console commands and their shortcuts in more detail in Chapter 8.

---

You can type and execute commands in the console

*Figure 3-5. You can manually call commands in the console to output values at runtime*

## Changing a Value at Runtime

A useful command you can type in the console is expression (or expr for short). It lets you change the value of a variable at runtime: this way you can experiment and test different values without having to rebuild and restart your app. Let us try this: put a breakpoint at the line where we call print inside the updateDayOfWeek method (Figure 3-6). When the debugger stops at the breakpoint, type the following:

```
expression dayOfTheWeek.text = "day for coffee"
```

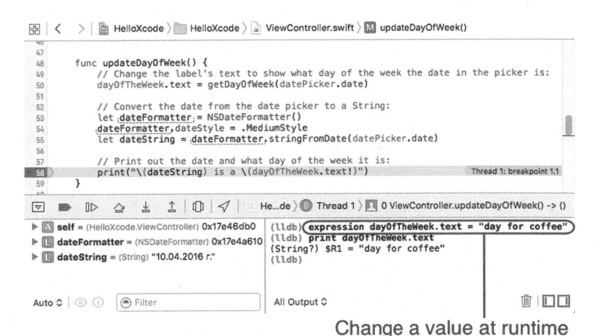

Change a value at runtime

*Figure 3-6. Use the expression command to set an expression's value at runtime*

This will change the label's text to "day for coffee."

■ **Warning** You may find that the expression command doesn't always have an effect: Xcode sometimes optimizes where values are copied and read from, which gets in the way of changing them at runtime.

## Inspecting Memory

You can see what an expression looks like in memory at a given point of the execution by right-clicking it in the Variables view and selecting **View Memory of "nameOfTheExpression"**.

■ **Note** The **View Memory of** option may not always work for Swift data structures. This has been a known issue since Xcode 6. Apple suggests a workaround for this, which we will see how to implement in Chapter 8.

Let us see what the dateString variable looks like in memory. We declared dateString in the updateDayOfWeek method. Set a breakpoint at the line after the variable's declaration and run the app in the debugger. When the breakpoint is hit, find dateString in the Variables view, right-click it, and select **View Memory of "dateString"** (Figure 3-7).

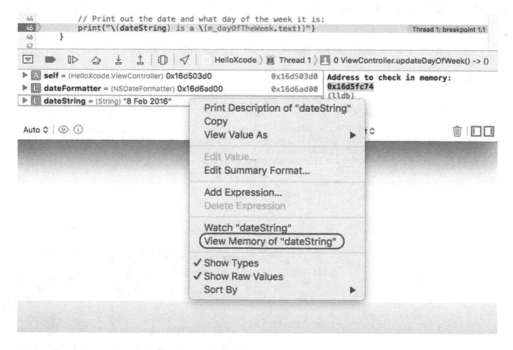

***Figure 3-7.*** *You can see the memory layout of an expression in the Variables view*

This will load the memory view in the Editor. If it looks like Figure 3-8, then you have nothing further to do: you can see the memory layout of dateString as hexadecimal numbers on the right and as characters on the left.

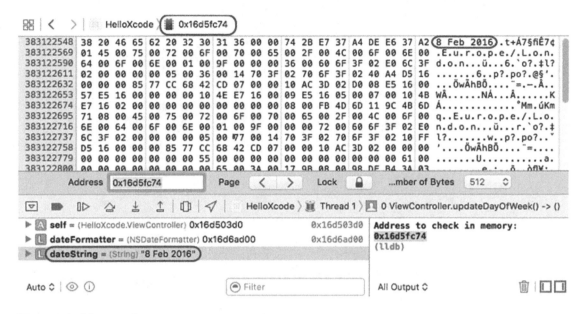

***Figure 3-8.*** *Memory view*

If, however, instead of lots of memory addresses and data you see a blank window and the address shown on top is 0x0, we will show you how to work around that when we get into more advanced debugging topics in **Chapter 8**.

# Summary

With **Chapters 1**, **2**, and **3** in the bag you are now set to start implementing and testing apps for iOS with Xcode. In this chapter we covered the basic use of Xcode's debugger—your best friend when it comes to making sure code does what you intend it to do. We saw how to manage breakpoints, how to step through code, and how to inspect and change runtime information.

Before we plunge into migrating your whole workflow to Xcode, we have a few more useful tools to show you in **Chapter 4**, which will help you with further diagnosing your apps and with releasing them to the app store.

# CHAPTER 4

■ ■ ■

# Additional Development Tools

So far in this part of the book we covered the essentials: the development tools you must have in order to program apps for iOS. Xcode is a big package and this is only a small part of what it has to offer. In this last chapter of **Part I** we continue to unwrap this package and familiarize ourselves with the integrated development environment (IDE).

In this chapter you will do the following:

- Learn about version control.

- Modify one of Xcode's game templates.

- Measure the game's performance and make improvements.

- Discover how Xcode can support your app development every step of the way.

When you are done, you will have an app project, which is version-controlled and will have gained experience in profiling it.

## Keeping Track of Changes

Keeping a history of changes in your source code and having it backed up on a regular basis is vital for creating an effective workflow. This is traditionally done via *version control*, also known as *source control* or *revision control*.

You have probably used a version control system (VCS) in your development practice. But in case you are new to it: version control is a system that keeps track of changes in files over time. Work files are kept in a repository and there are specific rules for how they are accessed: in order to modify part of a project, a developer needs make the modification in a local copy. Then the developer needs to commit the modification to the repository. This leaves a record of what the change was, when it was made, and by whom. In this way code is backed up along with the history of how it evolved. You can go back and inspect older versions of the project to see where a bug first appeared, for example.[1] You can also correct changes you made by mistake. When more than one person modifies the same file, a VCS assists with merging these changes, so that no one's work gets lost. Not only can code evolve linearly over time but it can branch out into different versions when necessary. For instance, if you want to keep the latest released version of an app stable but also want to introduce new features in the new version, you can make the changes in a new branch: this is a copy of the project, which evolves separately and can be optionally merged back into the main source tree.

There are three types of VCSs with respect to where the files and versioning information are stored:

- **Local**. A local VCS is useful if you work on your own and want to take advantage of the automatic backup and tracking of changes in your code.

---

[1]And, more important, who introduced it.

© Radoslava Leseva Adams and Hristo Lesev 2016
R. L. Adams and H. Lesev, *Migrating to Swift from Flash and ActionScript*,
DOI 10.1007/978-1-4842-1666-8_4

- **Centralized**. Centralized VCSs help with collaboration by keeping source code in a repository on a server and requiring that each developer check out a copy of the file they currently work on.

- **Distributed**. Distributed systems push this requirement further: each collaborator needs to have a local copy of the whole repository and first commit changes to it before pushing them to the central repository. This creates multiple source code backups, which eliminates issues with a VCS server being down, for example. It also allows developers to take advantage of version control locally without muddying everyone else's waters until they are confident in their changes.

Xcode offers version control from within the IDE and supports two distributed VCSs: Git and Subversion. We will have a look at how to use Git by setting up a project that uses source control.

In Xcode create a new game project: from the main menu select **File ➤ New ➤ Project...** and then **iOS ➤ Application ➤ Game**. Name it FibonacciSpaceships, make sure its **Language** is set to Swift and set **Game Technology** to SpriteKit (Figure 4-1).

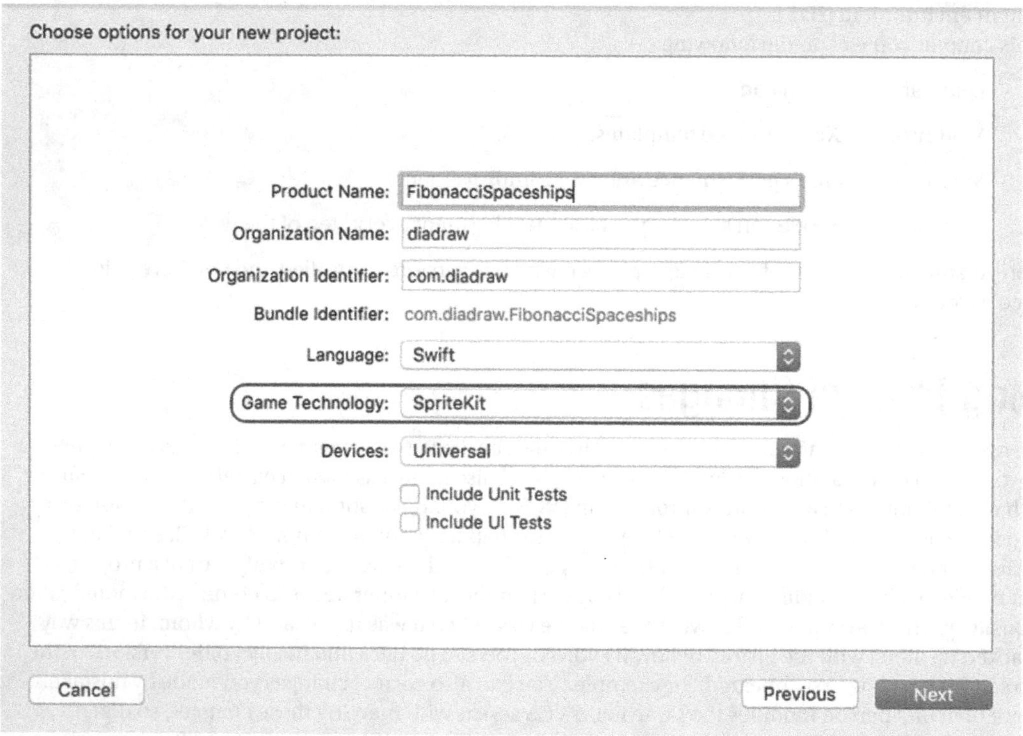

*Figure 4-1.* *Creating a new game project*

At the last step of the wizard set **Source Control** to **Create Git repository on My Mac** (Figure 4-2).

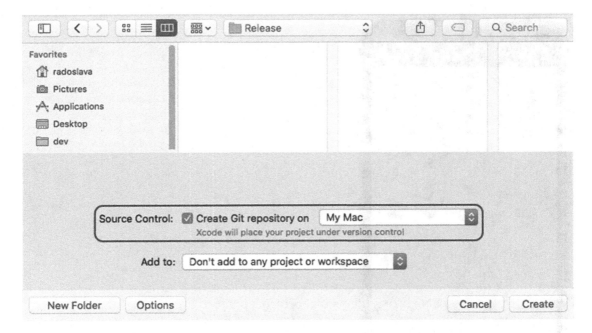

***Figure 4-2.*** *Putting a new project under version control*

When the project appears in Xcode, you will see that quite a lot has already been done: there are a couple of source code files, storyboards, and even assets. Run the app to see the result: there is a gray background with the words "Hello, World!" in the middle of the screen and whenever you tap, a rotating spaceship appears under your finger (Figure 4-3).

***Figure 4-3.*** *The SpriteKit game project out of the box*

It would be a good idea to have a look at where Xcode has created the repository for our project. In order to see it, navigate to the project folder in the Terminal app on your Mac and list the files in it by running

```
ls -a
```

The –a option instructs the ls command to show all files, including invisible ones. This reveals an otherwise hidden folder, called .git, where the local repository for our project is (Figure 4-4).

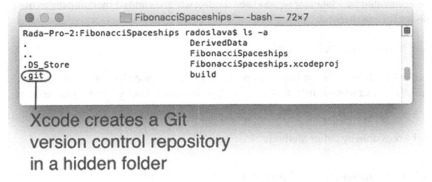

Xcode creates a Git
version control repository
in a hidden folder

*Figure 4-4.* *Inspecting the GIT repository that Xcode has created*

You can inspect .git further by navigating to it and running the ls command again or by running open
.git, which will show the folder's contents in Finder. Be careful not to manually change any of the files you
find there—this job is best left to the VCS.

Let us make some modifications to the source code in Xcode and see how Git handles these. We will give
each spaceship a code name. The code name will be the Fibonacci number, which corresponds to the order
in which the ship was added to the scene.[2] The text on the screen will change to greet each spaceship with its
code name when it first appears. So, for the first and the second ship the text will read "Welcome, 1!"[3]; for the
third it will change to "Welcome, 2!," for the eighth, to "Welcome, 21!," and so on. Just because we can.

In the Project navigator open GameScene.swift. It contains a class definition, which looks like Listing 4-1
(we have omitted the method implementations for brevity).

*Listing 4-1.* The Definition of the GameScene Class

```
import SpriteKit

class GameScene: SKScene {
    override func didMoveToView(view: SKView) {
        /* method definition */
    }

    override func touchesBegan(touches: Set<UITouch>,⏎
        withEvent event: UIEvent?) {
        /* method definition */
    }

    override func update(currentTime: CFTimeInterval) {
        /* method definition */
    }
}
```

---

[2]Fibonacci numbers form the following sequence: 0, 1, 1, 2, 3, 5, 8, 13, 21 . . ., where each number after the first two is
calculated as the sum of the previous two numbers in the sequence.
[3]These two will wreck havoc in space traffic control.

The text on the screen is controlled by a label (of type SKLabelNode), which is added dynamically to the scene on this line in the didMoveToView method:

```
let myLabel = SKLabelNode(fontNamed:"Chalkduster")
```

The first modification we will do is to make myLabel a property of the GameScene class. At the moment it is a local variable in didMoveToView. Cut its definition and paste it outside the method, so that the GameScene class looks like Listing 4-2.

***Listing 4-2.*** Making myLabel Accessible by Other Methods

```
class GameScene: SKScene {
    let myLabel = SKLabelNode(fontNamed:"Chalkduster")

    override func didMoveToView(view: SKView) {
        myLabel.text = "Hello, World!"
        myLabel.fontSize = 45
        myLabel.position = ↵
            CGPoint(x:CGRectGetMidX(self.frame), y:CGRectGetMidY(self.frame))

        self.addChild(myLabel)
    }

    // The rest of the class definition
}
```

We will add two more properties to GameScene: a variable that will keep track of how many spaceships have been added to the scene and a constant to limit their number to a maximum of 47. (The 47th number in the Fibonacci sequence is the last one we can store in an unsigned integer before we get overflow.) Add these two under the definition of myLabel as shown in Listing 4-3.

***Listing 4-3.*** Adding Properties to GameScene to Keep Track of Spaceships

```
let myLabel = SKLabelNode(fontNamed:"Chalkduster")
var spaceshipCount: UInt = 0
let maxSpaceships: UInt = 47
```

Next, modify the touchesBegan method to do the following. At the start it needs to check how many spaceships have been added to the scene and not allow more than the maximum we just defined. If another spaceship can be added, it needs to give it a code name and use that code name to display a greeting. The rest of the method we will leave as it is. Listing 4-4 shows you the modified version of touchesBegan.

***Listing 4-4.*** Modifying touchesBegan to Greet Each New Spaceship

```
override func touchesBegan(touches: Set<UITouch>, withEvent event: UIEvent?) {
    if spaceshipCount >= maxSpaceships {
        // If we have reached the maximum number of spaceships,
        // stop adding them to the scene.
        return
    }

    for touch in touches {
        let location = touch.locationInNode(self)
```

```
    let sprite = SKSpriteNode(imageNamed:"Spaceship")

    sprite.xScale = 0.5
    sprite.yScale = 0.5
    sprite.position = location

    let action = SKAction.rotateByAngle(CGFloat(M_PI), duration:1)

    sprite.runAction(SKAction.repeatActionForever(action))

    self.addChild(sprite)

    // Keep track of how many spaceships there are:
    spaceshipCount += 1

    // Give the newcomer a code name:
    let spaceshipCodeName = findFibonacciNumber(atPosition: spaceshipCount)

    // Greet the newcomer with its code name:
    myLabel.text = "Welcome, \(spaceshipCodeName)"
  }
}
```

Finally, let us implement a method, which will take a spaceship index and produce a code name by finding the corresponding Fibonacci number (Listing 4-5). It is called findFibonacciNumber and we already added a call to it in touchesBegan.

***Listing 4-5.*** Implementing findFibonacciNumber

```
func findFibonacciNumber(atPosition position: UInt) -> UInt {
    // The first two Fibonacci numbers are 0 and 1:
    if position <= 1 {
        return position
    }

    // After the first two, each number in the Fibonacci sequence
    // is calculated as the sum of its two preceding numbers
    // by calling findFibonacciNumber recursively:
    let fibonacciNumber = ↵
        findFibonacciNumber(atPosition: position - 1) + ↵
        findFibonacciNumber(atPosition: position - 2)

    return fibonacciNumber
}
```

Save the changes to GameScene.swift and notice how an "M" appears next to its name in the Project navigator (Figure 4-5).

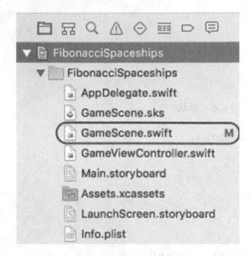

*Figure 4-5.  An M appears next to GameScene.swift to let you know it has been modified*

"M" stands for "modified" and this is Git telling us that we need to review our changes and commit them to the repository. Let us do that. From Xcode's main menu select **Source Control ➤ Commit...** Figure 4-6 shows you the commit window. On the left there is a list of files, which have changed. When you select one of the files, you can see two versions of it, called *revisions*, side by side. In the left half of the window is the version you just modified and in the right half, the last version that was committed to the local repository. Individual changes are highlighted, so you can quickly locate them. There is space at the bottom of the screen for typing a message: this is a short description of the changes you are about to commit. It will appear in the history of the committed files in the repository and make it easier for you to track how they evolved over time and why certain modifications were made. Click the **Commit 1 File** button to send your changes to the local repository.

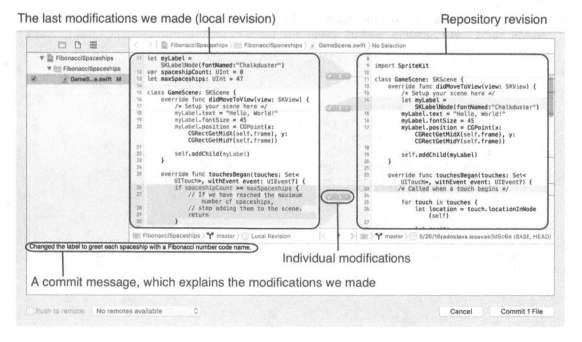

*Figure 4-6.  The commit window shows you the changes you made*

Let us have a look at the history of our project now. From Xcode's main menu select **Source Control ➤ History...** This opens the history window, which shows a list of revisions. You can see the initial commit that Xcode made for us when it created the project, as well as the commit we last made (Figure 4-7).

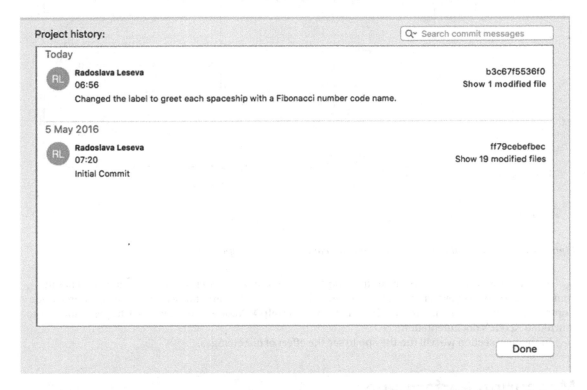

**Figure 4-7.** *The history window shows a list of the commits that were made to the repository*

Next to each revision in the list there is a button, which lets you browse and see what changes were committed. If you click **Show 3 modified files** next to the latest revision, you will see something very similar to the commit window we used earlier, this time read-only (Figure 4-8).

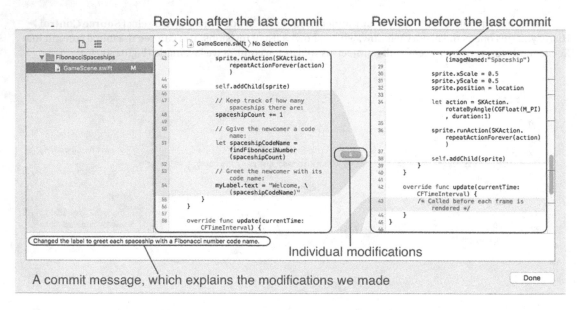

***Figure 4-8.*** *Inspecting the changes that were last committed to the repository*

You are now all set with version control. You can go back in time with revisions or create branches in your repository to test new functionality. For details on how to do this and more refer to "Using Source Code Control" in Xcode's manual. It is available online or from **Help ➤ Xcode Overview** (see **Chapter 1** for how to download Xcode's documentation).

In the next section we will run the app to see the effect of our changes.

# Measuring Performance

If you run the app we just made, you will notice that we did not cover ourselves in glory with the change we introduced to it. As you keep tapping the screen and adding more spaceships, each new spaceship takes longer and longer to appear and the action on the screen "hiccups" just before a new spaceship is spat out. In this section we will see how you can measure your source code's performance to find bottlenecks and make improvements.

Xcode comes with a large set of tools, called Instruments, which help you collect data about your code: its speed, memory usage, utilization of system resources and network connections, and even how its user interface behaves. The instruments are available from Xcode's main menu: **Xcode ➤ Open Developer Tool… ➤ Instruments**. You can also run your project through a particular instrument by selecting **Product ➤ Profile**.

Let us do just that: with the FibonacciSpaceships project open in Xcode select **Product ➤ Profile**. This will build the project and open the Instruments window, where you can choose what kind of data to collect. Note that the list you see does not show the instruments themselves but templates, each of which has been configured to work with a particular instrument.

Another thing to note is that you need to profile (i.e., run and collect statistics about) your app on the types of devices you expect users to have, as its performance in a simulator and on a device can differ quite a lot. As you can see in Figure 4-9, the FibonacciSpaceships project has been prepared for profiling on an iPad running iOS 9.3.1. For the same reason it makes sense to profile a release, rather than a debug build, so a release build is what Xcode produces when you build your project for profiling.

Your project has been built for profiling on a specific device

Choose a profiling template for: ▌ Radoslava's iPad (9.3.1) ⟩ ◮ FibonacciSpaceships

Standard    Custom    Recent                                              ⊝ Filter

| Blank | Activity Monitor | Allocations | Automation | Cocoa Layout | Core Animation |
|---|---|---|---|---|---|
| Core Data | Counters | Energy Log | File Activity | GPU Driver | Leaks |
| Metal System Trace | Network | OpenGL ES Analysis | System Trace | System Usage | Time Profiler |
| Zombies | | | | | |

◷ **Time Profiler**
Performs low-overhead time-based sampling of processes running on the system's CPUs.

Cancel    Choose

*Figure 4-9.* *Xcode's instrument templates*

Select the **Time Profiler** and click **Choose** to load the profiler template. The Time Profiler has a **Record** button: clicking it will run the project on your device and start recording performance statistics (Figure 4-10).

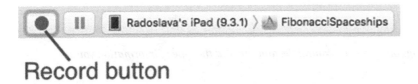

# Record button

*Figure 4-10.* *Click the Record button to start profiling the app*

When you start the profiler you will see the Details pane and the CPU Usage graph change: the Details pane shows stack traces of the threads running in your app (see **Chapter 7** on threads and concurrency) and CPU Usage tracks the load on the processor as your app runs. Give the app a hard time: tap away and don't go gentle on the tapping—add ships until the user interface visibly slows down. You will probably see that the CPU is working quite hard—something like Figure 4-11.

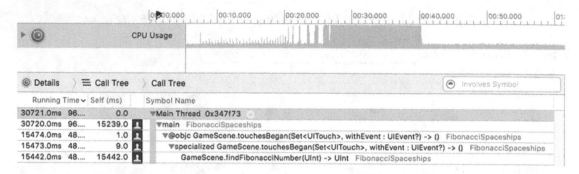

*Figure 4-11.* *The Call Tree and CPU usage show real-time information about the game's performance*

The pane on the right-hand side lets you set up how data is recorded and displayed. You can also use it to see details about the recording once it is in progress or has completed. Select **Display Settings** as shown in Figure 4-12.

*Figure 4-12.* *The Display Settings pane lets you control the amount and the type of information you see*

Let us have a look at the **Call Tree** options in the Display Settings pane.

- **Separate by Thread**. This gives you the option of seeing separate call trees for each of the threads running in the app. Leave it unchecked for this project.

- **Invert Call Tree**. By default the calls at the bottom of a stack trace are showed on top of the tree. This option inverts it. Check it to see how the methods we defined in GameScene.swift show up at the top. Then leave it turned off.

- **Hide System Libraries**. This option is useful when you want to focus exclusively on calls made to your code and not have to hunt for them in a big list of calls to system libraries. Turn this option on.

- **Flatten Recursion**. This option lets you see recursive functions as single entries, instead of one big tree of calls. To see what it does, find `GameScene.findFibonacciNumber` in the call tree and expand it, then turn Flatten recursion on and off. Leave the option unchecked.

- **Top Functions**. This option switches between including time spent only in a function itself and including time spent in functions it calls. Leave it turned off.

Next, open the **Extended Detail** pane as shown in Figure 4-13. It shows the heaviest stack trace and what a surprise to find our `findFibonacciNumber` method on top of it...

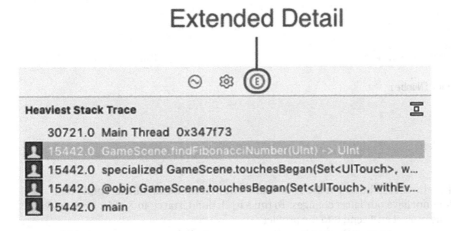

*Figure 4-13.* *The Extended Detail pane lets you drill down and find details about the call stack*

If you look at the call tree in the main window, you will see that `findFibonacciNumber` and the method that calls it, `touchesBegan`, are where the app has spent most of its time. Right-click `findFibonacciNumber` and from the pop-up menu select **Reveal in Xcode**, as shown in Figure 4-14. This takes us back to `GameScene.swift` in Xcode, where we can make improvements to the culprit for the hiccups in the user interface.

*Figure 4-14.* *You can navigate from the Call Tree back to the source code*

Let us change findFibonacciNumber into something more efficient. Listing 4-6 shows you the iterative version of the method. Replace findFibonacciNumber with it and let us have another go at profiling the app to see if this has improved performance.

**Listing 4-6.** Implementing an Iterative Version of findFibonacciNumber

```
func findFibonacciNumber(atPosition position: UInt) -> UInt {
    var fibonacciNumber = position

    if position > 1 {
        var a: UInt = 0
        var b: UInt = 1

        for _ in 2...position {
            fibonacciNumber = a + b
            a = b
            b = fibonacciNumber
        }
    }

    return fibonacciNumber
}
```

Note that if you clicked the Record button in the Time Profiler now, it would run the last build that Xcode sent to it, which does not have our latest changes. To run a fresh build, start it in Xcode: **Product ➤ Profile**. This will rebuild the project and send it to the profiler.

Start a new recording session and once the app launches, tap away until the greeting in the middle of the screen stops changing. The difference is noticeable in the app's performance: no more hiccups.[4] You can also see the difference in the CPU Usage graph in the Time Profiler, where you can visually compare recording sessions (Figure 4-15).

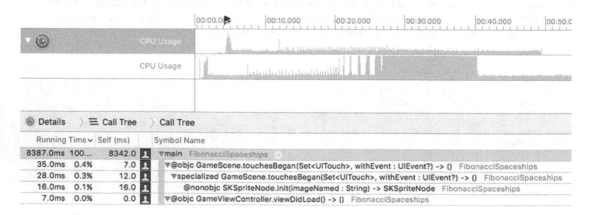

**Figure 4-15.** *Visually comparing recording sesssions*

---

[4]If you knew all along what would happen ever since we first implemented that wretched recursive function, apologies for the anticlimax. We are happy to receive "I told you so" e-mails.

Something else has changed too, though. Have a look at the call tree on Figure 4-15 to see if you can spot it. findFibonacciNumber has disappeared. Although actual timings will probably differ, the call probably disappeared from your profiler session too. This missing method is a good excuse to make a note about how Xcode's Time Profiler works.

There are various ways to collect statistical data about source code. The two most widely used are *instrumentation* and *sampling*. Following is a brief description of both methods.

- **Instrumentation**. With instrumentation additional code is inserted into the binary, in order to track how long a certain function call takes or how many times the call was made. The information collected in this way can be very precise down to lines of code, but at a cost: the inserted code adds time and memory overhead.

- **Sampling**. Sampling uses a different principle: execution is interrupted at regular intervals and call stack snapshots are taken to see what is running at that particular moment. This sacrifices precision but can give a feel for where time is spent and reveal problem areas. Xcode's Time Profiler uses sampling and probes an app every millisecond by default. So if a function takes less than that and is not called many times, it is likely to be missed by the sampler, which is the case with findFibonacciNumber.

You can control the sample interval from the Record Settings pane (Figure 4-16). The shortest interval you can set it to is half a millisecond (500 μs).

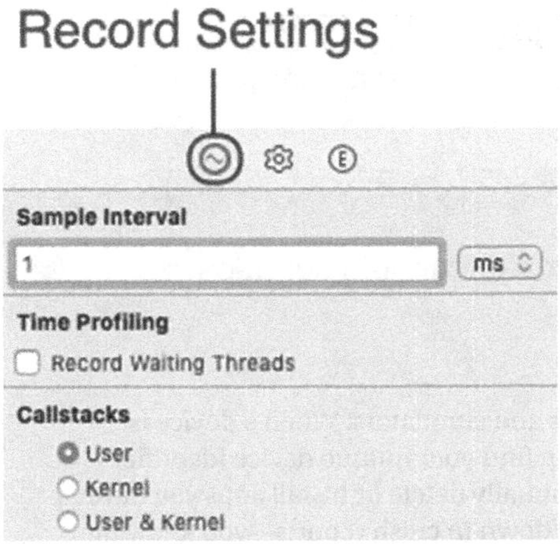

*Figure 4-16. Setting how frequently the Time Profiler samples the code*

Before closing the project, you can save the statistics from the Time Profiler to a .trace file. And do not forget to commit the optimized function to Git.

With this short tutorial we have barely scratched the surface of what is available through Xcode's instruments and profilers. A whole book can be dedicated solely to that. It is important, however, to know what is available and where to go for more information when you need it. Xcode's manual is a good place for that.

# Managing Devices

Back in **Chapter 2** we had a brief look at Xcode's Devices window. It can be your friend when it comes to managing development devices and gathering information about your apps, so we will have a more detailed overview of it. Figure 4-17 points out the main things with which it can help you.

**Figure 4-17.** *The Devices window*

On the left side of the Devices window there is a list of devices and simulators. When a device is selected, details about it are shown on the right side. There you can find your unique device identifier (UDID) or take screenshots of apps running on it. You can also manually delete or install apps you have developed and want to test. Viewing device logs can help you drill down in crash reports—you know the kind of crash that is hard to reproduce in debug builds.

In the device console at the bottom you can see real-time information about processes that are running on the device. In the past this was especially useful for tracking installation issues, when an app would fail to install on a device. In its latest version Xcode has become better at letting you know when there is a problem and what the problem is, but it is still a good idea to know where to dig for more information. Keep in mind that this console receives messages from pretty much everything that is active on the device at any given moment, so you may have to find your way through quite a lot of noise (or what appears to be noise when you are interested in what the matter is with a particular app). One useful tip is to use the search bar on top of the console (make it show up with **Cmd + F**) and search for the name of the app, about which you need information.

At the bottom of the left pane there is a settings button, which lets you inspect the provisioning profiles installed on a device (we became familiar with provisioning in **Chapter 2**) (see Figure 4-18).

***Figure 4-18.*** *Viewing the provisioning profiles, which are installed on a device*

# More Development Tools

Xcode offers a collection of other tools you might find useful at different stages of the development process. We will finish the chapter with a summary of some of the most widely used ones and a pointer for where you can find more information.

- **Application Loader**, available from **Xcode ➤ Open Developer Tool ➤ Application Loader**. This is the tool traditionally used for uploading builds to the App Store, as well as any in-app-purchase content. Some of its functionality now overlaps with Organizer.

- **Organizer**, available from **Window ➤ Organizer**. The Organizer window helps you manage your *archives* (i.e., app release builds) and lets you upload them to Apple's App Store.

- **File Merge**, available from **Xcode ➤ Open Developer Tool ➤ File Merge**. This tool lets you compare files side by side and merge changes in them. It is similar to the file comparison we saw in the commit window of Xcode's source control, but a bit more sophisticated than it. It lets you pick and choose changes and is very useful for merging different branches of code together.

- **Tools for internationalization**. As the name suggests, this is not a single tool but a whole set, which can help you make your app available on different markets around the world. You can get help not just with translations but with adapting your user interface to different layouts (e.g., making sure it displays right-to-left languages correctly) and using the relevant metric system and currency. Refer to the "Internationalization and Localization Guide," which comes with Xcode's documentation.

There is also a huge list of additional tools on Apple's web site. Selecting **Xcode ➤ Open Developer Tool ➤ More Developer Tools…** from Xcode's main menu will take you there.

# Summary

Now that you have completed **Part I** of the book you should have a good overall idea of what Xcode can do for you and where things are. In this chapter we explored some tools, which a lot of other IDEs do not include: integrated version control and profilers for measuring performance. We also had a peek at what else is available with Xcode and where to find more tools.

Of course, no amount of theory beats practice, so enough of the introductions, let us get on with work. We will see you in Part II, where we get on with app development by exploring options for user inferface (UI) design first.

# PART II

■ ■ ■

# Workflow Migration

# CHAPTER 5

■ ■ ■

# "Hello, Swift!"—A Tutorial for Building an iOS App

Xcode and the iOS SDK encourage you to use certain software design patterns when structuring and implementing an app. We are about to have a look at these patterns and learn how to take advantage of them. If you have fought your way through any of the theory books on design patterns[1] and your first thought is "Oh, no, not another one!," fret not. The goal of this chapter is that you learn by doing rather than by reading through pages of theory. We will make an app project and along the way cover the basics you will need for iOS app development in Xcode: from how to structure your project to how to work with storyboards and make your user interface (UI) adaptive.

In this chapter you will do the following:

- Learn about several software design patterns: *Delegation, Target-Action* and *Model-View-Controller (MVC)*.

- Learn how to structure your apps to take full advantage of MVC.

- Handle image assets in Xcode and create a custom view class.

- Use *Auto Layout* and *Size Classes* to make responsive UIs for different screen sizes.

When you are done, you will have an app with an adaptive UI that will run on any iOS device. We will have it display a cute panda and let the user change the panda's name.

## Developing a Project for the iOS

In Chapter 2 we had a go at setting up, provisioning, and running an iOS app, which didn't require a single line of code on your part. You saw how Xcode can generate and structure a working project for you and where the main tools at your disposal are. Now we will set up another app and will first spend some time dissecting the project and files that Xcode creates automatically: knowing how your project is structured will give you the best start.

---

[1]"The gang of four" famously opened their book on design patterns with "Don't worry if you don't understand this book completely on the first reading. We didn't understand it all on the first writing!" Erich Gamma, Richard Helm, Ralph Johnson, and John Vlissides, *Design Patterns: Elements of Reusable Object-Oriented Software* (Addison-Wesley 1995).

© Radoslava Leseva Adams and Hristo Lesev 2016
R. L. Adams and H. Lesev, *Migrating to Swift from Flash and ActionScript*,
DOI 10.1007/978-1-4842-1666-8_5

# Xcode mobile project anatomy

Create an iOS Single View Application project (**File ➤ New ➤ Project**, then **iOS ➤ Application ➤ Single View Application**) and name it **iOSProject**. Select **Swift** as the language and set **Devices** to **Universal**. Click **Create** and let us see what Xcode has generated for us: there are a bunch of Swift files, folders, a storyboard, and resource files in Project navigator.

## iOSProject

This is the root entry in the Project navigator and represents the project we have just created. It contains all source files, resources, and build settings.

## iOSProject Group

All project files are organized in groups. A group is used to keep files that logically belong together, but it doesn't have to correspond to an actual folder in the file system. You can create a new group by right-clicking inside Project navigator and selecting **New Group** from the pop-up menu.

## AppDelegate.swift

This file contains a single class, called AppDelegate, which serves as a helper to the application and gets notified about changes in the application's state. This class, in other words, acts as a *delegate* for the app, which gives it a special role. Following is a short explanation of the *Delegation design pattern*, which you will encounter many times in the iOS SDK.

---

## DELEGATION DESIGN PATTERN

The **Delegation design pattern** is used a lot in the iOS SDK. Its idea is to allow an object to delegate one of its tasks to a helper. The helper object provides an implementation for performing the task. In other words, the responsibility for the decision making is delegated to the helper object.

Let us take the class called UIApplication as an example. It is part of the iOS SDK and represents your app. Being part of the SDK, it needs to be pretty generic and leave room for you to define the behavior of your own app. For example, what happens before an app gets closed may vary: you may want to save the level a user reached in a game or to let go of the microphone or the camera. UIApplication can't provide for every possible scenario, so instead of deciding what should happen upon termination, it hands over that task to a helper class, which you implement: AppDelegate. If you have a look at the class in AppDelegate.swift you will see a method called applicationWillTerminate. As its name suggests, this method will be called just before the app terminates: this is UIApplication delegating the task to your class, so you can implement the behavior you need.

You have noticed that UIApplication is a class that has already been defined in the iOS SDK, whereas AppDelegate is part of your code (albeit generated for you by Xcode): you can name it Eric, if you like. For UIApplication to know how to hand over a task to AppDelegate or to Eric, as it happens, AppDelegate or Eric needs to be delegable (i.e., each needs to have a certain interface that can take tasks).

This is where *protocols* come in. A protocol defines an interface, which a type (a class, a structure, or an enumeration) can implement. That type is then said to *conform* to the protocol. In our case `AppDelegate` conforms to the `UIApplicationDelegate` protocol: `applicationWillTerminate`, as well as the rest of the methods which have been stubbed out for us to implement are part of the interface that `UIApplicationDelegate` delegate defines and that `UIApplication` expects to talk to.

For the time being you can think of *protocols* as an analogy to ActionScript's *interfaces*. You can find more on protocols in Chapter 21.

## ViewController.swift

Every screen (view) in the app is paired with a controller class. A controller supplies the view with data, responds to user actions, and is in charge of behavior when transitioning between screens. If you open `ViewController.swift` you will see a `ViewController` class already defined for you, which has a couple of methods:

- `viewDidLoad`: this method is called after the view has been created and loaded on screen. Here you can add code for the initial setup of your view: show user information, for example.

- `didReceiveMemoryWarning`: when called, this method gives you a chance to save any critical data and release resources when the operating system is running low on memory. Your app may get slapped on the wrist otherwise and get closed down.

Both of these methods override those in `UIViewController`: this class is part of the iOS SDK and is the base class that your `ViewController` inherits.

You can override another couple of methods of `UIViewController`, in order to customize what the view does just before and just after it is shown on screen:

- `viewWillAppear`: here you can perform operations before the view becomes visible. For example, you can refresh the displayed data.

- `viewDidAppear`: it is called when the view has just become visible. It may be a good place to notify the user if any heavy tasks are taking place, like fetching data from a server.

## Main.storyboard

A *storyboard* defines the app's user interface. Everything you create with the Interface builder: every screen, control, and so on. is stored inside this file. If you open a storyboard file in a text editor you will see that it is an XML file, containing the descriptions of UI elements, transitions, and connections.

Typically there will be one main storyboard per project. However, for applications with lots of screens or for situations where workload needs to be distributed between developers you can divide the UI between several storyboards.

## LaunchScreen.storyboard

This is the storyboard for your launch screen. Before iOS 8.0 this used to be a bunch of launch screen images instead.

## Assets.xcassets

This is not a single file, but a resource bundle, which contains the image assets for the app. It can contain your app's icon, launch screen, and all the images or textures that will be used in the views. In the Editor you can manage the bundle and provide different image resolutions for different screen sizes. We will see how to use image assets in the example later in this chapter.

## Info.plist

This file stores the settings of your app and lists the capabilities or *entitlements* that the app needs, for example the capability of using cloud services. The format of the file is XML key-value pairs.

Next comes the practical part: we will add an image and will get familiar with the Model-View-Controller paradigm by creating a custom View and Controller, as well as a custom Model, which will provide data to be displayed by the View.

## Using Assets

Apps often use a lot of images as part of their UI. We will see how to add and manage them.

First let us find an image that we can use in the example. If you go to `pixabay.com`, you can find thousands of free images under the Creative Commons license. I'm a bear lover, so I searched for "panda bear cute." Find your equivalent to a cute panda and download it[2]—any JPEG or PNG will do. I renamed the downloaded file to bear.png for short and this is how I will refer to it in the steps that follow.

Let us add bear.png to the project's assets. Click **Assets.xassets** in Project navigator to open the Asset Catalog editor. From there right-click inside the left panel and choose **Import** (Figure 5-1).

---

[2]Here is the link to the image I'm using, in case you want to download the same one: `https://pixabay.com/en/panda-bear-cute-happy-young-151587`.

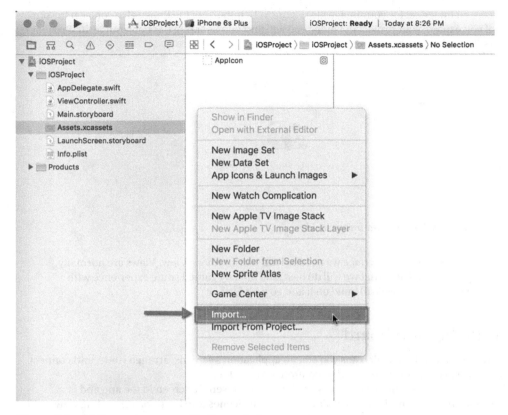

***Figure 5-1.*** *Adding an image asset to the project*

Find the image file using the Open dialog (Figure 5-2).

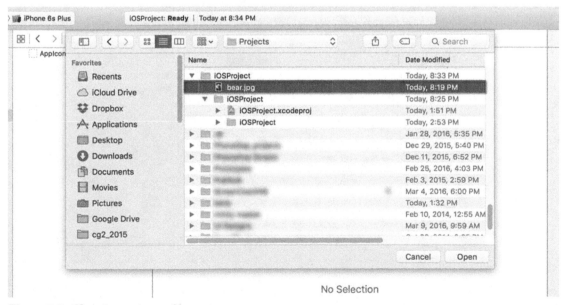

***Figure 5-2.*** *Choosing an image file*

This will create an image set for your image file (Figure 5-3). Importing the image also copies it in your project on disc: if you explore your project in Finder, you will find that bear.png has been put in iOSProject/Assets.xcassets/bear.imageset.

***Figure 5-3.*** *An image set with the panda image inside*

To show this image on the user interface we need to load it in an Image View. Views are normally composed on a storyboard, so that's what we will do next. You already gained some experience with storyboards from **Chapter 2**. Here we will build on it and go a bit further.

## Working with the Storyboard

Xcode has a powerful visual editor, which lets you edit an application's screens, arrange views, and connect UI elements with code in the corresponding view controller source file.

A storyboard consists of a sequence of scenes. Each scene represents a screen in the app and is composed of views such as buttons, labels, text views, and so on. Scenes also have corresponding view controller source files.

Transitions between scenes are also defined on the storyboard, using *segue* objects. Figure 5-4 shows an example of a storyboard with views, scenes and transitions between them.

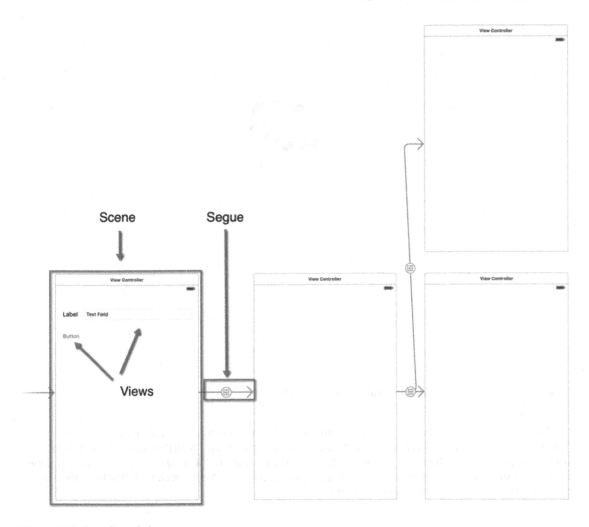

***Figure 5-4.*** *Storyboard elements*

I know what you are thinking: can I create UI programmatically? The answer is yes, you can. Storyboards are usually preferred however. Not only do they let you rapidly design UI by dragging and dropping components onto a scene, but they also help visualize the appearance and the flow of your app.

Before we start creating the UI, let me make a quick note about the word "view" and its usage. In this chapter depending on the context a view can refer to an element of the user interface of the application, an implementation of type that inherits UIView class or an abstract entity, which displays information to the user.

Let us add an Image View to show the panda: Figure 5-5 illustrates the steps. Select Main.storyboard to open it in the storyboard editor. In Object library find an Image View and then drag and drop it onto the scene: initially it's just a rectangle, which says "Image View." To load the picture of the panda, with the Image View selected open Attributes inspector and set the **Image** drop-down to "bear." The image is likely to be stretched and look out of proportion. In Attributes inspector set **Mode** to Aspect Fit to fix that.

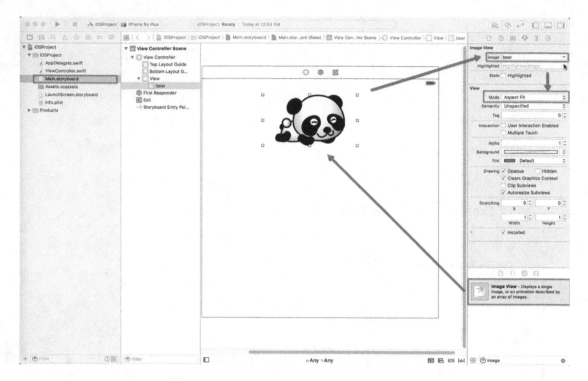

***Figure 5-5.*** *Add an Image View and display an image in it*

Let us finish designing the UI by adding a Label and a Text Field below the panda Image View. In Object library search for a Label and drag and drop it onto the storyboard. With the Label selected go to Attributes inspector and change its text to "My name is." If the Label's text appears shortened, resize the label horizontally until you see the text without trailing ellipses (Figure 5-6). Now search for a Text Field view in the Object library and drag and drop it below the label.

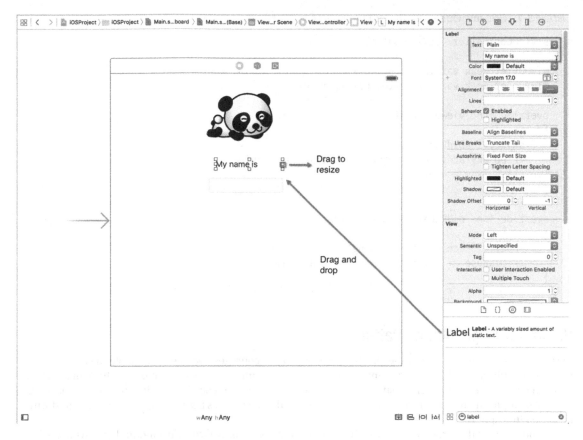

**Figure 5-6.** *Add a label view and resize it*

For now, do not worry if the UI is aligned or not: we will take care of this later on in the chapter.

Next are outlets and actions: you saw how to create them in **Chapter 2**, now we will see why we need them.

## Creating Outlets

All UI elements (views) we add onto the storyboard are instantiated as objects in memory when the app starts. The instances are created behind the scenes and we can't access them unless we create references to them, called *outlets*.

An outlet is typically added as a property in a view controller class. It is marked with the @IBOutlet attribute, which makes it accessible to the storyboard: this serves as a connection between the storyboard and the code.

Create outlets for the Label and the Text Field in the ViewController class in ViewController.swift the way we learned to do it in **Chapter 2**: open Main.storyboard and ViewController.swift side by side in Assistant editor and Ctrl+drag each UI element into the definition of the ViewController class. Name the Label outlet label and the Text Field outlet textField.

The ViewController class should now look like this (Listing 5-1):

***Listing 5-1.*** Creating Outlets for the UI Elements

```
class ViewController: UIViewController
{
    @IBOutlet weak var label: UILabel!
    @IBOutlet weak var textField: UITextField!

    override func viewDidLoad()
    {
        super.viewDidLoad()
        // Do any additional setup after loading the view,
 // typically from a nib.
    }

    override func didReceiveMemoryWarning()
    {
        super.didReceiveMemoryWarning()
        // Dispose of any resources that can be recreated.
    }
}
```

## Using the Target-Action Pattern

*Target-Action* is another design pattern, which the iOS SDK encourages you to use. It enables a system of objects to notify each other that an event has occurred and to target that event to an object that can act on it. You will typically see the pattern in situations where the app needs to react to an action done by the user, for example, tapping a button. The button view that receives the tap notifies a *target* object, which can perform an *action* in response.

In our context the target object is the ViewController instance. We will add a method to it, which will serve as the action to be performed when the user enters text in the text field: you can think of it as an event handler. This method has the following signature and is marked with the @IBAction attribute, which serves as a link between the storyboard and the code.

***Listing 5-2.*** Signature of an Action Method

```
@IBAction func actionName(sender: AnyObject)
```

You gained some experience with adding actions to view controllers from **Chapter 2**. Here is a quick reminder for how to do it: with Main.storyboard and ViewController.swift opened side by side, Ctrl+drag the Text Field from the storyboard into the definition of ViewController. Set the **Connection** in the pop-up dialog to **Action**, set **Event** to **Editing Changed**, name the action nameHasChanged, and click **Connect** to create the action method in ViewController (Figure 5-7).

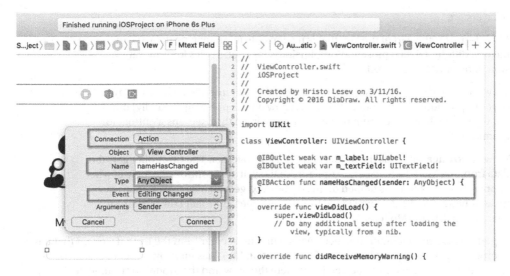

**Figure 5-7.** *Creating an action*

Leave action body empty for now. We will add logic to it in the next section, which shows you how to divide your code into layers of responsibilities with the *Model-View-Controller* pattern.

# Model-View-Controller Design Pattern

This is the third pattern, which abounds in iOS programming and the iOS SDK is designed to let you take advantage of it. Whole applications are designed using this pattern. MVC is not new to the Flash and ActionScript world, so you may have already used it a number of times. The next section provides a quick intro, in case you would like a refresher.

## MVC in Theory

The idea behind MVC is that the application is separated into three different functional layers: a model layer, which manages data; a view layer, which shows the data; and a controller layer, which controls how data is interacted with (Figure 5-8).

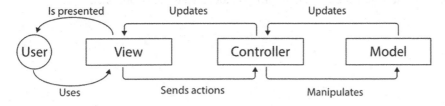

**Figure 5-8.** *Model-View-Controler pattern*

The three layers are

- **Model**—this is the part of the app that is responsible for managing data. It can include different data representations, business logic, and rules for how data is stored, retrieved, and edited.

- **View**—this is what the user sees on the screen: the user interface. The View layer of your app should care about how it looks (how data is presented visually) but not where the data comes from or what happens when the user taps a button, for example.

- **ViewController**—it binds the Model and the View together. The Controller gets the data from the Model and uses it to update the View. It also controls the logic of what happens when a button is tapped or an edit box text gets changed. When the user makes changes to the data presented by the View, the Controller commits these changes back to the Model.

The MVC pattern is such a common practice, that it won't be very far from the truth if we said that it is present in any program with a graphical user interface. Note that MVC has many incarnations, each of which is subtly different from the rest. You will find versions where the View and the Model communicate directly, for example. Here we have presented Apple's implementation of the pattern.

---

## ACTIONSCRIPT ANALOGY

Those of you who have worked with Adobe Flash Builder will already be familiar with structuring a project using the MVC paradigm. A typical application project in Flash Builder consists of an .mxml file, which represents the View; an ActionScript class, which serves as the Controller and often another class for the Model.

---

Let us structure our project in a way that will illustrate how MVC is meant to be used in iOS mobile apps.

# Creating a Model

We will start by creating separate groups in the project tree for each part of the MVC triad. While this is not mandatory, it is considered to be a good practice to logically separate files for easy navigation around the project.

Create three new file groups by right-clicking the iOSProject folder in Project navigator and selecting **New Group** from the context menu (Figure 5-9). Name the groups Model, View, and Controller.

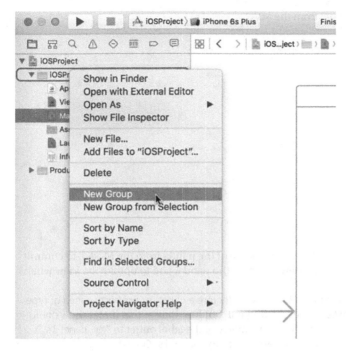

***Figure 5-9.*** *Creating a new file group*

As the names of the file groups imply, each group will hold the source files of the corresponding part of the MVC pattern. Drag the `ViewController.swift` file to move it to the Controller group. The project tree should look like Figure 5-10.

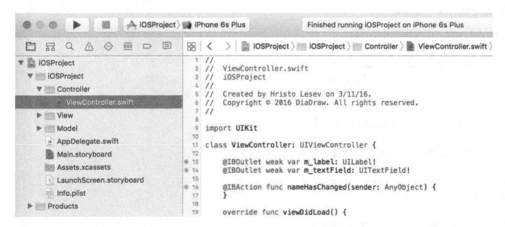

***Figure 5-10.*** *Move ViewController.swift file to Cotroller group*

Next we will create a Panda class that will hold data about our panda and will act as the Model in the application. Right-click the Model group and choose **New File** from the context menu. In the wizard that appears choose **iOS ➤ Source ➤ Swift file** and name the file `Panda.swift`. Inside we will define the Panda class. The class will have one property of type `String` for the name of the panda: not a huge amount of data, but this will suffice to illustrate how to separate the data into the Model layer of the app. You can see the Panda class in Listing 5-3.

*Listing 5-3.* Panda Class Representing the Model from the MVC

```
import Foundation

class Panda {

    var name : String

    init( pandaName : String ){

        name = pandaName
    }
}
```

# Setting Up the Controller

Next comes the Controller. The Controller's task is to load the name of the panda from the Model, to commit the changes back to the Model when the user types a new name for the panda, and to update the View when the panda's name changes (Listing 5-4).

Open `ViewController.swift` in the Code editor. First we will declare a constant property panda of type Panda and will set its name in the initializer to Cute. Not too original, but hey, look at that image: how could one resist? Go to the `viewDidLoad()` function and set the text property of the label outlet to `"My name is \(panda.name)"` so when the app starts the label on the screen will say `My name is Cute`

The last thing to do in the Controller is to edit the model and to refresh the Label view when a change has been made. Remember the `nameHasChanged(:)` *action* we created earlier? It is called every time the user changes the text in the Text Field view. This is where we will update the data in the Model: that is, we set the name property of panda to what the user typed in the Text Field, which we access through the `textField` outlet. After the Model has been updated, we change `label` to show the modified data.

*Listing 5-4.* Filling Up the Controller

```
class ViewController: UIViewController {

    @IBOutlet weak var label: UILabel!
    @IBOutlet weak var textField: UITextField!

    //
    let panda : Panda = Panda(pandaName: "Cute")

    @IBAction func nameHasChanged(sender: AnyObject) {

        //Edit the model when text field view changes
        panda.name = textField.text!

        //Display the new name of the panda
        label.text = "My name is \(panda.name)"
    }

    override func viewDidLoad() {
        super.viewDidLoad()
```

```
        //Display panda's name when the view is loaded
        label.text = "My name is \(panda.name)"
    }

    override func didReceiveMemoryWarning() {
        super.didReceiveMemoryWarning()
        // Dispose of any resources that can be recreated.
    }
}
```

## Creating a View

The final piece of the MVC puzzle is the View. While there are plenty of ready-to-use view components, there will be times when you need to implement a view with custom design and functionality. The good news is that you do not need to start writing the view from scratch, but you can use an existing view and extend it in a subclass. This is what we will do here. Imagine we want all of our panda images to have rounded corners and on a green background. The iOS SDK UIImageView class has properties that control the background and the radius of the corners, but if we want all panda images in the project to be rounded and green by default we can achieve this by creating a new view class.

Add a new file to the View group in the Project navigator. When the new file wizard appears select **iOS ➤ Source ➤ Cocoa Touch Class** and click Next. At the next step set the class name to RoundedImageView and make it a subclass of UIImageView. Click Next to create the new Swift file.

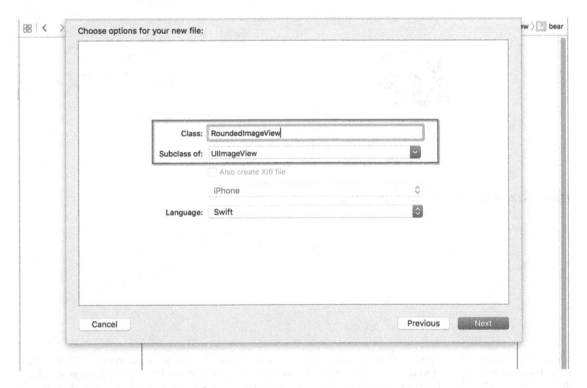

***Figure 5-11.*** *Create a custom view class*

When you open the new file, you will see that Xcode has already generated most of the code for the class. What is left for us to do is to access and modify the properties of the parent class that control the appearance of the view. We will do this in the awakeFromNib() method (Listing 5-5), which is called when the view is loaded from the Interface Builder archive.[3] In this method we will modify the view a bit by setting its color to green and its corner radius to 10.0. We will also get the Image View to clip itself, so we can see the rounded corners.

***Listing 5-5.*** RoundedImageView Class Implemetation

```
class RoundedImageView: UIImageView {

    override func awakeFromNib() {
        self.backgroundColor = UIColor.greenColor()
        self.layer.cornerRadius = 10.0;
        self.clipsToBounds = true;
    }
}
```

To use the newly created view class, open Main.storyboard and select the Image View. Open the Identity inspector and change Class to RoundedImageView as shown in Figure 5-12.

***Figure 5-12.*** *Setting custom class to the image view*

---

[3]During the build phase of the project all views and storyboards you have created are archived in .nib files. When a .nib file is loaded in memory, all of its contents get unachieved or *awakened*. If instead of a .nib you stumble upon an .xib, do not panic: they both have the exact same information inside; just store it in a different way. So you can think about .nib and .xib as synonyms.

Now if you run the app in the simulator you will see how our cute panda sits on top of a green background with rounded corners (Figure 5-13).

**Figure 5-13.** *The app running in a simulator*

So far in this chapter you learned how to structure your project using the MVC paradigm, what the Delegate pattern is, how to lay out the UI, and how to connect it to code using outlets and actions.

# UI Layout Techniques

Now it is time to see how to align the views on the screen and how to set up the UI to look good on different screen sizes.

## Auto Layout

When you design the UI of an application, you need to consider what its UI will look like on devices with different screen sizes and resolutions. Making it adaptive to different screen orientations is also a good thing: *Auto Layout* is a tool that does that by automatically recalculating the size and position of every element on the screen, taking into account any predefined constraints you have set.

## FLASH ANALOGY

If you have experience with Flex, you have definitely used layouts before. Flex uses several different layout containers: absolute, horizontal, vertical, tile, and so on. Each of them resizes and repositions the views it contains the way its name suggests. You can think of an Auto Layout as a layout container, but with more general rules, where each view is aligned and sized relative to its neighbors.

We will do a bit of planning for the UI of our app. Let's say we want the panda image to be horizontally centered on the screen and to have its top edge at 20 pixels from the top of the screen. We also want the vertical gap between all views to be 20 pixels. The Label view will take all the available width of the screen and the width of the Text Field view will be half of the width of the Label. See the UI sketch in Figure 5-14.

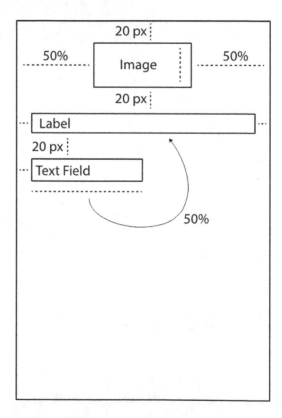

***Figure 5-14.*** *Sketching out the sizes and positions of the elements in the app's UI*

We also want these constraints to hold on every iOS device and for every screen orientation. If your lips are forming the question "Why?!," let's assume that this is what the client who has commissioned this app wants. This probably raises another "Why?!," but let's not go there. . . .

To see what the design looks like on different devices while we are still working on it, toggle the storyboard Preview window (Figure 5-15): select **Main.storyboard** and open the Assistant editor. Find the Assistant menu button and select **Preview ➤ Main.storyboard**.

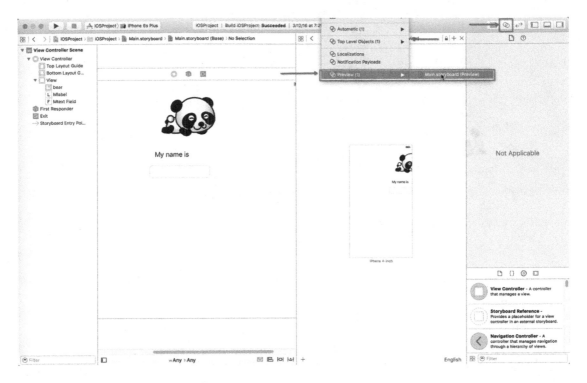

**Figure 5-15.** *Show the Preview window*

You can add multiple previews for different devices by clicking the + button at the bottom. Click it and select iPad and iPhone5.5 from the pop-up menu (Figure 5-16). You can see how the panda is not centered on the iPhone preview and all of the views (Image View, Label, and Text Field) appear clipped.

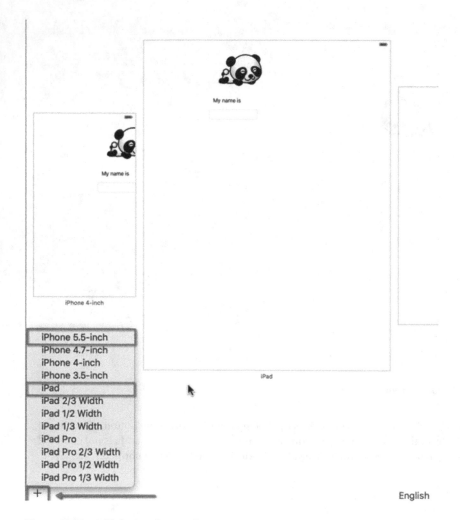

**Figure 5-16.** *Add devices for preview*

Let's add some constraints that will keep the views aligned. You can think of a constraint as a rule that you want a view to follow. For example, you can say that you want the top edge of the view to be positioned at a certain distance from the top edge of the screen or that two views should always maintain the same height.

All of the constraints put together form a system of linear equations. When solved, they result in actual numbers for the views' widths, heights and positions. Solving the system is Auto Layout's job.

There are two types of constraints. The first type is applied to a single view, for example, to give it a fixed width or height. The second type is defined as requirements for one view, relative to another view.

You had a go at using the Auto Layout tools back in **Chapter 2** and we will put them to use again. Start by selecting the Image View and click the Pin button. Set **Spacing to nearest neighbor** to 20 pixels to the top of the scene. Set **Height** to 98 pixels, tick **Aspect ratio,** and click **Add 3 Constraints**. You will see the constraints appear in the document outline on the left (Figure 5-17). A note: we only added the Aspect ratio constraint temporarily: it will prevent Auto Layout from stretching the image while we are adding other constraints (i.e. while the system of equations is still underdefined); we will get rid of it later.

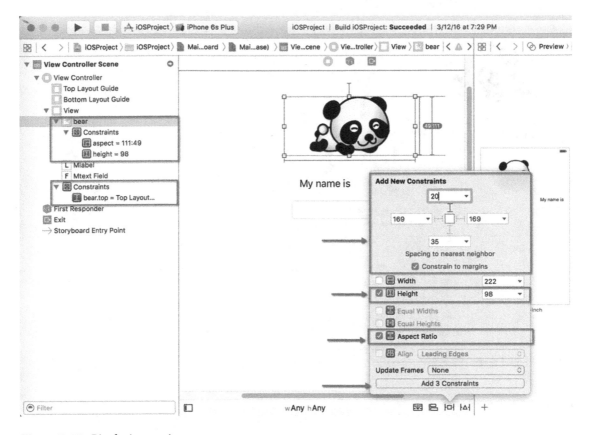

***Figure 5-17.*** *Pin the image view*

Next, select the Label and open the Pin dialog again. Pin the Label at 20 pixels vertically away from the Image View by setting the top **Space to nearest neighbor** to 20 pixels. Set the left and the right spaces to 10 pixels each: this will be the distance that the Label will maintain from the edges of its parent view. Click **Add 3 constraints** to apply them to the scene (Figure 5-18).

***Figure 5-18.*** *Pin the label view*

Pin the Text Field 20 pixels away from its nearest neighbor at the top and at 10 pixels from the left and from the right edge of its parent view.

To set the width of the Text Field to half that of the Label, select both views, open the Pin dialog and check the **Equal Widths** checkbox, then click **Add 1 Constraint** (Figure 5-19).

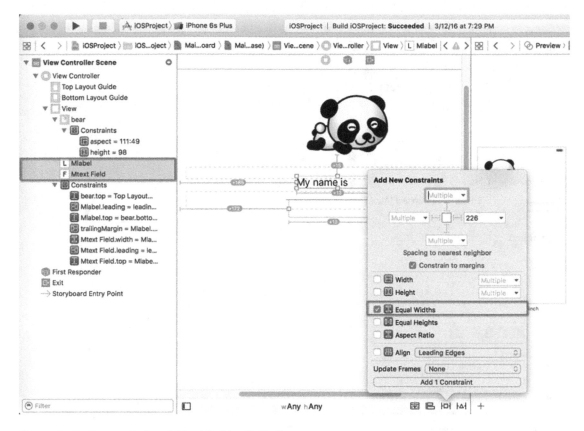

**Figure 5-19.** *Constrain the width of the Text Field view*

Setting the two UI elements to have equal widths when we are aiming to have one of them half the width of the other may seem a bit confusing. We will fix this in a minute.

With the Text Field selected open Size inspector (Figure 5-20), find the **Equal Widths** constraint, and double-click to edit it.

**Figure 5-20.** *Size inspector*

The first three fields in the Equal Widths Constraint form determine the two UI elements that the constraint will take into account or affect (Figure 5-21): **First item** should be set to **Mlabel.Width** and **Second Item** should be set to **MText Field.Width**.

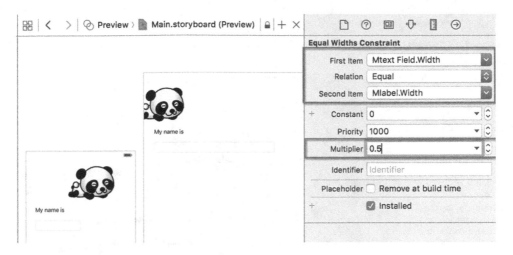

**Figure 5-21.** *Adjusting the width multiplier*

If you have a look further down the form, you will see a setting called **Multiplier**: this is what will help us set the correct proportion for the widths. The Multiplier setting is used to calculate a property proportional to another property. In this case it will be used for setting the width of the Text Field proportional to the width of the Label. The Multiplier, as its name implies, multiplies the selected property of the **Second Item** and applies the result to the selected property of the **First item**. We can set the Multiplier value to any floating point number: 1.0 means that the two properties should be equal. To make Text Field half the width of the Label, we need to set Multiplier to 0.5.

The last thing left to do is to center the panda horizontally on the screen. Select the Image View and its parent view (the screen in this example) and click the **Align** button (Figure 5-22). Tick **Leading Edges** and **Trailing Edges** and click **Add 2 Constraints**.

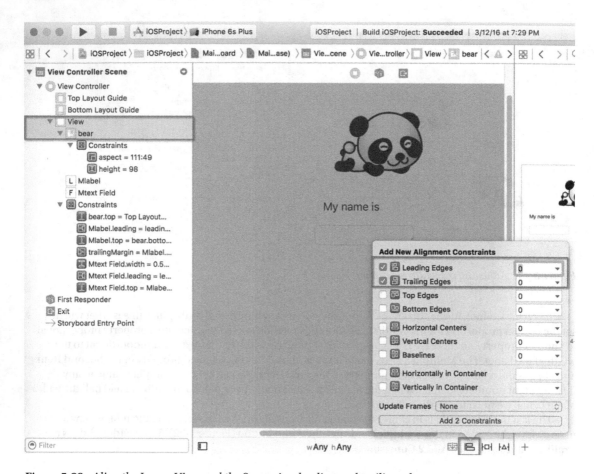

**Figure 5-22.** *Align the Image View and the Superview leading and trailing edges*

In the Document outline panel select the leading edge constraint you just created (Figure 5-23). Then, with the constraint selected, in Size inspector set **Second item** to **Superview.Center.X** and **Multiplier** to 0.5. This sets the left edge of the Image View in the middle of the first 50% of its containing view.

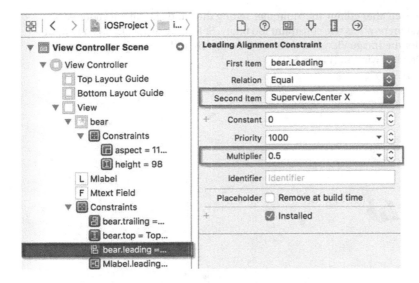

*Figure 5-23.* *Align the Image View's leading edge to 50% to the left of the Superview center*

To actually center the Image View, we have to set its right edge to be in the middle of the second 50% of its containing view. To apply this logic select the **Trailing Edge** constraint in Document outline (Figure 5-24), then in Size inspector set **Second item** to **Superview.Center.X** and **Multiplier** to 1.5.

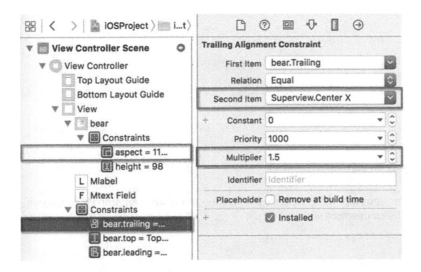

*Figure 5-24.* *Align Image View trailing edge to 50% to the right of the Superview center*

You may have noticed that even after editing the Multiplier setting the panda is still not centered properly. This is because the system now has one constraint too many. Select the Aspect Ratio constraint that we temporarily set earlier for the Image View and delete it. Now you should see the panda image centered on all devices in the Preview window (Figure 5-25).

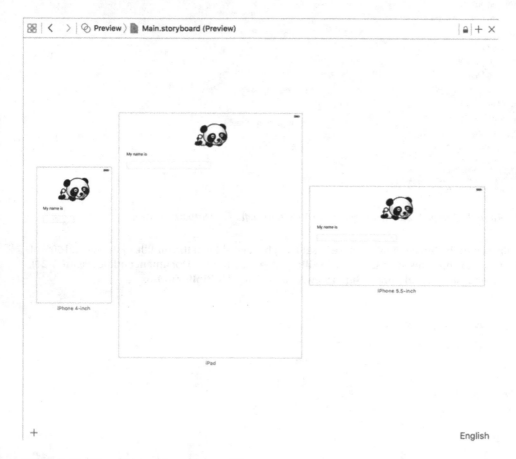

***Figure 5-25.*** *The app's user interface on different screen sizes*

And thus we made the UI of the app responsive. Next we will see how to enhance an Auto Layout, so we can fully master the real estate of different screen sizes.

## Size Classes

Having an adaptive UI is not always the whole story. Sometimes you want your application to make different use of different screen sizes and change its look (not just resize itself) depending on what device and what orientation it is used in. For example, a video chat app that shows video in its top half and a text area for typing in its bottom half on an iPad and on an iPhone in portrait orientation may be better presented with the video view taking the whole screen when the iPhone is rotated to landscape. Before iOS 8 providing these two different looks meant creating and maintaining two storyboards, which often resulted in duplicated work.

Size Classes were introduced to help with that. Here the word "class" is used to mean "category" rather than the object-oriented programming concept. They work together with Auto Layout: instead of having the same constraints apply to your UI all the time, you can categorize them. In other words, you can choose a constraint to only be applied in a certain case by setting it to belong to a given Size Class.

There are two main types of Size Classes: horizontal and vertical. They can be set to one of three options: Regular, Compact or Any. Each combination corresponds to a different device and screen orientation, summarized in Table 5-1.

***Table 5-1.*** *Size Classes–Devices Correspondence*

| | | Horizontal Size Class | |
|---|---|---|---|
| **Vertical Size Class** | | Regular | Compact |
| | **Regular** | Device: iPad<br>Orientation: portrait, landscape | Device: iPhone<br>Orientation: portrait |
| | **Compact** | | Device: iPhone<br>Orientation: landscape |

We will set constraints for the cute panda app and classify them with Size Classes to get a different look on the iPad. Imagine a client called to ask that only on the iPad all views be moved toward the bottom of the screen by 500 pixels.

Before we set the new constraints, we need to specify that we are now designing for the iPad screen size. With the storyboard open click the Size Class button and select Regular row and Regular column (Figure 5-26).

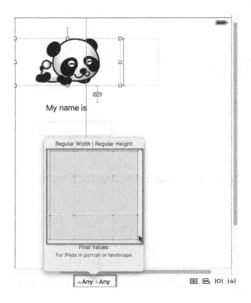

***Figure 5-26.*** *Set Size Classes to match iPad (Regular | Regular)*

Select the panda image view and pin its top at 500 pixels from the top edge of its parent view (Figure 5-27). You might notice that the bottom bar of the Interface builder has changed to blue: this is Xcode's way of reminding us that we are working in a Size Class mode different than Any | Any.

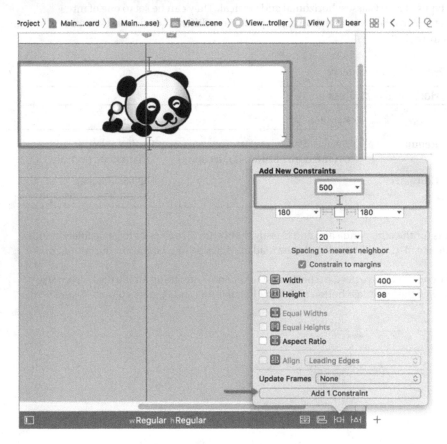

**Figure 5-27.** *Pin the Image View to Top with 500 pixels for the iPad*

Now if you look at the Preview window, you will see how all the views appear lower down only on the iPad preview (Figure 5-28).

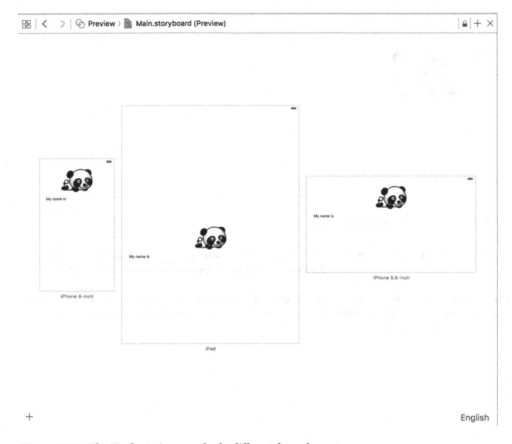

***Figure 5-28.*** *The iPad preview now looks different from the rest*

This is the power of Size Classes.

## Resolving Layout Issues

While designing the UI of the app you will inevitably stumble upon some red and orange lines around some of the view elements (Figure 5-29). This is how Interface Builder informs you about possible issues in the layout that you must consider resolving.

***Figure 5-29.*** *Constraints issues indicator lines*

The orange lines are used as a warning that there might be a missing constraint or that the Interface Builder has a suggestion for changing a constraint value. The red lines appear when there are conflicting constraints.

There are two ways to handle layout issues. You can try to edit the constraints manually until the Interface Builder is satisfied, or you can use the Resolve Auto Layout Issues tools, a button placed at the bottom of the storyboard editor panel (Figure 5-30).

***Figure 5-30.*** *Resolve Auto Layout Issues*

There are several options from which we can choose:

- **Update Frames**. This will update the frame of the selected view to match the constraints that were added.

- **Update Constraints**. This will do the opposite and change the values of the constraints to match what you see in the scene.

- **Add Missing Constraints**. If the applied constraints are not enough to resolve the layout, this operation will try to add the necessary constraints in order to satify the layout engine.

- **Reset to Suggested Constraints**. This will replace all constraints applied to the selected view with new ones suggested by the layout engine.

- **Clear Constraints**. This does what its name implies and removes all constraints from the selected view.

Try to avoid issues by adding just enough constraints to the views. If you add too little, you will create ambiguities; if you overconstrain the views, the chance to have conflicting constraints increases.

# Summary

In this chapter you saw how to apply three different design patterns, very much encouraged and employed by the iOS SDK: Delegation, Target-Action, and Model-View-Controller.

You used the MVC pattern to structure an application and implemented a custom view in it. You then made its UI responsive and adaptive with Auto Layout and Size Classes.

You should be proud of yourself. Now buckle up and prepare to enter the deep waters of the advanced UI presented in the next chapter.

# CHAPTER 6

■ ■ ■

# Adding a More Complex UI

In this chapter we dig deeper in designing user interfaces (UIs) for iOS with Swift by making another app. There is a lot of ground to cover both on the UI front and on the language front. To make things easier, we will point out some of the Swift concepts that may look new or strange, explain them along the way, and let you know where you can find more information.

In this chapter you will do the following:

- Learn how to add views to your app and transition between them.

- Try out different navigation patterns.

- Learn how to pass data between view controllers.

- Learn one more way of making adaptive UIs.

- Learn how to work with a table view and use it to present interactive choices.

- Handle user settings.

- Learn how to customize your app's launch screen.

- Learn about the Observer design pattern.

- Create and manage a UI programmatically.

- Learn how to use annotations to make your code easier to navigate.

When you are done, you will have an app that lets you collect votes from your friends when trying to decide where to go for dinner or which film to see.

---

■ **Swift reference**   Look for notes like this one throughout the chapter. They contain brief descriptions of Swift language features that we use in the code and will point you to the relevant chapters in Part IV, which is dedicated to language migration. Or, if you would prefer to dig into the language first, you can go to Part IV of this volume (chapters 17 to 22) and come back to the tutorials in this chapter later with an even better understanding of Swift.

---

## Setting Up the App

In the course of this chapter we will develop two versions of the same app:

- a Lite version, which lets users vote on a single topic and shows them the results of the vote; and

© Radoslava Leseva Adams and Hristo Lesev 2016
R. L. Adams and H. Lesev, *Migrating to Swift from Flash and ActionScript*,
DOI 10.1007/978-1-4842-1666-8_6

- a Pro version, which adds a settings screen and also allows for new voting topics and choices to be created.

Both apps will start off with the same logic and UI and on top of that we will add Lite and Pro functionality. In this section we will build this common logic and UI in a project, which we will later clone to create the two different versions of the app.

Start by making a new Single View Application iOS project in Xcode (**File ➤ New ➤ Project...**, then **iOS ➤ Application ➤ Single View Application**). Call it SimpleVote and set its language to Swift. This will create the boilerplate project, with which you are intimately familiar by now (Figure 6-1).

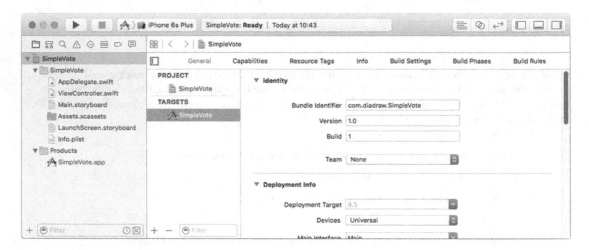

***Figure 6-1.*** *The boilerplate Single View Application project*

# Defining a Data Model

The voting app will use a simple data model, which contains a topic for the vote, a list of choices, and the number of participants who cast their votes or abstained. Each choice has a title and keeps track of how many votes it receives.

Let us define a *structure* that will represent a choice first. Create a new group in your project and call it Data model. Select the new group and create a new Swift file in it (**File ➤ New ➤ File... ➤ iOS ➤ Source ➤ Swift File**). Call the file Choice.swift. Then add the following definition (Listing 6-1).

***Listing 6-1.*** Defining a Structure to Represent a Choice for Voting

```
struct Choice {
    let title: String
    var votes: Int = 0

    init(title: String) {
        self.title = title
    }
}
```

The Choice structure represents a single option users can vote on. It has a constant member, called title, which we can set to "Pizza," "Thai food," and so on, and a variable member votes, which keeps track of how many votes the choice has received. The init method we have added is similar to a constructor in ActionScript: in Swift it is called *initializer* and its purpose is to ensure that all properties of Choice have initial values.

---

■ **Swift reference**   For the moment you can think of structures as similar to classes: they are types, which keep together data (member variables and constants) and behavior (methods). We look at structures and initializers in detail in Chapter 21.

---

Add another Swift file to the Data  model group and call it VoteData.swift. Let us define another structure in it, called VoteData. This one will store the vote topic and choices, as well as information on a voting session: how many participants there were and how they voted (Listing 6-2).

*Listing 6-2.*  Defining a Structure for Keeping Data on the Voting Session

```swift
struct VoteData {
    // Set a default topic for voting:
    var topic = "Which one would you choose?"

    // An array of choices for voting:
    var choices: [Choice] = []

    // The number of participants, who voted or abstained:
    var participants = 0

    var votes: Int {
        get {
            var numVotes = 0

            // Each choice keeps track of the number of votes
            // it receives, so just sum them all up:
            for choice in choices {
                numVotes += choice.votes
            }

            return numVotes
        }
    }

    var abstains: Int {
        get {
            // Work out how many participants abstained:
            return participants - votes
        }
    }

    mutating func resetVotes() {
        // Clear the vote information for a new session:
        participants = 0

        for i in 0 ..< choices.count {
            choices[i].votes = 0
        }
    }
}
```

Before we put this structure to use, let us look at its members and what each of them does, clarifying a few Swift concepts along the way.

The first property in VoteData is topic and is initialized with a literal string. The initialization helps the Swift compiler infer the type of topic.

---

■ **Swift reference**   Swift is a strongly typed language, but you do not have to explicitly declare types if they can be inferred. For more information on type inference, see Chapter 19.

---

The second property, choices, is an array of Choice instances. The following line,

```
var choices: [Choice] = []
```

declares choice and also initializes it with an empty array.

---

■ **Swift reference**   For details on arrays and other container types see Chapter 19.

---

The votes and abstains members are *computed properties*.

---

■ **Swift reference**   A computed property is like a hybrid between a property and a method: it does not store its value but rather works it out it on the fly. For more details see Chapter 21.

---

The resetVotes method has been defined with the keyword mutating, because inside it we change the properties of VoteData. Its task is to clear the data about the last voting session, so the user can start a new one.

---

■ **Swift reference**   By default, methods defined in a structure have read-only access to the structure's properties. To allow modification, a method must be declared as mutating. See Chapter 21 for more information.

---

The for loop in resetVotes uses the *half-open range operator* (..<). The syntax you see is equivalent to this for loop declaration in ActionScript:

```
for (var i : int = 0; i < choices.count; i++)
```

---

■ **Swift reference**   Range operators in Swift define intervals of values you can iterate over. For details on how they work see Chapter 18, and for more information on loops see Chapter 20.

---

## Adding a Custom View Controller

If you open the main storyboard of the project, Main.storyboard, you will see that there is currently a view controller on it: it controls the view of the app's main screen. In Project navigator there is also a source file, called ViewController.swift. It contains the definition of ViewController: a class, which inherits UIViewController—the base class for view controllers in the iOS SDK. The view controller on the storyboard and the ViewController class are not one and the same, but they are linked—we will see how shortly.

So far in the examples in this book we have modified and added code to `ViewController`. This time we will create our own class and will link it with the view controller on the storyboard.

In Project navigator create a new group, call it `View controllers` and add a new Swift file to it. Name the file `VoteViewController.swift`. Your project should now look like Figure 6-2.

*Figure 6-2.* *The app project with the new view controller*

Open `VoteViewController.swift` and replace the following line,

```
import Foundation
```

with Listing 6-3, which declares `VoteViewController` as a subclass of `UIViewController`.

*Listing 6-3.* Declaring a Custom View Controller

```
import UIKit

class VoteViewController: UIViewController {
}
```

---

■ **Tip**    `Foundation` and `UIKit` are both iOS SDK frameworks. The `Foundation` framework contains the basis of Objective-C classes and `UIKit` defines classes that deal with the user interface, such as `UIViewController`.

---

Next we will connect the main screen of the app with our custom `VoteViewController` class. Open `Main.storyboard` in the Editor and select the view controller, which is on it. With the controller selected, open the Identity Inspector, locate the **Custom Class** section, and set **Class** to `VoteViewController` (Figure 6-3).

> ■ **Tip**    It may be easier to select the view controller in the Document Outline (Figure 6-3).

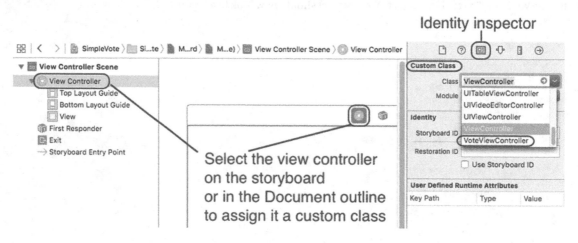

*Figure 6-3.*  *Assigning a custom class to the view controller on the storyboard*

We have now replaced the `ViewController` class. Let us delete it. In Project navigator right-click `ViewController` and select **Delete** from the pop-up menu (or press Backspace). You will see a dialog, which asks whether you want to delete the file or to remove its reference from the project. Go ahead and click **Move to Trash** (Figure 6-4).

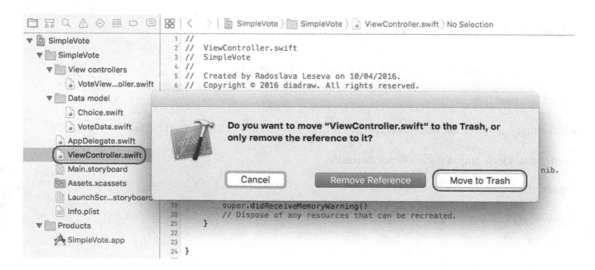

*Figure 6-4.*  *Deleting the view controller file generated by Xcode*

Now run the app on your iOS device or in the simulator to make sure it compiles and runs without errors.

## Designing the Vote View UI

We will now design the UI of the view, for which our Vote View Controller is responsible. This time we will use *stack views*: yet another technique for making UIs adaptive, which is good to have under your belt.

Open Main.storyboard in the Editor. In Object library find a Vertical Stack View and drag it onto the view on the storyboard (Figure 6-5).

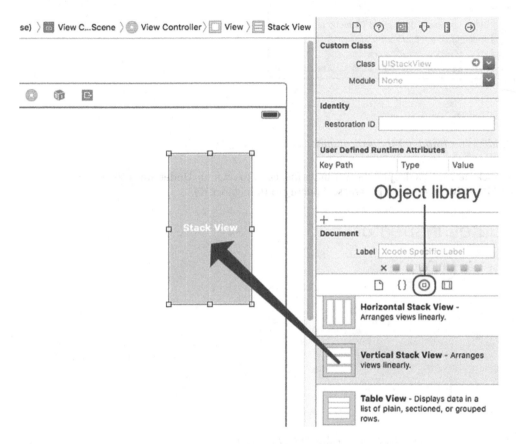

***Figure 6-5.*** *Adding a Vertical Stack View to the storyboard*

---

### FLEX ANALOGY

A Vertical Stack View is similar to the VerticalLayout class from the Spark library in Flex. It is a container view, which arranges its children vertically and repositions and resizes them to adapt to the available space. You can define rules about how elements are sized and positioned and set spacing between them.

---

Add constraints for the stack view: set the distance between it and the top and bottom layout guides to 20 and set zero for the distance between it and the parent view leading (left) and trailing (right) margins. Have a look at **Chapter 2** if you need a reminder for how to do that. When you are done, four constraints should appear under the stack view in the Document outline (Figure 6-6).

111

Vote View Controller Scene
Vote View Controller
Top Layout Guide
Bottom Layout Guide
View
Stack View
Constraints
Stack View.top = Top Layout Guide.bottom + 20
trailingMargin = Stack View.trailing
Stack View.leading = leadingMargin
Bottom Layout Guide.top = Stack View.bottom + 20
First Responder
Exit
Storyboard Entry Point

***Figure 6-6.*** *Adding constraints for the vertical stack view*

With the stack view selected, open the Attributes inspector to set it up. Under **Stack View** leave **Alignment** and **Distribution** both to Fill and set **Spacing** to 10 (Figure 6-7).

Attributes inspector
Stack View
Axis
Vertical
Alignment
Fill
Distribution
Fill
Spacing
10
Baseline Relative

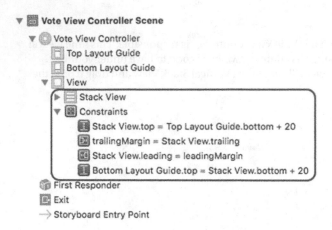

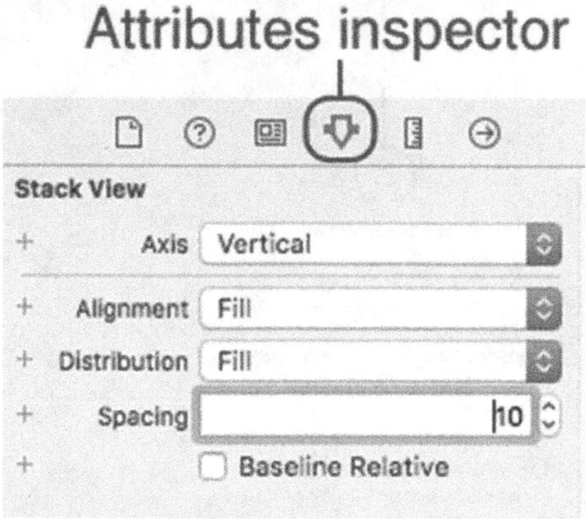

***Figure 6-7.*** *Set up the vertical stack view in the Attributes inspector.*

Now let us add more UI elements: drag a Label, a Table View, and a Horizontal Stack View from the Object library and position them in this order from top to bottom in the vertical stack view.

Constrain the height of the label and the height of the horizontal stack view to 30.

Select the horizontal stack view and set **Stack View ➤ Distribution** to Fill Equally and its **Spacing** to 10.

Add two buttons to the horizontal stack view and set their titles to Abstain and Vote: you can double-click each button on the storyboard and type a title directly. Alternatively, you can set their titles in the Attributes inspector under **Button ➤ Title**.

Have a look at Figure 6-8 to check if your storyboard looks like it.

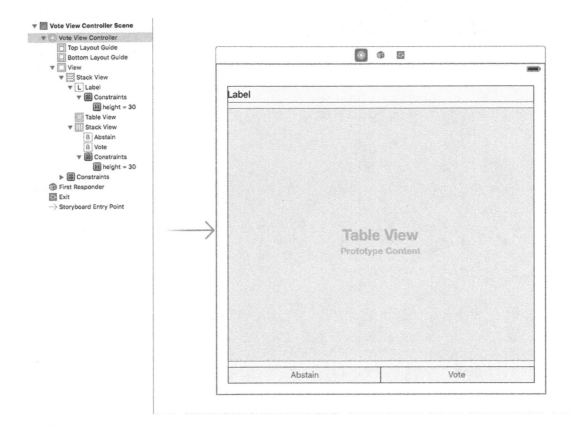

**Figure 6-8.** *The vote view on the storyboard*

If you run your app now it should look like Figure 6-9.

**Figure 6-9.** *The vote view at runtime*

The buttons we added show just titles by default. To make them more visible, let us add borders. Back on the storyboard in Xcode, if you select one of the buttons and have a look at the Attributes inspector, however, you will notice that there are no properties exposed that allow us to control borders. This is a good excuse to get familiar with another of Xcode's features: the *User Defined Runtime Attributes*, which you will find in the Identity inspector. Here you can set properties that would be available at runtime. The format is key-type-value, where the key, called *Key Path*, is the fully qualified property name: it could be a property of the class we are modifying or a property of one of its members.

In this case we will be setting up properties of UIButton's layer member. This is an instance of the CALayer class, which manages the visual content of a view. UIButton inherits its layer property from UIView—the base class for user interface elements in iOS.

Select the Abstain button and in the Identity inspector find the **User Defined Runtime Attributes** section. Click the + button to add an attribute and set its **Key Path** to layer.borderWidth, its **Type** to Number, and **Value** – to 1. Add another Number attribute, called layer.cornerRadius, and set its value to 6 (Figure 6-10).

Do the same for the Vote button.

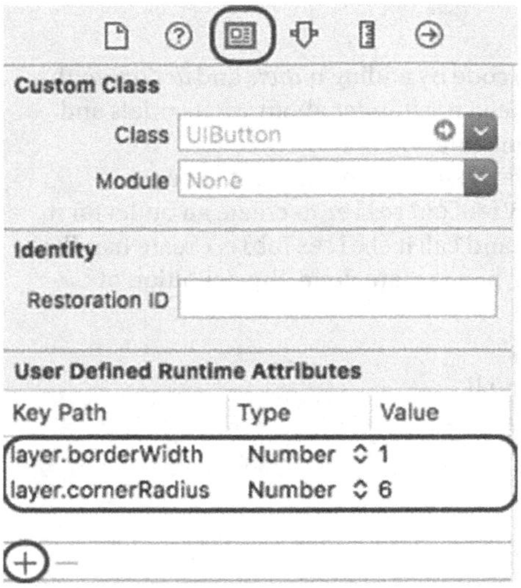

**Figure 6-10.** *Adding a runtime attribute to show a border around the button*

Run the app to see the buttons styled with a border (Figure 6-11).

**Figure 6-11.** *The buttons with borders*

# Linking the UI with the View Controller

In this section we will wire the UI we created on the storyboard to code by adding *outlets* and *actions* to the VoteViewController class. Have a look back at **Chapter 2** if you need a reminder about what outlets and actions are, how to create them, and how to work with the Assistant editor.

Open Main.storyboard and VoteViewController.swift side by side in the Assistant editor. Ctrl-drag the label from the storyboard into the definition of VoteViewController to create an outlet for it and call the outlet topicLabel. Create an outlet for the table view and call it choicesTable. Create handlers for the Touch Up Inside action for the Vote and Abstain buttons. When you are done, the definition of VoteViewController should look similar to Listing 6-4.

***Listing 6-4.*** VoteViewController with Outlets and Actions Added to It

```
class VoteViewController: UIViewController {
    // MARK: Outlets
    // The label shows the topic of the vote.
    @IBOutlet weak var topicLabel: UILabel!

    // The table lists the choices for voting
    // and lets the user select one.
    @IBOutlet weak var choicesTable: UITableView!

    // MARK: Actions
    @IBAction func vote(sender: AnyObject) {
        // User has voted.
        // TODO: Increment the votes for the selected choice.
        // TODO: Increment the number of participants.
        // TODO: Clear the selection to prepare for the next participant.
    }

    @IBAction func abstain(sender: AnyObject) {
        // User has decided not to vote.
        // TODO: Increment the number of participants.
        // TODO: Clear the selection to prepare for the next participant.
    }
}
```

What your version is probably missing are the comments. Some of those deserve a special mention here: the MARK and TODO annotations can help you navigate your code in the *Jump bar*. The Jump bar is located at the top of the Editor and is called thus for a reason: it lets you quickly jump to specific places in your project and in your code (Figure 6-12).

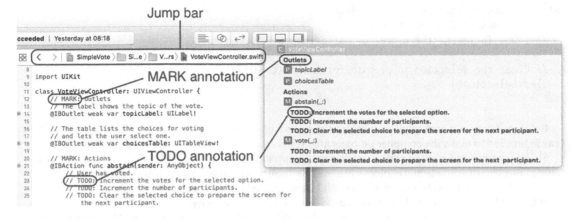

***Figure 6-12.*** *Using annotations to organize your code*

For an annotation to show up in the Jump bar it must appear in a comment (this can be a single-line comment or a comment block) and must be followed by a colon; it does not have to be the first string in the comment. You can use the following annotations:

- `// MARK: Heading`. This will create a section heading in the Jump bar. It is good practice to keep related methods under the same heading.

- `// MARK: - Heading`, `// MARK: Heading -`, or `// MARK: - Heading -`. These will add separators before, after, or before and after a heading.

- `// TODO: Reminder about an unfinished task`.

- `// FIXME: Reminder about a known issue`.

---

■ **Tip**　Use `MARK`, `FIXME,` and `TODO` annotations to organize your code and make it easy to navigate.

---

Let us replace a couple of the `TODO` annotations with code. Use the Jump bar to go to the following line in the vote action:

```
// TODO: Clear the selection to prepare for the next participant.
```

Add a call to a function, named `clearSelection:` we will implement it later on, when we learn how to work with the table view. Remove the `TODO` annotation, but leave the comment in as documentation. Do the same in the `abstain` action (Listing 6-5).

***Listing 6-5.*** Replacing TODO Annotations

```
// MARK: Actions
@IBAction func vote(sender: AnyObject) {
    // User has voted.
    // TODO: Increment the votes for the selected choice.
    // TODO: Increment the number of participants.

    // Clear the selection to prepare for the next participant:
    clearSelection()
}
```

```
@IBAction func abstain(sender: AnyObject) {
    // User has decided not to vote.
    // TODO: Increment the number of participants.

    // Clear the selection to prepare for the next participant:
    clearSelection()
}
```

Before we move on with implementing how choices will appear on the screen, let us add another call to clearSelection to make the compiler properly angry.

Shortly we will add another view controller to our app to show results from the vote. We want the vote screen to be clear of any selected choices whenever we return to it. To achieve that, a good place to call clearSelection is in the view controller's viewWillAppear method. It is inherited from the base class, UIViewController, and is called every time the view is about to be displayed.

Let us add an override for viewWillAppear. Add another MARK annotation, which will let us keep base class overrides together (Listing 6-6). Let us also add a TODO annotation as a reminder for something else we will want to do when the view appears: restart voting by clearing the results of the last vote.

***Listing 6-6.*** Override the View Controller's viewWillAppear Method and Clear the Vote Screen

```
// MARK: UIViewController
override func viewWillAppear(animated: Bool) {
    // Call the base class method first
    // to make sure we won't miss out on any preparation done by it:
    super.viewWillAppear(animated)

    // Then clear the selection:
    clearSelection()

    // TODO: reset the vote results
}
```

# Handling Choices with a Table View

As an ActionScript developer you may be used to presenting mutually exclusive choices with radio buttons, especially if you have developed desktop apps. However, radio buttons are well suited to a precise mouse cursor and less so to a chunky thumb on a small phone screen. The iOS SDK offers several different controls that help implement the same logic and feel more natural under the hand: you can use a segmented control (UISegmentedControl)—like the All/Missed filter controls in your recent iPhone calls list; a picker (UIPickerView) like the date picker we used in **Chapters 2** and **3**; or a table view (UITableView), which we are about to use.

The UITableView control is designed for presenting lists of items and receiving[1] user interaction, including making mutually exclusive selections, so it will do very well for handling votes.

Let us start setting up our table view by making sure it only allows one item to be chosen at a time: with the table view selected on the storyboard, open the Attributes inspector find **Table View ➤ Selection** and set it to Single Selection.

The next thing we will set up would be the table cells.

---

[1]It is worth making a distinction between receiving and handling user interaction events. The table view receives but does not handle gesture events. Instead, it uses delegation to hand over this task (we covered the Delegation design pattern in Chapter 5). A delegate needs to conform to the UITableViewDelegate protocol.

## Designing the Cells

Select the table view on the storyboard. In the Attributes inspector set **TableView ➤ Prototype Cells** to 1. This will add a Table View Cell entry under Choices Table in the Document outline. Select the new cell (this might be easier to do in the Document outline than on the storyboard) and in the Attributes inspector set **Table View Cell ➤ Style** to Basic (Figure 6-13).

When you change the cell style, you will see the cell change on the storyboard: now it says "Title." Cells in a table view can have very sophisticated design with various other UI controls added to them (image views, blocks of styled text, rating controls, etc.). A basic cell only has a label in it: this is what we will use to display choices for voting.

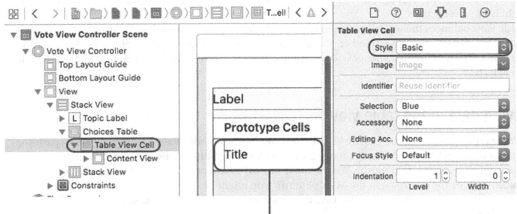

A basic style prototype cell with a label

*Figure 6-13.* *Adding a basic prototype cell*

Next, set the cell's **Identifier** to ChoiceCell in the Attributes inspector (Figure 6-14).

*Figure 6-14.* *Setting up the prototype cell*

In the next section we will see what we have just done and why.

## How Cells Work in a Table View

Table views in iOS are optimized for displaying large lists of ordered items. Also, as we mentioned earlier, each cell in the table can be designed to have a very custom look: you can add all sorts of UI elements to it. Cells in the same table don't even have to all look the same, but can each have a different layout.

The way to achieve this is to design what a *prototype cell* for each separate layout you want to display in the table. Think of it as designing a custom view that will be shown when a cell is displayed. The cell Identifier property we set in the previous section is used to distinguish between these custom views.

For performance reasons table views are designed to reuse cell objects. Say you have a list of 100 items you want to display in a table view. Out of the 100 only a few would be visible on the screen at any time, so memory-wise it would not be very effective to keep cell instances for all of them. On the other hand, each time you scroll up or down to see more items, creating cells from scratch for those that have just come into view might hurt performance.

A table view balances those time and memory costs by reusing cells: once they have been requested and created, the table view keeps a number of cell objects at hand (in a queue) that can be used again and again. It is only their content that changes: for example, instead of recreating a label in the cell, the table view will change its text.

## Displaying data in the table view

UITableView is designed to be used as the View in the now familiar Model-View-Controller (MVC) pattern, which we discussed in **Chapter 5**. Being merely a view, its responsibility is to display data but not to provide it. For that it relies on an external source. We will make our VoteViewController that source. "But isn't VoteViewController the *controller* in the MVC pattern?" you might be thinking. . . . You are right, this sounds confusing. But bear with me: in this case the view controller's role as a data source is to be the vehicle for the data from the data model it contains.

To start with, let us assign the view controller to the dataSource property of the table view (Listing 6-7). For that purpose we will override UIViewController's viewDidLoad method and do the assignment in it. You have already used viewDidLoad in previous chapters: it is called when the view has been loaded for displaying for the first time.

*Listing 6-7.* Set VoteViewController as the Data Source for the Table View

```
// MARK: UIViewController
override func viewDidLoad() {
    // Call the base class method first
    // to make sure we won't miss out on any preparation done by it:
    super.viewDidLoad()

    // This will cause the methods required
    // by the UITableViewDataSource to be called:
    choicesTable.dataSource = self
}
```

If you Cmd + click dataSource in the line of code we just added to see its definition, you will see that it is of type UITableViewDataSource?. UITableViewDataSource is a protocol from the iOS SDK, which provides an interface that the table view knows how to use to query for data. For VoteViewController to be used as the data source for the table view, it needs to conform to this protocol.

---

■ **Swift reference** -For details on protocols see Chapter 21 and for the meaning of the question mark after UITableViewDataSource see Chapter 19.

---

To make `VoteViewController` conform to `UITableViwDataSource`, we will first add the protocol to the view controller's inheritance list:

```
class ViewController: UIViewController, UITableViewDataSource {
```

Then we will implement two of the protocol's methodsw, which the table view will call when it is about to display its cells and needs to know what data to put in them.

The first method, `tableView(_:numberOfRowsInSection:)`, tells the table view how many rows to display in each of its *sections*. Here a section represents a group of rows, for example, the group for contacts starting with the letter "A" in your address book.

The second method, `tableView(_:cellForRowAtIndexPath:)`, fires each time a cell from the table needs to be shown on the screen. This is where we take advantage of the reusing of cells we saw in the previous section: instead of creating a new cell each time, we call the table view's `dequeueReusableCellWithIdentifier` method, which will only create a cell from scratch if there is not one available in the queue. Every time after that we will have a ready-made instance we can just populate with data. Listing 6-8 shows the implementation of both methods.

*Listing 6-8.* Implementing Methods of the UITableViewDataSource Protocol

```
// MARK: UITableViewDataSource
func tableView(tableView: UITableView,
            numberOfRowsInSection section: Int) -> Int {
    // Query the data model for the number of choices to present for voting:
    return choiceCount
}

func tableView(tableView: UITableView,
    cellForRowAtIndexPath indexPath: NSIndexPath) -> UITableViewCell {
    // Ask the table view for a cell that looks like
    // the one we prototyped ("ChoiceCell"):
    let cell = tableView.dequeueReusableCellWithIdentifier("ChoiceCell", ↵
        forIndexPath: indexPath)

    // Fill in the cell with data from the data model:
    setUpCell(cell: cell, atRow: indexPath.row)

    return cell
}
```

The two methods access a property, `choiceCount` and a method, `setUpCell`, which we have not implemented yet. We will take care of this in the next section.

## Adding Placeholders for Querying the Data Model

The property and the method that we now need to define will both access the data model: choiceCount is responsible for telling the table view how many rows to display and setUpCell populates a given cell with data. The Lite and the Pro versions of our app will each deal with the data model differently and so will need slightly different implementations for choiceCount and setUpCell. So at this stage of the app development we will just add placeholders and provide implementation later on for each app version.

Let us define choiceCount as a computed property to VoteViewController and annotate it with MARK: Data. For the moment we will have it return 1 (Listing 6-9).

*Listing 6-9.* Adding a Placeholder for the Number of Options for Voting

```
// MARK: Data
var choiceCount: Int {
    get {
        // Query the data model for the number of choices for voting.
        // TODO: Replace this row with a query to the data model:
        return 1
    }
}
```

Next, add a placeholder for the setUpCell method under the same annotation (Listing 6-10). It takes two parameters: an instance of UITableViewCell and the row that the cell is on. The row number lets find the relevant item in the choices array in the data model we defined back in Listing 6-2.

*Listing 6-10.* Adding a Placeholder for Filling in Vote Options

```
func setUpCell(cell cell: UITableViewCell, atRow row: Int) {
    // TODO: Populate the cell with data
}
```

## Clearing the Selection in the Table

Remember the calls to clearSelection we added earlier, when we were setting up the UI? We will implement clearSelection here to do what it says: if the user has tapped a cell in the table to select it, this method will clear this selection, so that the next user can vote. Add this method under MARK: Helper methods (Listing 6-11).

*Listing 6-11.* Clearing the Selection in the Table View

```
// MARK: Helper methods
func clearSelection() {
    if let selectedIndexPath = choicesTable.indexPathForSelectedRow {
        choicesTable.deselectRowAtIndexPath(selectedIndexPath, animated: true)
    }
}
```

## Adding a Second View

Add a new Swift file to the View controllers group in your project and name it ResultsViewController. swift. Open the new file and replace the import Foundation line with the class declaration from Listing 6-12: we are declaring another UIViewController subclass.

*Listing 6-12.* Declaring a View Controller Class, Which Will Be in Charge of the Results View

```
import UIKit

class ResultsViewController: UIViewController {
}
```

---

■ **Tip**    You can also let Xcode declare the class for you when you add the new file. To do that, from the main menu select **File ➤ New…**, then **iOS ➤ Source ➤ Cocoa Touch Class** and in the wizard set **Subclass of** to UIViewController. This will create the new class and stub out the following two methods: viewDidLoad and didReceiveMemoryWarning.

---

Next, we will add a view controller to the storyboard, which we will link with this new class. Open Main.storyboard, find a View Controller element in the Object library, and add it to the storyboard. Then add a Vertical Stack View to the new view controller and set the same constraints we used for the vertical stack view in Vote View Controller: set the distance between the stack view and the top and bottom layout guides to 20 and set zero for the distance between it and the parent view leading and trailing margins. In the Attributes inspector set the stack view's **Spacing** property to 10.

Add a Text View to the vertical stack view and in the Attributes inspector leave its **Text** property to Plain, but delete the default text it comes with. Uncheck **Editable** and **Selectable** in the **Behavior** section: we will use this text view as read-only (Figure 6-15).

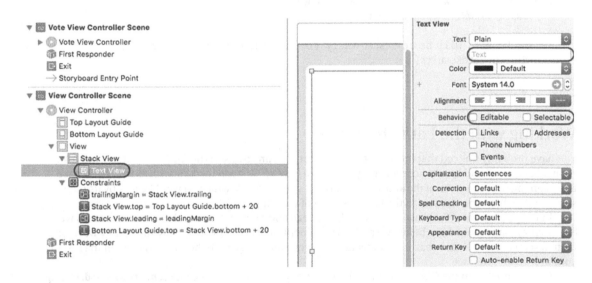

*Figure 6-15.* *Setting up the text view*

Let us link the new UI elements we just added with the ResultsViewController class. On the storyboard select the new view controller (or select it in the Document outline) and in the Identity inspector, under **Custom Class**, set its **Class** to ResultsViewController.

Open Main.storyboard and ResultsViewController.swift side by side in the Assistant editor and Ctrl + drag the text view from the storyboard into the definition of the ResultsViewController class to create an outlet for it. Name the outlet resultsTextView (Listing 6-13).

*Listing 6-13.* Adding an Outlet for the Text View

```
class ResultsViewController: UIViewController {
    // MARK: Outlets
    @IBOutlet weak var resultsTextView: UITextView!
}
```

Add a placeholder method for presenting the results of a vote and call it `displayVoteResults`: we will add different implementations for it in the two versions of the app. Then add an override for `UIViewController`'s `viewWillAppear` method and in it call `displayVoteResults`—we want to refresh the information every time we switch to this view. The definition of `ResultsViewController` should now look like Listing 6-14.

*Listing 6-14.* Adding a Placeholder for Displaying Vote Results

```
class ResultsViewController: UIViewController {
    // MARK: Outlets
    @IBOutlet weak var resultsTextView: UITextView!

    // MARK: Data
    func displayVoteResults() {
        // TODO: Display a vote summary in resultsTextView
    }

    // MARK: UIViewController
    override func viewWillAppear(animated: Bool) {
        super.viewWillAppear(animated)

        // Results will be refreshed every time the view appears on screen:
        displayVoteResults()
    }
}
```

# Working with the Launch Screen

You have probably noticed that the `SimpleVote` project contains two storyboard files created by Xcode: `Main.storyboard` and `LaunchScreen.storyboard`. We have so far been working with `Main.storyboard` to design the user interface of the app. `LaunchScreen.storyboard` is what you would guess by its name: a storyboard, where you can design the launch screen of your app.

In Project navigator find `LaunchScreen.storyboard` and open it. It should look familiar: this is what `Main.storyboard` looked like before we added UI elements to it. We will not do anything fancy with the launch screen, just a little tweak to demonstrate that you can work with it the way you do with the rest of your app's user interface.

Drag a Label from the Object library and drop it onto the view on `LaunchScreen.storyboard`. Change the label's title to Cast your vote! and click the Align button at the bottom of the editor to constrain the label to the middle of its containing view both vertically and horizontally. When you are done, your storyboard and Document outline should look like Figure 6-16.

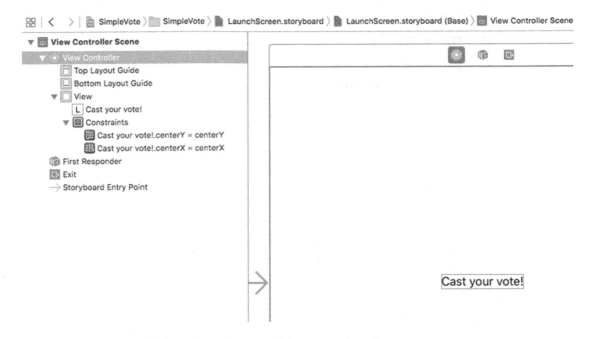

*Figure 6-16.* *Designing the launch screen in LaunchScreen.storyboard*

If you run your app now, you should see Cast your vote! for a few seconds before the main screen of the app loads.

# Developing VoteLite

In the Lite version of our application we will hard-code data for voting on, enable voting, and show results. For transitioning between the vote view and the results view we will initially set up segues and will then see how adding a navigation bar can save some of the work.

## Setting up the VoteLite Project

We will reuse the code and user interface we created in our SimpleVote project. This requires a bit of work, as there is no straightforward way to duplicate a project in Xcode. Following are the steps for setting up the new project and adding the files we created or modified in the first part of this chapter.

1. Create a new Single View Application project (**File ➤ New ➤ Project... ➤ iOS ➤ Application ➤ Single View Application**) and call it VoteLite.

2. In Project navigator select and delete ViewController.swift the way you did in SimpleVote (Figure 6-4).

3. Open both projects in Finder and copy the following files and folders from SimpleVote/SimpleVote to VoteLite/VoteLite (Figure 6-17):

   • The Base.lproj folder, which contains the storyboard files. When asked, agree to replace the Base.lproj folder in VoteLite.

- `Choice.swift`

- `VoteData.swift`

- `VoteViewController.swift`

- `ResultsViewController.swift`

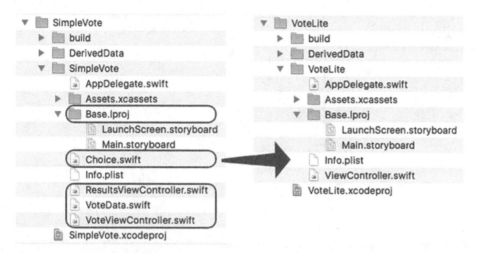

*In Finder copy the storyboards and the custom souce files into the new project folder*

***Figure 6-17.*** *Copying the reusable source and storyboard files in Finder*

4. Now let us add the newly copied files in Xcode and structure the project:

   a. Back in Xcode create two file groups and name them `Data model` and `View controllers`.

   b. Right-click the `Data model` group and from the popup menu select **Add Files to Vote Lite...** (or, with the group selected, use Xcode's main menu: **File ➤ Add Files to Vote Lite...**).

   c. Then, from the dialog select `Choice.swift` and `VoteData.swift`. Add `VoteViewController.swift` and `ResultsViewController.swift` to the `View controllers` group.

Your project's structure should now resemble Figure 6-18.

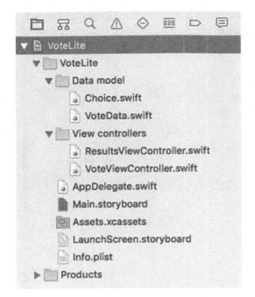

***Figure 6-18.*** *VoteLite in Project navigator*

5. Clean the project (**Product ➤ Clean**). This will remove any files that normally result from a build or are created by Xcode when it initially sets up your project. (If you are curious, have a look at the project's build and DerivedData folders beforehand. Even before you build the project for the first time they contain intermediate and cached files.)

6. Build and run the VoteLite app. It should now look identical to SimpleVote.

## Adding Buttons to Trigger Transitions

We will add a button to each of the screens in our app and will use the buttons for navigating between the two screens.

Open Main.storyboard and from the Object library drag a Button control and drop it at the bottom of the vertical stack view in Vote View Controller. Title the button See results and add a border and corner radius to it the way we did for the buttons in the SimpleVote project.

---

■ **Tip**    It might be easier to drop the button in the tree in the Document outline.

---

Do the same in Results View Controller: add a button at the bottom of the vertical stack view and style it with a border and corner radius. Title this one Back to voting (Figure 6-19). Add a height constraint to each of the buttons and set it to 30.

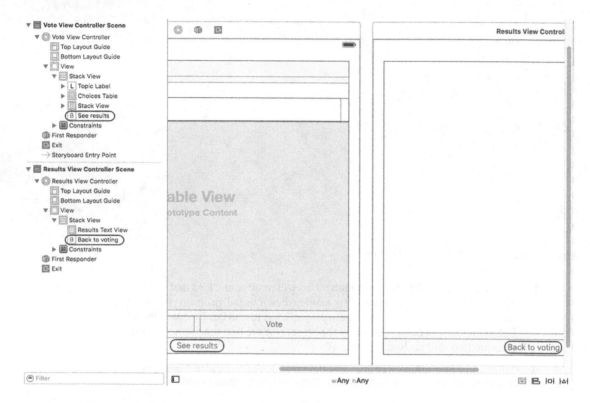

**Figure 6-19.** *The two buttons on the storyboard and in the Document outline*

■ **Tip** If a newly added UI element initially appears in a funny place on the storyboard, select the view controller whose view you added it to and click the Resolve Auto Layout Issues button. Then from the pop-up menu select All Views in * View Controller ➤ Update Frames.

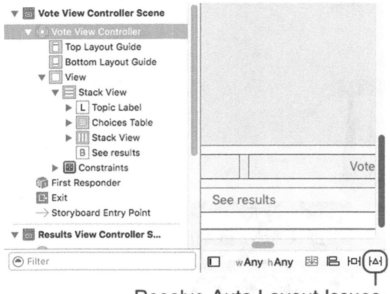

Resolve Auto Layout Issues

We will now add *segues*: transitions between the two views. A segue can be defined programmatically or in Interface builder. We will use Interface builder in this tutorial, so we can visualize the transitions.

First, let us make the See results button trigger a transition to the results view. Open Main.storyboard; in the Document outline select the See results button and Ctrl + drag from it to the Results View Controller (you can also do this on the storyboard). From the pop-up menu select **Action Segue ➤ Show** (Figure 6-20).

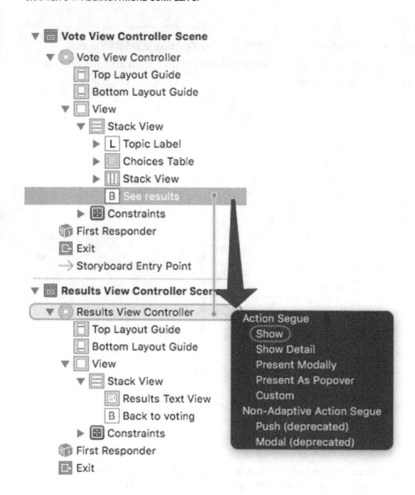

***Figure 6-20.*** *Adding a segue between the two app screens*

# Transitioning between views with segues

You will see the segue on the storyboard show up as an arrow between the two view controllers. It will also appear in the Document outline (Figure 6-21).

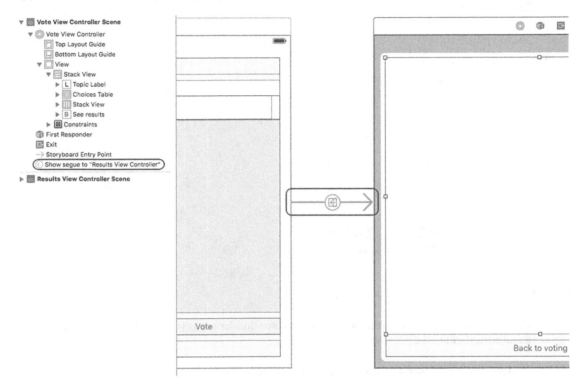

***Figure 6-21.*** *The segue on the storyboard and in the Document outline*

Run your app and tap the See results button to test the segue. This should take you to the results view. But hey, you are locked there and you can't go back!

We will remedy that with an *unwind segue*. An unwind segue is a way of "exiting" a view to return to the view that was shown before it. It is set up somewhat differently from the *show segue* we created earlier. While we did not have to write any code to make that segue work, to implement an unwind segue, we will first need to create an action that handles it. Note that this action needs to be in the view controller we want to transition back to, not the one that triggers the transition.

Open `VoteViewController.swift`, the view controller our unwind segue will lead back to, and add this action method to the `VoteViewControler` class (Listing 6-15). We do not need to add any more code to make the segue work.

***Listing 6-15.*** Adding an Unwind Segue to VoteViewController

```
// MARK: Segues
@IBAction func unwindToVoting(unwindSegue: UIStoryboardSegue) {
}
```

Now let us create the unwind segue and connect it with this action. Open `Main.storyboard`. In the Document outline select the Back to voting button and Ctrl + drag from it to the Exit icon of Results View Controller. When you release the mouse, you should see a pop-over, which lists the `unwindToVoting` action under **Action segue** (Figure 6-22).

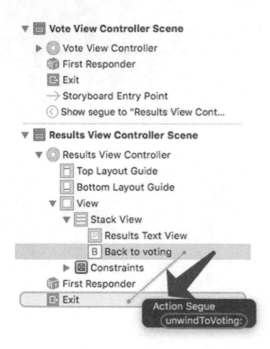

**Figure 6-22.** *Creating an unwind segue*

In order to let you select the appropriate action, Interface Builder scans your code for methods with this signature and adds them to the pop-over list:

```
@IBAction func unwindMethodName(unwindSegue: UIStoryboardSegue)
```

Select unwindToVoting and the unwind segue will appear in the Document outline at the bottom of the Results View Controller Scene. Run the app again to test going back and forth between the two views.

# Displaying Data

It is time to make this app do something useful. To start with, we will hard-code some data in VoteViewController.

Open VoteViewController.swift and add a property of type VoteData to the ViewController class. Then add a method, called createVoteData, in which we will populate the VoteData instance with a topic for voting and some choices (Listing 6-16).

*Listing 6-16.* Hard-Coding Data in the VoteViewController Class

```
// MARK: Data
var voteData = VoteData()

func createVoteData(){
    voteData.topic = "Gandalf or Dumbledore?"
    voteData.choices = &#x00E5;
        [Choice(title: "Gandalf"), Choice(title: "Dumbledore")]
}
```

---

■ **Swift reference**   In Listing 6-16 you can see the syntax for initializing an array in Swift: `[item1, item2, ...,` `itemN]`. For details on how to create and use arrays see Chapter 19.

---

Then, let us make a call to `createVoteData` in the view controller's `viewDidLoad` method we overrode earlier. We will also set the label at the top of the view to display the vote topic (Listing 6-17).

***Listing 6-17.*** Calling the createVoteData to Initialize

```
override func viewDidLoad() {
    // Call the base class method first
    // to make sure we won't miss out on any preparation done by it:
    super.viewDidLoad()

    // This will cause the methods required
    // by the UITableViewDataSource to be called:
    choicesTable.dataSource = self

    // Populate the model with data:
    createVoteData()

    // Get the label to display the vote topic
    // that was set in the data model:
    topicLabel.text = voteData.topic
}
```

Earlier in the chapter, when we set up the `SimpleVote` project, we added a couple of placeholders, whose role is to query the data model for data (see Listing 6-9 if you need a reminder). One was a property, `choiceCount`, which needs to work out how many choices there are to display in the table view. The other one was a method, `setUpCell`—it populates a given cell from the table view with data. Add the following implementation (Listing 6-18). Note the `textLabel` property of the cell that we set to display a choice: this comes from the label that the Basic cell style makes available to us.

***Listing 6-18.*** Implementing Methods for the UITableViewDataSource Protocol

```
var choiceCount: Int {
    get{
        // Query the data model for the number of choices for voting.
        // Replace this row with a query to the data model:
        return voteData.choices.count
    }
}

func setUpCell(cell cell: UITableViewCell, atRow row: Int) {
    // Populate the cell with data
    if row >= 0 && row < voteData.choices.count {
        let choice = voteData.choices[row]

        // textLabel is a property of the Basic table view cell:
        cell.textLabel?.text = choice.title
    }
}
```

## Taking Votes

Now that we have data and a topic with two choices for voting, let us implement the voting functionality. Use the Jump bar to locate the TODO annotations we left in the vote and abstain methods and let us replace these with code (Listing 6-19).

*Listing 6-19.* Implementing the Logic for the Voting

```
// MARK: Actions
@IBAction func vote(sender: AnyObject) {
    // User has voted.
    // Increment the votes for the selected choice:
    if let selectedIndexPath = choicesTable.indexPathForSelectedRow {
        assert(selectedIndexPath.row < voteData.choices.count)
        voteData.choices[selectedIndexPath.row].votes += 1
    }

    // Increment the number of participants:
    voteData.participants += 1

    // Clear the selected choice
    // to prepare the screen for the next participant:
    clearSelection()
}

@IBAction func abstain(sender: AnyObject) {
    // User has decided not to vote.
    // Increment the number of participants.
    voteData.participants += 1

    // Clear the selected choice
    // to prepare the screen for the next participant:
    clearSelection()
}
```

When the Vote button is tapped, we check if a row in the table has been selected. If it has, we find the corresponding choice and increment its votes. Then we increment the total number of participants in the vote. If the user taps Abstain, we just increment the total number of participants. At the end of both methods we clear the selection, so that the next user can vote.

With this functionality the user has two ways to abstain: by tapping the Abstain button or by leaving all choices unselected and tapping the Vote button. This implicit abstaining is not obvious and may even be confusing. Later on in the chapter we will improve this by alerting the users, so that they don't abstain accidentally.

---

■ **Swift reference**    The if let construct in Listing 6-19 does *conditional binding*. It is effectively a shortcut for doing several operations: first, declaring a constant, selectedIndexPath, then checking if choicesTable. indexPathForSelectedRow is nil and if it is not, making an assignment to the constant. Conditional binding works with Swift's Optional type. For more details see Chapter 19.

---

The line in vote, on which we call assert, is worth noting:

```
assert(selectedIndexPath.row < voteData.choices.count)
```

This is a basic check, which ensures that the selected cell is on a row that has a match in the voteData.choices array—that is, that we will not access an index in the array, which is out of bounds[2]. We will look at asserts in **Chapter 8**.

## Using Segues to Pass Data Between View Controllers

Let us take stock of the app we have created so far: it has a couple of views, has ways to transition back and forth between them, displays data, and lets the user vote. There is one thing missing: we have not yet implemented a way of showing the results of a vote. We will do so in this section. The implementation will use one of the segues to get the results to the relevant screen, which is one way of passing data between view controllers.

In order to be able to access a segue programmatically, we need to give it an identifier. Open Main.storyboard and select the segue we created for transitioning to the Results View Controller. In the Attributes inspector set **Storyboard Segue ➤ Identifier** to ShowResults (Figure 6-23).

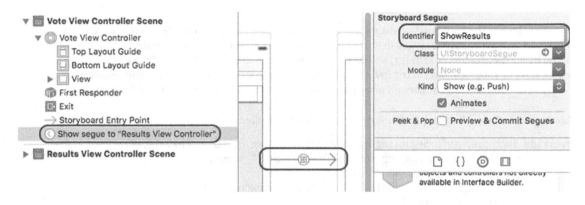

***Figure 6-23.*** *Adding an identifier to the segue*

Next, we will change the ResultsViewController to keep a copy of the vote data and display it. Open ResultsViewController.swift and add a VoteData member. Then replace the TODO annotation we added in displayVoteResults earlier in Listing 6-14 with the implementation from Listing 6-20.

***Listing 6-20.*** Displaying the Vote Results in a Text View

```
// MARK: Data
var voteData = VoteData() // This will receive a copy of the data

func displayVoteResults() {
    // Check if we have something to report and return if not:
    if voteData.participants == 0 {
```

---

[2]You can do better than calling assert here and extend the Array type to use indices in a safe way. If you are up for a little challenge, do a search on the Internet for "Swift safe array indexing" to see some cool implementations.

```
        resultsTextView.text = "No voting took place"
        return
    }

    // Create a string, which will accumulate a summary of the votes:
    var voteInformation = "Vote topic: \(voteData.topic)\n"

    voteInformation += "\nParticipants: \(voteData.participants)"
    voteInformation += "\nAbstained: \(voteData.abstains)\n"

    // Iterate through the options array
    // to read the votes each option received:
    for choice in voteData.choices {
        voteInformation += ↵
            "\n - \(choice.title) received \(choice.votes) votes"
    }

    // Display the string in the text view:
    resultsTextView.text = voteInformation
}
```

Now let us see how ResultsViewController can get a copy of the data for displaying. We will override a method, called prepareForSegue in VoteViewController,that will trigger the transition. This is a method of the base class UIViewController, so add its implementation under the MARK: UIViewController annotation in VoteViewController.swift. prepareForSegue is called before the segue passes navigation to its destination view controller and gives us access to this destination view controller (Listing 6-21).

***Listing 6-21.*** Overriding prepareForSegue in VoteViewController.swift

```
override func prepareForSegue(segue: UIStoryboardSegue, sender: AnyObject?) {
    // Check if we are preparing for the "ShowResults" segue:
    if segue.identifier == "ShowResults" {
        // Check if our destination is the ResultsViewController:
        if let resultsController =
            segue.destinationViewController as? ResultsViewController {
            // Copy data over to the results controller:
            resultsController.voteData = voteData
        }
    }
}
```

---

■ **Swift reference**    In Listing 6-21, in addition to the conditional binding in the second if statement, you can see an example of type casting. For more details and what the question mark after the as operator means see Chapter 19.

---

Finally, let us make sure that the voting session is reset every time we go back to the vote screen. Find the TODO annotation you added to VoteViewController's viewWillAppear method and replace it with a call to voteData.resetVotes() to clear the data from the last vote (Listing 6-22).

***Listing 6-22.*** Clear Vote Results Every Time We Go Back to the Vote Screen

```swift
override func viewWillAppear(animated: Bool) {
    // Call the base class method first
    // to make sure we won't miss out on any preparation done by it:
    super.viewWillAppear(animated)

    // Then clear the selection
    clearSelection()

    // Reset the vote results
    voteData.resetVotes()
}
```

Run your app and test it. You should be able to cast votes and see the results.

## Using a Navigation View Controller

As you might guess, the way we implemented navigation between our two views is not necessarily the most efficient. If we add more views to the app, it will quickly become hard work to create and maintain segues between all of them. Instead of doing all of this work ourselves, we can use a view controller, which manages some or all of the transitions between the views.

A navigation view controller is an example of that. It is a container view controller: instead of managing a single view, it manages many views and the transitions between them. The views are treated like a stack: there is a root view, which sits at the bottom of the stack and other views can be pushed on top (shown on the screen) or popped out of the stack (dismissed from the screen). The navigation view controller also decorates its child views with space for navigation controls—you will see what this looks like in a bit.

We will add a navigation view controller to the VoteLite app. Open Main.storyboard, select the Vote View Controller, and from Xcode's main menu select **Editor ➤ Embed in ➤ Navigation Controller**. This adds the navigation view controller to the storyboard, moves the storyboard entry point to it, and makes Vote View Controller a child of the navigation view controller. You will also see a navigation bar appear on top of the Vote View Controller (Figure 6-24).

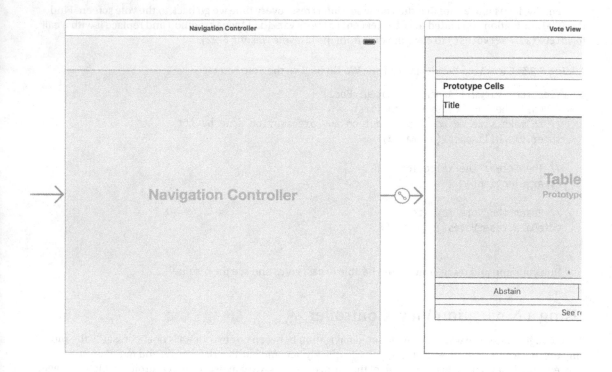

*Figure 6-24. Embedding the Vote View Controller in a navigation view controller*

If you ran the app now, you would notice a difference immediately: the Back to voting button has become obsolete, as a Back button appears on the navigation bar by default when we go to the vote results screen (Figure 6-25).

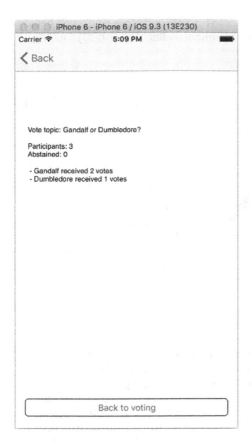

***Figure 6-25.*** *The navigation view controller adds a Back navigation button*

Let us make the Show results button obsolete too. First, we will add a title that will appear in the navigation bar of the vote view—this title will be used in navigation later. If you look at Vote View Controller in the Document outline, you will see that a Navigation Item has appeared in the tree. Select it and in the Attributes inspector set **Navigation Item ➤ Title** to Vote. Alternatively, you can double-click the navigation bar that has appeared on top of the Vote View Controller and set the title there (Figure 6-26).

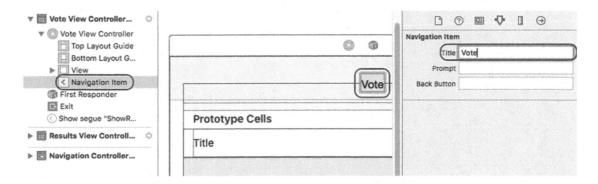

***Figure 6-26.*** *Adding a title to the navigation bar of Vote View Controller*

Next, find a Bar Button Item in the Object Library and drop it onto the right end of the navigation bar in the Vote View Controller or under **Right Bar Button Items** in the Document outline (Figure 6-27). Double-click to title it Results.

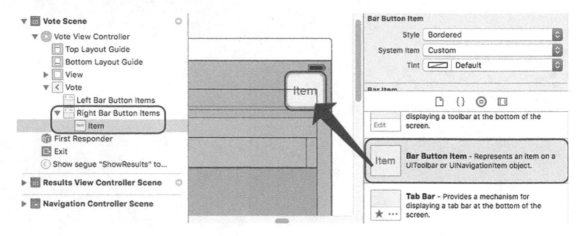

*Figure 6-27.* *Adding a bar button*

As magical as our navigation view controller is, this time we will need to help it work out where the bar button should lead. Select the bar button and Ctrl + drag from it toward the Results View Controller: you know how to do this two ways now: on the storyboard and in the Document outline. From the pop-up menu select **Action Segue ➤ Show** to create a segue to the results view. Select the segue and in the Attributes inspector set its **Identifier** to ShowResults. This is the same identifier we gave the segue triggered by the Show results button: reusing it will allow us to take advantage of the prepareForSegue method we implemented earlier in Listing 6-21.

If you run the app now, you should be able to go to the results screen by tapping Results on the navigation bar. When the results screen shows up, there should be a button for going back to the vote view, which reads < Vote (Figure 6-28).

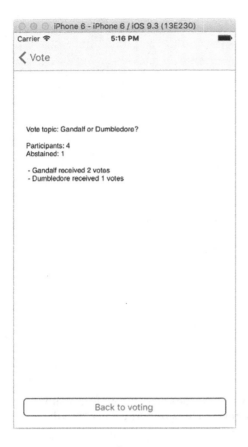

**Figure 6-28.** *Using the navigation view controller*

This completes our work on VoteLite and we are ready to move on to developing its Pro version.

# Developing VotePro

In the Pro version of the voting app we will add more screens to allow composing new votes and managing user settings. Even with only four screens using the navigation approach we applied to VoteLite would be counterproductive for managing the transitions between them.

The iOS SDK offers various *container view controllers*, which can manage multiple views. For example, your default mail client app uses *master-detail* design: the master view contains e-mail snippets and the detail view— the contents of the e-mail selected in the master view. The default weather app organizes its views as *pages*. Another popular app design is to make views accessible via *tabs*—this is what we are going to use for VotePro.

## Setting Up the VotePro Project

Once again we will reuse the code and UI we created in the SimpleVote project. Create a new Single View Application project and name it VotePro. Then repeat the steps we took for setting up VoteLite: delete ViewController.swift and add the files with custom code and UI from SimpleVote. Organize the files in two groups: View controllers and Data model. Add another group under View controllers and name it Containers. Your project should have the following structure (Figure 6-29).

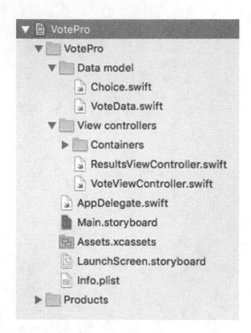

*Figure 6-29.* *VotePro in the Project navigator*

## Adding a Tab Bar Controller

Open Main.storyboard and select the Vote View Controller, then from Xcode's main menu select **Editor ➤ Embed In ➤ Tab Bar Controller**. This adds another view controller to the storyboard and moves the storyboard entry point to it (Figure 6-30).

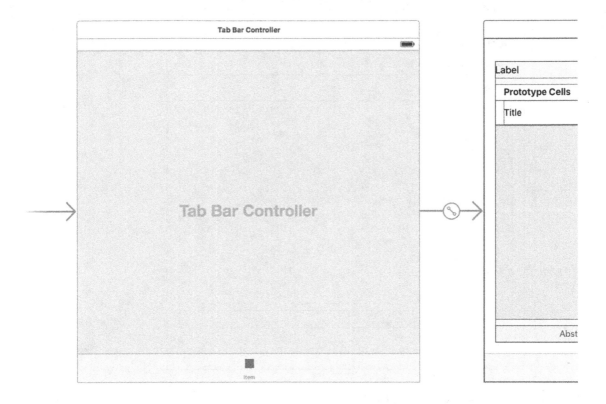

***Figure 6-30.*** *Adding a tab bar controller to the storyboard*

Notice also how a tab bar appears at the bottom of the Vote View Controller with an icon placeholder and a title Item. Double-click the title and change it to Vote (Figure 6-31).

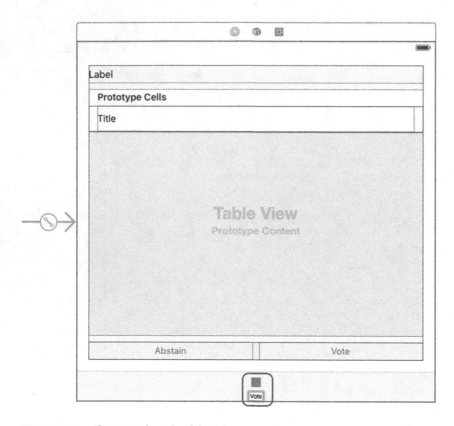

***Figure 6-31.*** *Changing the title of the tab*

So far we have a tabbed application with one tab. Let us add the Results View Controller to the list of controllers managed by the tab bar controller; this will make both our views accessible via tabs. Select the Tab Bar Controller either on the storyboard or in the Document outline and Ctrl + drag from it to the Results View Controller. From the pop-up menu select **Relationship Segue ➤ view controllers** (Figure 6-32).

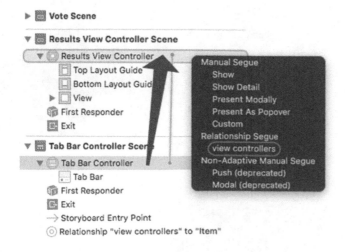

***Figure 6-32.*** *Adding the Results View Controller to the list that the tab view controller manages*

This will cause a tab bar item to appear at the bottom of Results View Controller too. Change its title to Results. Then run the app to test the navigation. You should see two tabs at the bottom of the app and be able to switch between the Vote and the Results screens (Figure 6-33).

***Figure 6-33.*** *Switching between views using tabs*

# Passing Data Between Tabs

A tab bar makes views in an app accessible in a random order. This means that when we add more views to our app, the user will be able to go from any view to any other view. So a transition between the Vote View Controller and the Results View Controller is no longer guaranteed and thus not a good place to pass data between them, unlike it was in VoteLite. Instead, we will keep the data someplace where both view controllers can access it.

One candidate is the tab bar controller. By adding the two view controllers to its list of managed view controllers we created parent-child relationships, where the tab bar controller is the parent. The base class UIViewController has a property, which will help us access this parent from our two child view controllers.

Let us create a class that we will link with the tab bar controller first. Add a new Swift file to the View controllers/Containers group in your project (**File ➤ New ➤ File... ➤ iOS ➤ Source ➤ Swift File**) and call it VoteTabBarController.swift.

Open VoteTabBarController.swift and replace the line

```
import Foundation
```

with the definition of the VoteTabBarController class from Listing 6-23. This class inherits
UITabBarController and overrides its viewDidLoad method to initialize an instance of VoteData. It is the
voteData property of VoteTabBarController that we want its child view controllers to access.

***Listing 6-23.*** Define the VoteTabBarController Class

```swift
import UIKit

class VoteTabBarController: UITabBarController {

    var voteData = VoteData()

    override func viewDidLoad() {
        super.viewDidLoad()

        voteData.topic = "Who would you have lunch with?"
        voteData.choices = [Choice(title: "Batman"), ↵
            Choice(title: "Wonder Woman"), Choice(title: "Superman")]
    }
}
```

On the storyboard select the tab bar controller and in the Identity inspector set **Custom Class ➤ Class** to
VoteTabBarController. This will link the tab bar controller on the storyboard with the class we just defined.

As a next step we will have both VoteViewController and ResultsViewController access their tab
view controller parent. Open VoteViewController.swift and add a *weakly referenced implicitly unwrapped
optional* for VoteTabBarController under the MARK: UIViewController annotation (Listing 6-24) and call it
tabManager. Initialize tabManager in VoteViewController's viewDidLoad method. Each UIViewController
has a tabBarController property, which gives it access to a tab bar controller, if it is embedded in one—this
is what we will use to initialize tabManager with.

***Listing 6-24.*** Add a Reference to the VoteTabBarController Instance in the VoteViewController Class

```swift
class VoteViewController: UIViewController, UITableViewDataSource {

    // MARK: UIViewController
    weak var tabManager: VoteTabBarController!

    override func viewDidLoad() {
        super.viewDidLoad()

        // Get a reference to the tab bar controller
        // and cast it to the class we created for it:
        tabManager = self.tabBarController as! VoteTabBarController

        // Access the vote data in tabManager
        // to initialize the topic label:
        topicLabel.text = tabManager.voteData.topic

        // This will cause the methods required
```

```
        // by the UITableViewDataSource to be called:
        choicesTable.dataSource = self
    }

    // The rest of the class definition
}
```

■ **Swift reference**   We threw in a couple of terms in the previous paragraph that need explaining. "Implicitly unwrapped" is term used for Swift variables and constants declared as Optional. An optional type has the option of having a value or having no value (i.e., being `nil`). Getting to the value, or finding out its absence, is called unwrapping. For details on how all this works and the syntax used see Chapter 19.

Another term that might need an explanation is "weak reference." In Chapter 21 we will see that, much like in ActionScript, class instances in Swift are always passed by reference, while other types are passed by value. In the example above this means that the assignment to `tabManager` does not cause a new instance of `VoteTabBarController` to be created; instead, it makes `tabManager` refer to the same instance that `self.tabBarController` does. A weak reference has memory-management implications. When the instance of `VoteViewController` gets deallocated, normally this will result in its properties being deallocated too. Making a reference weak prevents that. For more details on memory management, see Chapter 21.

Let us use `tabManager` to display choices in the table view. First, find the two placeholders, which we defined earlier to help display options in the table view: `setUpCell` and `optionCount`. Their implementation in Listing 6-25 will look very familiar: it is almost the same as what we provided in `VoteLite`, only this time `voteData` is accessed via `tabManager`.

***Listing 6-25.***  Display Vote Data in the Table View in VoteViewController

```
// MARK: Data
func setUpCell(cell cell: UITableViewCell, atRow row: Int) {
    // Populate the cell with data:
    if row >= 0 && row < tabManager.voteData.choices.count {
        let choice = tabManager.voteData.choices[row]
        cell.textLabel?.text = choice.title
    }
}

var choiceCount: Int {
    get{
        // Query the data model for the number of choices
        // to present for voting:
        return tabManager.voteData.choices.count
    }
}
```

Still in `VoteViewController.swift` find the `viewWillAppear` method and add a call to reset the number of votes, so that each transition to the vote screen will start a new voting session. The method should now look like Listing 6-26.

***Listing 6-26.*** Refresh the Topic Label and Start a New Session Every Time the View Appears on Screen

```
override func viewWillAppear(animated: Bool) {
    // Call the base class method first
    // to make sure we won't miss out on any preparation done by it:
    super.viewWillAppear(animated)

    // Then clear the selection
    clearSelection()
    tabManager.voteData.resetVotes()
}
```

We will implement the vote logic for the two action handlers we added earlier: vote and abstain. Use the Jump bar to find the two actions and add the code from Listing 6-27. This is again the same as the implementation we had in VoteLite, except for how we access voteData, which now lives in VoteTabBarController.

***Listing 6-27.*** Implement the Vote and Abstain Actions

```
@IBAction func vote(sender: AnyObject) {
    // User has voted.
    // Increment the votes for the selected choice:
    if let selectedIndexPath = choicesTable.indexPathForSelectedRow {
        assert(selectedIndexPath.row < tabManager.voteData.choices.count)
        tabManager.voteData.choices[selectedIndexPath.row].votes += 1
    }

    // Increment the number of participants:
    tabManager.voteData.participants += 1

    // Clear the selected choice to prepare the screen
    // for the next participant:
    clearSelection()
}

@IBAction func abstain(sender: AnyObject) {
    // User has decided not to vote.
    // Increment the number of participants.
    tabManager.voteData.participants += 1

    // Clear the selected choice to prepare the screen
    // for the next participant:
    clearSelection()
}
```

Next, open ResultsViewController.swift and add a reference to the tab bar controller, called tabManager. Then, add an overload for viewDidLoad and initialize tabManager in it (Listing 6-28).

***Listing 6-28.*** Add a Reference to the VoteTabBarController Instance in the ResultsViewController Class

```
class ResultsViewController: UIViewController{

    // MARK: UIViewController
```

```
weak var tabManager: VoteTabBarController!

override func viewDidLoad() {
    super.viewDidLoad()

    // Get a reference to the tab bar controller
    // and cast it to the class we created for it:
    tabManager = self.tabBarController as! VoteTabBarController
}

// The rest of the class definition
}
```

Now let us implement displayVoteResults—this method is currently a placeholder, which we added when we set up SimpleVote. The implementation looks the same as the one in the Lite version of the app, again, the only difference being how we access the data (Listing 6-29).

***Listing 6-29.*** Implement the Method That Will Display Vote Results in ResultsViewController

```
func displayVoteResults() {
    // Check if we have something to report and return if not:
    if tabManager.voteData.participants == 0 {
        resultsTextView.text = "No voting took place"
        return
    }

    // Create a string, which will accumulate a summary of the votes:
    var voteInformation = "Vote topic: \(tabManager.voteData.topic)\n"

    voteInformation += "\nParticipants: \(tabManager.voteData.participants)"
    voteInformation += "\nAbstained: \(tabManager.voteData.abstains)\n"

    // Iterate through the options array
    // to read the votes each option received:
    for choice in tabManager.voteData.choices {
        voteInformation += ↩
            "\n - \(choice.title) received \(choice.votes) votes"
    }

    // Display the string in the text view:
    resultsTextView.text = voteInformation
}
```

This is a good time to run the app, cast some votes, and switch between the tabs to see them update in real time.

## Showing Alerts

You are familiar with alerts: these are modal pop-up views, which you can use to show messages to the user or ask them to make a choice. We will create an alert to make the voting process a bit more user-friendly.

149

In the logic we implemented for voting in Listing 6-27 we increment the number of participants in the session when the Vote button gets tapped even if the user has not made a choice. And this, as we pointed out when we used the same logic in VoteLite, means that the user implicitly abstains, possibly without even realizing it. Showing an alert that warns the user about this abstention and asks if the user does want to abstain will make things more obvious and prevent abstaining by accident.

## FLEX ANALOGY

Alerts in the iOS SDK are similar to the Alert control in Flex, though the iOS ones are a bit more flexible. Excuse the pun. Whereas in Flex you are limited to one to three buttons to present different choices (usually a combination of OK, Cancel, Yes and No), you can add as many actions as you like to an iOS alert to handle multiple choices. It also allows you different alert styles, suited to mobile devices.

Let us modify the vote action to only increment the number of participants when an actual vote has been cast. Then make it show an alert if the user has not made a choice (Listing 6-30). To show the alert we will add a call to showAbsentVoteAlert—a function we will implement shortly.

***Listing 6-30.*** Modifying the Vote Action in VoteViewController to Alert the User If No Choice Was Made

```
@IBAction func vote(sender: AnyObject) {
    // User has voted.
    // Increment the votes for the selected choice:
    if let selectedIndexPath = choicesTable.indexPathForSelectedRow {
        assert(selectedIndexPath.row < tabManager.voteData.choices.count)
        tabManager.voteData.choices[selectedIndexPath.row].votes += 1

        // Increment the number of participants:
        tabManager.voteData.participants += 1
    } else {
        // The user tapped Vote, but didn't select an option to vote for.
        showAbsentVoteAlert()
    }

    // Clear the selected choice
    // to prepare the screen for the next participant:
    clearSelection()
}
```

The next piece of code in Listing 6-31 shows the implementation of showAbsentVoteAlert. It creates an instance of UIAlertController, an iOS SDK class, and sets it up to show a title and a message to the user.

Note that you can choose a style for the alert: you have a choice between UIAlertControllerStyle. Alert and UIAlertControllerStyle.ActionSheet. Alerts are like small dialogs: they pop up in the middle of the screen and are suited for short messages or choices between two options. Action sheets, on the other hand, emerge from the bottom of the screen on narrow screens or show as pop-overs on larger screens and are useful for longer lists of choices.

We will use the Alert style for our purposes. The alert will warn users that no choice was made and ask if they want to abstain, showing two choices: "No" and "Yes." These choices are represented by instances of the UIAlertAction class, which we add to the alert. An *alert action* shows up as a button that the user can tap. It has a title, a style, and a handler, which we can optionally implement to execute code when the option is tapped.

The style we can set for an action in the alert is of type UIAlertActionStyle and can be Default, Cancel, or Destructive. These styles define what the action buttons look like and in what order they appear in the alert. A *default action* represents the most likely choice a user would make (e.g., save her progress through a game). An example of a *destructive action* would be deleting photos from Camera Roll or cleaning up your inbox.

Add the code in Listing 6-31 to the VoteViewController class under MARK: Helper methods.

*Listing 6-31.* Showing an Alert

```
func showAbsentVoteAlert()
{
    // Create an alert to ask if they want to abstain:
    let alert = UIAlertController(title: "You didn't cast a vote", ↵
        message: "Do you want to abstain?", ↵
        preferredStyle: UIAlertControllerStyle.Alert)

    // Add a cancel action and a default action to the alert:
    // these will appear as buttons.
    let cancelAction = UIAlertAction(title: "No", ↵
        style: .Cancel, handler: nil)
    alert.addAction(cancelAction)

    // The default action will be trigerred when the uer wants to abstain.
    // Add a handler for that, so we can count this
    // toward the total number of participants:
    let defaultAction = UIAlertAction(title: "Yes", ↵
        style: .Default, handler: {
        // Increment the total number of votes:
        action in self.tabManager.voteData.participants += 1 } )
    alert.addAction(defaultAction)

    // Show the alert on screen:
    self.presentViewController(alert, animated: true, completion: nil)
}
```

---

■ **Swift reference**    If you have a look at how defaultAction is instantiated in Listing 6-31, you may find syntactic strangeness, namely, the code in the curly brackets after the handler label. This is a block of code is called when the user taps the button that represents defaultAction—in other words, it is an action handler. In this case it is implemented as a *closure*. We will look at closures and how to use them in Swift in Chapter 22.

---

Run the app, leave the choices in the table unselected, and tap the Vote button to see the alert pop up (Figure 6-34). Then do an experiment and change the style of the alert to ActionSheet. What does it look like now?

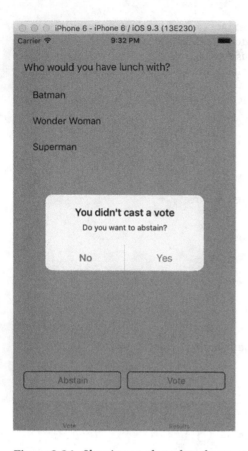

***Figure 6-34.*** *Showing an alert when the user taps the Vote button but has not voted*

## Working with User Preferences

In this section we will furnish the app with a Settings screen and learn how to use NSUserDefaults to store and read user preferences.

Start by adding another View Controller from the Object library to Main.storyboard. Then add the controller to the list of children of the tab bar controller (Ctrl + drag from the tab bar controller to the new view controller and from the pop-up menu select **Relationship Segue ➤ view controllers**). Set its tab bar item title to Settings.

You are now experienced with laying out user interface, so instead of walking you through each step, we will use a couple of diagrams to show you how to design the settings view.

First, find two Labels, a Switch and a Stepper in the Object library, and position them as shown in Figure 6-35.

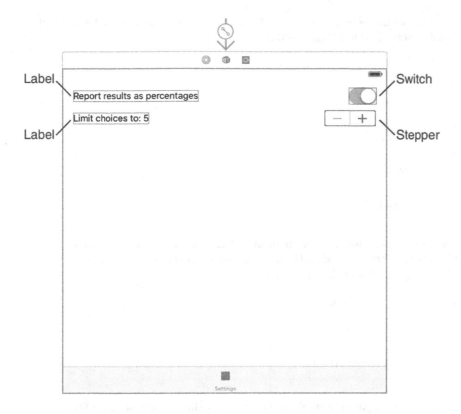

***Figure 6-35.*** *Designing the settings view*

Next, add the following constraints (Figure 6-36):

- Set the space to the leading margin to 0 for both labels.

- Set the space to the nearest neighbor at the top to 20 for both labels.

- Set the space to the trailing margin to 0 for the switch and for the stepper.

- Select the top label and the switch and align their vertical centers.

- Select the bottom label and the stepper and align their vertical centers.

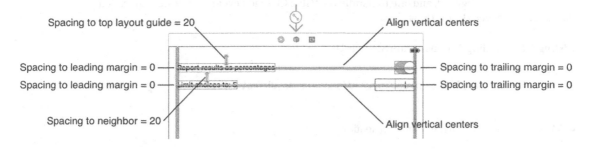

***Figure 6-36.*** *Adding constraints to the settings view*

Select the stepper and in the Attributes inspector set its Minimum value to 2, Maximum value to 5 and Current value to 5. Leave its Step setting set to 1 (Figure 6-37).

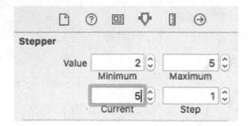

***Figure 6-37.*** *Setting up the stepper control*

Now let us back this all up with code. Add a new Swift file to the View controllers group in Project navigator and call it SettingsViewController.swift. Open the new file and declare a subclass of UIViewController, called SettingsViewController (Listing 6-32).

***Listing 6-32.*** Defining the SettingsViewController

```
import UIKit

class SettingsViewController: UIViewController {
}
```

Open Main.storyboard and SettingsViewController.swift side by side in the Assistant editor. First select the new view controller on the storyboard and set its Class to SettingsViewController (in the Identity inspector find the **Custom Class ➤ Class** setting). Then create the outlets for the switch, created the label for the maximum options setting and the stepper, and call them resultsAsPercentSwitch, maxOptionsLabel, and maxOptionsStepper, respectively (Listing 6-33).

***Listing 6-33.*** Adding Outlets for the Settings UI

```
// MARK: Outlets
@IBOutlet weak var resultsAsPercentSwitch: UISwitch!
@IBOutlet weak var maxChoicesLabel: UILabel!
@IBOutlet weak var maxChoicesStepper: UIStepper!
```

Add two actions: one to handle the Value Changed event for the switch, called resultsAsPercentToggled, and one to handle the Value Changed event for the stepper, called maxChoicesChanged (Listing 6-34).

***Listing 6-34.*** Adding Actions for the Settings UI

```
// MARK: Actions
@IBAction func resultsAsPercentToggled(sender: AnyObject) {
}

@IBAction func maxChoicesChanged(sender: AnyObject) {
}
```

# Storing User Preferences

We will implement these actions to save the user's preferences to the *defaults system*. This is Apple's term for the storage space specifically dedicated to keeping such information. We can access the defaults system with the help of the NSUserDefaults class, which has convenience methods for storing and retrieving values of various types.

Each value stored in the defaults system must be identified by a key, so we will define a couple of keys first: one for the value of the switch and one for the value of the stepper control. A key in this case is a string, which we need to choose. We will access these keys from several view controllers in our app: SettingsViewController will use them for writing to the defaults system and the ResultsViewController will need a read access, in order to decide how to present the results—as percentages or as number of votes. Later on, when we allow the user to set up his own vote topic and choices, the view controller that will help with that will need to know the maximum number of choices that the app allows.

To make the settings keys available to these view controllers, we will define them as constants in the VoteTabBarController class in VoteTabBarController.swift (Listing 6-35).

***Listing 6-35.*** Defining Keys for the User Settings in VoteTabBarController

```
class VoteTabBarController: UITabBarController {
    // MARK: Settings keys
    let resultsAsPercentKey = "ResultsAsPercent"
    let maxChoicesKey = "MaximumChoices"

    // The rest of the class definition
}
```

Go back to SettingsViewController.swift and add a reference to the VoteTabBarController instance the way we did for the other two view controllers. Don't forget to override UIViewController's viewDidLoad method and initialize the reference (Listing 6-36).

***Listing 6-36.*** Ading a Reference to the Tab Bar controller in SettingsViewController and Initializing It

```
// MARK: UIViewController
weak var tabManager: VoteTabBarController!

override func viewDidLoad() {
    super.viewDidLoad()

    // Get a reference to the tab bar controller
    // and cast it to the class we created for it:
    tabManager = self.tabBarController as! VoteTabBarController
}
```

Next we will add an implementation for the resultsAsPercentToggled action. It uses the setBool convenience method of the NSUserDefaults class to store the state of the switch (Listing 6-37).

***Listing 6-37.*** Saving the State of the Switch

```
@IBAction func resultsAsPercentToggled(sender: AnyObject) {
    // Get a reference to the defaults system
    let defaults = NSUserDefaults.standardUserDefaults()
```

```
// ... and use it to save the state of the switch:
defaults.setBool(resultsAsPercentSwitch.on, forKey: ↵
    tabManager.resultsAsPercentKey)
}
```

The implementation of the second action, maxChoicesChanged, uses setInteger—another method of the NSUserDefaults class—to save the value of the stepper. Note that the value we read from the stepper is of type Double, so we need to convert it to an integer before storing it (allowing 4.5 choices, for example, is not very meaningful). This action does one more thing: it calls updateMaxChoicesLabel—a method we will add next to show to the user the value that was set. Listing 6-38 shows the implementation of maxChoicesChanged.

***Listing 6-38.*** Saving the Value of the Stepper in SettingsViewController

```
@IBAction func maxChoicesChanged(sender: AnyObject) {
    // Get a reference to the defaults system
    let defaults = NSUserDefaults.standardUserDefaults()

    // The stepper value is of type Double,
    // but we want to store an Int, so create an Int:
    let maxChoices = Int(maxChoicesStepper.value)

    // Store the maximum preferred choices as an integer:
    defaults.setInteger(maxChoices, forKey: tabManager.maxChoicesKey)

    // Finally, update the label
    // to show the user the value they set:
    updateMaxChoicesLabel()
}
```

Next comes the implementation of updateMaxChoicesLabel. It is fairly simple: we read the value that the stepper has been set to and display as part of the maxOptionLabel's text (Listing 6-39).

***Listing 6-39.*** Updating the Label to Show the Value of the Stepper in SettingsViewController

```
// MARK: Helper methods
func updateMaxChoicesLabel() {
    maxChoicesLabel.text = "Maximum options: \(Int(maxChoicesStepper.value))"
}
```

# Loading User Preferences

Let us make sure that the settings screen displays the correct user preferences when it first loads. For that purpose we will use two of the convenience methods of NSUserDefaults for reading values: boolForKey and integerForKey.

The very first time we run the app there will be no keys and values stored in the system defaults for us to read. Conveniently, boolForKey and integerForKey both return values even if the relevant keys haven't been found, so we will have default settings to start with. However, note that the default value returned by integerForKey is 0, which is not a valid value for our purposes. Later on, when we allow the user to change the topic of the vote and add choices, we will want there to be at least two choices for voting on. We can also add a number to cap choices to. Let us do that by adding a couple of constants to VoteTabBarController in VoteTabBarController.swift (Listing 6-40)—we want to keep these data constraints with the rest of the data. Later on we will need to have them accessible from a new view, in which the user will set up their own vote.

*Listing 6-40.* Adding Constraints to the Data Model in VoteTabBarController

```
// MARK: Data constraints
let minChoices = 2
let maxChoices = 5
```

Back in `SettingsViewController.swift` add a helper function, called `loadSettings`, which queries the system defaults for the two settings we have stored. This will use two of the convenience methods of `NSUserDefaults` for reading values: `boolForKey` and `integerForKey`.

The very first time we run the app there will be no keys and values stored in the system defaults to read. Conveniently, `boolForKey` and `integerForKey` both return values even if keys haven't been found, so we will have default settings to start with. A detail to pay attention to: the default value returned by `integerForKey` is 0, which is not a valid value for our purposes. We want the choices for voting to be at least two, so we must check and adjust the result we get from `integerForKey` (Listing 6-41).

*Listing 6-41.* Displaying the Settings When the View Is Loaded by SettingsViewController

```
// MARK: Helper methods
func loadSettings()
{
    // Get a reference to the defaults system
    let defaults = NSUserDefaults.standardUserDefaults()

    // Read the Boolean stored for the state of the switch.
    // If no value is found for the key,
    // boolForKey will return false by default.
    resultsAsPercentSwitch.on = ↵
        defaults.boolForKey(tabManager.resultsAsPercentKey)

    // Read the value stored for the steper.
    // If no value is found, integerForKey will return 0.
    // When this is the case,
    // set the stepper to the maximum choices allowed.
    let maxOptions = defaults.integerForKey(tabManager.maxChoicesKey)
    maxChoicesStepper.value = ↵
        0 == maxOptions ? Double(tabManager.maxChoices) : ↵
        Double(maxOptions)

    // Update the label to show the value we set the switch to:
    updateMaxChoicesLabel()
}
```

We will call `loadSettings` from the view controller's `viewDidLoad` method to ensure that the view can display user preferences the first time it is loaded (Listing 6-42).

*Listing 6-42.* Updating viewDidLoad in SettingsViewController to Call loadSettings

```
override func viewDidLoad() {
    super.viewDidLoad()

    // Get a reference to the tab bar controller
    // and cast it to the class we created for it:
    tabManager = self.tabBarController as! VoteTabBarController
```

```
    // Query the system defaults for user preferences:
    loadSettings()
}
```

Let us see what the app looks like now. Run it, go to the Settings screen, and play with the values. Then quit and start the app again: the Settings screen should show the values you last set.

Before we move on, let us put one of the settings to use: we will change the results screen to show the votes as percentages or as numbers, depending on what the user prefers. Open ResultsViewController. swift and let us add a method similar to displayVoteResults, called displayVoteResultsAsPercentages (Listing 6-43). Note the use of NSNumberFormatter: this is an iOS SDK class, which helps with converting numbers to strings. In this case it formats Double values to show up to two digits after the decimal point when interpolated in a string.

***Listing 6-43.*** Adding a Method to ResultsViewController That Will Display the Vote Results as Percentages

```
func displayVoteResultsAsPercentages() {
    // Check if we have something to report and return if not:
    if tabManager.voteData.participants == 0 {
        resultsTextView.text = "No voting took place"
        return
    }

    // Create a string, which will accumulate a summary of the votes:
    var voteInformation = "Vote topic: \(tabManager.voteData.topic)\n"
    voteInformation += "\nTotal votes: \(tabManager.voteData.participants)"

    // Work out the percent of abstain votes:
    let abstainedPercent = 100 * Double(tabManager.voteData.abstains) / ↵
        Double(tabManager.voteData.participants)

    // Convert the percent to a string
    //  with precision of two digits after the decimal point:
    let formatter = NSNumberFormatter()
    formatter.maximumFractionDigits = 2
    let abstainedPercentString = formatter.stringFromNumber(abstainedPercent)!
    voteInformation += "\nAbstained: \(abstainedPercentString)%\n"

    // Iterate through the choices array
    // to read the votes each choice received:
    for choice in tabManager.voteData.choices {
        let choiceVotePercent = 100 * Double(choice.votes) / ↵
            Double(tabManager.voteData.participants)

        // Use the formatter to convert the percent information into a string:
        let choiceVotePercentString = ↵
            formatter.stringFromNumber(choiceVotePercent)!
        voteInformation += "\n - \(choice.title) received ↵
            \(choiceVotePercentString)% of the votes"
    }

    // Display the string in the text view:
    resultsTextView.text = voteInformation
}
```

Still in `ResultsViewController`, let us modify its `viewWillAppear` method to check the user settings and call the appropriate method for displaying the results (Listing 6-44).

***Listing 6-44.*** Modifying ResultsViewController to Take the User Preferences into Account

```
override func viewWillAppear(animated: Bool) {
    super.viewWillAppear(animated)

    // Get a reference to the defaults system
    let defaults = NSUserDefaults.standardUserDefaults()

    // Read the Boolean stored for the state of the switch.
    // If no value is found for the key,
    // boolForKey will return false by default.
    if defaults.boolForKey(tabManager.resultsAsPercentKey) {
        displayVoteResultsAsPercentages()
    } else {
        displayVoteResults()
    }
}
```

Run the app and see how the results screen changes according to what you do on the settings screen.

I have not forgotten about the user preference we added for limiting the maximum number of voting options. We will see what it's about in the next section, where we let the user set a new topic for the vote and define options.

# Creating and Managing UI Programmatically

Enough of this hard-coding nonsense. In this section we will make the app more dynamic and allow the user to change the voting topic and add choices.

This will be done on a separate tab in the app's interface, so put another view controller on the storyboard and then add it to the tab bar controller's list of controllers. Title it Create.

---

■ **Tip** You can drag and drop tab bar items in the tab view controller on the storyboard to change their order.

---

Add a Label, a Text Field, two Buttons, a Scroll View, and a Vertical Stack View to the view controller as shown on Figure 6-38. Note that the vertical stack view needs to be inside the scroll view.

Title the label Topic and the two buttons – + and -. We will use the buttons for adding and removing choices. Style them the way we did with the rest of the buttons in the app: in the Identity inspector add `layer.borderWidth` and `layer.cornerRadius` under **User Defined Runtime Attributes**, set their types to Number and their values to 1 and 6, respectively.

Select the stack view and, in the Attributes Inspector, set **Stack View ➤ Distribution** to Fill Equally and its **Spacing** to 10.

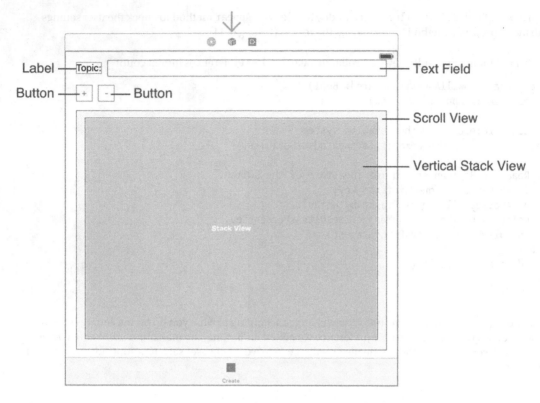

**Figure 6-38.** *Designing the Create view controller*

Constrain the UI elements, so that

- The vertical stack view fills up the scroll view (i.e., all of its edges go to the edges of the scroll view).

- The label, the + button, and the scroll view's leading edges are aligned and coincide with their parent view's leading margin.

- The vertical distance between the + button and the label is 20.

- The text field and the scroll view's trailing edges are aligned and coincide with the parent view's trailing margin.

- The distance between the bottom edge of the scroll view and the bottom margin is 20.

- The vertical distance between the scroll view and the + button is 20.

- The vertical centers of the label and the text field are aligned.

- The vertical centers of the two buttons are aligned.

---

■ **Tip** The storyboard is probably getting a bit crowded now. If you right-click somewhere outside a view controller, you can choose to zoom in and out, so that you get a better view and are able to arrange the view controllers in a convenient way. Double-clicking on the storyboard switches between 25% and 100% zoom.

---

Add a new Swift file to your project's View controllers group, called CreateViewController.swift, and in it declare a class, named CreateViewController, which inherits UIViewController (Listing 6-45).

*Listing 6-45.* Declaring CreateViewController

```
import UIKit

class CreateViewController : UIViewController {
}
```

Back on the storyboard set the **Class** property of the new view controller to CreateViewController. Then create outlets for the text field, the two buttons, and the vertical stack view and name them voteTopic, addButton, removeButton, and choicesView. Add actions for the two buttons' Touch Up Inside events and name them addButtonTapped and removeButtonTapped. Inside addButtonTapped make a call to createNewChoice and inside removeButtonTapped call removeLastChoice (Listing 6-46). The two calls we just added are to methods we will implement next.

*Listing 6-46.* Adding Outlets and Actions to CreateViewController

```
// MARK: Outlets
@IBOutlet weak var voteTopic: UITextField!
@IBOutlet weak var addButton: UIButton!
@IBOutlet weak var removeButton: UIButton!
@IBOutlet weak var choicesView: UIStackView!

// MARK: Actions
@IBAction func addButtonTapped(sender: AnyObject) {
    createNewChoice()
}

@IBAction func removeButtonTapped(sender: AnyObject) {
    removeLastChoice()
}
```

## Creating and Removing UI Elements at Runtime

The two methods we are about to implement will dynamically add or remove a text field from the screen, allowing the user to create or delete choices for voting on. We will first add an array, which will keep references to the text fields we create and delete. Add a MARK: Dynamic UI annotation and under it declare an empty array of type UITextField (Listing 6-47).

*Listing 6-47.* Declaring an Array to Keep Track of Dynamic UI in CreateViewController

```
// MARK: Dynamic UI
// This array keeps references
// to text fields we create at runtime:
var choiceTextFields = [UITextField]()
```

Add the definition of createNewChoice under MARK: Dynamic UI (Listing 6-48). The first three lines in this method create a new instance of UITextField and set it up. We set a text placeholder and assign our instance of CreateViewController as the delegate for the text field. We will see later on why we need the delegation and how to make it work.

For the moment let us concentrate on the dynamic UI: after the text field has been created, we add it to the choiceTextFields array, so we can keep track of it and then we call addArrangedSubView to place it on the vertical stack view. addArrangedSubView is a method of UIStackView, which will add the text field at the bottom of the subviews that the stack view manages.

The last call we make in this method, updateButtonState, is to another method that we will define later: its role is to keep track of whether the user is allowed to add or delete options, so it can enable or disable addButton and removeButton accordingly.

***Listing 6-48.*** Adding Text Fields at Runtime

```
func createNewChoice() {
    // Create and set up a new text field:
    let textField = UITextField()
    textField.placeholder = "Choice title"
    textField.delegate = self

    // Add it to the array of dynamic text fields:
    choiceTextFields.append(textField)

    // Add it to the vertical stack view:
    choicesView.addArrangedSubview(textField)

    // See if the addButton and the removeButton
    // need to be enabled/disabled:
    updateButtonState()
}
```

Next under the under MARK: Dynamic UI annotation comes the implementation of removeLastChoice. To remove the last text field we added on the screen, we first take its reference out of the choiceTextFields array and then we ask the vertical stack view to remove it from its list of arranged subviews. We assign nil to the reference, so that the instance it refers to it can be deallocated. Finally, we make a call to the function that will enable or disable the two buttons depending on how many choices (i.e., text fields) are left on the screen (Listing 6-49).

***Listing 6-49.*** Deleting Text Fields at Runtime

```
func removeLastChoice() {
    // Take out the last text field
    // we added to the array:
    var textField = choiceTextFields.popLast()

    // Remove it from the screen:
    choicesView.removeArrangedSubview(textField!)

    // Flag it for deallocating:
    textField = nil

    // See if the addButton and the removeButton
    // need to be enabled/disabled:
    updateButtonState()
}
```

■ **Swift reference**    The last two methods we added both use an array to add or remove items. You can find out more about arrays in Chapter 19.

The last method we will add under MARK: Dynamic UI is updateButtonState. It will dynamically enable or disable the add and remove buttons. We want the add button to be enabled only if the choices added on the screen are below the maximum we allow and we want the remove button to be enabled only if there are more choices than the minimum.

For working out the maximum number of choices we will check the user defaults system, where the Settings view may have stored a value set by the user. If no value is found, we can default to the constraints we defined on the data in VoteTabViewController. We will check these constraints to find out the minimum number of choices too (Listing 6-50).

***Listing 6-50.*** Enabling or Disabling the add and remove Buttons at Runtime

```
func updateButtonState() {
    // Check the user settings
    // for the maximum number of choices allowed:
    let defaults = NSUserDefaults.standardUserDefaults()
    var maxChoices = defaults.integerForKey(tabManager.maxChoicesKey)
    if maxChoices == 0 {
        // If no value was found,
        // take the data constraint from tabManager:
        maxChoices = tabManager.maxChoices
    }

    // Only enable the addButton if we are below the maximum:
    addButton.enabled = choiceTextFields.count < maxChoices

    // Only enable the removeButton
    // if we have more than the minimum choices allowed:
    removeButton.enabled = choiceTextFields.count > tabManager.minChoices
}
```

Listing 6-50 uses something we have not defined yet: tabManager. Let us fix that. Like we did in the rest of the view controllers, we will declare tabManager as a constant member and initialize it to refer to CreateViewController's tabBarController instance inside the viewDidLoad method (Listing 6-51).

***Listing 6-51.*** Adding a Reference to the Tab Bar Controller

```
// MARK: UIViewController
weak var tabManager: VoteTabBarController!

override func viewDidLoad() {
    super.viewDidLoad()

    // Get a reference to the tab bar controller:
    tabManager = self.tabBarController as! VoteTabBarController
}
```

We will do something else in `viewDidLoad` too: now that we have the means to dynamically create text fields, let us make sure that our view starts with text fields for the minimum number of choices we allow (Listing 6-52).

***Listing 6-52.*** Creating Text Fields for the Minimum Number of Choices

```
override func viewDidLoad() {
    super.viewDidLoad()

    // Get a reference to the tab bar controller:
    tabManager = self.tabBarController as! VoteTabBarController

    // Create text fields for the minimum number of choices
    // that make a valid vote topic:
    for _ in 1 ... tabManager.minChoices {
        createNewChoice()
    }
}
```

## Managing the Text Fields

Before we can build and run the app, we have to do some housekeeping. Remember that line in the `createNewChoice` method that we promised to explain later?

```
textField.delegate = self
```

In fact, even if you tried very hard to forget it, the compiler did not let you, as it generated a compiler error at this line. Time to put things in order.

`UITextField` uses the Delegation design pattern that we learned about in **Chapter 5**. One of the reasons it needs a delegate is to dismiss the keyboard after the user finishes typing. We will make `CreateViewController` that delegate by first adding the `UITextFieldDelegate` protocol to its inheritance list:

```
class CreateViewController : UIViewController, UITextFieldDelegate {
```

And then we will implement `UITextFieldDelegate`'s method that decides whether a field should release the keyboard when the user taps the Return button (Listing 6-53).

***Listing 6-53.*** Implementing textFieldShouldReturn to Allow a Text Field to Release the Keyboard

```
// MARK: UITextFieldDelegate
func textFieldShouldReturn(textField: UITextField) -> Bool {
    // This will make the keyboard disappear
    // when the Return button is tapped in a text field:
    textField.resignFirstResponder()
    return true
}
```

Let us assign a delegate to the `voteTopic` text field. We will do this in the `viewDidLoad` method, which should now look like Listing 6-54.

*Listing 6-54.* Modifying viewDidload to Assign a Delegate to the voteTopic Text Field

```
override func viewDidLoad() {
    super.viewDidLoad()

    // Get a reference to the tab bar controller:
    tabManager = self.tabBarController as! VoteTabBarController

    // Create text fields for the minimum number of choices
    // that make a valid vote topic:
    for _ in 1 … tabManager.minChoices {
        createNewChoice()
    }

    // Set CreateViewController as the delegate of the text field,
    // so it can help it let go of the keyboard:
    voteTopic.delegate = self
}
```

You can now run the app and play with the dynamic user interface. Figure 6-39 shows you the Create screen with a new vote topic and options added at runtime.

*Figure 6-39.* *The Create screen with vote options added at runtime*

## Updating the Data Model

To finish off the app we will get `CreateViewController` to update the data model when the user creates a new topic and choices for voting, so that we can see the changes reflected in `VoteViewController`.

First we will add a helper method to `CreateViewController`, called `newVoteWasComposed`, which will check if the user created a valid vote: for that we want to have text in all of the text fields on the screen (Listing 6-55).

*Listing 6-55.* Adding a Method to CreateVewController to Check If a Valid Vote Was Created

```
// MARK: Helper functions
func newVoteWasComposed() -> Bool
{
    // Check if we have a valid topic and choices for voting.
    // If any text field has been left empty,
    // we assume the composing of the new topic was not finished.

    if voteTopic.text!.isEmpty {
        return false
    }

    for textField in choiceTextFields {
        if textField.text!.isEmpty {
            return false
        }
    }

    return true
}
```

Then let us add another helper function, which updates the data model (Listing 6-56).

*Listing 6-56.* Updating the Data Model from CreateViewController

```
func updateDataModel() {
    // Update the data in tabManager:
    tabManager.voteData.topic = voteTopic.text!

    tabManager.voteData.choices.removeAll(keepCapacity: true)

    for textField in choiceTextFields {
        tabManager.voteData.choices.append(Choice(title: textField.text!))
    }
}
```

We will call the two helper functions when the user exits the Create view—for that purpose we will override `UIViewController`'s `viewWillDisappear` method (Listing 6-57).

*Listing 6-57.* Updating the Data Model When the View in CreateViewController Is About to Disappear

```
override func viewWillDisappear(animated: Bool) {
    super.viewWillDisappear(animated)
```

```
    if newVoteWasComposed() {
        updateDataModel()
    }
}
```

Let us add an override for `viewWillAppear` too. In it we will update the state of the two buttons for adding and removing options, in case the user changed preferences for the maximum number of choices (Listing 6-58).

***Listing 6-58.*** Updating the Buttons on the UI When the View in CreateViewController Appears on Screen

```
override func viewWillAppear(animated: Bool) {
    super.viewWillAppear(animated)

    // Update the add and remove buttons,
    // in case the user changed preferences
    // on the Settings screen:
    updateButtonState()
}
```

Run the app and test it. You will probably notice that there is something missing: you can create a new vote topic and options, but when you switch to the vote screen, the old vote is still there. We will add the missing piece of the puzzle in the next section.

# Sending Notifications

As an ActionScript developer you are intimately familiar with sending and receiving events. In this section we will see how we can send events in iOS in order to notify parts of our code about changes in other parts of the code.

To send a notification on iOS we will use `NSNotificationCenter`—a class from the SDK, which uses the *Observer design pattern.*

---

■ **Note**    In the Observer design pattern there are two sets of players: an object, which can send notifications, and observers that can subscribe to receive these notifications. The notifying object maintains a list of its observers and uses an event system to let them know when an event occurs that they are interested in.

---

`NSNotificationCenter` lets us send notifications, which are identifiable by their name. So let us define a name for the notification we will use to let the vote view controller know that there have been changes in the data model. We will do this in `VoteTabBarController` to keep the notification name together with the rest of the data-related code (Listing 6-59).

***Listing 6-59.*** Defining a Notification Name in VoteTabBarController

```
class VoteTabBarController: UITabBarController {
    // MARK: Notifications
    let dataChangedNotificationName = "Vote data changed"

    // The rest of the class definition
}
```

Next, we will add a subscription for this notification in VoteViewController's viewDidLoad method. Open VoteViewController.swift and modify viewDidLoad as shown in Listing 6-60.

***Listing 6-60.*** Subscribing for Notifications in VoteViewConroller

```
override func viewDidLoad() {
    // Call the base class method first
    // to make sure we won't miss out on any preparation done by it:
    super.viewDidLoad()

    // Get a reference to the tab bar controller
    // and cast it to the class we created for it:
    tabManager = self.tabBarController as! VoteTabBarController

    // This will cause the methods required
    // by the UITableViewDataSource to be called:
    choicesTable.dataSource = self

    // Subscribe for notifications about changes in the data model:
    let notificationCenter = NSNotificationCenter.defaultCenter()
    notificationCenter.addObserver(self, ↵
        selector: #selector(self.dataChanged), ↵
        name: tabManager.dataChangedNotificationName, ↵
        object: nil)
}
```

If you look at the call to notificationCenter.addObserver, you will notice strange syntax in the selector parameter:

```
#selector(self.dataChanged)
```

Let us first explain #selector.

---

■ **Swift reference**  Selectors are a way of identifying methods to be called and are an Objective-C legacy. Originally they could be used with string literals to select methods by their names at runtime.

---

Then we need to implement the method we pass to the selector parameter in addObserver. This method will be the notification handler for when the data model has changed–add it under MARK: Helper methods (Listing 6-61). In it we do two things: let the table view know that it needs to reload the data in its cells and refresh the text of topicLabel to show the new voting topic.

***Listing 6-61.*** Adding a Notification Handler in VoteViewController

```
func dataChanged() {
    // This will get the table view
    // to request new data for its cells:
    choicesTable.reloadData()

    // Access the vote data in tabManager
    // to initialize the topic label:
    topicLabel.text = tabManager.voteData.topic
}
```

The last thing we need to do in order to enable this notification system is to send an actual notification. Let us do this after we update the data model in CreateViewController's viewWillDisappear method (Listing 6-62).

**Listing 6-62.** Sending a Notification from CreateViewController

```
override func viewWillDisappear(animated: Bool) {
    if newVoteWasComposed() {
        updateDataModel()

        // Notify observers that data has changed:
        let notificationCenter = NSNotificationCenter.defaultCenter()
        notificationCenter.postNotificationName( ↵
            tabManager.dataChangedNotificationName, object: nil)
    }
}
```

Let us run the app and create a new topic for voting (Figure 6-40).

**Figure 6-40.** *The finished app*

And with this we wrap up our voting app. There are more thing we could do to make it foolproof, which we will leave to you, curious reader. . . as if you need more excuses to go deeper into Swift. For example, you could modify the Create screen to reflect changes in the user preferences: if the setting for the maximum number of choices is set lower than the options that were last created, you could remove options, start with a clean slate, or show a warning.

# Summary

For the sake of getting some exercise and fresh air, we hope you did not go through this chapter in one sitting. That was a lot of work to do. But hey, wasn't it worth it!

With this last app in your arsenal you now know how to choose a navigation pattern for your applications, how to pass data between views, how to handle user settings, and how to have the flexibility of creating and managing UIs programmatically.

In the next chapter we will turn our attention to the nonvisual side of app development and see what concurrency is and how it can help you. And also when to steer clear of it.

# CHAPTER 7

■ ■ ■

# Concurrency

Imagine that you share a house with three housemates: Alice, Bob, and Charles; the house is a mess and you want it cleaned up for your mother's visit on the weekend. You could do it all yourself, starting with the kitchen, moving on to the bathroom, then the hallway, and so on. Or you could recruit your housemates and give each of them tasks: Alice could tidy up the living room, Bob could vacuum it, and Charles could dust, while you water the plants, for example. Then all of you could get on with the kitchen, where you wash the dishes, Alice sweeps the floor, Bob takes out last night's beer bottles to be recycled. . . . Or, better still: you give each housemate a room to clean up and leave them to it. That would work well with Alice's sleeping until midday, Bob's intolerance of Charles, and your fear of spiders (best to leave the bathroom to someone else). Your only worry is making sure there is no contention over shared resources like the vacuum cleaner . . .

Breaking up a job into tasks, which can be done more or less independently of one another, rather than in a particular order, makes a system *concurrent*. This makes sure that higher-priority tasks are not slowed down by waiting for lower-priority tasks to complete[1] and even creates the possibility of tasks being done simultaneously and saving time.

In this chapter you will do the following:

- learn about designing concurrent apps and the benefits and challenges this involves.

- gain understanding of concurrency and multithreading concepts.

- design and implement an app that does the same job in both concurrent and nonconcurrent ways, so you can contrast the two.

When you are done, you will have an app that searches for prime numbers in several different ways and also lets you cancel a lengthy search.

## Understanding Concurrency

Concurrency is something that you need to consider at the design level of your app, before you start coding. Dividing functionality into tasks that can be run concurrently requires a lot more work and possibly a lot of code rewriting if done in an already existing code base than when you start fresh.

---

[1]Your mother may never even peek into Charles's room, but the living room needs to be spotless.

© Radoslava Leseva Adams and Hristo Lesev 2016
R. L. Adams and H. Lesev, *Migrating to Swift from Flash and ActionScript*,
DOI 10.1007/978-1-4842-1666-8_7

---

**ACTIONSCRIPT ANALOGY**

Although its implementation is quite subtle, the idea of concurrency is built into ActionScript. There are a lot of asynchronous application programming interface (API) calls in both Flash and Flex that make sure that user interface does not get blocked by slow operations. If you have developed desktop apps, you may have also used `Worker` objects, which wrap sets of tasks in code that can be run in the background.

---

## Benefits of Concurrency

Although it is not trivial, the effort of writing concurrent code usually pays off in one or more of the ways shown in the following list:

- **User interface responsiveness**. It is best to keep computationally heavy work and user interface (UI) updates separate, so that the UI does not freeze while the heavy work is being done. Similarly, UI should be kept interactive and responsive while your app waits for a response from a remote server, for example.

- **Better resource utilization**. In the last scenario waiting for a server response would keep the CPU (central processing unit) idle, unless your app can do other useful work in the meantime. For instance, instead of waiting for an entire audio file to download, in order to be played, your app could download a chunk of it and start playing it while the rest of the file is being downloaded.

- **Improved performance**. On multicore systems, such as today's iPhones and iPads, designing concurrent tasks makes it possible to run them in parallel, thus saving time. It is important to keep in mind that just because tasks can run at the same time does not mean that they will–more on that next.

## Challenges of Concurrency

Designing concurrent apps has its flipside too–here are some of the challenges to keep in mind.

- **Parallelism is not guaranteed.** Unless you are prepared to exercise very low-level control of scheduling, running, and synchronizing tasks, when and for how long each one runs is up to the operating system. Your job as a programmer is to write code that *can* be run in parallel if needed.

- **Improved performance is not a given either.** It is worth measuring your app's performance of critical jobs before and after you break them down into concurrent tasks. Too much granularity can often hurt, rather than improve speed.

- **Dealing with dependencies is important**. Tasks designed to serve the same job are rarely completely independent of each other. It is especially important to consider scenarios where two or more tasks can get in a *deadlock*, each waiting for the other one to complete, in order to continue.

- **Managing shared resources is important**. Tasks might need to access the same files, network connections, data in memory, or other resources. You need to make sure that this does not lead to data corruption, where more than one task modifies the same resource at the same time, or to inconsistencies, where reading data happens before writing to it has finished.

- **Debugging can be tricky**. When there is more than one task running at the same time, it can be challenging to replicate and trace errors in your code, because how things happen is related to timing and order.

# A few words on multithreading

Concurrency is traditionally linked with multithreaded programming. When making iOS apps you certainly have the option of accessing and using threads. Apple has also provided higher-level technologies, which can save you a lot of work related to thread scheduling and synchronization. We will use one of these technologies, Grand Central Dispatch (GCD), to build a concurrent app in the later part of this chapter. GCD itself uses threads, so it is worth understanding how these work, as this underpins GCD's principles. Moreover, whether you write multithreaded code or not, your apps are multithreaded, as a lot of iOS SDK calls run their tasks on different threads.

When you start an app on your iOS device, it runs in a *process*. Each process is virtually independent of anything else that runs on the device: it has its own chunk of memory, which no other process can access and can pretend that it is the only thing running on the system.

Code in a process runs in one or more *threads*. You can think of a thread as a sequence of CPU instructions to be executed one after the other. A process has at least one thread of execution. When there are multiple threads, one of them is designated as *the main thread*. The main thread is where code that updates the UI usually runs. Other tasks can be assigned to different threads and be run at the same time or seemingly at the same time as the code on the main thread. Each thread has its own stack for instructions but does not have designated memory–threads share the same memory space.

Executing threads "seemingly at the same time" is what happens on single-core machines. As there is only one CPU, which can execute a single instruction at a time, it is impossible to have instructions run in parallel. Instead this is simulated: when a thread runs, a chunk of its instructions are executed, then the thread is *put to sleep* (i.e., paused), while a chunk of instructions from another thread are executed, then the second thread is put to sleep, so another one can run... This going to sleep and waking up require work: before it is paused, the running thread needs to save its state (its stack) and then needs to retrieve it when it is woken up, so it can continue from where it left off. This is called *context switching* and is one of the prices you pay for using multiple threads: saving and retrieving state takes additional time and memory. In the house-cleaning example this would be similar to the scenario, where all of your housemates have found better places to be and have left you to tidy up on your own. You could run multiple tasks at a time and try to wash the dishes and dust in parallel: you start the tap, put dishwashing liquid on the sponge, wash one dish, then put the sponge down, rinse your hands, turn the tap off, pick up the dust cloth and dust the top of the bookshelf; then start the tap again, put dishwashing liquid on the sponge. All of the preparation to wash a dish or to dust a shelf is what you do to switch contexts and in this case creates a lot of unnecessary overhead–you would probably be better off if you washed all of the dishes and then got on with dusting. Figure 7-1 illustrates this: threads running on a single-core CPU, rather than the house cleaning drama.

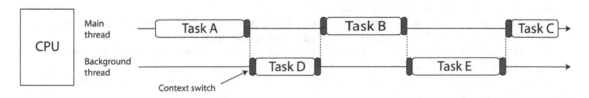

***Figure 7-1.*** *Multiple threads running on a single-core machine*

On multicore machines there is the option to run more than one task at a time (Figure 7-2): Alice can do the dishwashing, while you dust.

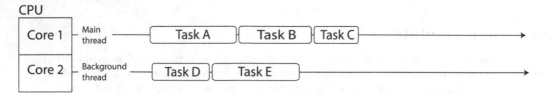

***Figure 7-2.*** *Multiple threads running on a dual-core machine*

When more than one thread can execute a piece of code, this code needs to be *thread-safe*. This means guaranteeing that there will be no unwanted side effects, such as data corruption or crashes, caused, for example, by a thread trying to access a variable that another thread has not yet finished initializing. Or Bob pulling the stepladder away just as you are about to climb on it to dust the chandelier.

Another couple of tricky situations that need to be considered with multithreading and when designing concurrent code in general are *deadlocks* and *race conditions*.

Deadlocking happens when two or more threads (or tasks) are paused and wait for each other to finish before they can continue execution. Say, Bob has kindly agreed to do the dishes and is waiting for you to return the dishwashing liquid, which you grabbed to treat a suspicious stain on the carpet. You, however, (prudently) want to use rubber gloves to do this, so you decide to wait until Bob has finished washing the dishes has and taken the gloves off.

A race condition typically arises when more than one thread or task can access and modify shared memory (or another resource) and the state of this memory can vary depending on who got to it first (i.e., it ends up being unpredictable). If two of your housemates decided to rearrange the bookshelves and Alice started ordering the books alphabetically, but Bob rearranged them by color and size at the same time,[2] Alice and Bob would be in a race condition and the final state of the bookshelves would be anybody's guess.

When you work with multiple threads, their scheduling is typically done by the operating system, but the communication between threads and ensuring their safety is up to you.

Apple's GCD saves you some of this work by helping you think about your code in terms of tasks and queues of tasks, rather than low-level threads and their relation to hardware. In order to explore GCD and see what is available through it, we will design an app that uses it to accomplish a task concurrently. The next section will guide you through setting up the app.

# Setting Up the App

The app we will use to demonstrate some of GCD's concurrency techniques will find and display all prime numbers smaller than a number chosen by the user.

To start, create a new iOS Single View Application project in Xcode and name it `FindPrimeNumbers` (**File ➤ New ➤ Project...**, then **iOS ➤ Application ➤ Single View Application**).

Open `Main.storyboard` and add three labels, a slider, a switch, a text view, a progress view, and two buttons. Figure 7-3 shows you how to lay out these UI elements and what names to give to the outlets you create for them in `ViewController.swift`. Don't forget to constrain the layout, so that it adapts its size to different screens (see **Chapter 5** for how to work with *Auto Layout* and *Size Classes*).

---

[2]Considering that you grew up with a mother whose visit requires such levels of preparations, it is little wonder that you ended up with pedantic housemates. Sorry.

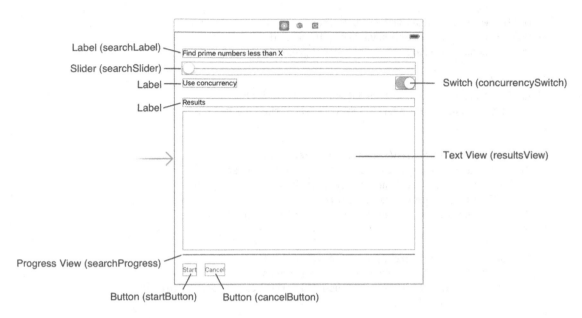

Label (searchLabel) — Find prime numbers less than X

Slider (searchSlider) —

Label — Use concurrency

Label — Results

Switch (concurrencySwitch)

Text View (resultsView)

Progress View (searchProgress) — Start  Cancel

Button (startButton)   Button (cancelButton)

***Figure 7-3.*** *Laying out the app screen on the storyboard*

When the app is run, the user will move the slider to select a number and tap the Start button to get a list of all prime numbers smaller than the chosen one. Tapping the Cancel button will stop a search for prime numbers.

Some of the UI elements will need their properties set up in the Attributes inspector. The list below will guide you through doing this.

- Select the text view, delete its default text under **Text View ➤ Text** and uncheck **Editable** and **Selectable** under **Text View ➤ Behavior**.

- Select the slider and set **Minimum** to 2, **Maximum** to 100, 000 and **Current** to 200 under **Slider ➤ Value**.

- Select the progress view and set **Progress View ➤ Progress** to 0.

In `ViewController.swift` add actions for the Touch Up Inside events for both buttons and call them `startSearch` and `cancelSearch`, respectively. Then add an action for the Value Changed event of the slider and call it `searchValueChanged`.

The definition of `ViewController` should now look like Listing 7-1. We have added `MARK` annotations to organize the code and `TODO` annotations to help us plan what we need to do next. See **Chapter 6** for a reminder about how these can help you navigate your source files more easily.

***Listing 7-1.*** Adding Outlets and Actions to ViewController.swift

```swift
class ViewController: UIViewController {

    // MARK: Outlets
    @IBOutlet weak var resultsTextView: UITextView!
    @IBOutlet weak var searchLabel: UILabel!
    @IBOutlet weak var searchSlider: UISlider!
    @IBOutlet weak var cancelButton: UIButton!
```

```
@IBOutlet weak var startButton: UIButton!
@IBOutlet weak var concurrencySwitch: UISwitch!
@IBOutlet weak var searchProgress: UIProgressView!

// MARK: Actions
@IBAction func searchValueChanged(sender: AnyObject) {
    // TODO: Update the search label to show the new value.
}

@IBAction func startSearch(sender: AnyObject) {
    // TODO: Reset any previous results shown on the screen.
    // TODO: Check if the concurrency switch is on.
    // TODO: Start a prime number search.
    // TODO: Enable the Cancel button if cancel is allowed.
}

@IBAction func cancelSearch(sender: AnyObject) {
    // TODO: Cancel the search for prime numbers
    // TODO: Update the screen to show that the search was cancelled.
    // TODO: Disable the Cancel button.
}

// MARK: UIViewController
override func viewDidLoad() {
    super.viewDidLoad()

    // TODO: Disable the Cancel button initially.
    // TODO: Make sure that the search label and the slider are in sync.
}

override func didReceiveMemoryWarning() {
    super.didReceiveMemoryWarning()
}
}
```

Let us take care of some of these TODOs, which we have left sprinkled around the code. First we will implement a method to keep the search label and the search slider in sync: when the user moves the slider, the label will update to show the new value that the slider was set to (Listing 7-2).

*Listing 7-2.* Updating the Search Label When the Slider Is Moved

```
// MARK: User interface helper methods
func updateSearchLabel() {
    searchLabel.text = "Find prime numbers less than ↵
        \(Int(searchSlider.value))"
}
```

Another couple of UI helper methods will take care of displaying the result from a search and resetting the screen before a new search begins (Listing 7-3). We will implement the search for prime numbers to produce an array of them, which can then be passed to the displayResults method shown in the listing.

***Listing 7-3.*** Displaying and Resetting the Search Results

```
func displayResults(resultsArray primes: [UInt]) {
    if primes.isEmpty {
        resultsTextView.text = "No prime numbers were found."
        return
    }

    // Iterate through the primes array and construct a string,
    // which will be displayed in the text view:
    var resultStr = "\(primes.count) prime numbers were found:\n\n"
    for i in primes.indices {
        resultStr += "Prime [\(i + 1)] = \(primes[i])\n"
    }

    resultsTextView.text = resultStr

    // Reset the two buttons, so we can start another search:
    cancelButton.enabled = false
    startButton.enabled = true
}

func resetResults() {
    // Delete the results of the last search:
    resultsTextView.text = ""
    searchProgress.progress = 0.0
}
```

---

■ **Swift reference**   `displayResults` in Listing 7-3 takes an array of unsigned integers as a parameter. See Chapter 19 for information on arrays and other collection types in Swift.

---

Let us add one last method to the user interface helpers: this one will update the progress view and the text view to show the percentage of work done during a prime number search (Listing 7-4).

***Listing 7-4.*** Showing Progress

```
func displayProgress(amountDone: Float) {
    searchProgress.progress = amountDone
    resultsTextView.text = "Progress: \(Int(100.0 * amountDone))%"
}
```

Now let us put to use some of the methods we have just added. We will add calls to `updateSearchLabel` to the `searchValueChanged` action and to `viewDidLoad`. Inside `viewDidLoad` we will also disable the Cancel button (Listing 7-5).

***Listing 7-5.*** Adding Calls to updateSearchLabel

```
// MARK: Actions
@IBAction func searchValueChanged(sender: AnyObject) {
    updateSearchLabel()
}
```

```
// MARK: UIViewController
override func viewDidLoad() {
    super.viewDidLoad()
    // Do any additional setup after loading the view,
    // typically from a nib.

    updateSearchLabel()
    cancelButton.enabled = false
}
```

Next come a couple of functions that will help us with the search for prime numbers: findPrimeNubersInRange takes a range of unsigned integers and iterates through them: if a number is found to be prime, it gets added to an array, which the method then returns as a result. findPrimeNumbersInRange calls isItPrime-a method, which performs a brute-force[3] check on a given number and returns true if the number is prime (Listing 7-6).

***Listing 7-6.*** Defining Methods for Finding Prime Numbers

```
// MARK: Prime numbers helper methods
func isItPrime(number number: UInt) -> Bool {
    // We know that 0 and 1 are not prime:
    if number < 2 {
        return false
    }

    // Do a brute-force check for the rest of the numbers:
    for div: UInt in 2 ..< number {
        if (number % div) == 0 {
            return false
        }
    }

    return true
}

func findPrimeNumbersInRange(range r: Range<UInt>) -> [UInt] {
    // We will collect the results in this array:
    var primeNumbers = [UInt] ()

    for i in r {
        if isItPrime(number: i) {
            primeNumbers.append(i)
        }
    }

    return primeNumbers
}
```

---

[3]A number is prime if it is greater than 1 and has no positive divisors other than 1 and itself. isItPrime naively iterates through the interval [2, number)–that is, starting at and including 2 and up to, but not including, number–to check if number has any divisors in it.

---

■ **Swift reference**    The code in Listing 7-6 makes use of the `Range` type, which defines an interval of values. You can see how a range can be defined and iterated through in the `for-in` loop of the `isItPrime` method: `2 ..< number` uses the half-open range operator to define a range starting at and including `2` and up to, but not including `number`. For details on Swift's range operators see Chapter 18. For interesting ways of using them in cycles and switch statements see Chapter 20.

---

Run the app on a device or in Xcode's simulator to test the UI. Does the search label update when you move the slider?

Next we will add two method placeholders: one to search for prime numbers and display the results sequentially and one that will use concurrency to do the same thing (Listing 7-7). Implementing and contrasting these methods are the main goals of this chapter.

*Listing 7-7.*  Adding Placeholders for Trying Out Concurrent and Nonconcurrent Searches for Primes

```
// MARK: Search for prime numbers without concurrency
func findPrimeNumbersLessThan(number limit: UInt) {
    // Make sure we have been given a valid limit:
    assert(limit > 0)

    // TODO: Find all prime numbers smaller than limit and display them.
}

// MARK: Search for prime numbers, using concurrency
func concurrentlyFindPrimeNumbersLessThan(number limit: UInt) {
    // Make sure we have been given a valid limit:
    assert(limit > 0)

    // TODO: Find all prime numbers smaller than limit and display them.
}
```

Before we get on with implementing these two methods, let us add calls to them in the action we created for the Start buttons: find `startSearch` and replace the `TODO` annotations in it with the code from Listing 7-8.

*Listing 7-8.*  Implementing the Start Button Action

```
@IBAction func startSearch(sender: AnyObject) {
    // Reset any previous results shown on the screen.
    resetResults()

    // Check if the concurrency switch is on
    // and start a search for prime numbers accordingly:
    if concurrencySwitch.on {
        concurrentlyFindPrimeNumbersLessThan(number UInt(searchSlider.value))

        // Enable the Cancel button, so we can cancel a concurrent search:
        cancelButton.enabled = true
```

```
    // Make sure we can't hit Start again before the search has completed:
    startButton.enabled = false

} else {
    findPrimeNumbersLessThan(number: UInt(searchSlider.value))
  }
}
```

The app has been set up. Run it to make sure that there are no compile errors and then let us get on with implementing the main part of it: finding prime numbers in several different ways.

## Nonconcurrent Implementation

We will first see how the search for prime numbers might work without any concurrency. The implementation of findPrimeNumbersLessThan is simple: obtain an array of prime numbers from findPrimeNumbersInRange and then pass it to displayResults (Listing 7-9).

*Listing 7-9.* Searching for Prime Numbers Without Employing Concurrency

```
// MARK: Search for prime numbers without concurrency
func findPrimeNumbersLessThan(number limit: UInt) {
    // Make sure we have been given a valid limit:
    assert(limit > 0)

    // Find all prime numbers smaller than limit:
    let primes = findPrimeNumbersInRange(range: 0...(limit - 1))

    // and then display them:
    displayResults(resultsArray: primes)
}
```

Run the app, make sure that the **Use concurrency** switch is turned off, and tap the **Start** button. You do not have to move the slider very far up before you notice that it takes a while for the results to appear and that the user interface freezes while the search is under way. In the next section we will see how splitting the work into concurrent tasks can help keep the user interface responsive, while a lengthy search is in progress.

## Concurrent Implementation with GCD

GCD is one of the libraries that Apple has provided to help with concurrent programming. It adds an abstraction layer above raw threads and saves you the need to think about how threads and their interactions are managed. Instead, you are encouraged to imagine your app's functionality as individual tasks, which can be placed on queues for execution. Each app (process) has a main queue, on which tasks end up by default, unless you dispatch them to a different queue to be done concurrently.

---

■ **Note**   Calls that modify the UI can only be executed on the main queue.

---

When choosing a queue to dispatch tasks to, we have the option of using one of the queues that iOS already has running, called *global queues*, or to create a custom one.

Queues can also be *serial* or *concurrent*. A serial queue waits for a task to finish before it starts the next one, so all tasks are guaranteed to start and finish in FIFO (first in, first out) order. The main queue is an example of a serial queue: tasks on it are executed one by one.

In contrast, a concurrent queue starts its tasks in FIFO order but does not wait for one task to finish before it can start the next one. So, if tasks A, B, and C were queued in that order, the queue will start A, start B, and finally start C. However the order in which they finish may be different: if task C is shorter, it may complete before A or B, for example.

Figure 7-4 shows you the difference between serial and concurrent queues.

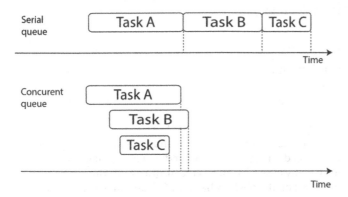

*Figure 7-4.* *Contrasting serial and concurrent queues*

It is worth mentioning that there is not necessarily a one-to-one correspondence between queues and threads. A serial queue will typically run one thread, but a concurrent queue might employ multiple threads to run its tasks. This is managed for you by GCD and you rarely have to think about the underlying threads in a queue.

With this in mind let us see how we can keep the UI responsive, while the search for prime numbers is going on in the background.

## Performing a Search in the Background

A simple way of concurrently searching for prime numbers is to split the job into two tasks: one to find prime numbers and another one to show the results on the screen. The task of displaying the results will need to be part of the main queue, as it involves updating the UI. The search however can be performed on a concurrent queue. Listing 7-10 shows you the implementation, which we explain step by step below.

*Listing 7-10.* Adding the Search Task to a Background Queue

```
// MARK: Search for prime numbers, using concurrency
func concurrentlyFindPrimeNumbersLessThan(number limit: UInt) {
    // Make sure we have been given a valid limit:
    assert(limit > 0)

    // Obtain a reference to one of the existing queues:
    let queue = ↵
        dispatch_get_global_queue(QOS_CLASS_USER_INITIATED, 0)
```

```
// Create a block of code that will be added to the queue:
let block = dispatch_block_create(DISPATCH_BLOCK_INHERIT_QOS_CLASS) {
    let primes = self.findPrimeNumbersInRange(range: 0...(limit - 1))

    // When the search is done,
    // obtain a reference to the main queue
    // and dispatch the task of updating the UI to it:
    let mainQueue = dispatch_get_main_queue()
    dispatch_async(mainQueue, {
        self.displayResults(resultsArray: primes)
    })
}

// Add the code block to the background queue,
// so it can be scheduled for execution:
dispatch_async(queue, block)
}
```

First we obtain a reference to one of the global queues, using the GCD function `dispatch_get_global_queue` and specifying an identifier for the queue we need. The queue identifier distinguishes between queues by the *quality of service (QOS)* they offer. Quality of service affects the priority with which tasks in the queue are run. How tasks are run also has an effect on the device's battery life. You can normally choose between the following QOS classes[4]:

- `QOS_CLASS_USER_INTERACTIVE`. Tasks with this QOS are treated as critical for keeping UI responsive and are thus executed with the highest priority for accessing system resources. They are the most energy-hungry.

- `QOS_CLASS_USER_INITIATED`. Tasks on such a queue have usually been triggered by a user action and the user is assumed to be waiting for a result. They get a relatively high priority for execution but are not treated as critical.

- `QOS_CLASS_UTILITY`. This QOS is for tasks that may or may not have been initiated by the user and have even lower priority. This allows them to be executed in a way that preserves energy (i.e., battery life).

- `QOS_CLASS_BACKGROUND`. Tasks in background queues are run with the lowest priority and in the most energy-efficient way. This QOS is for doing work from which the user does not expect an immediate result and may not even be aware of altogether.

Our intent is for the user to start the search for prime numbers and keep the user interface responsive while he or she waits for the result, so we request a queue with `QOS_CLASS_USER_INITIATED`.

Next, we define the task that we will put on the queue and assign it to a constant called `block`. This is done by creating a *dispatch block*: a piece of code that can be assigned to a variable or a constant and be passed around as an argument to function calls.

Inside the code block we call the `findPrimeNumbersInRange` method we implemented earlier and when it returns its result, we create another task that will display it on the screen. We add this task to the main queue, as it needs to update the UI. Note that we can define a block of code inline without assigning it to a variable or a constant first–this is what the curly brackets in the call do:

```
dispatch_async(mainQueue, {/*Code for the task comes here*/})
```

---

[4]The word "class" here comes from "classification" and is not to be confused with the Object-Oriented concept.

Finally we call `dispatch_async`, which adds the task in `block` to the queue to be executed (Listing 7-10).

---

■ **Swift reference**   The code that is assigned to `block` and the code that is added to the main queue in Listing 7-10 have both been defined as closures and need to access methods and properties of `ViewController` through its implied property, called `self`. For more information on closures in Swift see Chapter 22 and for what the `self` property is see Chapter 21.

---

Run the app again and this time start the search for prime numbers with the **Use concurrency** switch turned on. There is an improvement: finding prime numbers still takes a while, but the app's user interface does not freeze.

# Displaying Progress

It would be nice to inform the user about how the search is going while he or she waits for the results. For that purpose we will first overload the `findPrimesInRange` function to report progress as it goes, which can then be displayed on the screen. We will have progress reported in a callback that is passed as an argument to the function.

On Listing 7-11 we first create a `typealias` (i.e., an alias for the type of callback we want to use), in this case a function that takes one argument of type `Float` and does not return a result. We then define `findPrimeNumbersInRange` to be almost like the original version we coded earlier, but with one extra argument that takes the callback, which is called with progress information as the search for prime numbers is going on.

*Listing 7-11.* Defining a Search Method That Reports Progress

```
// Define an alias for the callback
// we want to use to report progress:
typealias ProgressHandler = (Float) -> ()

func findPrimeNumbersInRange(range r: Range<UInt>, ↵
    progressHandler: ProgressHandler) -> [UInt] {
    // We will collect the results in this array:
    var primeNumbers = [UInt] ()

    for i in r {
        if isItPrime(number: i) {
            primeNumbers.append(i)

            // Calculate the proportion of work done
            // and call the progress handler
            let progress = Float(i - r.first!) / Float(r.count)
            progressHandler(progress)
        }
    }
}
```

```
// Job done:
progressHandler(1.0)

return primeNumbers
}
```

---

■ **Swift reference**   This version of findPrimeNumbersInRange is an overload of the original one: they both have the same name, but their signatures differ. When we call findPrimeNumbersInRange the compiler knows which version to use, based on the number of arguments we pass. More on overloading functions in Chapter 17 and on overloading operators in Chapter 18.

---

A quick note on syntax: we defined the typealias in Listing 7-11 for ease of reading, but this is not compulsory. Instead, you can declare findPrimeNumbersInRange like this by using the callback signature as the second argument's type:

```
func findPrimeNumbersInRange(range r: Range<UInt>, ↵
    progressHandler: ((Float) -> ())) -> [UInt]
```

All we need to do in our concurrentlyFindPrimeNumbersLessThan method is call the new overload of findPrimeNumbersInRange and pass it the displayProgress method we defined earlier; the rest of the code is exactly the same as it was (Listing 7-12).

*Listing 7-12.*  Modifying concurrentlyFindPrimeNumbersLessThan to Use the New Search Method

```
// MARK: Search for prime numbers, using concurrency
func concurrentlyFindPrimeNumbersLessThan(number limit: UInt) {
    // Make sure we have been given a valid limit:
    assert(limit > 0)

    // Obtain a reference to one of the existing queues:
    let queue = dispatch_get_global_queue(QOS_CLASS_USER_INITIATED, 0)

    // Create a block of code that will be added to the queue:
    let block = dispatch_block_create(DISPATCH_BLOCK_INHERIT_QOS_CLASS) {
        let primes = ↵
            self.findPrimeNumbersInRange(range: 0...(limit - 1), ↵
                progressHandler: self.displayProgress)

        // When the search is done,
        // obtain a reference to the main queue
        // and dispatch the task of updating the UI to it:
        let mainQueue = dispatch_get_main_queue()
        dispatch_async(mainQueue, {
            self.displayResults(resultsArray: primes)
        })
    }
```

```
// Add the code block to the background queue,
// so it can be scheduled for execution:
dispatch_async(queue, block)
}
```

Before you can safely run the app, however, there is something we need to do. Can you guess what it is? Have a look at Listing 7-13 to see if you guessed right.

***Listing 7-13.*** Ensuring That Displaying Progress Happens on the Main Queue

```
func displayProgress(percent amountDone: Float) {
    dispatch_async(dispatch_get_main_queue(), {
        self.searchProgress.progress = amountDone
        self.resultsTextView.text = "Progress: \(Int(100.0 * amountDone))%"
    })
}
```

The displayProgress method we defined earlier updates the UI, so we need to ensure that the update happens on the main queue. We have changed displayProgress and wrapped the UI modifications in a dispatch_async call that adds them to the main queue.

## Controlling Access to Shared Resources with Dispatch Barriers

If we had to check a huge interval of numbers to find out which ones are prime, we could divide the job even further. Instead of having one task that iterates over all of the numbers, we could split the interval between several tasks–if run in parallel, they could, in theory, complete the job faster.

I hedged with throwing "in theory" there, as there is no universal recipe for improving performance. Making tasks more granular is a double-edged sword: it could speed up your code, but it could also just as easily slow it down if there is a lot of synchronization to do. Sharing resources between tasks is one tricky situation, which might require synchronization techniques that get in the way of performance.

In this section we will contrive a scenario to demonstrate how we can control access to shared resources between tasks with *dispatch barriers*. We will split the search for prime numbers into several tasks, which we will add to a queue to be run concurrently. But we will require that all results are combined in the same array in the end (and will not care if we end up with a sorted array of prime numbers or not). Access to this array will need to be limited to one task at a time within the queue–this is achieved by putting the code that modifies the array in a dispatch_barrier_async call.

Dispatch barriers are normally used to synchronize tasks in the same queue. The code in the barrier is executed only after all previous tasks that were submitted to the queue have finished. No other tasks are started before the barrier code completes.

We will do a few changes to concurrentlyFindPrimeNumbersLessThan to illustrate this. Listing 7-14 will guide you through these modifications.

***Listing 7-14.*** Splitting the Search for Prime Numbers into Subtasks

```
// MARK: Search for prime numbers, using concurrency
func concurrentlyFindPrimeNumbersLessThan(number limit: UInt) {
    // Let us split the search into four:
    let concurrentTaskCount: UInt = 4
    // Based on the numer of concurrent tasks we want,
    // calculate the size of the interval
    // that each task will need to search through:
    let rangeSize = limit / concurrentTaskCount + limit % concurrentTaskCount
```

```
// Keep track of how many tasks have completed:
var tasksDone: UInt = 0

// An array to combine results in the end:
var primes = [UInt]()

// Create a custom concurrent queue:
let queue = ↵
    dispatch_queue_create("com.diadraw.primeNumberSearchQueue", ↵
        DISPATCH_QUEUE_CONCURRENT);

for i in 0 ..< concurrentTaskCount {
    // Work out the interval for the search:
    let rangeStart = i * rangeSize
    if rangeStart >= limit {
        // If we have already covered the whole interval,
        // mark the task as complete:
        tasksDone += 1
        continue
    }
    let rangeEnd = min(UInt(rangeStart + rangeSize - 1), limit - 1)

    // Define a block of code to perform the search:
    let block = dispatch_block_create(DISPATCH_BLOCK_INHERIT_QOS_CLASS) {
        let primesInCurrentRange = ↵
            self.findPrimeNumbersInRange(range: rangeStart ... rangeEnd)

        // Set a barrier around writing to the primes array,
        // so that no more than one task can write to it
        // at the same time:
        dispatch_barrier_async(queue, {
            primes.appendContentsOf(primesInCurrentRange)

            // Keep track of how many tasks have completed:
            tasksDone += 1

            // When we've got the last chunk of results in, display them:
            if tasksDone == concurrentTaskCount {
                dispatch_async(dispatch_get_main_queue(), {
                    self.displayResults(resultsArray: primes)
                })
            }
        })
    }

    // Add the block to the background queue:
    dispatch_async(queue, block)
}
}
```

First we declare an array of unsigned integers, called `primes`, which will contain the results from all the tasks–this will be the shared resource between the queues. We also add a constant, `concurrentTaskCount`, which will determine into how many subtasks we want to split the search for prime numbers –let us arbitrarily set it to 4. In a loop from zero to `concurrentTaskCount` we do mostly the same as before: define a code block, which calls `findPrimeNumbersInRange` and receives from it an array of prime numbers. This time we will have several blocks, each of which does the search in its own subinterval of numbers. Instead of displaying the results as soon as they arrive, however, each task will add its results to the `primes` array and only when all tasks are done will we send the results to the main queue to be displayed on the screen. This is the code we put in a dispatch barrier.

Something to note about dispatch barriers is that they only make sense to use with custom concurrent queues. As a barrier serializes access to a resource, it will not make a difference on a serial queue. Put on a global queue, barriers are likely to be ignored: the priority of iOS's scheduler is to keep things running and not allow your app to block the execution of other processes. For that reason, instead of requesting a reference to a global queue like we did earlier, Listing 7-14 creates a custom queue with `dispatch_queue_create`.

In this version of `concurrentlyFindPrimeNumbersLessThan` we have opted out of displaying progress to keep things simple.

## Cancelling Lengthy Tasks

It is nice to allow the user to cancel a task that can take a while, especially if the user managed to start it accidentally or with the wrong input. You know the moment of "Oh, £@%^. I meant to download the latest Xcode, not all of the 'X-Men' series. . . ."

Let us modify the `concurrentlyFindPrimeNumbersLessThan` method, so that tasks can be cancelled. In order to do that, we will need access to the blocks of code that we add to the queue outside of `concurrentlyFindPrimeNumbersLessThan`. To help with that we will define an array to keep references to them. Add this array, called `blocks`, as a property to `ViewController` (Listing 7-15).

***Listing 7-15.*** Defining an Array to Keep References to the Code Blocks That Are Running Concurrently

```
// MARK: Search for prime numbers, using concurrency
// An array of execution blocks:
var blocks = [dispatch_block_t]()
```

The only modification we need to make to `concurrentlyFindPrimeNumbersLessThan` is at the end of the `for-in` cycle that creates and adds each code block to the queue. Find this line,

```
dispatch_async(queue, block)
```

and replace it with the code after the last comment in Listing 7-16. In this new version we first add a reference to the block of code in the blocks array, so we can access it for cancellation later. Then we send it to the concurrent queue, but instead of `dispatch_async`, we call `dispatch_after`. This call delays the execution of the block with a given time interval, specified in nanoseconds. Note that this is not a guarantee that the task in the block will be executed exactly after that long but only that it will not start before the time interval has passed.

We have added this delay, so we can test the cancellation. One thing to keep in mind when cancelling tasks in a queue is that they can only be cancelled *before* they have started executing. Cancelling a task that is already running has no effect. The five-second delay we have added should give us enough time to tap the Cancel button and see the effect. To reflect that, a nice addition to the UI would be to disable the Cancel button once the concurrent tasks start executing. We have omitted this from Listing 7-16, in order to keep it simple, and are leaving it as a little homework to you.

***Listing 7-16.*** Modifying concurrentlyFindPrimeNumbersLessThan, So That We Can Test Cancelling Tasks

```
func concurrentlyFindPrimeNumbersLessThan(number limit: UInt) {
    // Make sure we clear the blocks array from any old task references:
    blocks.removeAll()
    // The rest of the code below this line stays the same.

    for i in 0 ..< concurrentTaskCount {
        // The rest of the code in the for-in loop stays the same.

        // Add the block to the queue, but after a delay:
        blocks.append(block)

        let delayInSeconds = 5.0
        let startTime = dispatch_time(DISPATCH_TIME_NOW, ↵
            Int64(delayInSeconds * Double(NSEC_PER_SEC)))
        dispatch_after(startTime, queue, block)
    }
}
```

Now let us implement the actual cancellation. Find the cancelSearch action we added earlier and replace the TODO annotations inside it with the code from Listing 7-17. As you can see, cancelling a block of code is quite simple–it is done with a call to dispatch_block_cancel.

***Listing 7-17.*** Cancelling the Execution of Blocks of Code

```
@IBAction func cancelSearch(sender: AnyObject) {
    // Cancel any blocks that have not been run yet:
    for block in blocks {
        dispatch_block_cancel(block)
    }

    // Update the screen to show that the search was cancelled.
    resultsTextView.text.appendContentsOf("\nSearch cancelled.")

    // Disable Cancel, but enable Start:
    cancelButton.enabled = false
    startButton.enabled = true
}
```

Run the app, set the search limit with the slider, and tap the Start button. If you tap the Cancel button within five seconds after that, you should be able to cancel the search.

# If You Do Need to Use Threads

You might find yourself in a situation where you do need lower-level control over the concurrency in your apps. Apple's *Threading Programming Guide,* available online at https://goo.gl/A2Z7zh, will help you get familiar with and start using threads on iOS with Swift.

# Measure, Measure, Measure

A parting word on concurrency: when doing optimizations in your code, it is always a good idea to measure its performance before and after making changes. What sometimes seems like a more efficient way of doing things can surprise you by slowing your app down or making your UI appear less responsive than before. For example, you may find that while the search for prime numbers is going on in the background, trying to report each prime number as it is found may not work very well, as scheduling UI updates is not entirely up to you. This perceptively hurts performance: not only is more time spent constructing strings and sending them to the text view to be shown but also strings don't necessarily appear when you want them to.

While we are at it, here are some observations and measurements from the various versions of `concurrentlyFindPrimeNumbersLessThan` that we implemented in this chapter. I timed how long it took to find all prime numbers smaller than 100, 000 on an iPad 3:

- The version, in Listing 7-10, which defines one task to search for prime numbers in the background did its job in about 80 seconds.

- The version, in Listing 7-14, which runs four tasks to do the same job took about 40 seconds.

- Splitting the job between more tasks hardly gains us any improvement at all: 10 tasks took 37 seconds and 100 took 34 seconds.

The initial 50% increase in speed is better than nothing, but it may not be enough to justify making code more complex.

# Summary

In this chapter we covered some of the techniques and abstractions that Apple has provided to help Swift developers design concurrent applications. We outlined the pros and cons of writing concurrent code and put it to the test with the help of GCD. We hope it will be a good starting point for your exploration of this wide and varied subject.

In the next chapter we will look at some of the tools that Swift and Xcode can offer in order to help you write better and more robust code.

# CHAPTER 8

■ ■ ■

# Debugging and Testing Your App

Migrating your workflow to Xcode and Swift would not be complete without an overview of the tools available to help you diagnose issues, debug and test your code.

In this chapter you will do the following:

- See how to use Xcode's debug gauges to track your app's usage of CPU, energy, memory and other system resources.

- Learn about setting up different types of breakpoints.

- Try out debugger commands.

- Implement a workaround for the Memory view issue we discovered in **Chapter 3**.

- See techniques for debugging concurrent code.

- Explore Xcode's automated testing framework and add tests to your project.

When you are done, you will have moved your workflow to Xcode and iOS with Swift and will be ready to move on to real-world app development with **Part III**.

## Preparing the Project

In order to try the more sophisticated features of the debugger and to see how automated testing works in Xcode, we will use the app we created in the previous chapter as our guinea pig. In that app the user moves a slider to choose a number and then starts a search for all prime numbers smaller than the chosen number (Figure 8-1). In **Chapter 7** we implemented a couple of different ways of structuring the search: with and without concurrency.

© Radoslava Leseva Adams and Hristo Lesev 2016
R. L. Adams and H. Lesev, *Migrating to Swift from Flash and ActionScript*,
DOI 10.1007/978-1-4842-1666-8_8

*Figure 8-1.* *The FindPrimeNumbers app*

To prepare for the tutorials in this chapter, make a backup copy of the FindPrimeNumbers project from **Chapter 7** and then open FindPrimeNumbers.xcodeproj in Xcode.

# Making the Best of the Debugger

If by now Xcode is beginning to seem less like a Swiss Army knife and more like a space shuttle, you are not far from the truth. It is equipped with so many gadgets you may not need to leave it for weeks, and you may never reach for a tool outside it. While the last statement may or may not be true in your case, it is worth getting to know the shuttle's equipment and the various ways it can help you write better code. In this part of the chapter we look at some useful debugger features and techniques you can use to diagnose issues in your apps.

## Inspecting the Debug Gauges

We will first run the FindPrimeNumbers project without making any changes to it and have a look at the Debug navigator. At the top there is a list of debug gauges, which show you how the state of system resources changes over time as your app is running. You can inspect processor load (CPU), memory usage, energy impact, disk usage, traffic over the network, iCloud, and graphics processing unit (GPU) usage.

For example, when you initially run the app, it hardly uses any CPU time at all. But set it up to do a lengthy prime number search by moving the search slider up and you will see some impact on the CPU (Figure 8-2).

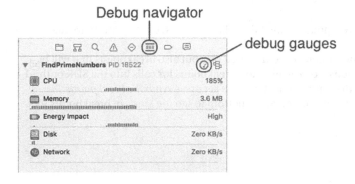

*Figure 8-2. Show or hide the debug gauges at the top of the Debug navigator*

When you select a gauge, the Editor changes to show you a detailed report of the respective system resource (Figure 8-3).

*Figure 8-3. Select a gauge to see a detailed report in the Editor*

Note how, for some gauges, a button appears at the top left of the Editor, called **Profile in Instruments**. Clicking it prepares your project for profiling and launches Xcode's instruments, which include profilers for time, memory, and network usage among other things. We had a look at these in **Chapter 4**.

## Setting up breakpoints

Back in **Chapter 3** we learned how to add breakpoints in the Editor. Let us now see what control we have over them.

You can add breakpoints not only at lines of code in your source files but also breakpoints that will be triggered by events, such as errors or exceptions. You can also add breakpoints for calls into the SDK or third-party libraries, for which you may not have the source code: these are set up as *symbolic breakpoints*.

Open the Breakpoint navigator and click the + button at the bottom to see the kinds of breakpoints that are available (Figure 8-4).

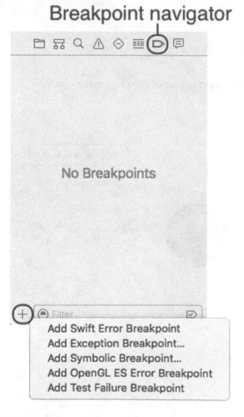

*Figure 8-4. Adding a breakpoint in the Breakpoint navigator*

Let us add a symbolic breakpoint to see how these work. Select **Add Symbolic Breakpoint...** from the pop-up menu you saw in Figure 8-4. We will have the debugger stop inside the isItPrime method we implemented in the ViewController class, but only after it has been called 100 times. In the setup dialog set **Symbol** to isItPrime and **Ignore** to 100 times before stopping.

Apart from determining when the breakpoint will be hit, we can also set up actions to be triggered when it happens. Let us set up two actions: one will play a sound to alert us when the debugger stops at the breakpoint and the other one will execute a command. Click the **Add Action** button next to **Action**. Set **Action** to Sound and choose one of the available sound effects (we like the frog . . .) Then click the + button on the right of the sound action you just added, in order to add another one. Select Debugger Command as the action type and in the text field underneath put the following command:

```
expr "Checking if \(number) is prime"
```

Figure 8-5 shows how the breakpoint is set up.

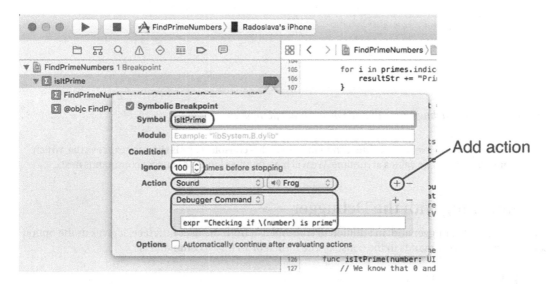

***Figure 8-5.*** *Setting up a symbolic breakpoint*

Run the app through the debugger and when it loads, tap the Start button. After a few moments there should be a (slightly shy sounding) frog call and you should be able to see the result of the command in Xcode's console (Figure 8-6).

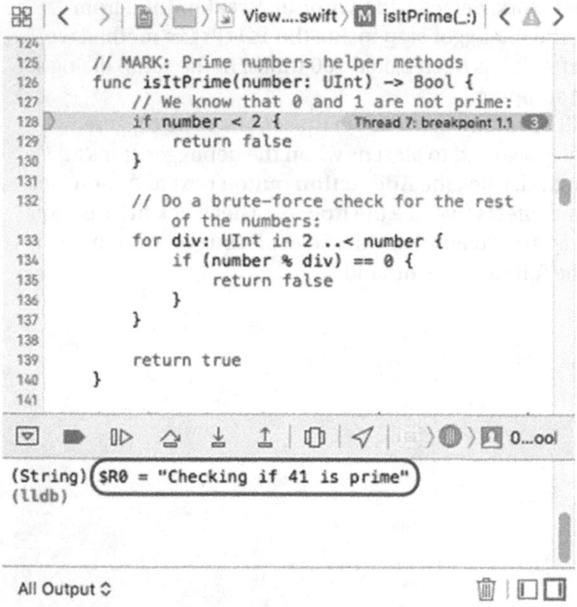

```
⊞ | < > | ▤ ⟩▤⟩ ▤ View....swift ⟩ Ⓜ isItPrime(_:) | < ⚠ >
124
125     // MARK: Prime numbers helper methods
126     func isItPrime(number: UInt) -> Bool {
127         // We know that 0 and 1 are not prime:
128 ▷      if number < 2 {            Thread 7: breakpoint 1.1 ◀③
129             return false
130         }
131
132         // Do a brute-force check for the rest
                of the numbers:
133         for div: UInt in 2 ..< number {
134             if (number % div) == 0 {
135                 return false
136             }
137         }
138
139         return true
140     }
141

 ⊡  ▶  ◗▷  △  ±  ⬆  ◫  ◁  ⟩◉⟩ ▨ 0...ool

(String) $R0 = "Checking if 41 is prime"
(lldb)

All Output ⇕                              🗑 | ⬜⬜
```

***Figure 8-6.*** *Executing a debugger command when a breakpoint is hit*

What we just did was to execute a debug command in Xcode's console: expr is short for expression, which we used in **Chapter 3** to change values at runtime. We will have another look at debugger commands next.

## Communicating with the Debugger

Xcode uses the LLDB debugger and, in addition to controlling it from the user interface, it gives us the option to talk to it by running commands in the console. The format of an LLDB command is:

```
command options -- arguments
```

The double dash (--) serves as a divider between any options and arguments you may pass to the command.

Let us try a few commands. With the debugger paused at the breakpoint we defined earlier type this in the console:

```
e self
```

This command uses an abbreviation: e is another short form of expression. You can see the result in the console: expression infers the meaning of self from the context, in which we have paused the debugger, and prints out a hierarchical description of the instance of ViewController we are using (Figure 8-7).

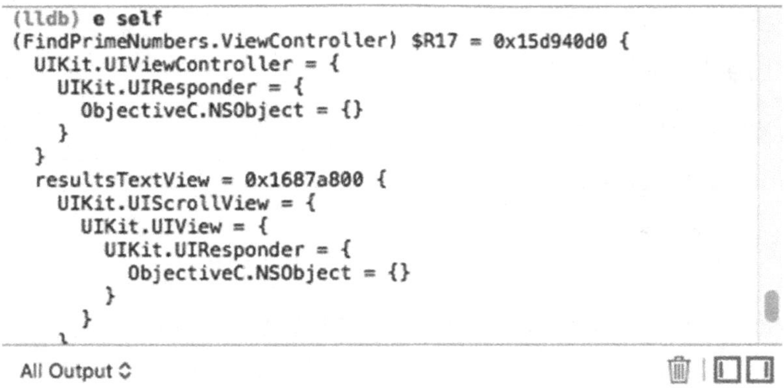

```
(lldb) e self
(FindPrimeNumbers.ViewController) $R17 = 0x15d940d0 {
  UIKit.UIViewController = {
    UIKit.UIResponder = {
      ObjectiveC.NSObject = {}
    }
  }
  resultsTextView = 0x1687a800 {
    UIKit.UIScrollView = {
      UIKit.UIView = {
        UIKit.UIResponder = {
          ObjectiveC.NSObject = {}
        }
      }
    }
```

All Output ◇                                        🗑 | ▢▢

***Figure 8-7.*** *Printing out a description of ViewController's instance*

Let us try another one:

e -O -- self

Executing this evaluates self again, this time only displaying a top-level description of the ViewController object without its members: <FindPrimeNumbers.ViewController: 0x15d940d0>.

The last version of the command we ran is equivalent to

po self

Here po is a shortcut for e -O (the command expression, run with the option -O). In fact, the print command we used in **Chapter 3** to print out values of objects is also a variation of the same command and is equivalent to expression --.

Here are a couple more commands for you to try when the debugger stops at the breakpoint in isItPrime:

finish

The finish command is a shortcut for thread step-out. It completes the running of the current function (stack frame) and goes back to its caller. When you run it, you will see execution go to findPrimeNumbersInRange and pause there.

continue

This command is short for process continue and instructs the debugger to proceed with the execution until another breakpoint is hit.

You can, of course, use the debugger user interface (UI) to control execution, as shown in Figure 8-8.

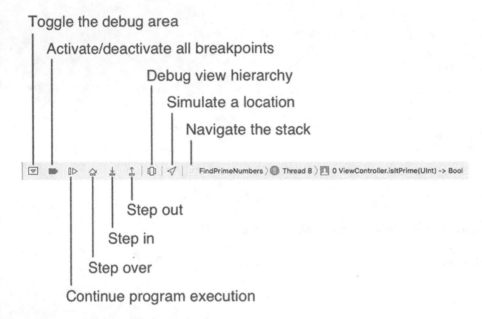

Figure 8-8. *Using the debugger controls*

Finally, if you remember only one LLDB command, make it this one:

```
help
```

As its name suggests, `help` will give you a hand with any other command you may want to learn about. Running `help` will print out a list of all available commands and `help command-name` will give you details about the options and syntax for a particular command.

## Checking the Type of a Symbol

In the previous chapters we mentioned a few times and you have seen in examples that you do not always need to specify a type when you declare a symbol (a constant, a variable, a function, etc.) The Swift compiler is good at inferring type from the context, in which a symbol is declared (see **Chapter 17** for details). The code that you end up with if you omit all type declarations wherever possible can be very concise, but also a bit harder to read. It can also leave you wondering about what type a symbol is.

There are a couple of ways to reveal the type of a symbol at runtime while the debugger is paused at a breakpoint. You can option-click the symbol in the Editor to see its declaration as shown in Figure 8-9.

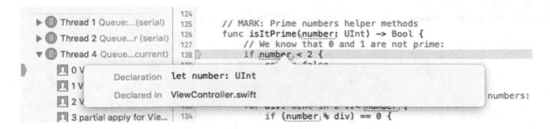

Figure 8-9. *Using Alt + click to see the declaration of a symbol*

You can also toggle symbol types in the Variables view: right-click inside the view and from the pop-up menu select **Show Types** (Figure 8-10).

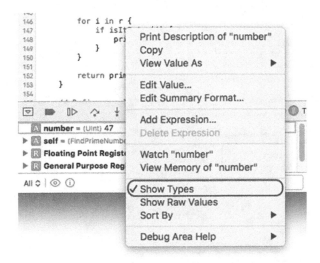

***Figure 8-10.*** *Showing symbol types in the Variables view*

---

■ **Tip** Before we move on it may be a good idea to disable the breakpoint we set for isItPrime. To do that, find the breakpoint in the Breakpoint navigator, right-click it, and select **Disable breakpoint**. This will leave the breakpoint in, in case you want to switch it on again by selecting **Enable breakpoint**. Note that you can also select **Delete breakpoint** when you want to remove a breakpoint permanently.

---

## Inspecting Memory—A Workaround

We have not forgotten our promise to show you how to inspect the memory of a symbol, in case the straightforward way we demonstrated in **Chapter 3** does not work. We will see how to deal with this scenario here.

First, let us set a breakpoint on this line in the displayResults method:

```
resultsTextView.text = resultStr
```

We want to see the memory of resultStr. Run the app through the debugger and when the breakpoint is hit, find resultStr in the Variables view. Right-click it and from the pop-up menu select **View Memory of "resultStr"** (Figure 8-11).

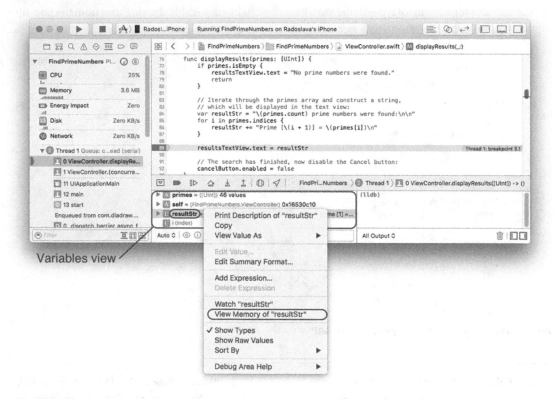

***Figure 8-11.*** *Selecting a variable in the Variables view to inspect in the Memory view*

If you remember back from **Chapter 3**, what we expect to see is the Memory view with the memory footprint of the variable. However, what you are likely seeing instead is this: the screenshot in Figure 8-12 shows the memory for address zero.

***Figure 8-12.*** *Inspecting the memory for a variable someitimes results in showing address 0x0*

This is a known issue, which Apple describes in the *Xcode 6 Release Notes* (`https://goo.gl/Pki8UV`):

*View Memory for Swift data structures in the debugger may show memory location zero.*

The following workaround is suggested:

*Pass the structure to a function expecting a reference to an UnsafePointer<Void>, and print it within the function. Enter this address as the memory location to view.*

Xcode is ever-evolving and helping make Swift development easier, so this issue will probably be fixed in a release very soon. Since it is still present in Xcode 7, however, let us see how to implement the suggested workaround.

Add the following method to the `ViewController` class (Listing 8-1):

***Listing 8-1.*** Printing Out the Address of a Symbol

```
// MARK: Debugging helper methods
func printAddressOf(symboToInspect: UnsafePointer<Void>) {
    print("Actual address in memory: \(symboToInspect)")
}
```

---

■ **Swift reference**     Pointers are part of Swift, in order to make it compatible and allow it to interact with C and Objective-C code. For the most part you will rarely need to use pointers, but it is worth being aware of how they work. A pointer is an object, which keeps the memory address of another object and thus "points" to it. Using pointers can save both time and memory when large objects have to be passed around. It is much more expensive to copy an object and all its data than to copy its address and dereference it (i.e., find the object by its address). There are risks when using pointers, however. For example, a pointer can hold an address of an object, which was deallocated or can point to memory that has not been initialized yet. The name of Swift's `UnsafePointer` type signals just that: this type of pointer does not automatically change when changes happen at the memory location, to which it points.

---

Let us add a call to `printAddressOf` just after we have finished composing `resultStr` in the `displayResults` method as shown in Listing 8-2.

***Listing 8-2.*** Adding a Call to printAddressOf

```
func displayResults(primes: [UInt]) {
    if primes.isEmpty {
        resultsTextView.text = "No prime numbers were found."
        return
    }
```

```
// Iterate through the primes array and construct a string,
// which will be displayed in the text view:
var resultStr = "\(primes.count) prime numbers were found:\n\n"
for i in primes.indices {
    resultStr += "Prime [\(i + 1)] = \(primes[i])\n"
}

// Workaround for the Memory view issue:
printAddressOf(resultStr)

resultsTextView.text = resultStr

// The search has finished, now disable the Cancel button:
cancelButton.enabled = false
}
```

Now, with the breakpoint we added earlier still in place, run the app through the debugger, and tap the Start button. When the breakpoint is hit, have a look at the console: there you should see the result of the print statement we put in the body of printAddressOf:

```
Actual address in memory: 0x15bace14
```

The hexadecimal number you see is the memory location (address) of the resultStr variable.[1] We will copy and paste it in the **Address** field in the Memory view as shown in Figure 8-13. Hit Enter and you should now see the memory footprint of the variable: it is shown as hexadecimal numbers on the left and as string in the right part of the Memory view.

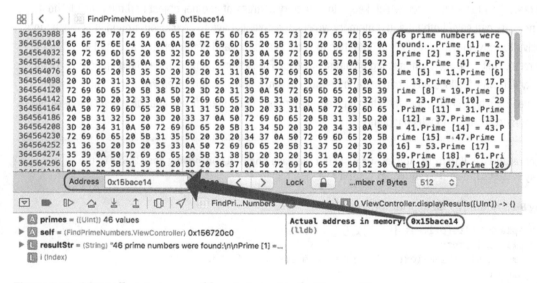

***Figure 8-13.*** *Manually entering an address to inspect in the Memory View*

---

[1]Note that the actual address in memory will most likely be different on your device and may change between runs of the application.

■ **Tip**   Now that you have implemented the official workaround, here are a couple of quicker ways to get the address of a symbol, which don't require additional code.

With a breakpoint active, you can print out the address in the console by running the following command:

```
po resultStr._core._baseAddress
```

Alternatively, you can expand `resultStr` in the Variables view, right-click its `_baseAddress` and from the menu select **Print Description of _baseAddress**. This too will print the address in the console, which you can then copy and paste in the Memory view.

# Debugging Concurrent Code

In **Chapter 7** we implemented a method, called `concurrentlyFindPrimeNumbersLessThan`, to look for prime numbers smaller than a given number. It keeps the UI responsive by creating a new custom concurrent queue, which is separate from the main execution queue, and using it to execute tasks to search for prime numbers. (Have a look at **Chapter 7** for a reminder of how queues work on iOS.) Each concurrent task searches for prime numbers in a portion of the range between zero and the given number and collects its results in an array. When a task completes, it adds those results to another array, which accumulates the prime numbers found by all tasks. In order to restrict access to this array to one task at a time, we put a dispatch barrier around the code, which accesses it.

To see how we can inspect concurrent code, we will do something naughty. You probably remember when we discussed deadlocks in **Chapter 7**: when two or more tasks each wait for one another to finish, in order to continue execution, they are in a deadlock. We will introduce one to see how we can detangle it—useful to know when your app hangs, for example.

Let us make a few changes to the code, in order to artificially create a deadlock situation. Listing 8-3 shows the new implementation of the `concurrentlyFindPrimeNumbersLessThan` method.

***Listing 8-3.***   Modifying concurrentlyFindPrimeNumbersLessThan, So We Create a Deadlock

```
func concurrentlyFindPrimeNumbersLessThan(number limit: UInt) {
    // Make sure we clear the blocks array from any old task references:
    blocks.removeAll()

    // Let us split the search into four:
    let concurrentTaskCount: UInt = 4

    // Based on the numer of concurrent tasks we want,
    // calculate the size of the interval
    // each task will need to search through:
    let rangeSize = limit / concurrentTaskCount + limit % concurrentTaskCount

    // Keep track of how many tasks have completed:
    var tasksDone: UInt = 0

    // An array to combine results in the end:
    var primes = [UInt]()
```

```
    // Create a custom serial queue:
    let queue = ↵
        dispatch_queue_create("com.diadraw.primeNumberSearchQueue", ↵
            DISPATCH_QUEUE_SERIAL);

    for i in 0 ..< concurrentTaskCount {
        // Work out the interval for the search:
        let rangeStart = i * rangeSize
        if rangeStart >= limit {
            // If we have already covered the whole interval,
            // mark the task as complete:
            tasksDone += 1
            continue
        }
        let rangeEnd = min(UInt(rangeStart + rangeSize - 1), limit - 1)

        // Define a block of code to perform the search:
        let block = dispatch_block_create(DISPATCH_BLOCK_INHERIT_QOS_CLASS) {
            // Tasks have now started executing and we cannot cancel them,
            // so disable the Cancel button:
            dispatch_async(dispatch_get_main_queue(), {
                self.cancelButton.enabled = false
            })

            let primesInCurrentRange = ↵
                self.findPrimeNumbersInRange(range: rangeStart ... rangeEnd)

            // Perform the writing to the primes array synchronously,
            // so that no more than one task can write to it
            // at the same time:
            dispatch_sync(queue, {
                primes.appendContentsOf(primesInCurrentRange)

                // Keep track of how many tasks have completed:
                tasksDone += 1

                // When we've got the last chunk of results in, display them:
                if tasksDone == concurrentTaskCount {
                    dispatch_async(dispatch_get_main_queue(), {
                        self.displayResults(resultsArray: primes)
                    })
                }
            })
        }

        // Enqueue the block to be executed asynchronously:
        dispatch_async(queue, block)
    }
}
```

Let us walk through the changes we made and explain them. First, we replaced the custom concurrent queue with a serial one:

```
let queue = ↵
    dispatch_queue_create("com.diadraw.primeNumberSearchQueue", ↵
        DISPATCH_QUEUE_SERIAL)
```

Then, instead of putting the code, which writes to the results collection in a dispatch barrier (dispatch_barrier_async), we just dispatch it to the queue in a synchronous way:

```
dispatch_sync(queue, { /*Collect results and display them on the screen.*/ })
```

In the original implementation, at the end of the for-in loop, we used to add tasks to the queue after a delay. This time we enqueue each task immediately with dispatch_async for simplicity:

```
dispatch_async(queue, block)
```

Let us run the app and tap the Start button. Can you see what happens? Probably not, as nothing seems to be happening. To find out what is going on, we will pause the execution. Click the Pause button in the Debug area as shown in Figure 8-14.

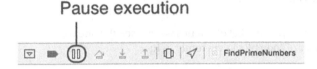

*Figure 8-14.* *Pausing the debugger*

This immediately changes the view to show the Debug navigator, as if we have hit a breakpoint. Let us now have a look at the Debug navigator: underneath the debug gauges there are stack traces, listed by thread. Each stack trace shows what code a particular thread was running when we paused the execution. Use the button at the top right-hand corner to switch to viewing queues (select **View Process by Queue** from the pop-up menu) as shown in Figure 8-15.

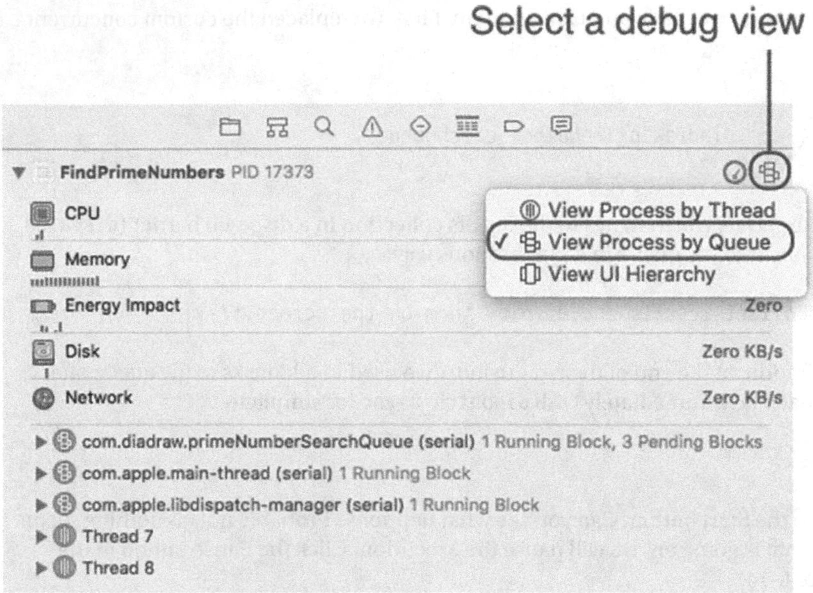

**Figure 8-15.** *Switch the debug view to show dispatch queues*

Inspecting queues takes us to more familiar territory. In the list of queues we can see the one we created, listed with its name, its type, and the number of code blocks currently in it:

```
com.diadraw.primeNumberSearchQueue (serial) 1 Running Block, 3 Pending Blocks
```

Let us expand the queue entry and see the call stack for each of the blocks. At the top there is a call to semaphore_wait_trap. The cogwheel icon next to it means that this is a system call.

---

■ **Tip** For a full list of debugger icons, see *Debugging with Xcode* in Apple's online documentation at https://goo.gl/3cgkSt.

---

In order to understand what semaphore_wait_trap means, let us explain what *semaphores* are. This is a technique for controlling access to common resources from multiple threads or processes. Say we have a block of code and want to ensure that only one thread at a time can execute it, such as when we write results to the primes array in the concurrentlyFindPrimeNumbersLessThan method. A semaphore could be a Boolean flag, which signals true if the code is available for running. When a thread begins executing the block, the semaphore flag is set to false and any other thread that needs to execute the same block of code will be suspended and wait until the flag becomes true again. The call to semaphore_wait_trap at the top of the stack means that the thread, on which the custom queue has placed our block of code, is currently suspended and waiting for a semaphore to signal that it is allowed to continue execution. For information on threads and queues look back at **Chapter 7**.

If we look down the call stack, shown in Figure 8-16, we can find where in our code the execution has been suspended. Calls that are made into our (user) code appear with a blue icon with a person outline on it. The topmost one we can see reads

```
ViewController.(concurrentlyFindPrimeNumbersLessThan(UInt) -> ()).(closure #1)
```

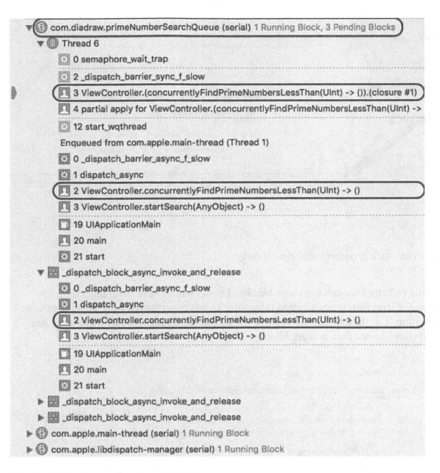

**Figure 8-16.** *Inspecting the call stack*

If you click on this call, you will be taken to a line of code in the Editor (Figure 8-17). This line of code happens to be at the end of the block of code we enqueued synchronously on our serial queue. We did that in order to make sure that only one task can modify the `primes` array at a time and write its results to it.

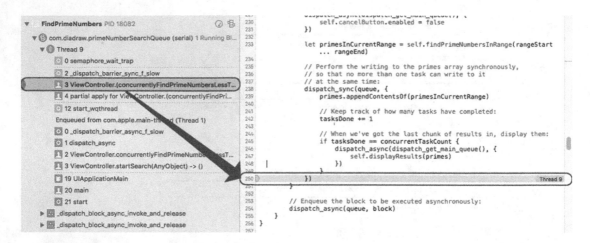

***Figure 8-17.*** *Going from the call stack to a particular line of code*

Looking further down the call stack we can see more blocks of code, which have been placed on the same queue. Do you see how the icon next to each call in these blocks has been grayed out? This is because the blocks are pending execution (i.e., they are not running at the moment). In Figure 8-18 we can see four blocks of code, one of which contains another, nested, block.

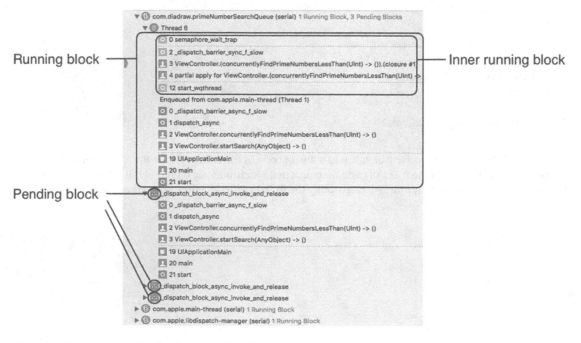

***Figure 8-18.*** *Inspecting blocks of code on the call stack*

It is only the nested block (marked as "Inner running block" in Figure 8-18) that is active. This is the block we matched to the `dispatch_sync` call in `concurrentlyFindPrimeNumbersLessThan`. Listing 8-4 shows it in context.

***Listing 8-4.*** The Block of Code, Which Is Currently Running

```
func concurrentlyFindPrimeNumbersLessThan(limit: UInt) {
    // ...

    for i in 0 ..< concurrentTaskCount {
        // ...

            // Perform the writing to the primes array synchronously,
            // so that no more than one task can write to it
            // at the same time:
            dispatch_sync(queue, {
                primes.appendContentsOf(primesInCurrentRange)

                // Keep track of how many tasks have completed:
                tasksDone += 1

                // When we've got the last chunk of results in, display them:
                if tasksDone == concurrentTaskCount {
                    dispatch_async(dispatch_get_main_queue(), {
                        self.displayResults(primes)
                    })
                }
            })
        }

        // ...
    }
}
```

This block of code is nested inside the definition of the `block` constant: another code block, which we later add to the same queue by calling `dispatch_async` (Listing 8-5).

***Listing 8-5.*** The Outer Block of Code, Which Is Pending Execution

```
func concurrentlyFindPrimeNumbersLessThan(limit: UInt) {
    // ...

    for i in 0 ..< concurrentTaskCount {
        // ...

        // Define a block of code to perform the search:
        let block = dispatch_block_create(DISPATCH_BLOCK_INHERIT_QOS_CLASS) {
            // The definition of the block,
            // containing the nested call to dispatch_sync from Listing 8-4
        }
```

```
        // Enqueue the block to be executed asynchronously:
        dispatch_async(queue, block)
    }
}
```

If you click the top user call in the grayed-out part of the call stack as shown in Figure 8-19, it will take you to that same line.

```
dispatch_async(queue, block)
```

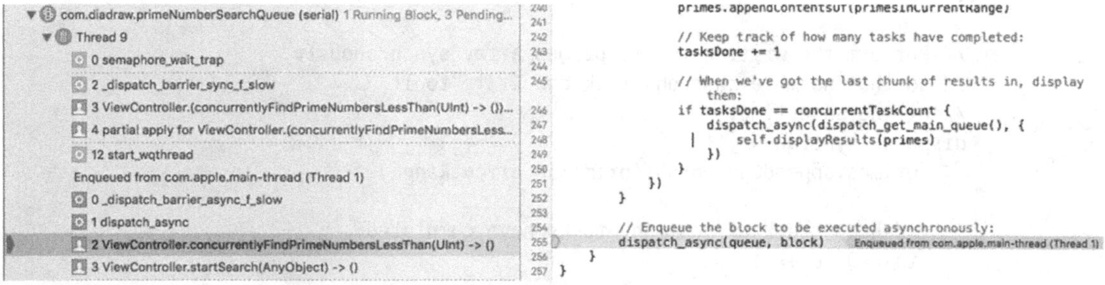

***Figure 8-19.*** *Finding out where the block of code is waiting*

Here is what has happened. We create the first block of code and dispatch it asynchronously on our custom serial queue. The block starts executing and gets to the inner block of code, which it tries to dispatch to the same queue synchronously. Before that inner block of code can start execution, however, it needs to wait for the block, currently executing, to finish. But for that to happen, the inner block of code must be executed. Thus the two blocks of code end up in a deadlock.

Diagnosing deadlocks, race conditions, and other conflicts in concurrent code is not easy. Finding a call to `semaphore_wait_trap` is not necessarily an indication of a deadlock. Instead, the waiting block of code might just temporarily have ended up there until the resource it needs becomes available. However, it is a good place to start and if you find your app spending a long time in such calls, a deadlock could be a primary suspect.

# Testing Your Code

Testing is an important part of any development workflow and does not necessarily have to happen at the end of a development cycle. In fact, proponents of Test-Driven Development (TDD) like Kent Beck would urge you to "[not] write a line of new code unless you first have a failing automated test."[2] Coming up with a test strategy and designing tests before you have even written the code has important benefits.

- It forces you to consider real-world usage and corner cases in advance.

- Tests can document your intentions for the code you are about to write.

- Regularly running automated tests can help with catching issues with newly checked-in code early and save development time.

---

[2]Kent Beck, *Test-Driven Development by Example* (Boston: Addison Wesley, 2002).

- The tests you design might even uncover bugs! It is important to keep in mind the old principle that no amount of testing can prove your code bug-free. Testing can only prove bugs' existence.

There is always a trade-off between the amount of time invested in designing and putting test strategies in practice and the time it takes you to maintain your code without testing.[3] It would be hard for an integrated development environment (IDE) to offer automated tools for any test imaginable. For example, user experience is best evaluated through . . . well, letting users experience your app and give you feedback. What Xcode has to offer via its XCTest framework, however, makes certain types of tests so easy to automatically integrate in your projects that it would be inexcusable not to put them to use. The types of tests you can include are

- **Unit tests**. Apple divides these into *functional unit tests* and *performance tests*. Functional unit tests exercise part of your code by running it and comparing the output to an expected result—that is, they treat code as a black box. Performance tests help you measure how long it takes your code to perform selected tasks and keep track of whether performance changes over time.

- **User interface tests**. Xcode lets you record a sequence of actions that a user would perform in the UI and define the expected state of the app after these actions. The sequence can then be replayed automatically, in order to check if the app is in the expected state.

We will add two unit tests: a functional one and a performance one to the same project we have been abusing in the previous sections of this chapter.

Tests are usually created in a separate project target. If you ticked the **Include Unit Tests** box when you created the project for **Chapter 7**, a test target has already been created for you by Xcode. To check if this is the case, in Project navigator select the main project and see if FindPrimeNumbersTests appears under Targets in the Editor. You should also be able to see FindPrimeNumbersTests in the project tree as shown later on in Figure 8-21.

If there is no test target in the project, let us create one. With the FindPrimeNumbers project open in Xcode select **File ➤ Target...** Then, at the first step of the wizard select **iOS ➤ Test ➤ iOS Unit Testing Bundle** (Figure 8-20).

---

[3]As testing consultant and speaker James Lyndsay puts it: "An organisation's greatest investment in testing with any tool is likely to be the cost of understanding the tool and developing plus maintaining the tests."

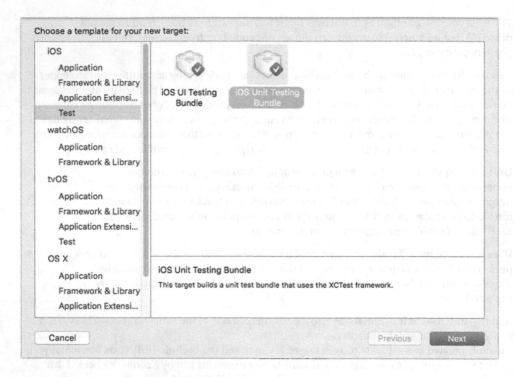

**Figure 8-20.** *Adding a unit testing bundle to your project*

At the next step the wizard offers to name the new target after the project with Tests appended to the name (i.e., FindPrimeNumbersTests). Accept that, as well as the rest of the settings that have been set by default, then click **Finish**.

The new target is added to the project with its own Info.plist settings file and a source file, called FindPrimeNumbersTests.swift (Figure 8-21).

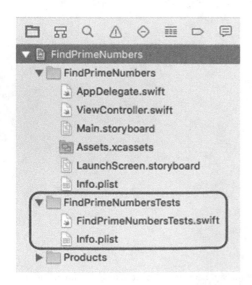

**Figure 8-21.** *The test target in the Project navigator*

Inside `FindPrimeNumbersTests.swift` you will find the definition of a class, called `FindPrimeNumbersTests`. It is a subclass of `XCTestCase` from the XCTest framework in the iOS SDK.

---

## FLASH ANALOGY

Flash Builder offers `FlexUnit`—a unit test environment, which lets you generate and run tests within the IDE.

---

This is what `FindPrimeNumbersTests` looks like out of the box (Listing 8-6).

***Listing 8-6.*** FindPrimeNumbersTests, Defined by Xcode

```
class FindPrimeNumbersTests: XCTestCase {

    override func setUp() {
        super.setUp()
    }

    override func tearDown() {
        super.tearDown()
    }

    func testExample() {
    }

    func testPerformanceExample() {
        self.measureBlock {
        }
    }
}
```

The `testExample` and `testPerformanceExample` methods are where we add test code. The other two methods, `setUp` and `tearDown`, are called before and after each of the test methods are run and we can use them to do initialization and cleanup.

You can add as many test methods as you need to. As a general rule, make each method test one thing and one thing only and keep related tests together (i.e., as methods of the same `XCTestCase` subclass).

Before we add our first test, let us see how the test code can access the code in the app target. In Swift, *access control* is defined in terms of source files and *modules*. A module is a collection of source files that are built and shipped together as an application or as a framework. By default, only declarations, which are made `public`, are visible (i.e., accessible) to code outside the module where they have been defined (more details on that in **Chapter 17** and **Chapter 21**). This means that the test module we added does not see the source code in our app module by default. In order to give it access to them, we need to import the app module, `FindPrimeNumbers`, in our test code with the `@testable` keyword. Open `FindPrimeNumbersTests.swift` and add the following line at the top of the file under `import XCTest`:

```
@testable import FindPrimeNumbers
```

This line does two things: it lets the test code know about the app code but also gives it access even to entities in `FindPrimeNumbers`, which have been declared `private`.

Next, we will add an instance of ViewController as a property to the FindPrimeNumbersTests class and initialize it inside the setUp method (Listing 8-7). Note that this will create a new instance of the class every time we run a test. Although this is not too much of a hassle for our simple scenario, it is good to keep in mind. Depending on what you test, you may or may not want to start with a fresh instance before each test case is run.

*Listing 8-7.* Adding an Instance of ViewController

```
var viewController: ViewController!

override func setUp() {
    super.setUp()

    let storyboard = UIStoryboard(name: "Main", bundle: NSBundle.mainBundle())
    viewController =
        storyboard.instantiateInitialViewController() as! ViewController
}
```

## Adding a Functional Unit Test

Let us now add a test. Replace the testExample method in FindPrimeNumbersTests with the method from Listing 8-8.

*Listing 8-8.* Adding a Test

```
func testIsItPrime_0() {
    let result = viewController.isItPrime(number: 0)
    XCTAssertFalse(result)
}
```

testIsItPrime_0 tests the isItPrime method of ViewController by treating it like a black box. It calls isItPrime with zero as the parameter and expects to receive a negative result. The result is checked in the XCTAssertFalse call. If the argument of XCTAssertFalse evaluates to false, the test passes, otherwise the test fails.

---

■ **Swift reference** The XCTAssertFalse call in Listing 8-8 uses an *assertion*: a programming technique that helps you state and check assumptions about the correctness of your code.

In general, an assertion takes a Boolean argument and does nothing if this argument evaluates to true, but in the case of false it alerts you by outputting a diagnostic message and throwing an error or even terminating the app. Using assertions helps you define clear responsibilities for each function you implement. Say that a function relies on a certain condition to be true, in order to do its job—for example, a variable having a value and not being nil. Instead of silently handling the case when the variable is nil and allowing it to cause issues down the line, the function can assert for the condition and alert you sooner and closer to the cause of the trouble. It is important to note that assertions are a debugging technique and are disabled (i.e., do nothing) when your app is built for release. This means that your diagnostic code can be left in without bloating the final product. Remember, assertions are a diagnostic tool rather than a tool for error handling.

To use assertions in your functional code, call the global `assert` function, like we did in `findPrimeNumbersLessThan` in the `ViewController` class.

When writing tests, you have a whole arsenal of convenience assertions at your disposal: they are part of the `XCTest` framework and are prefixed with `XCT`. We just used `XCTAssertFalse`, which, in contrast to traditional assert statements, expects its argument to evaluate to `false`. You can also use `XCTAssertTrue`, the more general `XCTAssert`, `XCTAssertEqual`, and so on. For a full list have a look at the `XCTTest` API (application programming interface).

---

The Test navigator offers you a dashboard for running and inspecting the results of your tests. New tests normally appear in the navigator as you add them in the code and save your changes. You can also make sure that the list in the navigator is up to date by running a build from Xcode's main menu: **Product ➤ Build For ➤ Testing**. As Figure 8-22 shows, each test appears with a button next to it, which lets you run it separately from the rest of the suite.

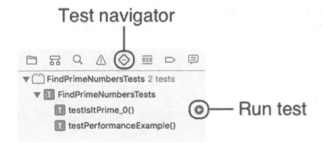

*Figure 8-22.* *Tests appear in the Test navigator*

When you click the button, Xcode builds the project, installs it on your device (or in a simulator), and runs the test. You will see your app loading and then quickly disappearing, as this test does not actually take very long.

If the test passes, a green tick appears next to its name in the Editor and in the Test navigator (Figure 8-23).

```
29    func testIsItPrime_0() {
30        let result = viewController.isItPrime(0)
31        XCTAssert(result == false)
32    }
```

*Figure 8-23.* *A test is marked with a green icon when it has passed*

You can add more tests as a homework exercise: for example, make sure you run `isItPrime` with other interesting cases: 1, 2, `UInt.max`, a large prime number . . .

## Adding a Performance Test

In order to see how performance tests work, we will replace testPerformanceExample with our own test, called testPerformanceFindPrimeNumbersInRange. You can see its implementation in Listing 8-9. There is an interesting call to note there: self.measureBlock is a method of the base XCTestCase class, which measures the performance of the code block inside the curly brackets that follow it. In our test we will measure how long it takes ViewController's findPrimeNumbersInRange method to find the prime numbers between 0 and 1000.

***Listing 8-9.*** Adding a Performance Test

```
func testPerformanceFindPrimeNumbersInRange() {
    self.measureBlock {
        self.viewController.findPrimeNumbersInRange(range: 0...1000)
    }
}
```

When you run the test, you will again see your app appearing on the device or in the simulator and then disappearing after the test has run. Xcode actually executes the test ten times in a row and calculates the average running time and the standard deviation for those runs.

Results are conveniently reported in the Editor next to the test declaration (Figure 8-24). When you click the results, a pop-up dialog shows you a more visual representation. The first time you run the test, there is no baseline to compare the results to, and so you are prompted to set it. Once set, it will be used as a criteria for the test passing: this way you will be alerted if the code you are testing suddenly becomes much slower as the project evolves.

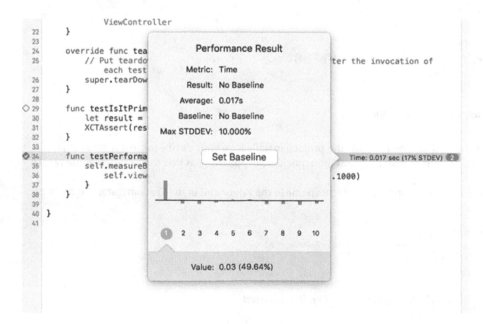

***Figure 8-24.*** *Displaying performance test results*

# Tracking Code Coverage

In addition to automating part of your testing process, Xcode can help you keep track of how much of your code is actually exercised by automated tests. To enable this from the main menu select **Product ➤ Scheme ➤ Edit Scheme** and then open the **Test** scheme. Enable **Gather coverage data** next to **Code Coverage** (Figure 8-25).

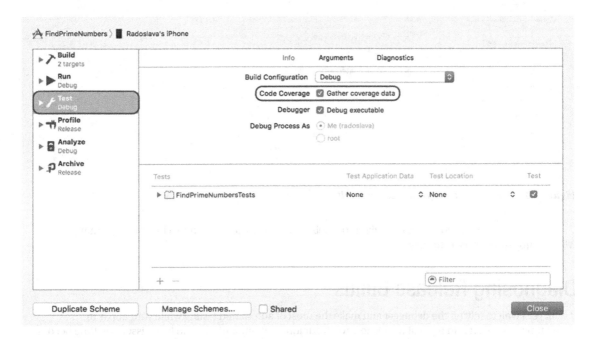

***Figure 8-25.*** *Enabling Xcode to gather code coverage data*

After you have run a test, open the Report navigator, select the test report, and then go to the Coverage pane in the Editor. This will show you visually how much of the code is currently covered by tests (Figure 8-26).

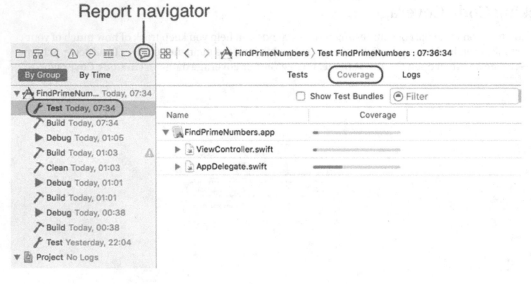

**Figure 8-26.** *Displaying performance test results*

As you can see, the coverage for FindPrimeNumbers can be improved quite a lot. We hope that you would enjoy doing this as homework.

## Diagnosing Release Builds

It is all very well to rely on the debugger and make the most of automated testing while your app is in development. Once it is in the real world, however, your job for maintaining it and fixing issues on time becomes a bit harder, as you rely on user feedback. You will probably not be surprised that Apple has provided tools and services for that too. Apple makes it easy for users to report issues and for you to track and fix them. We will close this chapter with a few words on a couple of tools that help you maintain your release builds.

- **TestFlight**. This is a service, available to members of the iOS Developer Program. It makes it very easy for beta testers to install your app on their devices and send you feedback, crash logs, and usage statistics.

- **The Organizer window**. Once you have published your apps in the App Store, you can receive crash reports in Xcode's **Window ➤ Organizer ➤ Crashes**. These are *symbolicated* for you by Xcode—that is, the addresses from the crash report are linked with lines of code to allow you to inspect and diagnose issues.

## Summary

This is the final chapter in **Part II** of this book, which helps you port your workflow and start making the most of what Xcode has to offer to iOS developers. Here we covered some powerful features of the debugger and ways they can help you keep an eye on how your app utilizes system resources, step through your code with sophisticated breakpoints, and detangle concurrent code issues. We also had a look at Xcode's automated test frameworks and how they can be a valuable asset to your workflow.

You are now ready to move on to the more exciting **Part III**, where we will build some fun apps. The first one will allow users to send e-mail and text messages, as well as make phone calls from within the app.

# PART III

# Making Apps with Swift—Applied Examples

# CHAPTER 9

■ ■ ■

# Communicating: E-mail, Text Messages, and Calls

In their early days mobile phones were used only for making calls and later on for sending short text messages. Today we don't even call them phones any more: a mobile device is a computer that fits in your pocket. Still, communication is one of the core purposes of a mobile device and this is what we will focus on in this chapter by making an app that can make phone calls and send e-mail and text messages (SMS, or short message service).

In this chapter you will do the following:

- Learn how to use the `MessageUI` framework for composing and sending e-mail and text messages.

- Learn how to make a phone call from an app.

- Learn how to work with the iOS address book, iterate through contacts, and read contact information with the `AddressBookUI` framework.

- Build an app that does all of the above.

When you are done, you will have an app that can send e-mail and text messages, can make phone calls, lets you choose contact info from the address book, and assists you with message composition.

## Setting Up the App and Designing the UI

The app you will develop has two main objectives. The first one is to help the user compose and send messages without leaving the app. The second objective is to make sending messages quicker by presenting the main bits of information already populated: the recipient's address or phone number, a template for the message body, and so on.

Start by creating a Single View iOS application project (**File ➤ New ➤ Project...**, then **iOS ➤ Application ➤ Single View Application** ) and naming it `MessageComposer`. We will design the user interface (UI) of the application as part of the setup, so we can focus on code in the rest of the chapter.

Figure 9-1 shows you what the UI will look like: on the left there is a mock-up with the UI elements you will need to place in the view on the storyboard and on the right is a screenshot of the storyboard with the elements already positioned on it.

© Radoslava Leseva Adams and Hristo Lesev 2016
R. L. Adams and H. Lesev, *Migrating to Swift from Flash and ActionScript*,
DOI 10.1007/978-1-4842-1666-8_9

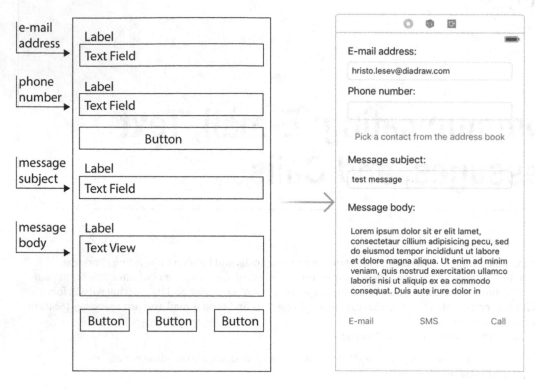

***Figure 9-1.*** *The app's user interface*

Open `Main.storyboard` and arrange the UI as shown in Figure 9-1 by adding three text fields, a text view, four buttons, and four labels. The text fields and the text view will be used for inputting a message and information about the recipient. Do not forget to add constraints, so that the app adapts its look to whatever device it runs on. If you need a reminder for how to set constraints and make an adaptive UI, have a look at **Chapter 5**.

Next, open `ViewController.swift` and import the `MessageUI` framework to start with. Then create outlets for all the text fields you added to the storyboard (see **Chapter 2** for how to create outlets). Your code should look like Listing 9-1.

***Listing 9-1.*** Adding Outlets for the Text Fields to the ViewController Class

```
import UIKit
import MessageUI

class ViewController: UIViewController {

    @IBOutlet weak var recipientEmail: UITextField!
    @IBOutlet weak var phoneNumber: UITextField!
    @IBOutlet weak var messageSubject: UITextField!
    @IBOutlet weak var messageBody: UITextView!

    //The rest of the code goes here
}
```

With the UI of the app laid out we are ready to focus on writing code and adding functionality to the app.

# Composing and Sending E-mail

Making it easy for the user to send an e-mail without leaving your app has two advantages: it is convenient for the user and allows you to spread the word about your app and brand by providing a custom template for the message body.

The MessageUI framework offers an easy way of doing that: it lets you show the standard iOS e-mail composer UI within your app with the help of a view controller class, called MFMailComposeViewController. We will see how to use it in a bit.

The e-mail interface will be shown when the user taps the E-mail button on the app's screen, so let us first add a handler for that. On the storyboard select the button and create a Touch Up Inside action for it, called sendEmail, in ViewController.swift. (For details on how to create actions for storyboard elements see **Chapter 2**.)

Listing 9-2 has the implementation you should put inside the action. First, we check if the device has been set up to send e-mail by calling canSendMail—a static method of the MFMailComposeViewController class. If sending e-mail is possible, we create an instance of MFMailComposeViewController, set it up, and present it on screen.

The setup includes providing initial values for the e-mail's subject (setSubject), body (setMessageBody), and recipients (setToRecipients). To fill these in, we use the text that the user has provided in the text fields and the text view we added to the app earlier. Note that setToRecipients takes an array of String: this lets you specify more than one e-mail recipient. We get an array, containing all the recipients' e-mails by dividing the original string into substrings using comma as the separator.

You can be creative with the message body and use HTML tags to make it prettier, include hyperlinks, and so on. To turn HTML on, you need to set the second parameter of setMessageBody to true. We will keep things simple in this example and only use plain text.

When all the setup is done, the e-mail composer is shown on screen with presentViewController.

*Listing 9-2.* Creating and Configuring an E-mail Composer Instance

```
@IBAction func sendEmail(sender: AnyObject) {
    //Check if the device is configured to send e-mail
    if MFMailComposeViewController.canSendMail() {
        let emailController = MFMailComposeViewController()
        //Set a delegate responsible for the dismissal of the view controller
        emailController.mailComposeDelegate = self

        //Extract recipients in an array of String items
        //by dividing the string using comma as a separator
        let recipientList = ↵
                recipientEmail.text!.componentsSeparatedByString(",")
        //Use the resulting array to set the To field
        emailController.setToRecipients(recipientList)
        //Copy the subject from the messageSubject text field
        emailController.setSubject(messageSubject.text!)
        //Copy the message body from the messageBody text view
        emailController.setMessageBody(messageBody.text, isHTML: false)

        //Show emailController on the screen
        presentViewController(emailController, animated: true, completion: nil)
    }
    else {
        print("Cannot send e-mail.")
    }
}
```

You may have noticed that there is a line in Listing 9-2 I haven't explained yet:

```
emailController.mailComposeDelegate = self
```

We talked about *delegation* in **Chapter 5**. It is a design pattern, which is used a lot in the iOS SDK and lets an object delegate tasks to another object. In this case the mail composer will delegate to our ViewController class the task of handling what happens when the user is done composing an e-mail. For the delegation to work, ViewController needs to have an interface that the mail composer recognizes, so we will have it *conform* to the MFMailComposeViewControllerDelegate *protocol*, which is part of the iOS SDK. Let us add the protocol to ViewController's inheritance list:

```
class ViewController: UIViewController, MFMailComposeViewControllerDelegate {
```

---

■ **Note** For more information on protocols and conforming to them, see Chapter 21.

---

The protocol we have just added requires that any conforming type implement a method, named mailComposeController(_:didFinishWithResult:). This method serves as a callback and is executed when the user decides whether to send, save, or delete the e-mail by tapping one of the buttons in the mail composer: Send or Cancel. The user's decision is delivered in one of the callback's parameters, called result of type MFMailComposeResult. For simplicity, all our callback will do is print the result from the user's choice and dismiss the mail composer (i.e., hide it from the screen). You can see the implementation in Listing 9-3.

*Listing 9-3.* Dismissing the E-mail Compose View Controller

```
func mailComposeController(controller: MFMailComposeViewController, ↵
        didFinishWithResult result: MFMailComposeResult, error: NSError?) {

    //Print the result of the user's action
    switch (result) {
    case MFMailComposeResultCancelled:
        print("Cancelled.")
    case MFMailComposeResultSaved:
        print("Saved as a Draft.")
    case MFMailComposeResultSent:
        print("Sent.")
    case MFMailComposeResultFailed:
        print("Failed \(error?.localizedDescription)")
    default:
        print("Result code: \(result.rawValue)")
    }

    //Dissmiss the view controller from the screen
    controller.dismissViewControllerAnimated(true, completion: nil)
}
```

That's it: you have an app that lets the user send e-mail with just a few lines of code. Now let us run it and test it by sending an e-mail or two.

■ **Caution**    At the time of this writing there is a bug in the iOS 9 simulator, which results in a crash when you try to use MFMailComposeViewController. Apple is aware of it and will likely provide a fix in the next simulator update. If you do get a crash in the simulator, you can test the app on a device instead. See Chapter 2 if you need a reminder for how to deploy apps on an iOS device.

Run the application; fill in the e-mail address, subject, and body fields; and tap the E-mail button. You should see the e-mail compose view controller modally presented on the screen (Figure 9-2) and be able to send an e-mail by tapping Send.

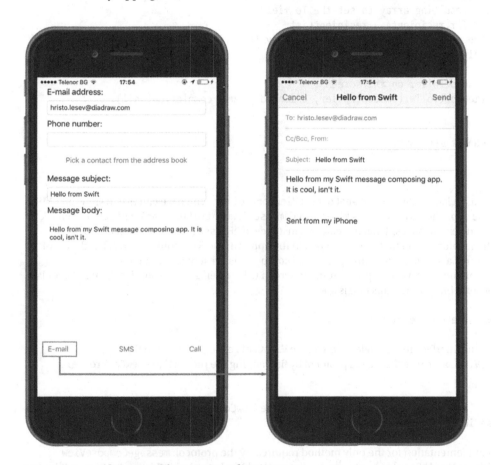

***Figure 9-2.*** *Sending e-mail from your application*

## Composing and Sending SMS

Sending text messages from your app is so similar to sending e-mail, you are likely to have a déjà vu while writing the code.

To start with, create an action handler for the Touch Up Inside action of the SMS button you added to the storyboard earlier. Call the action handler sendSMS. Now look at Listing 9-4, which shows the implementation of sendSMS: does it look familiar?

*Listing 9-4.* Create and Configure SMS Compose View Controller

```
@IBAction func sendSMS(sender: AnyObject) {
    //Check if the device can send SMS
    if MFMessageComposeViewController.canSendText() {
        let smsController = MFMessageComposeViewController()
        //Set a delegate responsible for the dismissal of the view controller
        smsController.messageComposeDelegate = self
        //Extract recipients in an array of String items
        //by dividing phoneNumber using comma separator
        let recipientList = phoneNumber.text!.componentsSeparatedByString(",")
        //Use the resulting array to set the To field
        smsController.recipients = recipientList
        //Copy the message body from the messageBody text view
        smsController.body = messageBody.text

        //Show smsController on the screen
        presentViewController(smsController, animated: true, completion: nil)
    }
    else {
        print("Cannot send sms.")
    }
}
```

The iOS SDK has a class, called `MFMessageComposeViewController`, which we can use to show an SMS composer inside the app. The code first calls `MFMessageComposeViewController.canSendText()` to check if the device can send text messages. Then it creates an instance of `MFMessageComposeViewController` and sets it up with the information that the user typed in the app's UI: the SMS content (body) and a list of recipients in the form of a `String` array. Finally, the SMS composer is presented on the screen.

The task of dismissing the SMS composer from the screen will be delegated to our `ViewController` class by the SMS composer, which is what this line is about:

```
smsController.messageComposeDelegate = self
```

To implement the interface for the delegation, make `ViewController` conform to the `MFMessageComposeViewControllerDelegate` protocol by first adding the protocol to `ViewController`'s inheritance list:

```
class ViewController: UIViewController, MFMailComposeViewControllerDelegate, ↵
MFMessageComposeViewControllerDelegate {
```

Then add an implementation for the only method required by the protocol: `messageComposeView Controller(_:didFinishWithResult:)`. You can see the method implemented in Listing 9-5: again, it looks very similar to the callback method we implemented for handling e-mail sending in the previous section. In it we print the result from the user's action and dismiss the SMS composer from the screen.

*Listing 9-5.* Dissimss the SMS Compose View Controller

```
func messageComposeViewController(controller: MFMessageComposeViewController, ↵
                        didFinishWithResult result: MessageComposeResult) {
```

```
//Print the result of the user's action
switch (result) {
case MessageComposeResultCancelled:
    print("Cancelled.")
case MessageComposeResultSent:
    print("Sent.")
case MessageComposeResultFailed:
    print("Failed.")
default:
    print("Result code: \(result.rawValue)")
}

//Dissmiss the view controller off the screen
controller.dismissViewControllerAnimated(true, completion: nil)
}
```

When you run the app on your device and tap the SMS button, you should see the message compose view controller appear as shown in Figure 9-3.

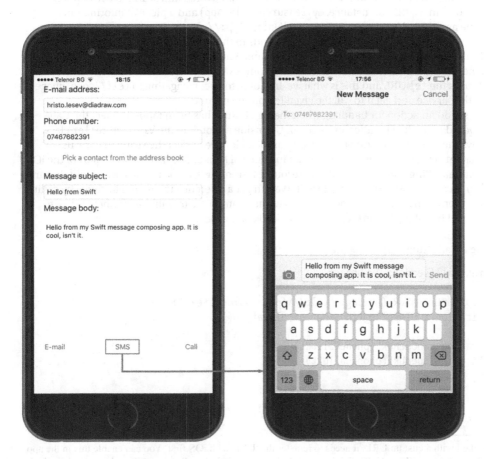

***Figure 9-3.*** *Compose SMS view controller*

> ■ **Note** In order to test sending text messages you will need to run the app on an iPhone with a SIM card. The simulator will not do in this case. If you try to run the app in the simulator or on a phone without a SIM card the `MFMessageComposeViewController.canSendText()` will always returns `false`.

# Making a Call

Initiating a telephone call from an app is actually pretty easy and can be done with a single line of code. There is no dedicated iOS SDK framework specifically for making phone calls. Instead, to call a number, you need to treat it like a URL (uniform resource locator).

The same way that a URL scheme like `http` lets you open a web browser and navigate to a web page by doing `http://mywebsite.com/mywebpage`, defining a custom URL scheme for an app allows that app to be opened and to receive information from other apps.

Let us say, for example, that you are building a treasure-hunting app, which leads the user to discover a prize by following clues that you have hidden in the local park. You could encode the clues in QR codes and attach them to trees, benches, and posts in the park, which can be uncovered and scanned with a phone. Each QR code could contain a URL (for instance, `myTreasureHuntingApp`) and a piece of information (say, `clue_1`), which can be assembled in a string: `myTreasureHuntingApp://clue_1`. The first part of the string, the URL followed by //, tells iOS to look for an app that responds to this URL and start it.[1] The second part is much a command-line parameter list that you can pass to an app when you start it.

Most of the standard applications and services that iOS comes with have custom URLs. The service for making phone calls uses the `tel` URL and this is what we are going to use: navigating to `tel://some_phone_number` should start the service and get it to call the given telephone number.

We will again first add an action for handling when the Call button has been tapped. Select the Call button on the storyboard and add a handler for its Touch Up Inside action it to the `ViewController` class.

Listing 9-6 shows the implementation of the action handler. First we extract the string that the user typed in the phoneNumber text edit and use it to create an instance of `NSURL`. The `NSURL` class is part of the iOS SDK, which helps with handling and parsing paths to resources—remote and local. The URL we obtain can be used to ask our application instance to navigate to it. We can get a reference to our app instance by calling iOS SDK's `UIApplication.sharedApplication()`. Before we navigate to the telephone number URL, we check if it's actually valid by calling `UIApplication`'s `canOpenURL` method.

***Listing 9-6.*** Making a Call Using a URL Scheme

```
@IBAction func makeCall(sender: AnyObject) {

    if let phoneCallURL = NSURL(string: "tel://\(phoneNumber.text!)") {
        let application = UIApplication.sharedApplication()

        if application.canOpenURL(phoneCallURL) {
            application.openURL(phoneCallURL)
        }
    }
}
```

---

[1]For an app to be invoked with a custom URL, it needs to register this URL with iOS first. You can enable this in the app settings. For more information see "Using URL Schemes to Communicate with Apps" on Apple's web site: `https://developer.apple.com/library/ios/documentation/iPhone/Conceptual/iPhoneOSProgrammingGuide/Inter-AppCommunication/Inter-AppCommunication.html#//apple_ref/doc/uid/TP40007072-CH6-SW1`.

■ **Note** As was the case with sending text messages, testing phone calls in your app will require the app to run on a device with a SIM card, rather than in a simulator.

Run the app on your phone, enter a valid telephone number in the Phone Number text field, and tap Call. This should start the call service (Figure 9-4).

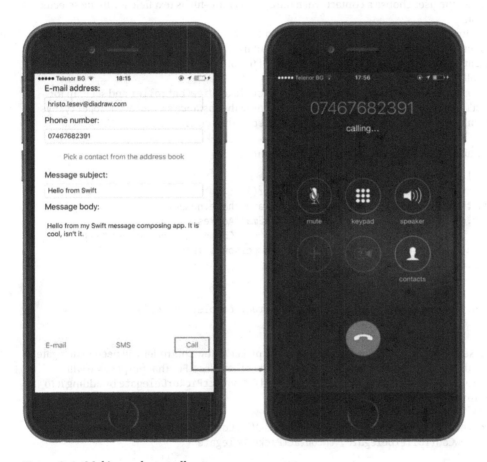

***Figure 9-4.*** *Making a phone call*

# Using the Address Book

There is one more thing we could add to our app to make it even more convenient for making phone calls and sending messages. Instead of having the user input phone numbers and e-mail addresses by hand, we could grab the information from the device's address book. You can think of the address book as a centralized database of contact information, which can be accessed by multiple applications.

iOS lets you access this information programmatically for reading and modifying contacts. If you choose to do that, your app will first need to ask the user's permission.

If your app doesn't need to browse through all of the contacts but just have them displayed on the screen for the user to select one, you can use a ready-made view controller, called CNContactPickerViewController, which is part of the AddressBookUI framework. It displays the standard iOS address book screen, where the user can browse through the contact list. In this case the app itself doesn't have access to the whole address book but gets a copy of the selected contact, so it doesn't need to ask for permission.

In this example we will have our app use CNContactPickerViewController to present an instance of it on the screen and let the user choose a contact. Then the app will auto-fill its text fields with the selected contact's information.

We start by first importing the ContactsUI framework and then adding an action handler for one of the buttons on the screen: in this action handler we will present the contact picker view controller. Add a handler to ViewController for the Touch Up Inside action of the button titled Pick a contact from the address book and call it selectContact.

Inside selectContact first obtain an instance of CNContactPickerViewController and set it up for displaying a contact's email address and phone number by setting the instance's displayedPropertyKeys property as shown in Listing 9-7. Then show the view controller on the screen.

*Listing 9-7.* Create and Configure a Contact Picker View Controller

```
@IBAction func selectContact(sender: AnyObject) {
    let contactPicker = CNContactPickerViewController()
    //Tell contactPicker that we want to use e-mail and phone number
    contactPicker.displayedPropertyKeys = [CNContactEmailAddressesKey, ↩
                                            CNContactPhoneNumbersKey]
    //Set a delegate which will recieve the selected person's info
    contactPicker.delegate = self

    //Show contactPicker on the screen
    presentViewController(contactPicker, animated: true, completion: nil)
}
```

When the user selects a contact in the contact picker, the picker's view controller will need to delegate the task of handling that contact's information to our ViewController class. For that purpose we will make ViewController conform to yet another protocol, called CNContactPickerDelegate by adding it to ViewController's inheritance list:

```
class ViewController: UIViewController, MFMailComposeViewControllerDelegate, ↩
MFMessageComposeViewControllerDelegate, CNContactPickerDelegate {
```

In Listing 9-7 you can see the line that sets our ViewController as the delegate for the contact picker view controller:

```
contactPicker.delegate = self
```

Now let us implement the callback that CNContactPickerDelegate requires, in order to pass contact information back to us: contactPicker(_:didSelectContact). The second parameter of the callback is an instance of CNContact, a class, which represents a record in the address book. We will use that instance to read the selected contact's e-mail address and telephone number and fill them in the main screen of our app (Listing 9-8).

An interesting thing to note here is how e-mail addresses and phone numbers are represented.

A contact in the address book can have multiple e-mail addresses (e.g., a work one and a personal one). We can access these e-mail addresses through CNContacts's emailAddresses property, which is an array of CNLabeledValue instances. CNLabeledValue is very similar to a key-value pair in that it combines a value with a given label, for example, '06658907432' and 'Work'. In our example we will use the first available e-mail address from the array.

A contact can also have multiple phone numbers stored for it, again labeled 'Work', 'Home', and so on. CNContacts's phoneNumbers property gives us access to them in the form of an array of CNPhoneNumber instances. We can get a phone number as a String by reading CNPhoneNumber's stringValue property (Listing 9-8).

***Listing 9-8.*** Reading Data from the Selected Contact

```
func contactPicker(picker: CNContactPickerViewController, ⏎
                                      didSelectContact contact: CNContact) {
    //Check if there are any e-mails for this contact
    if contact.emailAddresses.count > 0 {
        //Get the first e-mail entry
        let email = contact.emailAddresses.first?.value as! String
        //Show the e-mail address in the UI
        recipientEmail.text = email
    }

    //Check if there are any phone numbers for this contact
    if contact.phoneNumbers.count > 0 {
        //Get the first phone number entry
        let phone = contact.phoneNumbers.first?.value as! CNPhoneNumber
        //Extract a string from the phone number and show it in the UI
        phoneNumber.text = phone.stringValue
    }
}
```

Figure 9-5 shows you what you should see when you run your app with this last bit of functionality added to it. When you tap the Pick a contact from the address book button, the contact picker controller shows you all of your contacts. After you select one, you are taken back to the main screen of the app with the contact's information filled in.

***Figure 9-5.*** *Pick a person from the address book*

# Summary

In this chapter you saw how to use default iOS user interface to compose e-mails, send SMS, and make phone calls. You learned about the `MessageUI` framework and implemented a way of sending messages and making calls from within an app. As a bonus, you saw how to harness the `AddressBookUI` framework to read and display information about the user's contacts.

In the following chapter we continue the topic of communication and look at how to compose and post messages on popular social networks. Let me just update my Facebook profile first . . .

# CHAPTER 10

∎ ∎ ∎

# Getting Social: Posting to Facebook and Twitter

One of the significant events in the last decade was the rise of social networks. They transformed not only how we communicate with each other but also how ideas spread. If your app gives a compelling reason and an easy way for users to share thoughts and creations with their social network tribes, it can get the benefit of word of mouth and instantly be in front of the eyes of many more potential users.

In this chapter you will do the following:

- Learn how to use the Social framework to post messages to Facebook and Twitter from your app.

- Learn how to link a device with social media accounts.

- Build an app that posts messages to Facebook and Twitter using the Social framework built-in composer user interface (UI).

When you are done, you will have an app that can post messages to the two most popular social networks: Facebook and Twitter. Note that to be able to test the app you will need Facebook and Twitter accounts.

## Setting Up the App and Designing the UI

Apple recognized the power of the social media early on and introduced integration with Twitter as early as iOS 5. The next iOS release brought us the Social framework, which has continued to evolve since. In its current version the Social framework makes it easy to integrate several social network platforms with your app: Facebook, Twitter, Sina Weibo, and Tencent Weibo.

The app we are going to build will let the user compose and post messages with text and images to Facebook and Twitter. To do that we will use the built-in composer of the Social framework.

Create a Single View iOS application project (**File ➤ New ➤ Project...**, then **iOS ➤ Application ➤ Single View Application**). Name it SocialSharingApp.

Open Main.storyboard and place two buttons and a text view on the main view of the app, as shown in Figure 10-1. Have a look back at **Chapter 5** if you need a reminder for how to constrain the UI elements to make the design adapt to different screen sizes and orientations.

© Radoslava Leseva Adams and Hristo Lesev 2016
R. L. Adams and H. Lesev, *Migrating to Swift from Flash and ActionScript*,
DOI 10.1007/978-1-4842-1666-8_10

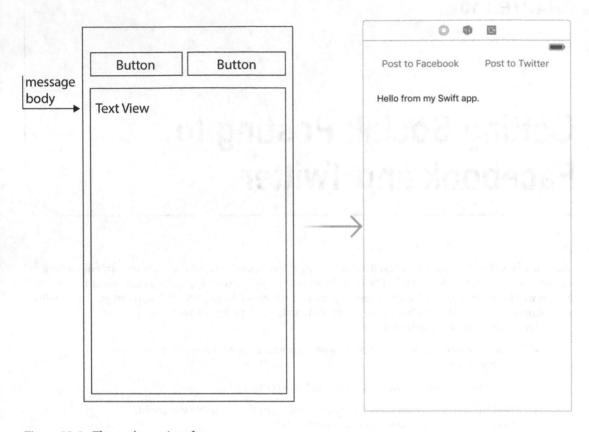

*Figure 10-1.* *The app's user interface*

Next, open ViewController.swift and first import the Social framework at the top of the file. This will let us use the application programming interface (API) that posts to social networks.

Then create an outlet for the text view and name it postBody. Add actions for the two buttons' Touch Up Inside events. (See **Chapter 2** for how to create outlets and actions.) Name the first action postToFacebook and the second action postToTwitter.

Your code should look like that in Listing 10-1.

*Listing 10-1.* Adding an Outlet and Two Actions to the ViewController Class

```
import UIKit
import Social

class ViewController: UIViewController {

    @IBOutlet weak var postBody: UITextView!

    //The rest of the code goes here

    @IBAction func postToFacebook(sender: AnyObject) {
    }
```

```
@IBAction func postToTwitter(sender: AnyObject) {
}

}
```

We will see how to post not just text but also pictures to social media. To keep things simple, we will add an image to the app's assets and include it in posts. If you did the tutorial in **Chapter 5**, you already know how to add an image as an asset: in Xcode's Project navigator open `Asset.xassets`, then drag and drop an image file inside (Figure 10-2). We will use the same cute panda image we used there (you can download it from `https://pixabay.com/en/panda-bear-cute-happy-young-151587`; rename the file to `bear.png` to keep it short).

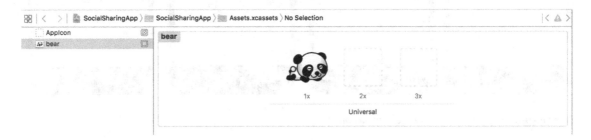

***Figure 10-2.*** *Adding a panda bear image to the project's assets*

# Configuring Your Social Media Accounts on a Device

To be able to post a message to Facebook or Twitter from our app, the user must link iOS with his or her social media accounts first, using the device settings.

Stepping into the user's shoes for a moment, let us do just that—you can use a device or one of the iOS simulators in Xcode. Go to **Settings** and find Facebook in the list. Tap it, enter your Facebook account details, and tap **Sign In**. On the next screen you will see a list of the ways that your device (or simulator) will be able to interact with your Facebook account. Tap **Sign In** again and you are ready. You can see the steps shown in Figure 10-3.

*Figure 10-3.* *Signing in with a Facebook account*

Repeat the same steps to link your device (or the simulator) with Twitter. You can follow Figure 10-4.

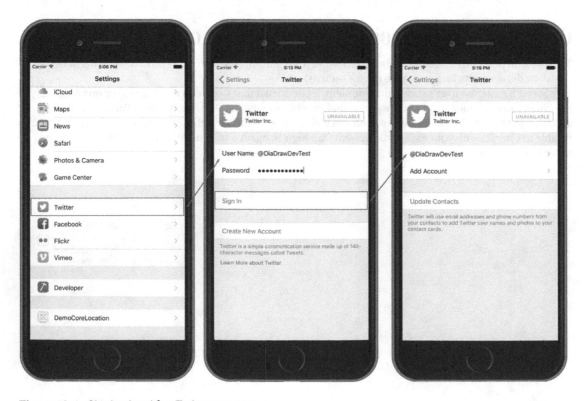

*Figure 10-4.* *Signing in with a Twitter account*

Before we continue with the back end of the application, make sure your device or the simulator is connected to both social networks. We will need that in order to share posts.

# Composing and Posting a Facebook Post

The Social framework has standard composer user interface, which we will use. It is controlled by the SLComposeViewController class and offers several helper methods that are designed to assist with writing a post, adding an image, creating hyperlinks, and handling user interaction. In fact, this is quite similar to how we used the MessageUI framework to compose and send e-mail back in **Chapter 9**.

Listing 10-1 will guide you through the implementation of posting a message on the user's Facebook timeline. Open ViewController.swift, find the postToFacebook action we added earlier and let us begin.

The first thing we do is call isAvailableForServiceType(_:)—a method of SLComposeViewController, which checks if a Facebook account has been set up on the device. Note the use of the SLServiceTypeFacebook constant: isAvailableForServiceType(_:) handles several different social networks, so we must specify which one we are interested in. To tell the composer view controller that we are interested in working with Facebook we use SLServiceTypeFacebook.

If a Facebook account has been found, we set up an instance of SLComposeViewController and present it on the screen.

The setup includes optionally providing default content for the post by calling setInitialText, addImage and addURL. To use it with addImage, we wrap our cute panda picture in an instance of UIImage and load it from the app's assets using its file name.

There is an interesting line towards the bottom of the listing: facebookVC's property completionHandler takes a block of code, which will be executed when the user finishes working with the composer either by posting to Facebook or by cancelling the post. We will look at that syntax in detail when we discuss *closures* in **Chapter 22**.

When all the setup is done the composer is shown on the screen with presentViewController.

***Listing 10-2.*** Setting Up a Compose View Controller to Post to Facebook

```
@IBAction func postToFacebook(sender: AnyObject) {
    //Check if a Facebook account has been set up
    if false == SLComposeViewController.isAvailableForServiceType( ➤ SLServiceTypeFacebook
) {
        print("Facebook service is not available.")
        return
    }

    //Create an instance of the view controller,
    //which will show the post compoer on the screen
    let facebookVC = SLComposeViewController( ↵
        forServiceType: SLServiceTypeFacebook)

    //Set post's message body
    facebookVC.setInitialText( postBody.text )
    //Add an image to the post
    facebookVC.addImage( UIImage(named: "bear") )

    //Add a url to the post
    let url = NSURL(string: "http://diadraw.com")
    facebookVC.addURL( url )
```

```
    //Handle post completion
    facebookVC.completionHandler = {
        result in

        switch result {
        case .Cancelled:
            print("Message cancelled.")
        case .Done:
            print("Message sent.")
        }
    }

    //Show facebookVC on the screen
    presentViewController(facebookVC, animated: false, completion: nil)
}
```

---

■ **Note**    You can add but also remove content from a post programmatically by calling removeAllImages and removeAllURLs. These are methods of the SLComposeViewController class.

Note also this line: facebookVC.completionHandler = { /*...*/ }. The curly brackets define a closure—a block of code that will be executed only after posting to Facebook completes. We will look at closures in detail in Chapter 22.

---

And that is all we need to do to allow the user to post to Facebook without leaving the app. Let us test it: run the application, fill in the message body, and tap the Post to Facebook button. The compose view controller will pop up as shown in Figure 10-5.

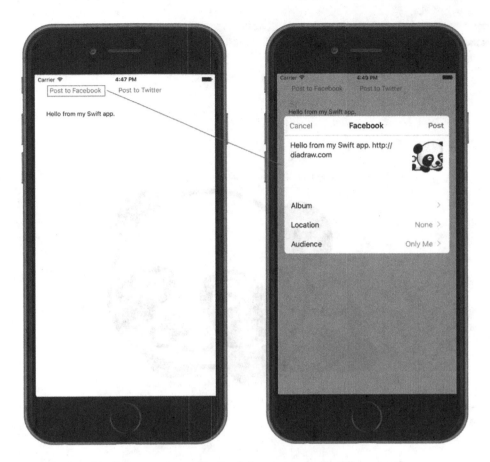

***Figure 10-5.*** *Posting a message to Facebook from your application*

Notice how you can tag your post with a geographical location and specify who can see it (define its audience). If the post contains an image, you can also add it to one of your Facebook photo albums.

Tap Post and open your Facebook account (use the Facebook app or a browser) to see the post with the smiling panda on your timeline (Figure 10-6).

*Figure 10-6.  See the post on your Facebook timeline*

# Composing and Posting a Twitter Message

We will use the same idea and code structure to create a post for Twitter as we did for Facebook. The implementation of the postToTwitter action is shown in Listing 10-3.

We start by checking if a Twitter account has been set up on the device. If there is one available, we proceed with setting up the composer UI and presenting it on the screen. Note that this time we instantiate SLComposeViewController with SLServiceTypeTwitter.

*Listing 10-3.* Setting Up a Compose View Controller to Post to Twitter

```
@IBAction func postToTwitter(sender: AnyObject) {
    //Check if a Twitter account has been set up
    if false == SLComposeViewController.isAvailableForServiceType( å SLServiceTypeTwitter )
{
        print("Twitter service is not available.")
        return
    }
```

```
    //Create a composer view controller
    let twitterVC = SLComposeViewController( ↵
forServiceType: SLServiceTypeTwitter)

    //Set post's message body
    twitterVC.setInitialText( postBody.text )
    //Add an image to the post
    twitterVC.addImage( UIImage(named: "bear") )

    //Add a url to the post
    let url = NSURL(string: "http://diadraw.com")
    twitterVC.addURL( url )

    //Handle post completion
    twitterVC.completionHandler = {
        result in

        switch result {
        case .Cancelled:
            print("Message cancelled.")
        case .Done:
            print("Message sent.")
        }
    }

    //Show twitterVC on the screen
    presentViewController(twitterVC, animated: false, completion: nil)
}
```

Let us test this. Run the app and tap the Post to Twitter button to see the composer UI show up on the screen (Figure 10-7). This being Twitter, you are limited to posts of up to 140 characters—notice how the Post button becomes inactive if you go over that count.

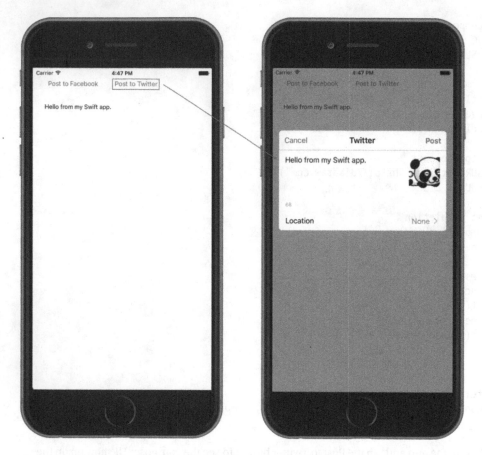

***Figure 10-7.*** *Posting a message to Twitter from your application*

If there is more than one Twitter account set up on the device, the composer UI will let the user choose which account to post to (Figure 10-8).

***Figure 10-8.*** *Choosing to which of the active Twitter accounts to post*

When you finish posting, you should see the new post in your Twitter account in a matter of seconds (Figure 10-9).

*Figure 10-9.  See the post in your Twitter account*

# Other Types of Interaction with the Social Medias

Besides posting to the user's timeline, the Social framework can help you with getting data back from social media platforms.

The SLRequest class can send HTTP requests to a social networking service. You can use it to retrieve user information from the HTTP API of each of the supported social media platforms. For example, you can send a request to Twitter and ask it to give you the activity feed for the currently logged in user.

Keep in mind that the SLRequest class is just a wrapper around the standard HTTP connection routines. The request endpoints and the format of the data returned by each social network service will be different.

# Summary

In this chapter you used the built-in iOS functionality for sharing information on Facebook and Twitter. You learned about the Social framework and created an app that uses it to let users create posts with text, images, and hyperlinks on their social network timelines.

In the next chapter you will see how to access the device motion sensors, how to get a GPS location, and how to show it on a map.

# CHAPTER 11

■ ■ ■

# Knowing Your Location

It's good to know where you stand. In this chapter—literally. A mobile app that helps you with that can be priceless: from being able to summon a taxi by just sending your location to the taxi company (useful when leaving drinking establishments in a not entirely verbal state) to finding your way to the family picnic before your cousins get to the marshmallows.

One of my friends laughed uncontrollably when he saw me using my phone as a spirit level to hang a picture on the wall. But, hey, isn't this the idea when you have a digital Swiss Army knife like the iPhone?

In this chapter you will do the following:

- Learn how to read the device's motion and location sensors.

- Set up a project that uses the accelerometer, the magnetometer, and the gyroscope sensors.

- Get familiar with the MapKit framework and how to use it to visualize your location on a map.

- Get your GPS location in real time.

When you are done, you will have two applications receiving data from the device's motion and location sensors. The first app is focused on using the accelerometer, the magnetometer, and the gyroscope for querying motion data. The second one asks the device for its GPS location and uses it to visualize your position on a map.

## Motion Sensors

Before we start talking to them, it would be good to get acquainted with the motion sensors that an iPhone or an iPad gives us access to and see the format of data they offer and its analogs in the physical world. There are three motion sensors at your disposal:

- **The accelerometer** gives you the changes in the device's position along the three Cartesian axes: x, y, and z, relative to the ground.

- **The gyroscope** measures the rate of rotation around the three axes.

- **The magnetometer** works like a digital compass and can tell you the direction of the Earth's magnetic North.

The data you get from the sensors is mapped to the x, y, and z axes, which run through the device as shown on Figure 11-1.

© Radoslava Leseva Adams and Hristo Lesev 2016
R. L. Adams and H. Lesev, *Migrating to Swift from Flash and ActionScript*,
DOI 10.1007/978-1-4842-1666-8_11

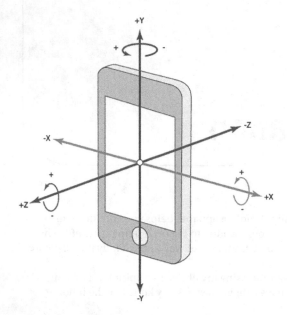

**Figure 11-1.** *Motion data representation*

Following is how the sensor's data values are measured:

- The *x axis* runs from left to right with negative values to the left of the device's vertical middle and positive ones to the right.

- The *y axis* runs from top to bottom with negative values running down from the device's center and positive ones running up.

- The *z axis* runs perpendicularly to the device's screen with negative values starting away from the device's back and positive ones running toward you from the screen.

The rotational data from the gyroscope is measured around each axis in radians with the direction of positive and negative angles as shown on Figure 11-1.[1]

The iOS SDK framework that gives you access to the data is called CoreMotion and gives you two options. You can listen for raw data provided separately by each of the sensors or you can receive processed data, which combines information from all of the sensors at once.

## Setting Up the App

Start by creating an empty *Single View Application* in Xcode. Name the project *DemoCoreMotion*. Locate the Main.storyboard file in the Project navigator and click to open it. Drag six Label components from the Object library onto the storyboard and arrange and name them as shown on Figure 11-2. To ensure that the labels are resized properly on different screen sizes select the View Controller element on the storyboard, click Resolve Auto Layout Issues button, and select Add Missing Constraints.

---

[1]You can also use *the right-hand rule* to determine the direction of positive and negative rotation: make a fist with your right hand and have your thumb point in the positive direction of the axis. The rest of your fingers will then point in the direction of growing angle values.

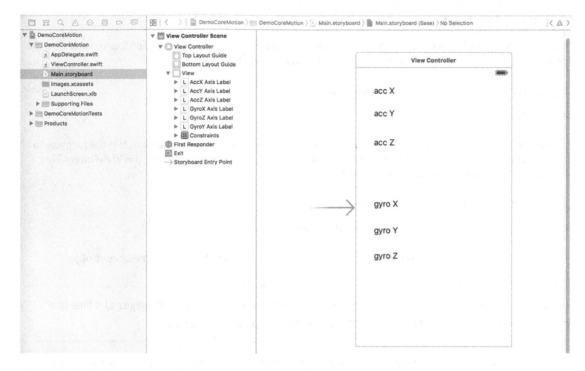

**Figure 11-2.** *Project storyboard*

---

■ **Tip**    For more information on constraints and storyboards, see Chapter 5.

---

The labels prefixed with *acc-* will output accelerometer data and the labels prefixed with *gyro-* will show gyroscope data.

To make use of these labels open the ViewController.swift file and add the corresponding *outlets* in the beginning of the ViewController class (Listing 11-1).

**Listing 11-1.** Add an Outlet for Each Label to the ViewController Class

```
class ViewController: UIViewController
{
    @IBOutlet weak var accXAxisLabel:  UILabel!
    @IBOutlet weak var accYAxisLabel:  UILabel!
    @IBOutlet weak var accZAxisLabel:  UILabel!
    @IBOutlet weak var gyroXAxisLabel: UILabel!
    @IBOutlet weak var gyroYAxisLabel: UILabel!
    @IBOutlet weak var gyroZAxisLabel: UILabel!

    // Leave the rest of the code inside ViewController unchanged
}
```

To connect each label with its corresponding outlet open Main.storyboard in the Standard editor and ViewController.swift in the Assistant editor. Then Ctrl + Drag each label from the storyboard to the corresponding outlet in the code.

# Motion Manager

To access the accelerometer and the gyroscope, you first need to import the `CoreMotion` framework. Add the line in Listing 11-2 to the `import` section of `ViewController.swift` file.

***Listing 11-2.*** Import the CoreMotion Framework

```
import CoreMotion
```

The `CMMotionManager` class, part of the CoreMotion network, enters the scene next. It is the gateway to the motion services provided by the iOS SDK. Create an instance of it as a member of the `ViewController` class right after the outlet declarations (Listing 11-3).

***Listing 11-3.*** Instantiate CMMotionManager

```
let motionManager : CMMotionManager = CMMotionManager()
```

This line declares the `mMotionMmanager` variable and initializes it to be a `CMMotionManager` object.

---

■ **Caution**    Apple's manual suggests that you only have one instance of `CMMotionManager` at a time and warns that having more than one can affect the rate at which motion data is received.

---

The code that works with the motion manager will go inside the `viewDidLoad()` function, as shown in Listing 11-4.

***Listing 11-4.*** Using the Motion Manager

```
override func viewDidLoad() {
    // This line was generated for us by Xcode:
    super.viewDidLoad()

    // Set data sampling rate for the two sensors:
    motionManager.accelerometerUpdateInterval = 0.1 // ten times per second
    motionManager.gyroUpdateInterval = 0.1 // ten times per second

    // Check if the device has an accelerometer:
    if motionManager.accelerometerAvailable {

        // An accelerometer is present, now start listening for updates:
        mMotionManager.startAccelerometerUpdatesToQueue( ↲
                NSOperationQueue.mainQueue()) {
            // Data is captured inside this closure (callback).
            data, error in

            // print acceleration (x, y, z) data:
            self.accXAxisLabel.text = "\(data!.acceleration.x)"
            self.accYAxisLabel.text = "\(data!.acceleration.y)"
            self.accZAxisLabel.text = "\(data!.acceleration.z)"
        }
    }
```

```
// Check if the device has a gyroscope:
if motionManager.gyroAvailable {

    // A gyroscope is present, now start listening for updates:
    motionManager.startGyroUpdatesToQueue(NSOperationQueue.mainQueue()) {
        // Data is captured inside this closure (callback).
        data, error in

        //print rotationRate (x, y, z) data:
        self.gyroXAxisLabel.text = "\(data!.rotationRate.x)"
        self.gyroYAxisLabel.text = "\(data!.rotationRate.y)"
        self.gyroZAxisLabel.text = "\(data!.rotationRate.z)"
    }
}
}
```

This code first sets the motion sensors' sampling rate to ten times per second. In other words, that's how often you will be getting updates about your device's position. Then it checks if the device actually has an accelerometer and if one is present, it calls CMMotionManager's startAccelerometerUpdatesToQueue method, which provides the updates. startAccelerometerUpdatesToQueue takes two parameters:

- A queue, on which to send the updates. In this example you will use the queue associated with the app's main thread.

- A closure (callback function) to receive and process the data. The closure takes two parameters: data and error. The next few lines of code use data.acceleration.x, etc. to extract data about the device's position and to update the top three labels on the screen.

---

■ **Tip**   For more information on closure syntax, see Chapter 22.

---

The exact same logic applies to getting data from the gyroscope. This time you are interested in data.rotationRate.x, data.rotationRate.y, and so on.

---

■ **Caution**   Apple strongly discourages using the .mainQueue for heavy data operations or for frequently updating data like that coming from the motion sensors, because this could affect the rendering of the user interface. With that in mind, this example uses the main thread to read the motion data in the example, in order to keep the focus on working with data, rather than on managing threads. For more information on using background threads see Chapter 7.

---

You are ready to start the app! It needs to run on an actual device, rather than in the simulator, in order to use the motion sensors. When the app starts, shake and move your device to see the accelerometer and gyroscope data updating on the screen between -1.0 and 1.0 for each of the three axes.

# Maps and Location

In this tutorial you will build an app that retrieves the current geo coordinates of the device and displays them on a map. Quite useful for building apps that show the user nearby restaurants, hotels, ATMs, and so on.

## Setting Up the App

Start by creating an empty *Single View Application* in Xcode. Name the project *DemoCoreLocation*.

Being able to display a map in your application requires the use of the MapKit framework. And, to be able to use that, you first need to add Maps to your app's *capabilities*. To do that select your project in the Project navigator, then in the list of targets select the target for your app, *DemoCoreLocation*. Click the *Capabilities* tab, scroll down to find Maps, and turn it on, as shown on Figure 11-3.

***Figure 11-3.*** *Adding map capabilities*

Note that when you turned on the Maps capability switch, the MapKit framework was automatically added to the project.

Find Main.storyboard in Project navigator and click to open it. Then drag the following user interface (UI) components from the Object library onto the storyboard and arrange them as shown in Figure 11-4:

- *Label*—it will display geo coordinates as plain text.

- *Button*—tapping it will retrieve the device's location. Set its caption to "Get location."

- *Map Kit View*—this will display a local map and the location of your device on it.

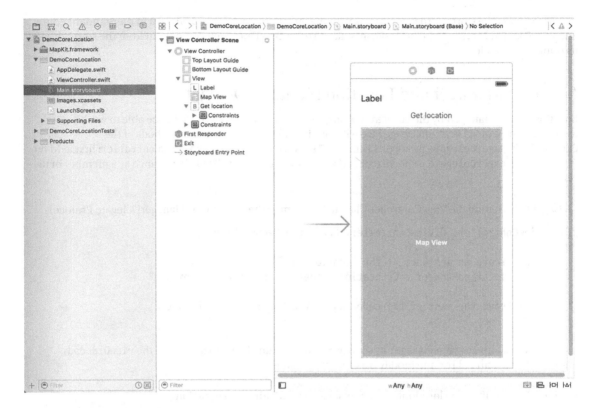

*Figure 11-4. DemoCoreLocation storyboard*

Do not forget to manually constrain all views in the storyboard or to use Xcode's Add Missing Constraints feature. Now open the ViewController.swift file from Project navigator and add the CoreLocation and MapKit frameworks to its import section (Listing 11-5). These contain the application programming interfaces (APIs) you will later work with.

*Listing 11-5.* Import the CoreLocation and MapKit Frameworks

```
import CoreLocation
import MapKit
```

Next, add the corresponding *outlets* to the top of the ViewController class and bind them to the UI components you placed on the storyboard. Listing 11-6 shows you how to define the outlets.

*Listing 11-6.* Add UI utlets to the ViewController

```
class ViewController: UIViewController {

    @IBOutlet weak var label: UILabel!
    @IBOutlet weak var mapView: MKMapView!
        // Leave the rest of the code inside ViewController unchanged
}
```

To connect the storyboard components with the outlets, open `Main.storyboard` in the Standard editor and `ViewController.swift` in the Assistant editor. Then Ctrl + Drag each component from the storyboard to its outlet in the code.

## Location Manager and Location Manager Delegate

Location data is managed by the `CLLocationManager` class. For `ViewController` to be able to work with an instance of `CLLocationManager` we will have it implement some of the methods of the `CLLocationManagerDelegate` protocol. Listing 11-7 shows you how to modify `ViewController`: first, add the `CLLocationManagerDelegate` protocol to it and then add a `CLLocationManager` instance as a member of the class.

***Listing 11-7.*** Getting the ViewController Class to Conform to the CLLocationManagerDelegate Protocol

```
class ViewController: UIViewController, CLLocationManagerDelegate {

    // Create an instance of the location manager class:
    let locationManager : CLLocationManager = CLLocationManager()

    // Leave the rest of the code inside ViewController unchanged
}
```

You will set up `locationManager` as soon as the app's main view is loaded. Find the `viewDidLoad` method of `ViewController` and modify it as shown in Listing 11-8.

***Listing 11-8.*** Configuring locationManager Inside the viewDidLoad() Function

```
override func viewDidLoad() {

    // This line was generated for us by Xcode:
    super.viewDidLoad()

    // Set this ViewController instance as the delegate
    // that will receive the location service callbacks:
    locationManager.delegate = self

    // Set the desired accuracy level:
    locationManager.desiredAccuracy = kCLLocationAccuracyBest

    // Ask the user for permission to use location services:
    locationManager.requestAlwaysAuthorization()
}
```

The first thing this code does is to set the location manager's delegate to `self`. This tells the Swift compiler to look for a specific location manager delegate function in the `ViewController` class. The next line sets the accuracy level (i.e., the precision with which you want location coordinates reported). Last, but not least, you need to ask the user to allow your app to use location services and this is what the last line of this setup does.

■ **Caution**    The LocationManager can use various techniques to determine your location, from Wi-Fi to GPS. Using the actual GPS of the device gives the most accurate results, but it can impact battery life dramatically. Apple states that the GPS chip is used when you set the `desiredAccuracy` property to less than 100 meters, so be aware and set it to lower accuracy when you can.

## Permissions

The user must give permission to your app to use location services. Prior to iOS 8 a prompt was shown automatically once the location manager made a query. In iOS 8 you need to add a couple of settings to your app in order for that to happen.

In Project navigator find and open the `Info.plist` file and add either one of the following keys or both: `NSLocationWhenInUseUsageDescription` and `NSLocationAlwaysUsageDescription` (Figure 11-5). As their names suggest, the first key requests permission to use location services only when the app is running and the second key asks if the app can track the user's location in the background. The value you define for each key is the message that will be shown in the permission dialog to let the user know how the app intends to use location services.

| Key | | Type | Value |
|---|---|---|---|
| ▼ Information Property List | | Dictionary | (17 items) |
| Localization native development region | ↕ | String | en |
| Executable file | ↕ | String | $(EXECUTABLE_NAME) |
| Bundle identifier | ↕ | String | com.diadraw.$(PRODUCT_NAME:rfc1034identifier) |
| InfoDictionary version | ↕ | String | 6.0 |
| Bundle name | ↕ | String | $(PRODUCT_NAME) |
| Bundle OS Type code | ↕ | String | APPL |
| Bundle versions string, short | ↕ | String | 1.0 |
| Bundle creator OS Type code | ↕ | String | ???? |
| Bundle version | ↕ | String | 1 |
| Application requires iPhone environment | ↕ | Boolean | YES |
| Launch screen interface file base name | ↕ | String | LaunchScreen |
| Main storyboard file base name | ↕ | String | Main |
| ▶ Required device capabilities | ↕ | Array | (1 item) |
| ▶ Supported interface orientations | ↕ | Array | (3 items) |
| ▶ Supported interface orientations (iPad) | ↕ | Array | (4 items) |
| NSLocationAlwaysUsageDescription | ↕ | String | Because I always want to know where you are |
| NSLocationWhenInUseUsageDescription | ↕ | String | I just want to know where you are |

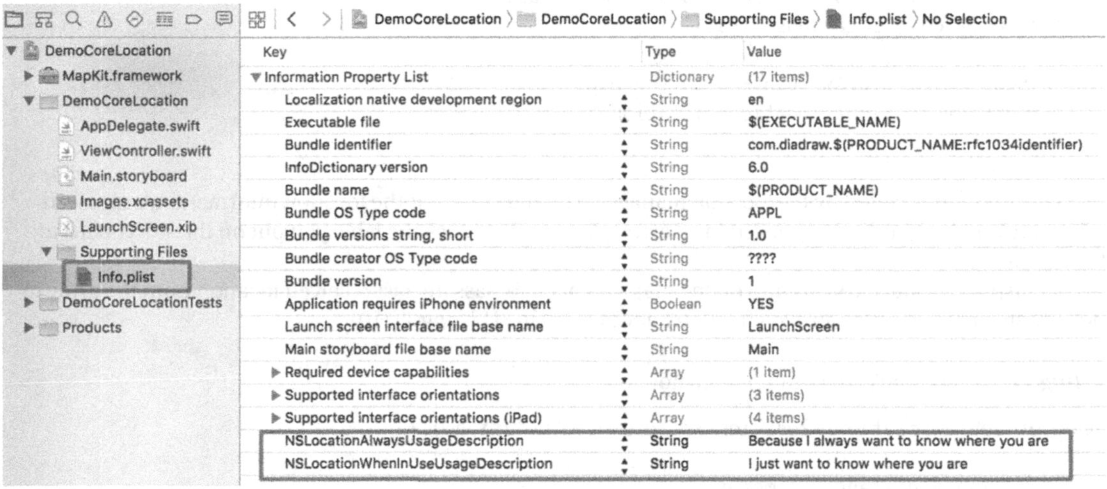

*Figure 11-5. Setting permission requests*

An important thing to note here is that if you don't define either of these keys in `Info.plist`, no prompt will be shown to the user, your application will not be granted permissions and will be unable to use the location service.

# Receiving Location Updates

Before your app is complete you will need to make sure that ViewController complies with the CLLocationManagerDelegate protocol. For that it will need to implement a function called locationManagerdidUpdateLocations, which takes two parameters:

- manager, which is a reference to the location manager that made a call to the delegate function;

- locations, an array composed of CLLocation elements that store the updated geo locations.

Listing 11-9 shows you the implementation of locationManagerdidUpdateLocations.

***Listing 11-9.*** Location Manager Delegate Function

```
func locationManager(manager: CLLocationManager, ↵
                    didUpdateLocations locations: [CLLocation]) {

    // Print out the location array:
    label.text = "locations = \(locations)"

    // Read the first set of locations from the array:
    let location = locations.first!

    // Show the device's location on the map:
    setMapViewLocation( location: location )
}
```

This method is called by the location manager, which passes to it the location information, expressed as latitude and longitude, and packed in an array. The function uses the label you put on the storyboard to display these.

To display the device's position on the map you need to pass the last received location from the array to the setMapLocation function, which you are about to define (Listing 11-10).

***Listing 11-10.*** setMapViewLocation Function

```
func setMapViewLocation( location location : CLLocation ) {

    // Define a distance in meters:
    let locationDistance : CLLocationDistance = 100;

    // Create a region on the map, the center of which is our location
    // and its radius - the distance we defined above:
    let region = MKCoordinateRegionMakeWithDistance(location.coordinate, ↵
                                        locationDistance, locationDistance)

    // Show the region on the map:
    mMapView.setRegion(region, animated: true)
}
```

This function uses the location data and a distance that you define to create a region on the map, which has its center at the given location and its radius—the given distance. The last line of this function asks the Map Kit View to show this location, using animation.

If you try to run the application at this point you will notice that a zoomed-out map is displayed, but nothing else happens. For your location to be found, you need to ask the location manager to do it for you. Let us do that on the touch event of the button you put on the storyboard.

With `Main.storyboard` open in the Standard editor and `ViewController.swift` open in the Assistant editor, select the button and open the Connections inspector panel on the right. Find the button's Touch Up Inside event and Ctrl + Drag it inside the `ViewController` class in the `ViewController.swift` file. This creates an action (event handler) for you. Name it `buttonTouched`, leave the rest of the settings in the pop-up dialog as they are and click Connect. Add the code in Listing 11-11 to the event handler.

**Listing 11-11.** Location Manager Start Update

```
@IBAction func buttonTouched(sender: AnyObject) {
    label.text = "Searching location…"
    locationManager.startUpdatingLocation()
}
```

When the user taps the button, the label will first tell them that the app is busy searching for the device's location. Then the location manager is asked to start updating the location data.

And voilà, your app is ready for testing (Figure 11-6).

**Figure 11-6.** *Running location app*

Enjoy.

# Summary

This chapter showed you how to use the CoreMotion, CoreLocation, and MapKit frameworks to capture the information from your device's motion sensors and to display your location on a map.

The next chapter will focus on how to take a picture with the camera and how to manipulate it.

# CHAPTER 12

■ ■ ■

# Working with the Camera and Images

When cameras were added to mobile devices and image-editing apps started appearing, we were all transformed into artists overnight. Taking a photo of an interesting object, applying a filter, and immediately sharing the resulting creation is so easy, it would probably inspire Andy Warhol to recreate his Marilyn Diptych. On the following pages we will see how to take pictures with the camera and edit them with the power of Swift.

In this chapter you will do the following:

- Learn about the Photos framework.

- See how to programmatically take photos with the camera and browse the gallery.

- Learn how to use the CoreImage framework to apply filters and edit photos.

- Learn how to save an image back to the gallery.

- Build an app that does all of the above.

When you are done, you will have an app that takes photos; lets users browse the gallery; and changes the color, brightness, and saturations of selected photos and saves them back to the gallery.

## Setting Up the App and Designing the UI

The app we are about to develop will let the user take a photo, make changes to it, and save the modified photo to the photo gallery.

Following is a list of the main features we will focus on:

- Taking a photo by using the camera user interface (UI) API (application programming interface) of the Photos framework.

- Choosing a photo from the gallery with the help of the default gallery browsing UI on iOS.

- Editing the brightness, contrast, and saturation of the photo by applying a filter.

- Saving the edited copy back to the photo gallery.

In Xcode create a Single View iOS application project (**File ➤ New ➤ Project...**, then **iOS ➤ Application ➤ Single View Application**) and name it ImageEditor.

© Radoslava Leseva Adams and Hristo Lesev 2016
R. L. Adams and H. Lesev, *Migrating to Swift from Flash and ActionScript*,
DOI 10.1007/978-1-4842-1666-8_12

Open `Main.storyboard` and position the UI elements to look like the right half of Figure 12-1. Add a Navigation Bar and drop a Bar Button Item on its right side, then add a Button, three Labels, three Sliders, and an Image view to the main view of the app. Constrain the layout to make it adaptive (see **Chapter 5** for a reminder of how to use Auto Layout and Size Classes to help with that).

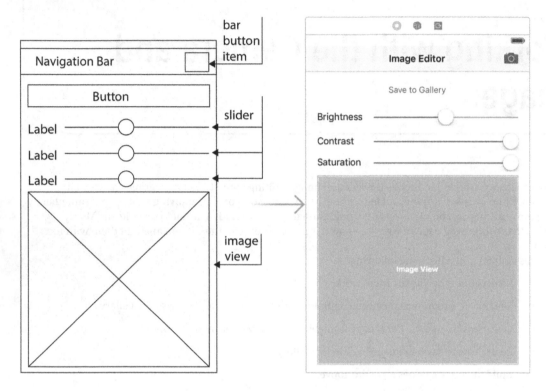

***Figure 12-1.*** *The app's user interface*

Title the three labels "Brightness," "Contrast," and "Saturation." The sliders next to each label will change the corresponding properties of the image we will load in the image view.

To add a camera icon to the bar button, select it and in the Attributes inspector set **System Item** to Camera.

Select the Image View and in the Attributes inspector set its **Mode** to Aspect Fit. This will ensure that the photo we choose to display will fit in the bounding box of the image view.

Adjust the range of each slider in the Attributes inspector:

- Select the brightness slider and set its **Minimum Value** to -1, **Maximum Value** to 1 and **Current** to 0.

- Select the contrast slider and set its **Current** to 1.

- Select the saturation slider and set its **Current** to 1.

Open `ViewController.swift` and add imports for the `Photos` and `CoreImage` frameworks. The `Photos` framework has the definitions of the default view controllers for taking pictures with a camera and for browsing the photo gallery. The `CoreImage` framework gives us plenty of image processing tools. Now get ready to add some actions.

Start with the button: create an action for its Touch Up Inside event and name it saveToGallery. For the Bar Button Item create an action named showChooseImageOptions. Add an action for the Value Changed event of each of the Sliders and call them brightnessValueChanged, contrastValueChanged, and saturationValueChanged, respectively. Then add an outlet for the Image View and call it imageView. Your code should look similar to that in Listing 12-1.

***Listing 12-1.*** Adding an Outlet and Actions to the ViewController Class

```
import UIKit
import Photos
import CoreImage

class ViewController: UIViewController {

    @IBOutlet weak var imageView: UIImageView!

    override func viewDidLoad() {
        super.viewDidLoad()
    }

    override func didReceiveMemoryWarning() {
        super.didReceiveMemoryWarning()
    }

    @IBAction func brightnessValueChanged(sender: UISlider) {
        // TODO: Adjust the filter's brightness property.
    }

    @IBAction func contrastValueChanged(sender: UISlider) {
        // TODO: Adjust the filter's contrast property.
    }

    @IBAction func saturationValueChanged(sender: UISlider) {
        // TODO: Adjust the filter's saturation property.
    }

    @IBAction func saveToGallery(sender: AnyObject) {
        // TODO: Save a copy of the filtered image back to the photo gallery
    }

    @IBAction func showChooseImageOptions(sender: UIBarButtonItem) {
        // TODO: Ask the user from where he wants to pick an image
    }
}
```

# Taking Pictures and Browsing the Gallery

Apple knows how important it is for developers to be able to use the device's camera in their apps. To allow easy access to it without the bother of setting up a UI, the iOS SDK provides a ready-made view controller. It is called UIImagePickerController and is part of the Photo framework.

The UIImagePickerController lets the user choose the source of an image: the device's built-in camera or the gallery. Once an image is chosen, it can be obtained programmatically via a method of the UIImagePickerControllerDelegate protocol. We will now see how to use the image picker controller in our app.

First we need to make our ViewController class conform to the UIImagePickerControllerDelegate protocol by adding the protocol to ViewController's inheritance list. In order to be used as a delegate for the image picker controller, ViewController will need to conform to one more protocol: UINavigationControllerDelegate.

---

■ **Caution**    This could be a potential point of confusion. Note that conforming to UINavigationControllerDelegate is required, in order to make ViewController a delegate for the image picker, not for the app's navigation bar.

---

We set ViewController as the delegate for the image picker controller in viewDidLoad. Then we implement one of the methods of UIImagePickerControllerDelegate, which receives a copy of the image that the user chose from the gallery or took with the camera: imagePickerController(_:didFinishPicking Image:_). You can see the implementation in Listing 12-2.

---

■ **Note**    For more information about delegation and how it works, see Chapter 5. We will look at protocols and conformance in Chapter 21.

---

*Listing 12-2.* Implementing UIImagePickerControllerDelegate Protocol and Setting Up the Image Picker

```
class ViewController: UIViewController, UINavigationControllerDelegate, ↵
    UIImagePickerControllerDelegate {

    //Create an instance of the image picking controller:
    let imagePicker = UIImagePickerController()

    override func viewDidLoad() {
        super.viewDidLoad()

        //Set the delegate, which will recieve the chosen image:
        imagePicker.delegate = self
        //Hide any editing options from the default UI:
        imagePicker.allowsEditing = false
    }

    func imagePickerController(picker: UIImagePickerController, ↵
        didFinishPickingImage image: UIImage, editingInfo: [String : AnyObject]?) {
        // TODO: Manipulate the image
    }

    //The rest of the code comes here
}
```

The imagePickerController(_:didFinishPickingImage:_) is called when the user has finished taking a photo with the camera or has picked one from the gallery. A copy of the image gets passed in the image parameter of the function. The parameter is of type UIImage. This means that the received image is ready to be used in the UI of our application.

To show the image picker UI on the screen we have to set it up first. Since we want to be able to obtain images from both the camera and the photo gallery, we will implement the setup logic in two separate functions. The functions are called openCameraVC and openGalleryVC, respectively. You can see the implementation in Listing 12-3.

*Listing 12-3.* Implementing openCameraVC and openGalleryVC Functions

```
func openCameraVC(action: UIAlertAction) ->Void {
    //Tell the image picker that we want to take a picture with the camera:
    imagePicker.sourceType = UIImagePickerControllerSourceType.Camera
    //Show imagePicker on the screen:
    presentViewController(imagePicker, animated: true, ↵
        completion: nil)
}

func openGalleryVC(action: UIAlertAction) ->Void {
    //Tell the image picker that we want to browse the photo gallery:
    imagePicker.sourceType = UIImagePickerControllerSourceType.SavedPhotosAlbum
    //Show imagePicker on the screen:
    presentViewController(imagePicker, animated: true, ↵
        completion: nil)
}
```

These two functions are very similar. First we set the sourceType property of the imagePicker to the location from which we want to obtain an image. Then we show the image picker view controller on the screen.

In order to let the user choose between taking a new photo and using one from the gallery, we will use an action sheet, which will show up when the user taps the camera button on the navigation bar. We will implement this in the showChooseImageOptions method we stubbed out earlier.

First we create an instance of the UIAlertController class, set its preferedStyle property to UIAlertControllerStyle.ActionSheet, and set up a message that the user will see.

---

■ **Note** UIActionSheet used to be a popular choice for showing action sheets, but it was deprecated in iOS 8. Since then, UIAlertController is what is used for the same purpose. For more details on using alerts, see Chapter 6.

---

Next we set alert actions to handle the three options. The first two actions, cameraAction and galleryAction, will result in calls to openCameraVC and openGalleryVC, respectively. The third alert action is called closeAction and is used to dismiss the action sheet. To do that we set its style property to UIAlertActionStyle.Cancel and provide an empty action callback.

Before we present the actions on the action sheet, it is a good idea to check if all of the options are actually available on the device. For example, the iOS simulator does not support camera, so in that case we can only offer the user to pick an image from the gallery. To perform the check we make a call to isSourceTypeAvailable—a static method of the UIImagePickerController class.

261

You can see the implementation of the showChooseImageOptions in Listing 12-4.

*Listing 12-4.* Setting Up an Action Sheet with Three Options

```
@IBAction func showChooseImageOptions(sender: UIBarButtonItem) {
    //Create an action sheet with options:
    let actionSheet = UIAlertController(title: "", message: "Get an image", ↩
        preferredStyle: UIAlertControllerStyle.ActionSheet)

    //Configure a new action for taking a photo with the camera:
    let cameraAction = UIAlertAction(title: "Use the camera", style: ↩
        UIAlertActionStyle.Default,handler: openCameraVC)

    //Configure a new action for picking an image from the gallery:
    let galleryAction = UIAlertAction(title: "From the gallery", style: ↩
        UIAlertActionStyle.Default, handler: openGalleryVC)

    //Configure an empty action to close the action sheet:
    let closeAction = UIAlertAction(title: "Done", style: ↩
        UIAlertActionStyle.Cancel){ (action) -> Void in
    }

    //Check if the device has a camera:
    if UIImagePickerController.isSourceTypeAvailable( ↩
        UIImagePickerControllerSourceType.Camera) {
        //Add the cameraAction to the action sheet
        actionSheet.addAction(cameraAction)
    }

    //Check if a gallery is available:
    if UIImagePickerController.isSourceTypeAvailable( ↩
        UIImagePickerControllerSourceType.SavedPhotosAlbum) {
        //Add the galleryAction to the action sheet
        actionSheet.addAction(galleryAction)
    }

    //Add the close action to the sheet:
    actionSheet.addAction(closeAction)

    //For devices with bigger screens
    //set the pop over controller to be the bar button instance.
    //This is needed by iOS to calculate the screen position
    //of the action sheet controler.
    if let popoverController = actionSheet.popoverPresentationController {
        popoverController.barButtonItem = sender
    }

    //Show the action sheet on the screen:
    presentViewController(actionSheet, animated: true, completion: nil)
}
```

If I were you, I would already be eager to see the result of all the code we wrote so far. In order to do that, we need to show an image on the screen: we will assign the UIImage that gets passed to imagePickerControl ler(_:didFinishPickingImage:_) to the image property of imageView (see Listing 12-5).

*Listing 12-5.* Showing an Image on the Screen

```
func imagePickerController(picker: UIImagePickerController, didFinishPickingImage image:
UIImage, ↵
    editingInfo: [String : AnyObject]?) {

    //Dismiss the image picker view controller:
    dismissViewControllerAnimated(true, completion: nil)

    //Show the image in the image view:
    imageView.image = image
}
```

Let us run the app and pick an image from the gallery, as shown in Figure 12-2.

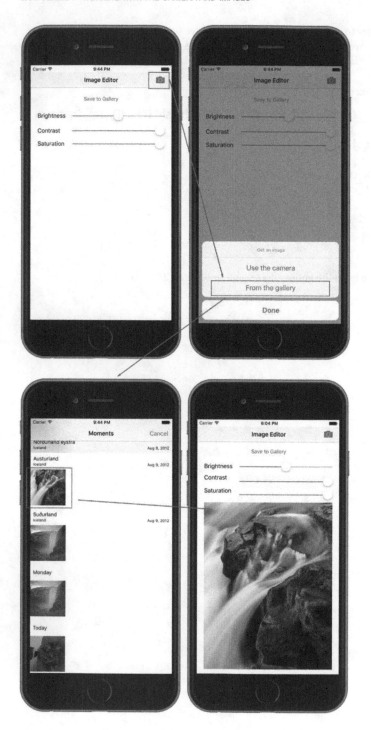

*Figure 12-2.* *Picking an image from the gallery*

Or you can take a photo with the camera as shown in Figure 12-3.[1]

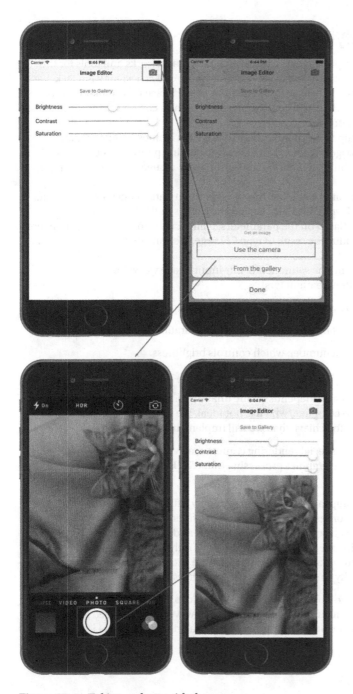

**Figure 12-3.** *Taking a photo with the camera*

---

[1]Thanks to Mushana the cat for agreeing to appear in the shot!

In the next section we will see how we can edit the image.

# Editing an Image by Applying a Filter

When it comes to editing an image Apple has provided us with an arsenal of frameworks and tools for the task. Their vast number can empower you, as well as make you wonder which one is best for what task. Each of the available frameworks comes with pros and cons in different areas of the image manipulation world. You can choose to edit an image pixel by pixel, use high-level frameworks such as CoreGraphics, CoreImage, ImageProcessingKit, or opt for third-party libraries.[2]

The best choice for what we want our app to do, manipulate an image's brightness, contrast, and saturation, would be the filters in the CoreImage framework. It offers outstanding performance, a great abstraction layer over the low-level image-editing operations, and comes with a huge number of ready-to-use filters.

A filter in the CoreImage framework is treated as a black box: it takes input data, processes it, and spits out an output image. All built-in filters are of type CIFilter. Their input comes in the form of one or more images and parameters in key-value format. Based on the parameters, a filter can combine the input images and make alterations. When it is ready, it produces a result of type CIImage. We can create a filter by passing a filter name to CIFilter's initializer.

To control the brightness, the contrast, and the saturation of our input image we will use the CIColorControls filter. It has the following input parameters:

- inputImage—a CIImage instance, which contains the original image data.

- inputSaturation—a floating point number, which controls saturation.

- inputBrightness—a floating point number, which controls brightness.

- inputContrast—a floating point number, which controls contrast.

The time needed for filtering an image heavily depends on the image size. For large-resolution files applying a filter could take several seconds to complete, which is not ideal. We would like the user to see results in real time, when they move a slider. To achieve that, we will implement a couple of tricks.

- The first trick involves the use of a special rendering context that will offload the work from the CPU and will use the graphics processing unit (GPU) of the device to do the calculations.

- The second trick is to make our app lazy and not actually apply a filter to the original image while it is being edited. In order to show the effects of a filter in real time, we will display a downsampled copy of the image as a preview and apply the filter to it. The heavy work of modifying the original file will be done only when the user decides to save the changes to the image. We will then show an activity indicator to let the user know that a potentially lengthy operation is in progress.

Let us start by declaring an instance of the CIFilter class and calling it colorFilter. Then we will need one UIImage instance for the original image and another one for the preview. We will also need an instance of the view controller, which will display the activity indicator. You can see all declarations in Listing 12-6.

---

[2]You can find more info about image manipulation frameworks here: https://developer.apple.com/library/ios/documentation/GraphicsImaging/Conceptual/CoreImaging/ci_intro/ci_intro.html.

*Listing 12-6.* Declaring Instances

```
//The filter we will use to controll the brightness, contrast and saturation of the image
let colorFilter = CIFilter(name: "CIColorControls")

//The original full sized image
var originalImage:UIImage?
//A downscaled image for preview
var previewImage:UIImage?

//An allert controller with activity indicator
//to show that the app is busy saving an image
var savingImageVC:UIAlertController?

//A context to render the filter on the GPU
var filterContext:CIContext = CIContext(EAGLContext: EAGLContext(API: .OpenGLES2), ↵
    options:[kCIContextWorkingColorSpace : NSNull()])
```

Note the use of the `filterContext` variable: by passing the `EAGLContext(API: .OpenGLES2)` as an argument we instruct the framework to perform calculations on the GPU instead of on the CPU. This is our first performance trick done.

As a next step we will take the image that the user has chosen with the image picker, make a downsampled copy of it, and feed it to the filter.

Find the `imagePickerController(_:didFinishPickingImage:_)` method. In it we will downsample the chosen image by drawing a scaled-down copy of it and converting it to a UIImage. We need to do the drawing inside a graphics context, which is managed by these two calls: `UIGraphicsBeginImageContextWithOptions` and `UIGraphicsEndImageContext`. To create a scaled-down copy of our image we call `drawInRect` and specify the size of the rectangle, in which the image should fit. We use `CGSizeApplyAffineTransform` to calculate the desired size of the image, so that it matches the size of `imageView`, where we show the preview. Finally, we store the two copies of the image as follows: the original is kept in the `originalImage` variable and the `previewImage` variable stores the smaller copy. We pass that smaller copy as an input to the filter. To set an input parameter we use the filter's `setValue(_:forKey)` function and specify the name of the parameter and its value. You can see the implementation in Listing 12-7.

*Listing 12-7.* Create a Preview for the Selected Image and Set It as an Input to the Filter

```
func imagePickerController(picker: UIImagePickerController, didFinishPickingImage image:
UIImage, ↵
    editingInfo: [String : AnyObject]?) {

        //Dismiss the image picker view controller
        dismissViewControllerAnimated(true, completion: nil)

        //Calculate a scale factor for the preview image
        //scale the original image so that it fits inside the imageView frame
        let scaleFactor:CGFloat = CGFloat(imageView.frame.size.height / image.size.height)

        //Calculate the size of the preview image
        let size = CGSizeApplyAffineTransform(image.size, ↵
            CGAffineTransformMakeScale(scaleFactor, scaleFactor))

        //Create a context to draw the image inside
```

```
UIGraphicsBeginImageContextWithOptions(size, false, CGFloat(0.0))
//Draw the image downsampled to the new size
image.drawInRect(CGRect(origin: CGPointZero, size: size))
//Get the downsampled image from the context
let scaledImage = UIGraphicsGetImageFromCurrentImageContext()
//Destroys the context
UIGraphicsEndImageContext()

//Store the original image from the gallery
originalImage = image

//Store the downsampled image and use it for preview
previewImage = scaledImage

//Set the preview image as an input image to the filter
colorFilter!.setValue(CIImage(image:previewImage!), forKey:kCIInputImageKey)

applyFilter()
}
```

At the end of the Listing 12-7 you might have noticed a call to a function, which we have not implemented yet: applyFilter. Its role is to get the output from the filter and display it on the screen. You can see the implementation in Listing 12-8.

*Listing 12-8.* Implementing the applyFilter Function

```
func applyFilter() {
        //Get the filtered (output) image
        if let ciiOutput = colorFilter?.valueForKey(kCIOutputImageKey) as? CIImage {
            //Create an CGImage using the provided context
            let cgiOutput = filterContext.createCGImage(ciiOutput, fromRect: ciiOutput.
            extent)

            //Create an UIImage from the CGImage
            let result = UIImage(CGImage: cgiOutput)

            //Show the output image in the image view
            imageView?.image = result
        }
}
```

Let us now set values for the brightness, contrast, and saturation properties. We will do this in the corresponding actions for each of the three sliders that we added in the beginning of the chapter (see Listing 12-9).

*Listing 12-9.* Setting the Brightness, the Saturation, and the Contrast Values

```
@IBAction func brightnessValueChanged(sender: UISlider) {
    //Change the brightness:
    colorFilter!.setValue(sender.value, forKey:"inputBrightness")
    //Apply the filter and show the result:
    applyFilter()
}
```

```
@IBAction func contrastValueChanged(sender: UISlider) {
    //Change the contrast:
    colorFilter!.setValue(sender.value, forKey:"inputContrast")
    //Apply the filter and show the result:
    applyFilter()
}

@IBAction func saturationValueChanged(sender: UISlider) {
    //Change the saturation:
    colorFilter!.setValue(sender.value, forKey:"inputSaturation")
    //Apply the filter and show the result:
    applyFilter()
}
```

Now run the app, pick an image from the gallery or take one with the camera and move the sliders. You will see how the filter is applied in real time (Figure 12-4).

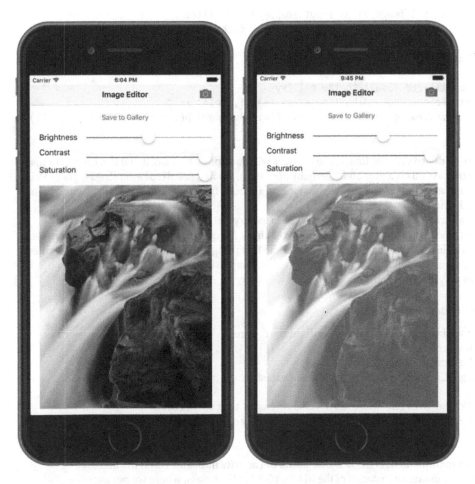

***Figure 12-4.*** *Editing an image*

One last thing before the end of the chapter: I promised you that we would save the edited image back to the gallery. Let us do that now. In ViewController.swift find the saveToGallery method and add the following lines of code to it (Listing 12-10):

**Listing 12-10.** saveToGallery Implementation

```swift
@IBAction func saveToGallery(sender: AnyObject) {

        //Check if there is an image to save
        guard let origImg = originalImage else {
            //If there is no image exit this function
            return
        }

        //Show the activity indicator
        savingImageVC = displaySavingImageActivity()

        //Set the original image as an input image to the filter
        colorFilter!.setValue(CIImage(image:origImg), forKey:kCIInputImageKey)

        applyFilter()

        //Save the filtered result to the gallery
        UIImageWriteToSavedPhotosAlbum(imageView.image!, self, ↵
            #selector(ViewController.image(_:didFinishSavingWithError:contextInfo:)), nil)
}
```

When the user decides to save the image, the changes will be applied to the original file, instead of just to the preview copy of it. As this is a potentially lengthy operation, we first call displaySavingImageActivity to show an activity indicator and inform the user that the app is busy filtering a large image. You can see its implementation in Listing 12-12.

The function that saves the filtered image to the photo gallery is UIImageWriteToSavedPhotosAlbum. It can notify us about whether saving was successful in a callback function, which is passed as a parameter. Listing 12-11 shows the implementation of the callback. The first thing we do when the callback is executed is to hide the activity view controller. Then we set the preview image as the input of the filter again, so the user can continue to play safely with the sliders.

**Listing 12-11.** Finish Image Saving Handler

```swift
func image(image: UIImage, didFinishSavingWithError error: NSError?, ↵
    contextInfo:UnsafePointer<Void>) {
        //Hide the activity indicator
        savingImageVC!.dismissViewControllerAnimated(true, completion: nil)

        //Set back the preview image as an input image to the filter
        colorFilter!.setValue(CIImage(image:previewImage!), forKey:kCIInputImageKey)
}
```

The last function to implement is the one that shows the activity indicator when the image is being saved. Inside we create an instance of the UIAlertController class, where we put an UIActivityIndicatorView and animate it (Listing 12-12).

*Listing 12-12.* Creating an Alert Controller with Activity Indicator

```
func displaySavingImageActivity() -> UIAlertController {
        //Create an alert controller
        let alertController = UIAlertController(title: "Saving image", message: nil,
            preferredStyle: .Alert)

        //Create an activity indicator
        let indicator = UIActivityIndicatorView(frame: alertController.view.bounds)
        indicator.color = UIColor.blackColor()
        indicator.autoresizingMask = [.FlexibleWidth, .FlexibleHeight]

        //Add the activity indicator as a subview of the alert controller's view
        alertController.view.addSubview(indicator)
        indicator.userInteractionEnabled = false
        indicator.startAnimating()

        //Show the alertController on the screen
        presentViewController(alertController, animated: true, completion: nil)

        return alertController
}
```

With this our image-editing application is ready and we can call it a day. Congratulations.

# Summary

In this chapter you saw how to use the built-in iOS functionality for taking photos, browsing the gallery, and editing images. You learned about the Photos and CoreImage frameworks and implemented a simple photo-editing app.

In the next chapter you will see how to build an app to persist data to files on the device and how to store and retrieve data remotely from the cloud.

# CHAPTER 13

■ ■ ■

# Working with Data

Working with data is a big part of app development. Anything from storing user preferences and achievements to providing larger storage for the users' artistic creations requires that you know how to work with data, how to store it locally, and how to offer your users the option to back it up in the cloud.

This chapter is split into two parts. In the first part we explore different ways of persisting local data on a device. The second part introduces iCloud—Apple's cloud solution. We will see how to set up an account for it and use it to store data remotely.

## Reading and Writing Data Locally

The iOS SDK offers several different ways of persisting data locally on the device's file system. The examples that follow will help explore them: we will save and read arbitrary data from a text file, then we will see how to serialize objects into files and into a key-value database.

### The iOS File System

Let us first have a look at how iOS manages files internally. As there can be lots of applications installed on a device and trying to read and write data to it, there are restrictions on which parts of the file system an application can access.

Every application has its own sandbox, which defines the disc locations that are available to it and is not accessible to other apps. The two directories where an app can store files and manage folders are called Documents and tmp. The Documents directory is where user-generated content goes—it persists between launches of the app. The contents of this folder can be made available to the user through file sharing and are backed up by iTunes. The tmp folder is used, as its name suggests, for storing temporary information that doesn't need to be kept between application launches.

There are three important classes that the iOS SDK offers for working with files and folders:

- **NSFileManager** is used to perform basic file and folder operations such as creating, moving, writing, and reading. It can be queried for the current working folder and offers folder management: creating and deleting folders and enumerating their contents.

- **NSFileHandle** is helpful with low-level file operations such as seeking a position in a file, appending new data, or reading and writing specific chunks of data from a file.

- **NSData** is used as a storage buffer: for example, it can store the contents of a file in memory.

© Radoslava Leseva Adams and Hristo Lesev 2016
R. L. Adams and H. Lesev, *Migrating to Swift from Flash and ActionScript*,
DOI 10.1007/978-1-4842-1666-8_13

■ **Note**    Path names in iOS use the standard UNIX convention, where each path component is separated with a forward slash /.

The applications you develop are installed in `/private/var/mobile/Containers/Data/Application/YourAppUniqueIDString.`

In the next section we will use the three classes we mentioned previously to create an application which stores a text file in the `Documents` folder and reads it back.

## Preparation: Setting Up the App

Our app will initially save a text file, which it will then read back. Later on in the chapter we will add more advanced functionality to it.

Start by creating a new Single View Application project in Xcode (**File ➤ New ➤ Project...**, then **iOS ➤ Application ➤ Single View Application**), named `LocalStorageDemo`. The app will have a very simple user interface (UI), consisting of a `UITextView` and two buttons: find these in the Object library and drag them onto the storyboard in `Main.storyboard` to make it look as shown on Figure 13-1. Change the button captions to read Open and Save and leave the text in the text view as it is.

***Figure 13-1.***  *LocalStorageDemo Application user interface*

Ctrl+drag the text view into the `ViewController` class definition in the `ViewController.swift` file to create an outlet for it, named `m_textView`. Then Ctrl+drag each of the buttons into `ViewController` to add handlers for their *Touch Up Inside* actions: name the actions `openTextFile` and `saveTextFile`, respectively.

■ **Tip**    See Chapter 2 if you need a reminder for how to create UI outlets and event handlers.

After the outlet and the two event handlers have been generated, the code in `ViewController.swift` should look like that in Listing 13-1.

*Listing 13-1.* ViewController.swift with an Outlet and Event Handlers for the UI

```
import UIKit
class ViewController: UIViewController {

    //Outlet for accessing the label and the date picker in Main.storyboard:
    @IBOutlet weak var textView: UITextView!

    @IBAction func openTextFile(sender: AnyObject) {
        //This method is called when the Open button is touched
    }

    @IBAction func saveTextFile(sender: AnyObject) {
        //This method is called when the Save button is touched
    }

    //The rest of the code goes here

}
```

Hit the run button to make sure that the app compiles and executes, although it doesn't do much at this point.

## Working with File Paths

We will use the NSFileManager class from the iOS SDK to help with the reading and the writing of files. For that purpose we need a reference to it in ViewController: declare a property of the ViewController class, named fileManager, and initialize it with the default file manager by calling the defaultManager method of the NSFileManager class. Then add a property of type String? to ViewController and name it localFilePath. We will use it to store the path to the file we write to and read from (Listing 13-2).

*Listing 13-2.* Obtaining a Reference of NSFileManager

```
//Obtain a reference of NSFileManager
let fileManager : NSFileManager = NSFileManager.defaultManager()

//A property to store the path to the file in the file system
var localFilePath : String?
```

The reading and writing will happen in a text file, called test.txt: let us initialize localFilePath with the path to test.txt right after the view has been shown on screen (in the viewDidLoad method of the ViewController class). We will store test.txt in the tmp folder of our application, but we don't need to remember or hard-code the full path to it: the NSTemporaryDirectory global function will help us with that. The NSURL class from the iOS SDK can then help us construct the full path to our file.

You can see this done on Listing 13-3: we create a constant, named tmpDirPath, of type NSURL and initialize it with the result from NSTemporaryDirectory. The next constant we create, fileURL, contains the full path to test.txt. Calling fileURL.path gives us the path to our file as a String.

*Listing 13-3.* Set the Path to the test.txt File

```
override func viewDidLoad() {
    super.viewDidLoad()

    //Get a URL path to the Application's tmp directory
    let tmpDirPath = NSURL(fileURLWithPath: NSTemporaryDirectory())

    //Append a file name to the path
    let fileURL = tmpDirPath.URLByAppendingPathComponent("test.txt")

    //Get the file path as string
    localFilePath = fileURL.path

    //Output the resulting path to the console
    print( localFilePath )
}
```

## Saving a Text File

We will add code to the saveTextFile action handler (see Listing 13-4), which will be executed when we tap the Save button. It will save the contents of the text view to test.txt. We will use the reference to NSFileManager we created earlier to do the file writing operation by calling its createFileAtPath method. This method kills two birds with one stone: it creates the file and writes bytes to it. There are a couple of things to note about createFileAtPath:

- It takes data in the form of NSData: this is another iOS SDK class, which serves as a byte buffer. In order to read and write text to it we will use UTF8 encoding.

- It returns a Boolean result, which indicates whether writing to the file was successful. This is quite useful, as a lot of things can go wrong during a file-write operation: we can run out of disc space, the path to the file might be incorrect, and so on. We will check the result of createFileAtPath and will show it to the user in an alert: this is done in the showMessage method we will implement later.

*Listing 13-4.* Save a Text File

```
@IBAction func saveTextFile(sender: AnyObject) {

    //Get the text from the text view
    //and encode it as NSData with UTF8 encoding
    let fileData : NSData! = ↵
        (textView.text as String).dataUsingEncoding(NSUTF8StringEncoding)

    //Try to create test.txt and add to it the contents of fileData
    let isOk = fileManager.createFileAtPath(localFilePath!, ↵
        contents: fileData, attributes: nil)

    //Test if file creation was successful and show an alert
    if isOk {
        showMessage( message: "File creation successful!" )
    }
```

```
    else {
        showMessage( message: "File creation unsuccessful!" )
    }

    //Print to the console for convenience
    print( isOk )
}
```

Next comes the implementation of the showMessage method (see Listing 13-5): it may look familiar from the example in **Chapter 5**.

***Listing 13-5.*** Implementation of the showMessage Method

```
func showMessage(message message: String) {
    //Instantiate an allert controller
    let alertController = UIAlertController(title: "Local Storage Demo", ↩
        message: message, preferredStyle: UIAlertControllerStyle.Alert)

    //Add a "Dismiss" button to the alert
    alertController.addAction(UIAlertAction(title: "Dismiss", ↩
        style: UIAlertActionStyle.Default,handler: nil))

    //Show the alert on the screen
    self.presentViewController(alertController, animated: true, ↩
        completion: nil)
}
```

Run the app, edit the text in the text view, and tap Save. You should see the *"File creation successful!"* alert. Next, we will read the file back.

## Reading a Text File

We will implement the file reading in the openTextFile action handler we added when we started the chapter: it will be called when the user taps the Open button. Listing 13-6 shows the implementation: we start clean by removing the current text from the text view: this way we can be confident that what we write to it next is the content of the file on disc and not what was previously in the view. Next we make sure that the file exists by calling NSFileManager's fileExistsAtPath method. If test.txt is where we expect it to be, we can proceed with the reading: another method of NSFileManager helps us with that—contentsAtPath. You may remember that to write it to the file, we had to convert the String from the text view into NSData (similar to ByteArray in ActionScript). Here we will do the reverse and convert the NSData obtained from calling contentsAtPath back to String before displaying it in the text view.

***Listing 13-6.*** Reading from a Text File

```
@IBAction func openTextFile(sender: AnyObject) {
    //Clear the text view content for convenience
    textView.text = ""

    //Check if the file exists
    if fileManager.fileExistsAtPath(localFilePath!) {
        //Read the contents of the file as NSData
        let dataBuffer = fileManager.contentsAtPath(localFilePath!)
```

```
        //Decode from UTF8 NSData back to NSString
        let dataString = NSString(data: dataBuffer!, ↵
            encoding: NSUTF8StringEncoding)

        //Put the decoded string in the text view
        textView.text = dataString as! String
    }
    else {
        showMessage( message: "File does not exist!" )
    }
}
```

This was easy, wasn't it? You now have an app that utilizes NSFileManager to read and write files. There aren't many limits to the contents of files on iOS: you can store text, images, binary blobs, and so on—anything that can be converted to bytes and put into NSData.

## Serializing Objects with NSCoder

One of the types of data you may want to store is the current state of your app: serializing the objects that are in play at a given moment is a convenient way of doing it. The NSCoding protocol form the iOS SDK can help with this: it allows classes to serialize and deserialize themselves into data, which can be stored on the device or transferred across a network.

---

### ACTIONSCRIPT ANALOGY

Adobe's JSON class helps with serializing ActionScript objects into JSON (Java Script Object Notation) format.

---

To try this out we will add a new class to the app we just made and have it conform to the NSCoding protocol. From Xcode's main menu select **File ➤ New ➤ File** and click **Swift file** to add a new file to the project. Name the file UserSettings.swift and click its name in Project navigator to open it. Add the UserSettings class definition from Listing 13-7 to the file. UserSettings will hold some user information: their name, their age, do they like pizza, and a list of school nicknames—never miss an opportunity for embarrassment.

***Listing 13-7.*** UserSettings Class

```
class UserSettings : NSObject, NSCoding {
    var userName : String
    var lovesPizza : Bool
    var age: Int
    var nickNames: [String]

    // Memberwise initializer
    init(userName: String, lovesPizza: Bool, age: Int, nickNames: [String]) {
        self.userName = userName
        self.lovesPizza = lovesPizza
```

```
        self.age = age
        self.nickNames = nickNames
}

//Print all properties of the class to a string
override var description: String {
        return "UserSettings: \(userName), \(lovesPizza), ↵
            \(age), \(nickNames)"
}

// MARK: NSCoding
}
```

You will see that we have defined UserSettings to conform to the NSCoding protocol. For that purpose it will need to implement two methods, initWithCoder and encodeWithCoder, which will be called when we want to serialize or deserialize instances of UserSettings. Let us add their implementations below the // MARK : NSCoding line.

encodeWithCoder takes an instance of NSCoder: this class offers convenience methods for serializing different types of data and their names as key-value pairs. You can see it in use for storing the user's age as an integer, the user's love for pizza as a Bool, and his or her name and the array of nicknames as generic objects. Copy the implementation from Listing 13-8 to the UserSettings file.

***Listing 13-8.*** Serializing of the UserSettings Class

```
func encodeWithCoder(coder: NSCoder) {
    coder.encodeObject(self.userName, forKey: "userName")
    coder.encodeBool(self.lovesPizza, forKey: "lovesPizza")
    coder.encodeInt(Int32(self.age), forKey: "age")
    coder.encodeObject(self.nickNames, forKey: "nickNames")
}
```

The deserialization of UserSettings will be done in an initializer method: it too takes an NSCoder instance as an argument. To read the data back, we will call NSCoder's decodeObjectForKey method. Note that this method returns an NSObject instance, which we will need to convert to the type we expect a given piece of data to be. You can see the implementation of the initializer in Listing 13-9.

***Listing 13-9.*** Deserializing of the UserSettings class

```
required convenience init?(coder decoder: NSCoder) {
    guard let userName = decoder.decodeObjectForKey("userName") as? String ↵
    else {
        return nil
    }

    let lovesPizza = decoder.decodeBoolForKey("lovesPizza");

    let age = decoder.decodeIntegerForKey("age");

    guard let nickNames = decoder.decodeObjectForKey("nickNames") as? ↵
    [String] else {
        return nil
    }
```

```
    self.init(
        userName: userName,
        lovesPizza: lovesPizza,
        age: age,
        nickNames: nickNames
    )
}
```

To test serializing and deserializing UserSettings (see Listing 13-10), let us create an instance of it in the viewDidLoad method of the ViewController class in ViewController.swift. We will store the instance's state in an XML file, called userSettings.xml and located in the app's tmp folder: this utilizes the NSKeyedArchiver class from the iOS SDK: it is a descendant of NSCoder and has convenience methods for storing and retrieving key-value pairs of information.

We will use NSKeyedArchiver for reading back the serialized object, after which we will output what we read into Xcode's console. Note that NSKeyedUnarchiver.unarchiveObjectWithFile: returns an NSObject, which we will need to cast to UserSettings.

*Listing 13-10.* Serializing and Deserializing of a UserSettings Instance

```
override func viewDidLoad() {
    ...
    //The rest of the method's implementation
    ...

    //Create an instance of the UserSettings class
    let userSettings = UserSettings(userName: "Julius Marx",
                                    lovesPizza: true,
                                    age: 32,
                                    nickNames: ["Groucho"])

    //A file path and name where the userSettings state will be stored
    let archivePath = ↵
        (tmpDirPath.URLByAppendingPathComponent("userSettings.xml")).path

    //Archive userSettings to a file
    NSKeyedArchiver.archiveRootObject(userSettings, toFile: archivePath!)

    //Unarchive the user settings from the file
    let unarchivedSettings : UserSettings = ↵
        NSKeyedUnarchiver.unarchiveObjectWithFile(archivePath!) as! UserSettings

    print(unarchivedSettings)
}
```

If you now run the app in debug mode you should see the following string printed in the console output window:

```
Julius Marx, true, 32, ["Groucho"]
```

## Persisting Data with NSUserDefaults

As usual in programming there is more than one way to skin a cat. Each iOS app has its own key-value database for storing simple data such as user preferences. The access to this database is managed by the NSUserDefaults class.

Listing 13-11 shows a modification of the code we added to viewDidLoad in ViewController: instead of writing to an XML file, it persists the state of the UserSettings object into the app's database. We get hold of the database by calling NSUserDefaults.standardUserDefaults and store the data under a key, which we will name my_userSettings. Storing data for a given key is achieved by calling one of the convenience methods: objectForKey, integerForKey, stringForKey, and so on. Reading data back can be done with one of the set*:forKey methods: setObject:forKey, setInteger:forKey, and so forth.

***Listing 13-11.*** Working with the User Defaults Database

```
//Create an instance of the UserSettings class
let userSettings = UserSettings(userName: "Julius Marx",
                                lovesPizza: true,
                                age: 32,
                                nickNames: ["Groucho"])

//Serialize userSettings to NSData constant
let settingsData = NSKeyedArchiver.archivedDataWithRootObject(userSettings)

//Put data in the User Defaults database under the key "my_userSettings"
NSUserDefaults.standardUserDefaults().setObject(settingsData, ↵
        forKey: "my_userSettings")

//Retrieve data from the User Defaults database
//associated with "my_userSettings" key
if let unarchivedData = ↵
    NSUserDefaults.standardUserDefaults().objectForKey("my_userSettings") as? ↵
    NSData {
    let unarchivedSettings = ↵
        NSKeyedUnarchiver.unarchiveObjectWithData(unarchivedData)
    print(unarchivedSettings)
}
```

## Dealing with Larger Data: A Word About CoreData

This chapter will not be complete if we do not mention CoreData. It is an object graph persistence framework, which is so powerful that it deserves a book of its own.

Why and where might you find CoreData useful? If you are working on a massive project with many sources of data and complex class hierarchies, CoreData gives you the ability to model relationships between data entities, manage their life cycles, persist them to XML files, and even do SQL queries on them.

# Working with the Cloud

Storing data in the cloud gives great power to developers. You can have your data available on multiple devices anywhere around the globe without the need to write a single line of server code.

To help developers embrace cloud technology Apple introduced *CloudKit*, a framework that directly interacts with Apple's iCloud servers. CloudKit provides a flexible application programming interface (API) and a dashboard that offers developers access to the data stored on Apple's iCloud servers. Over the next few pages we will discuss the basics of the CloudKit framework and will make a shopping list app that stores its data in the cloud.

---

■ **Note** Using iCloud requires that you enroll in Apple's iOS Development Program (`https://goo.gl/iDkemP`). This is a paid membership program, which you can add to your account on Apple's web site.

---

## CloudKit Basics

Let us first observe how the CloudKit framework is organized by looking at the most important classes for managing data in the cloud. There are several key concepts: *Containers*, *Records*, *Relationships*, and *Assets*. We will introduce each of them in turn, starting with *Containers*.

## Containers—How Data Access Is Organized

The data management and data access in iCloud have a similar feel to how we access data locally on the device in that each application has its own sandbox in the cloud. This sandbox is called a **Container** and contains the data that an app might need to store in the cloud. One significant difference, however, is that, unlike with local storage, several apps can share a storage container in the cloud, as long as they are all associated with the same development account.

Programmatically containers are represented by the CKContainer class, which is part of the CloudKit framework. Every app that uses iCloud has a designated default container object, which you can obtain by calling CKContainer.defaultContainer()(Listing 13-12).

*Listing 13-12.* Obtaining a Reference to the Default Container

```
let container = CKContainer.defaultContainer()
```

Figure 13-2 illustrates the structure of a container. It consists of several databases: a public one and multiple private ones. The public database is application-centric and is available to all users of the app, whereas each private database is associated with only one user and is only accessible to that user.

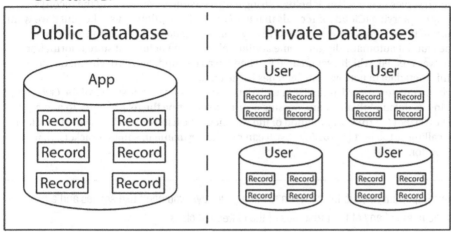

**Figure 13-2.** *CloudKit Container structure*

When an app is installed on a user's device, it can only see and access two databases: the public one and the private database for the user. CKContainer has helper methods, which allow us to talk to each database: publicCloudDatabase and privateCloudDatabase. Each of these methods returns a reference to a CKDatabase object (Listing 13-13).

**Listing 13-13.** Obtaining References to the Public and the Private Database

```
let publicDatabase = container.publicCloudDatabase
let privateDatabase = container.privateCloudDatabase
```

---

■ **Note**    There is a certain amount of data storage and data transfer available for free from Apple; going over that requires a paid subscription plan. As a rule of thumb, data stored in the public database counts toward the application's quota and data stored in the private database counts toward the user's quota. It's a good idea to try to minimize the amount of data you store in the user's private database to avoid forcing users to purchase additional storage space.

---

Be aware that you cannot delete a container. Once a container is created it will stay in iCloud forever, or at least until Apple decides to change how its cloud works. In other words, do not run around and create new containers without a good reason.

Next we will have a look at how data is represented inside a container's database.

## Records—How Data Is Represented

Data in the CloudKit databases is organized as records. A record is very similar to a key-value pair, where the value can take a variety of types: number, array, date, and time; location; binary blob; and many more. The key part of the pair is of type String, which consists of alphanumeric characters and starts with a letter.

The class that helps you work with records is called CKRecord. CKRecord instances have a property, called recordType, which serves as metadata: it holds a string with a custom description of the record's data. This gives us a way of querying iCloud for records that match this description. This is helpful if we want to query iCloud for certain record types only. You can give any valid string name as a record type. When a record is created in the cloud it automatically gets some additional metadata fields that store information about when the record was created, which user created it, when it was last updated, and who made the update. You can use this metadata to narrow your searches in the database.

Let us see how we can create a record and fill it in with data Listing 13-14). An instance of the CKRecord class is created by calling its default initializer and passing a string to describe the record type. To add a key-value pair we call the setObject(_:forKey:) method of the instance. The listing also shows you a shortcut alternative: instead of calling setObject(_:forKey:) you can put the key name in square brackets, [], and use the assignment operator.

---

■ **Note**   There are two important rules to follow when naming your keys: you can't use spaces and a key name must not match the name of any of the properties of the CKRecord class.

---

*Listing 13-14.* Creating a CKRecord Instance and Populating It with Data

```
let record = CKRecord(recordType: "Person")
record.setObject("Julius Marx", forKey: "name")
record["age"] = 30
record["nickname"] = "Groucho"
```

Each record has a unique ID, which is automatically assigned to it by the CloudKit framework at the time of initialization. You can set an ID yourself by using the initWithRecordType:recordID: initializer of the CKRecord class. When a record is received by the iCloud server its ID gets checked for uniqueness and if it is not unique the server throws an error.

Records can be organized in groups, called *zones*, which are represented by the CKRecordZone class. Every container has a default zone, which is used if you don't explicitly define one. Grouping records lets you define custom business logic and perform transactional operations on records in a zone. We won't use zones in this tutorial, but it's good to be aware of them, as they can be invaluable when it comes to segmenting big data.

# Defining Relationships Between Records

Imagine we have to create a music player application that will help users play their favorite songs of their favorite bands. We can design the underlying data model as records, which will represent a band, an album, or a song. In other words, each CKRecord in our model will have its recordType set to Bands, Albums, or Songs. If we had the record for a song, it would be useful to be able to work out what album it was released on and which band recorded it. To do that we will need to set relationships between the song, album, and band records.

In CloudKit relationships between records are managed by instances of the CKReference class. A CKReference object creates a many-to-one relationship between records in CloudKit's database. Records that refer to another record, which we will call the *target record*, need to contain a reference object, which in turn contains information about the target. Both the target and the referring records need to be in the same zone of the same database.

Listing 13-15 illustrates how references between records are created, using the example from the start of this section: we see how to create references from a song record to its respective band and album records.

***Listing 13-15.*** Creating a Reference Between Two CKRecords

```
let band = CKRecord(recordType: "Bands")
band["name"] = "Scorpions"

let album = CKRecord(recordType: "Albums")
album["name"] = "Crazy World"

let song = CKRecord(recordType: "Songs")
song["name"] = "Wind of Change"

let referenceBand = CKReference(recordID: band.recordID, ↩
    action: .DeleteSelf)
let referenceAlbum = CKReference(recordID: album.recordID, ↩
    action: .DeleteSelf)

song["inAlbum"] = referenceAlbum
song["byBand"] = referenceBand
```

You probably noticed a parameter called `action`, which we set when initializing `CKReference`. This is a property of the `CKReference` class, which defines what action needs to be taken when the target of the reference is deleted. We can choose between these two:

- `CKReferenceActionDeleteSelf`—deleting the target record deletes any records that contain that reference in one of their fields.

- `CKReferenceActionNone`—no action is taken.

## Assets—Storing Unstructured Data

Storing strings and numbers in the cloud is good, but how do we go about storing a large document like an image or a video file? To create such a record in the database, its value needs to be of type `CKAsset`. This class represents data stored in, typically, large files.

Listing 13-16 builds on the band-album example we used earlier and stores the album cover as an asset.

***Listing 13-16.*** Creating an Asset from an Image File

```
let albumCoverAsset = CKAsset(fileURL: coverImageURL)
album["coverImageAsset"] = albumCoverAsset
```

---

■ **Note** Even though we initialized the `CKAsset` class with a URL (uniform resource file) to a file, the URL itself is not stored in the cloud. Only the asset's data gets uploaded to the cloud.

---

## Saving and Deleting Records from the Cloud

CKRecord instances live in the application's memory and get deleted when the app closes. To persist a record to iCloud, we need to ask the database to which it belongs to save it on the server. For that purpose CKDatabase has a convenience method, called saveRecord(_:completionHandler:). Have a look at Listing 13-17 for how to use it. saveRecord's first argument is the record we want to persist and its second argument is a callback, also known as completion handler, which will be executed when the saving operation finishes. The callback's signature is (CKRecord?, NSError?): in it we get passed the record we tried to persist and an error object, which is set to nil if the saving was successful or contains information on what went wrong otherwise.

*Listing 13-17.* Save a CKRecord in the Server's Database

```
let privateDatabase = CKContainer.defaultContainer().privateCloudDatabase
let band = CKRecord(recordType: "Bands")
band["name"] = "Scorpions"

privateDatabase.saveRecord(band) { (record, error) -> Void in
    //Handle success or error response from the server
}
```

saveRecord(_:completionHandler:) is used for updating existing records in the database, as well as for persisting them for the first time.

To delete a record from the server we call CKDatabase's deleteRecordWithID(_:completionHandler:) method, which looks very similar to the method we used for saving: we pass in the record we want to delete and a callback function as arguments. The callback gets executed when the deletion is complete; it receives a reference to the record that we tried to delete and optional error information. We can see this in Listing 13-18.

*Listing 13-18.* Deleting a Record from the Cloud

```
privateDatabase.deleteRecordWithID(band.recordID) ↵
    {(recordID, error) -> Void in }
```

Note that saving and deleting are performed asynchronously over the network. As it is not in our control how long a response from the server may take, it is usually a good idea to notify the user with an activity indicator that a potentially lengthy operation is taking place.

## Retrieving Records from the Cloud

To get records from the cloud we need to perform a query, using CKQuery—another helper class from the CloudKit framework. Initializing a CKQuery instance takes the already familiar recordType and an instance of NSPredicate. NSPredicate is a powerful class that helps us specify how data should be retrieved from the database. It has its own query language, similar to using the WHERE clause in the structured query language (SQL) for those of you familiar with SQL.

Apart from narrowing down and filtering the data we fetch from the database, we can have the retrieved records sorted, using CKQuery's property sortDescriptors, which is an array of NSSortDescriptor objects.

Performing a query on the server is an asynchronous operation and, like the rest of the server-side calls we have made so far, requires that we implement a completion handler function that will be called once the query returns a result. We pass this completion handler to CKDatabase's performQuery(_:inZoneWithID:completionHandler:) method.

In Listing 13-19 you can see an example of a query that retrieves all records of type Bands from the server and sorts them by their name in ascending order. The result comes as an array of CKRecord objects, which is the first parameter of the completion handler closure we pass to privateDatabase.performQuery.

***Listing 13-19.*** Retrieve a List of Records from the Server

```
let fetchQuery  = CKQuery(recordType: "Bands", ↵
                         predicate: NSPredicate(format: "TRUEPREDICATE"))

fetchQuery.sortDescriptors = [ NSSortDescriptor(key: "name", ↵
                                ascending: true) ]

privateDatabase.performQuery(fetchQuery, inZoneWithID: nil) { ↵
                            (records, error) -> Void in }
```

## Common Error Messages

As you can see, all network operations we have done so far return their results in callback functions, which take optional NSError parameters. It's a good idea always to check if the error passed to the callback is nil and if it isn't, to inspect its error code. You can find a complete list of error codes in the definition of CKErrorCode. Following are some of the most common ones with suggestions about how to deal with them:

- **.BadContainer** or **.MissingEntitlement**. Check if you have specified a container in the iCloud entitlements section of your app matching the CKContainer object. Make sure that the container exists on the CloudKit Dashboard web site.

- **.NotAuthenticated** or **.PermissionFailure**. You might not have entered your iCloud credentials in the settings of your device yet. Go to device Settings > iCloud and see if an account has been assigned. Another reason to get one of these errors could be that iCloud is disabled on the device. Enable it in **Settings ➤ iCloud**.

- **.UnknownItem**. This usually means that you have requested a record type that doesn't exist on the server. Make sure you haven't made a typo when specifying the string for recordType and check the CloudKit Dashboard web site to make sure the string matches the records that are there.

I keep mentioning the CloudKit Dashboard but haven't told you what it is yet. This is a web-based admin panel that helps you manage data on the iCloud server. The rest of this chapter provides a more in-depth look at it.

## Building a CloudKit-Powered Application

At this point you should be familiar with the basic concepts in the CloudKit framework. Now let us put all of them into practice by building an app.

The app will maintain a simple shopping list, which the user will create by adding or deleting items from it. The app will persist this shopping list to the user's iCloud private account and will take care of synchronizing the user's local copy with the one in the cloud. When the app is run for the first time, it will be the user who creates the shopping list. After that, every time we start the application, it will retrieve the list stored on the server and show it to the user for modification.

I have divided the app implementation into three parts:

- **Setup**: we will set up the prerequisites necessary to enable an app to work with iCloud;

- **Data management**: this will require us to write some code for communicating with the iCloud;

- **User interface**: we will see how we can present data to the user.

---

■ **Note**    To be able to test the code in this tutorial you will need an Apple ID that's a member of the iOS Development Program.

---

## Preparation: Setting Up the App

First things first. Before we start coding, we need to perform several mandatory steps to enable CloudKit in our application.

Start by creating a new Single View Application project in Xcode and name it CloudKitDemo. Select the project in the *Project Navigator* and select the app from the list of targets. Open the General tab and set Team to the correct iOS development account (Figure 13-3).

***Figure 13-3.*** *Select an account in Team: it will need to be a member of Apple's iOS Development Program*

Next, open the Capabilities tab and find the iCloud setting. Toggle the switch to enable iCloud (Figure 13-4). This will add all the necessary entitlements to your application. It may take a few minutes for Xcode to create an app ID and authorize it to use iCloud. Note that this step will generate an error if the team/Apple ID you selected in the previous step is not a member of Apple's iOS Development Program.

***Figure 13-4.*** *Enable iCloud usage for the app target*

Tick the Key-value storage and CloudKit checkboxes (Figure 13-5). In this tutorial we will not share database containers with other apps, so leave the Use default container option checked.

***Figure 13-5.*** *The applciation's iCloud settings*

At the bottom of the settings you will see a button that says CloudKit Dashboard. Click it to go to the CloudKit Dashboard admin web page—it will load in a browser. Log in with your Apple ID.

---

■ **Note**    If your Apple ID is a member of multiple teams, you will need to first make sure that you are already logged into developer.apple.com and have chosen the right team. Otherwise you will see an error indicating that nothing has been set up yet.

---

## CloudKit Dashboard—Registering Record Type

The *CloudKit Dashboard* is the place where you can administer the app's back end in the cloud. It lets you manage database containers, zones, and record types; monitor data usage and data traffic; and get information about users.

Before we can store and fetch records from iCloud we need to create a new Record Type. Open the *CloudKit Dashboard* page and select *Record Type*s from the menu on the left as shown on Figure 13-6. Create a new record type by clicking the + button at the top of the page. Name the new record type ShoppingItem. Next you need to add fields to the record and specify their data type. Let us add a field of type String and name it "name." Finally, click the Save button at the bottom of the page to persist the changes.

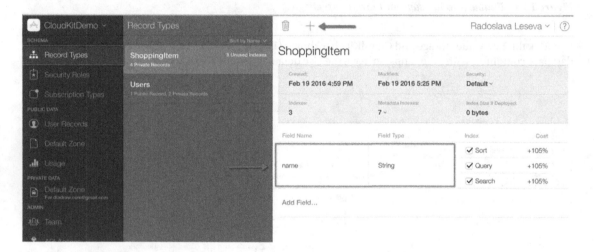

***Figure 13-6.*** *Create a new Record Type*

## Linking the Device with an iCloud Account

For our users to be able to use this application they should be logged in with their iCloud account on the device. You have to do the same in order to test the app whether on a device or in a simulator.

On your iOS device open **Settings ➤ iCloud** and make sure iCloud Drive is turned on (Figure 13-7). Then, if the account field is empty, fill in your or your Apple ID credentials to log in to iCloud.

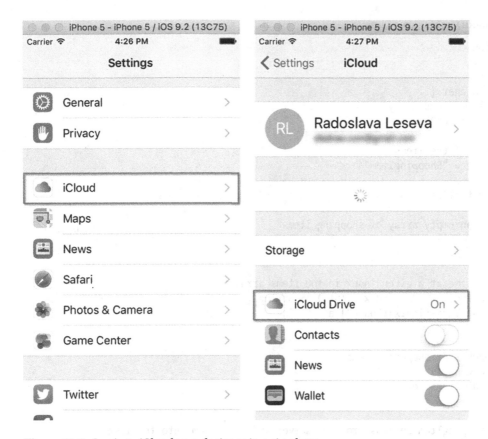

**Figure 13-7.** *Log in to iCloud on a device or in a simulator*

## Using the CloudKit Framework: Making a Cloud Data Manager

With the project and the new record type set up, it is time to start coding with the CloudKit framework. For clarity we will split the application's code into two layers. One layer will manage shopping list items and will communicate with the iCloud back end and other layer will take care of the user interface.

In this section we will create a class which will be responsible for

- storing all shopping list items and providing access to their names.

- adding an item to the list and sending it to the cloud.

- deleting an item from the list and syncing with the cloud.

- notifying the UI of the application whenever a response from the server arrives.

From Xcode's main menu select **File ➤ New ➤ File** and click **Swift fil**e to add a new source code file to the project. Name the file `CloudDataManager.swift` and click on its name in Project navigator to open it. Listing 13-20 shows the `CloudDataManager` class definition with all the methods stubbed out. We will add functionality to them in a minute. Note that in order to use CloudKit's API, we need to import the CloudKit framework at the top of the file.

*Listing 13-20.* CloudDataManager Class

```
import Foundation
import CloudKit

class CloudDataManager {
    //Shopping list items array
    var dataItems : [CKRecord]

    //Record Type of the items
    let recordType = "ShoppingItem"

    //Default initializer
    init() {
        //Create an empty array of shopping items
        dataItems = []
    }

    //Get item's name at a given index in the items array
    func getItemName( atIndex index : Int ) -> String {
        return dataItems[index]["name"] as! String
    }

    //Get the number of shopping items
    func getItemsCount() -> Int {
        return dataItems.count
    }

    //Get all ShoppingItem records from the server and load them into the list
    func fetchCloudItems( callback callback: (NSError?) -> Void ) {
        //Code of the method goes here
    }

    //Add a new shopping item to the list and sync with iCloud
    func addItem( itemName item : String, callback: (NSError?) -> Void ) {
        //Code of the method goes here
    }

    //Remove an existing shopping item from the list and sync with iCloud
    func removeItem( atIndex index : Int, callback: (NSError?) -> Void) {
        //Code of the method goes here
    }
}
```

In this class dataItems property is an array that stores the local cache for the shopping list items. There are two sets of methods in the class. The first set includes getItemName(:atIndex) and getItemsCount(), which act as a façade for dataItems. They are used to query the local cache and do not perform any network operations, so they are fast and synchronous.

The next three methods, `fetchCloudItems(:callback)`, `addItem(:itemName:callback)`, and `removeItem(:atIndex:callback)` perform asynchronous network operations and are potentially slow. Because of this, each of the methods takes a callback function as an argument, which is executed when the respective network operation is complete. We will later implement these callbacks to update the app's user interface.

We have the skeleton of the `CloudDataManager` class. Let us now focus on implementing its logic in each of the methods' stubs (Listing 13-21).

We will start with `fetchCloudItems(:callback)`. This method is called when the app launches: its purpose is to get all previously entered shopping items from the server if there are any. For that purpose we will create a query for retrieving all records of type `ShoppingItem`: this will be done with the help of an `NSPredicate` instance. In Listing 13-21 we set the `NSPredicate`'s filter to `TRUEPREDICATE`, which means "iterate through all records and fetch each one." The next step is to get the records sorted. Sorting will be performed on the records' "name" field in ascending order. The result of the query is returned in the `records` argument of the completion handler, implemented as a closure in this case.

---

■ **Note**    For details on how closures work in Swift, see Chapter 22.

---

In the completion handler we are going to update the local cache and signal the UI to show the updated shopping list. The logic of the code inside the closure is fairly simple: if the result contains any records, they are copied into the local list of items. Finally, the code calls the `callback` argument to communicate the changes with the UI. This is a pattern we will follow when implementing the rest of the methods that involve waiting for a response from the server.

*Listing 13-21.* Implementation of fetchCloudItems Method

```
func fetchCloudItems( callback callback: (NSError?) -> Void ) {
    //Get a reference of the user's iCloud database
    let privateDatabase = CKContainer.defaultContainer().privateCloudDatabase

    //Construct a query to get all the records of type "ShoppingItem"
    let fetchQuery  = CKQuery(recordType: self.recordType, ↵
                    predicate: NSPredicate(format: "TRUEPREDICATE"))

    //Sort fetched records by their name in ascending order
    fetchQuery.sortDescriptors = [ NSSortDescriptor(key: "name", ↵
                                    ascending: true) ]

    //Send the query to iCloud
    privateDatabase.performQuery(fetchQuery, inZoneWithID: nil) { ↵
        (records, error) -> Void in
        //Move the result records into the dataItems array
        if records!.count > 0 {
            for record in records! {
                self.dataItems.append( record )
            }
        }

        //Tell the UI to update itself
        callback(error)
    }
}
```

Next to implement is the addItem(:itemName:callback) method (Listing 13-22). This method is called every time the user adds an item to the shopping list and a new CKRecord instance needs to be created for it. Once this is done the new record is persisted to the cloud by the saveRecord call. We only add the new record to the local cache if saving it to the server was successful—we are notified about this in the completion handler we supply to saveRecord.

**Listing 13-22.** Implementation of addItem Method

```
func addItem( itemName item : String, callback: (NSError?) -> Void ) {
    //Get a reference of the user's iCloud database
    let privateDatabase = CKContainer.defaultContainer().privateCloudDatabase

    //Create a record of of type "ShoppingItem" and set its name
    let localRecord = CKRecord(recordType: self.recordType)
    localRecord["name"] = item

    //Ask iCloud to store the record
    privateDatabase.saveRecord(localRecord) { (record, error) -> Void in
        //If the response is ok add this record to the local list
        if let record = record {
            self.dataItems.append( record )
        }

        //Tell the UI to update itself
        callback( error )
    }
}
```

We will complete the CloudDataManager class with the implementation of the removeItem(:atIndex:callback) method (Listing 13-23). We ask the server to delete a record by calling deleteRecordWithID and passing the record's unique ID, which we can work out from the record's recordID property. The completion handler we supply follows a familiar pattern: if the deletion is successful, the local cache is updated and changes are reflected in the user interface.

**Listing 13-23.** Implementation of removeItemAtIndex Method

```
func removeItem( atIndex index : Int, callback: (NSError?) -> Void) {
    //Get a reference of the user's iCloud database
    let privateDatabase = CKContainer.defaultContainer().privateCloudDatabase

    //Get a record by its index in the local list
    let record = dataItems[ index ]

    privateDatabase.deleteRecordWithID(record.recordID) { ↩
      (recordID, error) -> Void in
        //Get the local index of the record that should be removed
        let recordIndex = self.dataItems.indexOf(record)
        //Remove the underlying record
        self.dataItems.removeAtIndex(recordIndex!)
```

```
        //Tell the UI to update itself
        callback( error )
    }
}
```

## Preparing the User Interface

We will use a Table View component to display the shopping list on the screen and two buttons that will let the user add and delete items.

In Xcode open the `Main.storyboard` file and make it look like the screenshot in Figure 13-8: first find a Navigation bar component in the Object library and drag it to the top of the scene. Then drag two Bar Button item components on top of it—place one on the left and one on the right. Select the left button and in the Attributes inspector select Edit from the System Item drop-down. This will change the caption of the button to **Edit**. Set System Item for the right button to **Add** and its caption will change into a big plus sign. These two buttons will let the user add and delete items from the list.

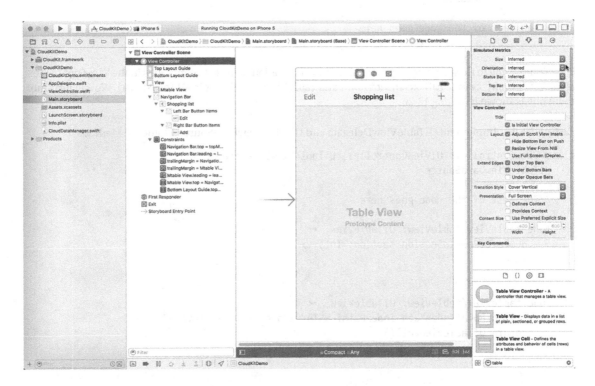

***Figure 13-8.*** *CloudKitDemo application user interface*

To finish building the UI drag and drop a Table view component under the Navigation and add constraints to it to take the remaining portion of the screen. Create a prototype cell and set its Identifier property to `ShoppingItemCell`.

---

■ **Note**    For more info about table views, prototype cells, cell reusing, and identifiers, see Chapter 6.

---

Drag the table view into the definition of the ViewController class in ViewController.swift to create an outlet. Name the outlet tableView (Listing 13-24).

***Listing 13-24.*** Create an Outlet for the Table View

```
@IBOutlet weak var tableView: UITableView!
```

## Creating Table View Data Source and Delegate

The table view needs to get its data from an object that conforms to the UITableViewDataSource protocol. To keep things simple, we will make the ViewController class our data source. To talk to the table view, we will also make it conform to the UITableViewDelegate protocol (Listing 13-25).

***Listing 13-25.*** Conform to UITableViewDelegate and UITableViewDataSource Protocols

```
class ViewController: UIViewController, UITableViewDelegate, ↩
    UITableViewDataSource {

    //The rest of the code goes here
}
```

Conforming to these two protocols requires implementation of these two methods in the ViewController class: tableView(_:numberOfRowsInSection:) and tableView(_:cellForRowAtIndexPath). We will just stub them out as shown in Listing 13-26.

***Listing 13-26.*** Implement UITableViewDelegate and UITableViewDataSource Protocols' Methods

```
class ViewController: UIViewController, UITableViewDelegate, ↩
    UITableViewDataSource {

    //The rest of the code goes here

    func tableView(tableView: UITableView, ↩
        numberOfRowsInSection section: Int) -> Int {
        return 0
    }

    func tableView(tableView: UITableView, ↩
        cellForRowAtIndexPath indexPath: NSIndexPath) -> UITableViewCell {
        return UITableViewCell()
    }
}
```

## Populating the Table View with Data

We are finally ready to fill the table view with data. First we need an instance of the CloudDataManager class, which will provide shopping items data: we will make this a property of the ViewController class, called cloudDataManager. The next step is to set the table view's data source and delegate properties to the ViewController class instance. We will do this in the viewDidLoad() method of ViewController (Listing 13-27).

*Listing 13-27.* Instantiate CloudDataManager and Fetch Shopping Items from the Server

```
class ViewController: UIViewController, UITableViewDelegate, ↵
    UITableViewDataSource {

    //Reference to the table view
    @IBOutlet weak var tableView: UITableView!

    //A reference to the data manager class
    let cloudDataManager = CloudDataManager()

    override func viewDidLoad() {
        super.viewDidLoad()

        //Set table view datasource and delegate
        tableView.delegate = self
        tableView.dataSource = self

        //Get all shopping list items from the server
        cloudDataManager.fetchCloudItems( callback: dataChanged )
    }

    //The rest of the code goes here
}
```

There is a method called dataChanged, which we haven't implemented yet. This method will be used as a callback for the CloudDataManager methods and will notify the UI to update itself when there is a response from the server.

Its implementation is pretty straightforward: if there was an error, we will print out information about in Xcode's console; otherwise we will update the table view (Listing 13-28). In iOS we are allowed to access the UI only on the main thread and we need do make sure the all related calls happen there. To execute a code block on the main thread we wrap it in a dispatch_async(dispatch_get_main_queue(),{() -> Void}) call. This function tells iOS to execute the code block nested inside on a specific thread of the app. dispatch_get_main_queue makes sure that the chosen thread is the main one.

*Listing 13-28.* Update the Table View Using a Callback Method

```
func dataChanged( error : NSError? ) {
    if let error = error {
        //If there is an error message print it in the console
        print(error)
    }
    else {
        //When there is a response do the logic in the main thread
        dispatch_async(dispatch_get_main_queue(), { å
          [weak self] () -> Void in
            //Refresh data in the table view
            self!.tableView.reloadData();
        })
    }
}
```

---

■ **Note**    There are a couple of interesting things to note in the code in Listing 13-28. First, we make a call to `dispatch_async`, which causes code to be executed on a particular queue. The code we pass will update the UI, so we select the main queue. We covered queues in Chapter 7—have another look if you need a reminder. The block of code that we want executed on the main queue is passed in as the second parameter to `dispatch_async` in the form of a closure—you can see it wrapped in curly brackets. Chapter 22 presents closures in detail. The last thing that may look strange at first is the reference to `[weak self]`, where `self` refers to the current instance of `ViewController`. As controversial as this looks, it is not a judgment on our class's character but has to do with memory management. As closures are independent objects, they retain strong references; that is, they obtain ownership of the objects they reference. To prevent that, we mark the reference as `weak`. You can read more on weak references and memory management in Chapter 21

---

Now let us populate the shopping items in the table view. First we need to provide the number of items so the table can ask the data source to construct the appropriate number of rows in the table. The number of rows is set in the `tableView(_:numberOfRowsInSection:)` method (Listing 13-29).

***Listing 13-29.*** Set Table View Rows Number

```
func tableView(tableView: UITableView, ↩
    numberOfRowsInSection section: Int) -> Int
{
    //Return shopping items number
    return cloudDataManager.getItemsCount()
}
```

The `tableView(_:cellForRowAtIndexPath:)` call gives us access to update a single cell in the table: we will fill in the new cells with the names of the items in the shopping list, as shown in Listing 13-30.

***Listing 13-30.*** Create a Cell and Set Its Label

```
func tableView(tableView: UITableView, ↩
    cellForRowAtIndexPath indexPath: NSIndexPath) -> UITableViewCell {
    //Create a new table cell for the row
    let cell = tableView.dequeueReusableCellWithIdentifier( ↩
                            "ShoppingItemCell", forIndexPath: indexPath)

    //Set the cell's label to be the name of the corresponding shopping item
    cell.textLabel?.text = cloudDataManager.getItemName( ↩
                                    atIndex: indexPath.row)

    return cell
}
```

Run the app and you will see an empty table (Figure 13-9). In the next section we will implement how items are added, so we can create our first shopping list.

*Figure 13-9.* *Empty table view*

## Adding New Items

Open Main.storyboard and ViewController.swift in the Assistant editor and create an Action handler for the plus button. Name this Action didTapAdd (Listing 13-31).

*Listing 13-31.* Add an Action Handler for Adding New Items

```
@IBAction func didTapAdd(sender: UIBarButtonItem) {
}
```

We will show an alert dialog to the user to type the new item's name. Listing 13-32 shows you how to create an alert dialog with a text field and two buttons: **Cancel** and **Add**.

*Listing 13-32.* Add Item Dialog Implementation

```
@IBAction func didTapAdd(sender: UIBarButtonItem) {
    //Create an allert controller dialog for adding new item
    let alertController = UIAlertController(title: "New Item", ↵
        message: "Tap in new item", preferredStyle: UIAlertControllerStyle.Alert)

    //Add a text field component to the dialog
    alertController.addTextFieldWithConfigurationHandler { ↵
        (UITextField) -> Void in }

    //Add a Cancel button to dismiss the dialog
    alertController.addAction(UIAlertAction(title: "Cancel", ↵
    style: UIAlertActionStyle.Default, handler: { ↵
        (action : UIAlertAction) -> Void in
    }))

    //Add an Add button to add new item
    alertController.addAction(UIAlertAction(title: "Add", ↵
    style: UIAlertActionStyle.Default, handler: { ↵
        (action : UIAlertAction) -> Void in

        //Get the item's name from dialog's text field
        let itemName = (alertController.textFields![0] as UITextField).text

        //Ask data manager to create new shopping item with the given name
        self.cloudDataManager.addItem( itemName: itemName!, ↵
            callback: self.dataChanged)
    }))

    //Show this dialog on the screen
    self.presentViewController(alertController, animated: true, ↵
        completion: nil)
}
```

Run the application and tap the + button. You should see the dialog prompting you to create a new item (Figure 13-10).

***Figure 13-10.*** *Add new item dialog*

## Deleting Items from the Table View

While adding a new item required us to write only one new method, deleting an item will require more work. We will add several new methods, but they will all be one-liners, I promise.

First create an Action handler for the Edit button in `ViewController.swift`. Name the Action `didTapEdit`. Inside this method we will toggle the `tableView.editing` property to `true` or `false` (Listing 13-33). Changing this property notifies the table that we want to edit its rows and causes each row to show a delete button.

***Listing 13-33.*** Edit Button Action

```
@IBAction func didTapEdit(sender: UIBarButtonItem) {
    //Toggle table view edit mode
    tableView.editing = !tableView.editing
}
```

When the table view is in edit mode it will ask the data source to verify if a given row can be edited. This would require implementing a method called `UITableViewDataSource tableView(_:canEditRowAtIndexPath)`. Since all of our shopping items can be deleted we will always return `true` (Listing 13-34).

***Listing 13-34.*** A Method That Checks If a Given Row in the Table Can Be Edited

```
func tableView(tableView: UITableView, ↵
    canEditRowAtIndexPath indexPath: NSIndexPath) -> Bool {

    //We can edit all the rows
    return true
}
```

When the user taps the delete button next to a row, the table view asks the data source to commit the deletion of the row. This is done inside the tableView(_: commitEditingStyle: forRowAtIndexPath) method (Listing 13-35). This method is used for committing any editing operations, so before proceeding further we will need to make sure that we are committing a deletion: the value of the editingStyle argument needs to be .Delete. Finally, we ask cloudDataManager to delete the corresponding shopping item.

***Listing 13-35.*** A Method for Deleting a Row

```
func tableView(tableView: UITableView, ↵
    commitEditingStyle editingStyle: UITableViewCellEditingStyle, ↵
        forRowAtIndexPath indexPath: NSIndexPath) {

    if UITableViewCellEditingStyle.Delete == editingStyle {
        //Ask the data manager to delete the coresponding shopping item
        cloudDataManager.removeItem( atIndex: indexPath.row, ↵
            callback: dataChanged)
    }
}
```

The app is now complete. Run it, tap Edit, and delete a row to see it vanish from the table view and from the iCloud servers (Figure 13-11).

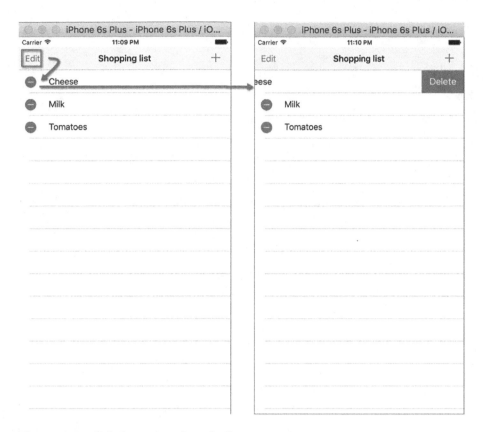

***Figure 13-11.*** *Deleting an item from the list*

# Summary

This chapter gave you the tools for working with files on the local device as well as storing and retrieving data from Apple's iCloud service. You saw a few different ways to persist data: as a binary blob, via serialization, and even via using the application's settings database.

With this knowledge we are ready to head off to the land of networking operations. See you there.

# CHAPTER 14

■ ■ ■

# Networking

Today most mobile applications are part of an ecosystem of different channels for presenting information to the user. Whether you are reading your e-mail or checking the weather forecast in a web browser, in a desktop client, or in a mobile app all the information and devices are connected via the invisible meta-space called Internet. In this chapter we will focus on how to connect to and retrieve information from a web service and load it into your app.

In this chapter you will do the following:

- Learn how to request and retrieve data from a web service.

- Learn how to create a network session and initiate a download task.

- Learn how to work with JSON (Java Script Object Notation) and how to convert it to Swift objects.

- Learn how to download an image from a URL (uniform resource locator) and how to display the image in a table view.

- Build an app that does all of the above.

When you are done, you will have an app that gets a weather forecast for a chosen place around the world. The forecast will be retrieved from an open online weather service using the network communication capabilities of iOS.

## Setting Up the App and Designing the UI

The app we are about to develop will let the user read the weather forecast for any known city around the world. The app will present the information as a five-day forecast, and the data for each day will be sampled every three hours. It will include the expected temperature and an icon to depict the weather conditions.

Start by creating a Single View iOS Application project (**File ➤ New ➤ Project...**, then **iOS ➤ Application ➤ Single View Application**) and naming it WeatherApp. We will design the user interface (UI) of the application as part of the setup, so we can focus on code in the rest of the chapter.

Figure 14-1 shows you what the UI will look like: on the left there is a mock-up with the UI elements you will need to place in the view on the storyboard and on the right is a screenshot of the storyboard with the elements already positioned on it.

© Radoslava Leseva Adams and Hristo Lesev 2016

R. L. Adams and H. Lesev, *Migrating to Swift from Flash and ActionScript*,

DOI 10.1007/978-1-4842-1666-8_14

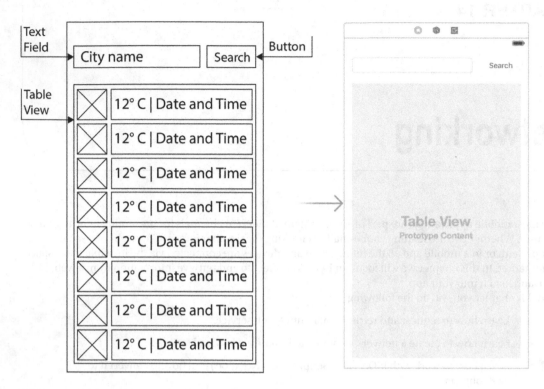

*Figure 14-1.* *The app's user interface*

As you can see in Figure 14-1, at the top of the screen there is a text field, which will be used to input the name of the city, for which we want to see a forecast, and a button to start a data search for it. The forecast results will be displayed in a table view, where each row will contain a piece of forecast information: the expected temperature, the day and the time, and an image that represents the weather conditions.

Open Main.storyboard and arrange the UI as shown in Figure 14-1 by adding a text field, a button, and a table view. Do not forget to add constraints, so that the app adapts its look to whatever device it runs on. If you need a reminder for how to set constraints and make adaptive UI, have a look at **Chapter 5**.

Next, open ViewController.swift and create two outlets, one for the city text field and another for the table view. Then create an action for the Search button's Touch Up Inside event. (See **Chapter 2** for how to create outlets and actions.) Your code should look like that in Listing 14-1.

*Listing 14-1.* Adding an Outlet and an Action to the ViewController Class

```swift
import UIKit

class ViewController: UIViewController {

    @IBOutlet weak var cityTextField: UITextField!
    @IBOutlet weak var tableView: UITableView!

    //The rest of the code goes here

    @IBAction func searchForCity(sender: AnyObject) {
    }

}
```

Next we will set up the app to connect to a web service. With iOS 9, Apple introduced a feature called App Transport Security (ATS). It forces apps to use the more secure HTTPS protocol by blocking less secure connections that use HTTP. This, on the one hand, is great, as it improves the security and privacy for your users' data. If you have control at the server end, you can help your app support ATS by setting up the server to use Secure Sockets Layer (SSL). This enables it to send and receive encrypted information. On the other hand, if your app needs to connect to a third-party service, which may or may not support SSL, you may want to bypass ATS.

To do this, open project's `Info.plist` file and add new key with name **App Transport Security Settings**, then add a subkey named **Allow Arbitrary Loads** and set its value to YES (Figure 14-2). This instructs the app to allow any network connections, including insecure ones.

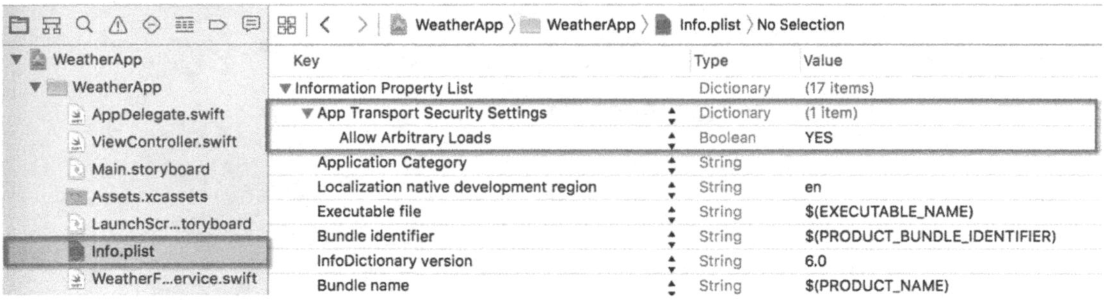

*Figure 14-2.* *Disable App Transport Security*

Note that ATS also allows you to configure behavior for individual domains and only allow non-SSL communications for certain ones (see `https://goo.gl/neuUz9` for more details).

With the app set up, let us have a look at the weather web service, which we will query for data.

# The Weather Forecast Web Service

The app will get its data from a public weather web service. There are a few of these available on the Internet. For this tutorial we will use OpenWeatherMap. We chose it because it

- has a free account option.

- offers plain and simple URL structure.

- returns data in JSON format.

- has an easy authorization policy: it uses only an application programming interface (API) key at the end of each request.

Before we can use OpenWeatherMap we have to create an account. Every account is given a unique application programming interface (API) key, which is used to authorize any apps you create that send queries to the server.

To create your free account open your favorite web browser and navigate to this URL: `https://home.openweathermap.org/users/sign_up`. The web site will ask you to enter a username, an e-mail address, and a password (Figure 14-3).

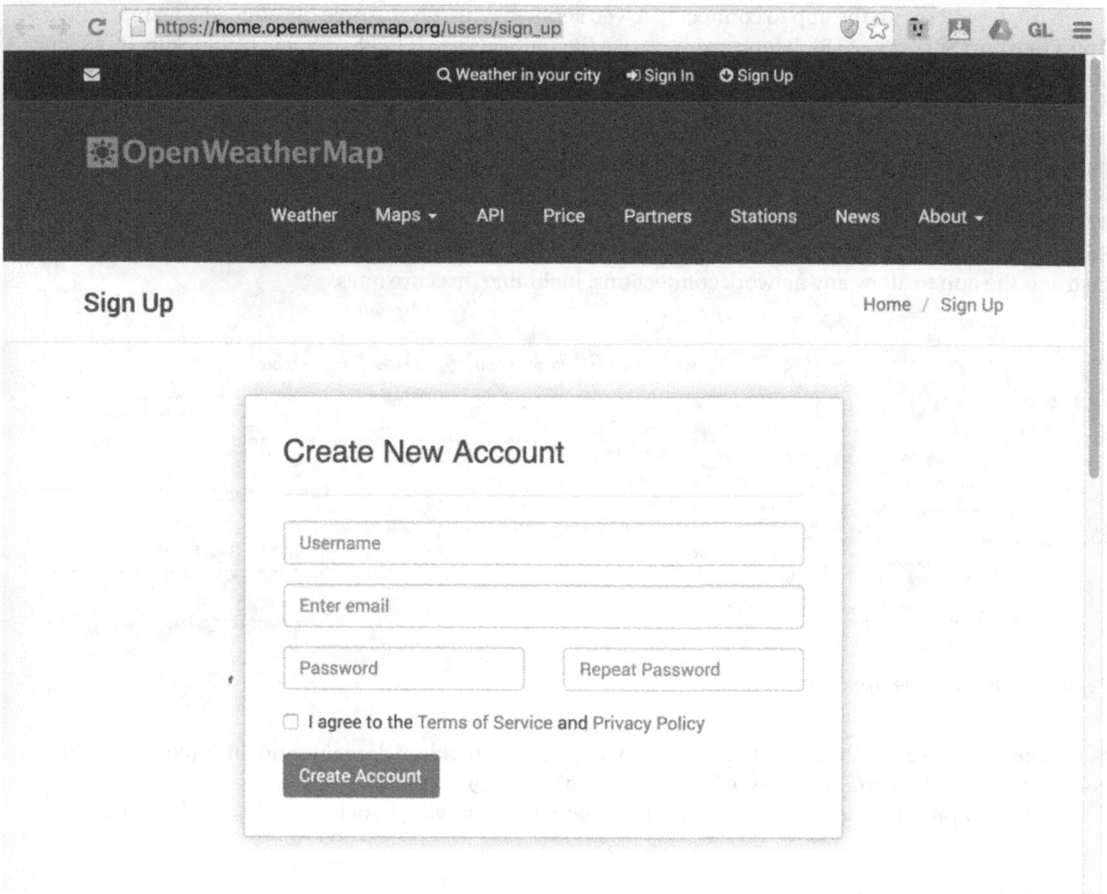

**Figure 14-3.** *OpenWeatherMap's account registration page*

Once your account has been created, you will be redirected to the account settings page. Here you can copy your API key (Figure 14-4). We will use the key later for authorizing the app's requests to the web service.

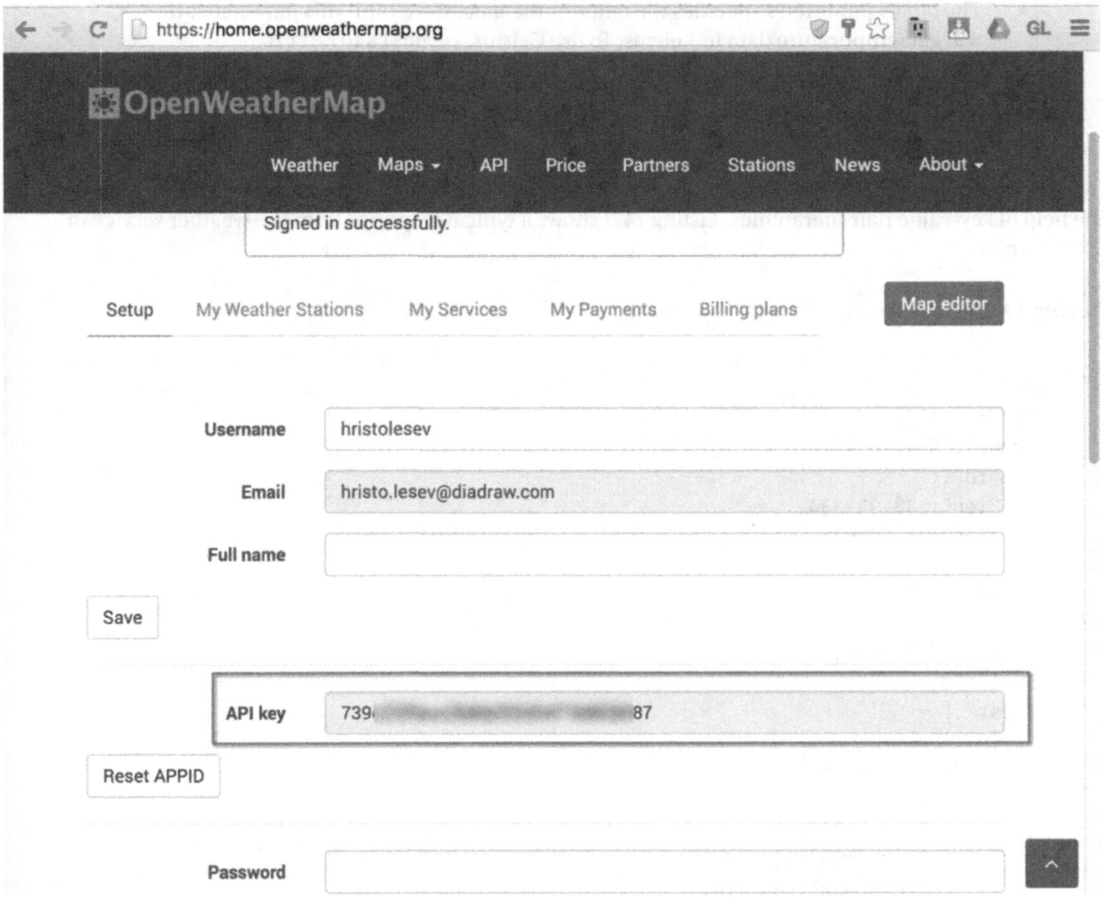

***Figure 14-4.*** *Get an OpenWeatherMap API key*

OpenWeatherMap offers an API that you can explore if you navigate to `http://openweathermap.org/api` in a web browser. The web site has a detailed manual, which explains how to connect to the service and retrieve weather information. In this tutorial we will focus on how to get the 5-day/3-hour forecast (i.e., a forecast for five days with data every three hours (see `http://openweathermap.org/forecast5` for more details).

According to the manual, to get a forecast for a given city using only its name, we need to send a request that has the following format:

`api.openweathermap.org/data/2.5/forecast?q={city_name}&units=metric&APPID={api_key}`

Let us dissect the request:

- `api.openweathermap.org/data/2.5/forecast` is the entry point URL for the 5-day/3-hour forecast service.

- The q parameter instructs the weather service that we want to search for a city by its name. The value of the parameter is the name of the city.

- The units parameter specifies the units for the data. If we omit this parameter, we will get temperature data in Kelvins. To use Celsius, set units to metric.

- The APPID parameter expects the unique API key from your account. This parameter needs to be appended to every request to OpenWeatherMap made by the app. If it is missing, the server will respond with an error string.

The response to this request will come in JSON format. JSON is a text format for describing objects with the help of key-value pair hierarchies. Listing 14-2 shows a typical response from the weather service in JSON format.

***Listing 14-2.*** JSON Weather Forecast Response

```
{
    "city":{
        "id":1851632,
        "name":"Shuzenji",
        "coord":{
            "lon":138.933334,
            "lat":34.966671
        },
        "country":"JP",
        "cod":"200",
        "message":0.0045,
        "cnt":38,
        "list":[
            {
                "dt":1406106000,
                "main":{
                    "temp":298.77,
                    "temp_min":298.77,
                    "temp_max":298.774,
                    "pressure":1005.93,
                    "sea_level":1018.18,
                    "grnd_level":1005.93,
                    "humidity":87,
                    "temp_kf":0.26
                },
                "weather":[
                    {
                        "id":804,
                        "main":"Clouds",
                        "description":"overcast clouds",
                        "icon":"04d"
                    }
                ],
                "clouds":{
                    "all":88
                },
                "wind":{
                    "speed":5.71,
                    "deg":229.501
                },
```

```
        "sys":{
            "pod":"d"
        },
        "dt_txt":"2014-07-23 09:00:00"
    }
 ]
}
}
```

JSON distinguishes the following data types: number, string, Boolean, object, and array. In Listing 14-2 an example of an object is the value following the `city` key. The weather forecast data is stored in the `list` array. Every object in the list describes a weather forecast for a certain time of the day.

To get the forecast, we need to read the values of the following keys from the JSON response:

- `temp`—the temperature of the air, measured in the units we specified in the request.

- `icon`—a string identifier, which contains an icon name. This name can later be used to download a weather icon.

- `dt_txt`—a timestamp in a string format.

In the next section we will create a data model class to contain the data, which we extract from the JSON server response.

# Preparing the Forecast Data Model

Following the Model-View-Controller (MVC) paradigm, we will create a model to store and work with the forecast data. For a reminder about MVC, see **Chapter 5**.

We will create two Swift classes to implement the data model. The first one will represent a single forecast item with all of its data properties. The second one will store a collection of forecast items and will provide helper functions to access those items. We will host both of the classes inside the same swift source file.

In Xcode add a new file to your project, name it `ForecastModel.swift`, and open it for editing.

Let us start with the first class, `ForecastItem`. You can see its definition in Listing 14-3. Each forecast item has several properties of type `String`: a temperature measurement, a day and time for the forecast, and an identifier for the weather image icon.

There is one more property, named `uiImageCache` of type `UIImage`. `UIImage` is a class from the UIKit framework, which stores image data and provides a number of helper functions for loading and displaying data from various formats, such as PNG or JPEG. We will use `uiImageCache` to store an icon for the forecast.

`ForecastItem` contains a helper method, which stores image data in `uiImageCache`: `addImageCache`. As we will see later, the image data we download comes in an `NSData` object. You can think of `NSData` as analogous to ActionScript's `ByteArray`. `addImageCache` uses `NSData` to construct a `UIImage` instance and store it in `uiImageCache`.

*Listing 14-3.* ForecastItem Class Implementation

```
import UIKit

public class ForecastItem {
    //Forecast temperature stored as String
    public var temparature : String
    //Forecast date and time entry
    public var dayAndTime : String
```

```
//Weather icon name
public var imageID : String
//Cached weather image
public var uiImageCache : UIImage?

init( temperature: String, dayAndTime : String, imageID : String) {
    self.temparature = temperature
    self.dayAndTime = dayAndTime
    self.imageID = imageID
    self.uiImageCache = nil
}

//Load image from data and cache it
public func addImageCache(fromData data : NSData) {
    //Create UIImage from NSData
    uiImageCache = UIImage(data: data)
}
}
```

Our app will show the weather forecast for five days and the data for each day will be sampled every three hours. This makes 8 forecast items per day or 40 items for the whole five-day period. The next class we are going to implement, ForecastModel, will be responsible for storing these items and for providing access to them to the other parts of the application. The class has four methods:

- getItem: atIndex, which returns a forecast data item from the list by its index.

- removeAll(), which removes all previously stored forecast items from the model.

- appendItem: newItem, which is used to populate the forecast list with new items.

- getItemCount(), which returns the number of the forecast items in the list.

You can see the implementation of ForecastModel in Listing 14-4.

***Listing 14-4.*** The ForecastModel Class

```
public class ForecastModel {

    //An array of forecast items
    private var forecastData : [ForecastItem]

    init() {
        forecastData = []
    }

    //Remove all forecast items
    func removeAll() -> Void {
        forecastData.removeAll()
    }

    //Get a forecast item at a given index in the forecastData array
    func getItem( atIndex index : Int ) -> ForecastItem {
        return forecastData[index]
    }
```

```
//Add a new forecast item to the list
func appendItem( newItem newItem : ForecastItem ) {
    forecastData.append(newItem)
}

//Get the number of forecast items
func getItemCount() -> Int {
    return forecastData.count
}
}
```

# Writing the Network Communication Logic

We will create another class that will be responsible for connecting to the remote server, getting data, and parsing it for the forecast model. This will help with keeping all network communication code in one place.

Add a new source code file to the project and name it WeatherForecastService.swift. Listing 14-5 shows the WeatherForecastService class definition with all the methods stubbed out. We will add functionality to them in a minute.

***Listing 14-5.*** WeatherForecastService Class

```
public class WeatherForecastService {

    //Path to the API entry point
    private let apiBasePath : String = ↵
        "http://api.openweathermap.org/data/2.5/"

    //Unique key to access the OpenWeatherMap service
    private let apiKey : String = "739c23f0ecc3b86bf0545471b*******"

    //An aray of data tasks
    var dataTasks = [NSURLSessionTask]()

    //Unique error domain of the app
    let errorDomain = "com.diadraw.WeatherApp.WeatherForecastService"

    //Enum of possible error conditions
    enum ErrorCode {
        case noForecastData(Int)
        case urlFormatError(Int)
        case serverError(Int, String)
        case jsonParsingError(Int, String)
    }

    //Get a forecast from OpenWeatherMap service
    //and populate the forecast model
    public func getForecast( forecastModel forecastModel : ForecastModel, ↵
        forCity city: String, completionHandler: (NSError?) -> Void) {
        //The body of the method goes here
    }
```

```
    //Request data from the server and decode it into an NSDictionary
    private func requestToServer( apiEndpoint url : NSURL, ↵
        completionHandler: (NSDictionary?, NSError?) -> Void ) {
        //The body of the method goes here
    }


    //Download a forecast PNG icon and cache it in the forecastItem
    public func downloadForecastImage( forecastItem forecastItem : ↵
        ForecastItem , completionHandler: (NSError?) -> Void ) {
        //The body of the method goes here
    }


    //Transforms ErrorCode to NSError
    func getNSError( fromCode errorCode:ErrorCode ) -> NSError {
        //The body of the method goes here
    }

    deinit {
        //The body of the method goes here
    }
}
```

The class has two constants that are used to build a connection string to the weather service. apiBasePath holds the entry point of the API. The apiKey property, as its name implies, holds the unique API key that we must use to connect to OpenWeatherMap.

For communicating with the weather service we will create several asynchronous tasks to retrieve data from the server. We will keep track of them in an array called dataTasks. This gives us control over safely stopping tasks that may still be running when the app is closed.

Retrieving remote data is not entirely in our control, however. During this process a number of errors may occur. We will use an enumeration for the error states that can happen during data retrieval and decoding.

There are five methods in the WeatherForecastService class.

- getForecast(:forCity:) initiates a request to the forecast API of the weather service and populates the forecast model with the data that comes back.

- downloadForecastImage(:) is called when we need to download an icon to depict the weather conditions.

- requestToServer(apiEndpoint:completionHandler) serves as a generic function that sends request to the web service API, waits for a response, and converts JSON into equivalent Swift objects.

- getNSError:fromCode transforms an error code into an NSError instance that will be used by other parts of the application to inform the user that something went wrong inside the WeatherForecastService class.

- deinit is the place where all open connections to the server and unfinished jobs will be closed.

# Downloading Images from a URL

We will start the implementation with downloadForecastImage(forecastItem: completionHandler). The purpose of this method is to download one of OpenWeatherMap's weather icons and to store the result into a forecast item. You can see the method implementation in Listing 14-6.

OpenWeatherMap offers a set of weather icons that can be used to visually illustrate forecast conditions: from clear sunny sky to heavy rain clouds. Weather images are stored in PNG format and can be accessed on the OpenWeatherMap server with the following URL scheme: http://openweathermap.org/img/w/{icon_file_name}.png, where weather_icon_file name comes from the imageID property of the ForecastItem class.

To download an image from the server we will use the NSURLSession class from the iOS SDK. It has methods, which can request and download data from URLs via various protocols like FTP, HTTP, HTTPS, and so on.

From a developer's point of view NSURLSession opens a session to a remote server in which we can create series of so-called *tasks*. Each task is responsible for performing a request to the server and asynchronously downloading the response data.

There are two ways to use NSURLSession. The first way is to create an instance and configure the session properties manually. The second way is to use a reference to a shared session that comes configured with default settings. What is the difference between the two ways and which one should we use? Creating and configuring a session manually could be a tedious process, but it gives us control. We can set a specific timeout for the request or specify if we want the session to stay alive even when the app is not running. A shared session, on the other hand, comes with predefined parameters and without the ability for background downloads, but it is a perfect choice if you just want to grab data from a URL without the need to manage configurations.

In our app we will go with the default shared session. To obtain a reference to a shared session just call the static sharedSession() method of the NSURLSession class.

We will create a data task constant of type NSURLSessionDataTask named downloadImageTask by calling the dataTaskWithURL(url:completionHandler) method of the session reference. The role of the data task will be to download data from a URL and to call a completion handler function when it is done.

There are three types of session tasks: data, upload, and download tasks. The main difference between them is where and how they store their end results. For example, a data task returns the server's response as an NSData object stored in memory, while a download task could save the data in a disc file.

We will use a *closure* as the completion handler, which will be called when there is a response from the server. (For more details on how closures work in Swift see **Chapter 22**.) Inside the closure we first check if there were any errors during the execution of the task. Then if there were no errors we pass the received data to forecastItem.addImageCache(:), which will convert the PNG information into a UIImage instance. Finally, we call completionHandler(:) (which is the second argument of the downloadForecastImage method) to signal to the other parts of the app that the download of the weather image has finished.

Now there is only one thing left to do: add the task to the task list and start it. To start a task, call its resume() method. The name of the method may sound a bit weird, but it does the job.

***Listing 14-6.*** Implementation of downloadForecastImage Method

```
//Download a forecast PNG icon and cache it in the forecastItem
public func downloadForecastImage( forecastItem forecastItem : ForecastItem , ⏎
    completionHandler: (NSError?) -> Void ) {
    //Get a URL to the weather image from the imageID string
    let url = NSURL(string: ⏎
        "http://openweathermap.org/img/w/\(forecastItem.imageID).png")
```

```
//Get a shared session instance and start a task
//to download the image data from the url
let downloadImageTask = NSURLSession.sharedSession().dataTaskWithURL(url!) {
(data, response, error) in

    if error == nil {
        print("Download Finished")

        //Get a UIImage from the returned data and cache it
        forecastItem.addImageCache(fromData: data!)
    }

    //The task is complete, call the completion handler
    completionHandler(error)
}

// Add the task to the tasks list
dataTasks.append(downloadImageTask)

//Start the download task
downloadImageTask.resume()
}
```

# Requesting JSON from a Server

Next to implement is requestToServer(apiEndpoint:completionHandler). This method is marked as private for the WeatherForecastService class and is called internally by the getForecast(:) method. Its purpose is to get JSON-encoded forecast data from the server and to convert it into an NSDictionary object, which will be used by getForecast to extract the forecast data.

In Listing 14-7 you can see the implementation of requestToServer. The function takes two parameters: an apiEndpoint, which is a URL referring to a specific API entry point, and a completionHandler to call when the request is complete. The result of the response and any error information are returned as parameters of the completion handler.

This function follows the logic that we used to implement downloadForecastImage: obtain a shared session, create a data task to download the response as NSData, and start the task. The interesting part is how we convert the JSON-formatted data to a dictionary object that we can use in Swift.

To convert JSON to a Swift object we use the NSJSONSerialization helper class from the iOS SDK. In fact, this class can also convert Swift objects to JSON-formatted strings. The function that performs the conversion is called JSONObjectWithData:data:options. As the first parameter to the function we pass the NSData object, returned from the server, which contains JSON data. The second parameter is of type NSJSONReadingOptions and allows us to configure how the internal JSON parser will process the input data. In this example we set its value to AllowFragments, which instructs the JSON parser to work even if the root-level data is not wrapped in an object or an array.

If there are any errors during the parsing JSONObjectWithData:data:options will throw an error, so we must wrap the call in a do-catch statement. You can find more information about the do-catch statements in **Chapter 17**.

Inside the body of the function there are several points of interest.

- First we must check the task completion handler's error parameter.

- Then we check if there is any data in the server's response.

- Next there is a check for whether the JSON object can be parsed and then we ensure that the result from the parser is of type NSDictionary.

- The last check is a precaution. From OpenWeatherMap API's documentation we know that the top-level item in the JSON that its server produces is expected to be an object, which corresponds to an NSDictionary object in Swift. If the result of the parsing is of some other type, then the JSON response probably has different format from what we expected.

In all those cases we call the getNSError:FromCode method to create an NSError instance, in which we describe the problem and call the requestToServer completion handler to notify the caller.

*Listing 14-7.* Implementation of requestToServer Method

```
//Request data from the server and decode it into an NSDictionary
private func requestToServer( apiEndpoint url : NSURL, ↵
    completionHandler: (NSDictionary?, NSError?) -> Void ) {

    //Get a shared session instance and define a task
    let task = NSURLSession.sharedSession().dataTaskWithURL(url) { ↵
        (data:NSData?, response:NSURLResponse?, error:NSError?) -> Void in

        guard error==nil else {
            //There was an error returned from the server
            completionHandler(nil, error)
            return
        }

        // Check for JSON serialization errors
        guard let unwrappedData = data else {
            completionHandler(nil, self.getNSError( ↵
                        fromCode: ErrorCode.jsonParsingError(50, ↵
                        "Unexpected data format.")))
            return
        }

        var jsonObject : AnyObject? = nil

        do {
            //Deserialize JSON data to a dictionary
            jsonObject = try ↵
                NSJSONSerialization.JSONObjectWithData(unwrappedData, ↵
                        options: .AllowFragments)
```

```
            //Check if the resulting object from the serialization
            //is a dictionary
            guard let deserializedDictionary = jsonObject as? NSDictionary ↵
            else {

                //We expected dictionary, but some other
                //object was returned. Return error.
                completionHandler(nil, self.getNSError( ↵
                            fromCode: ErrorCode.jsonParsingError(50, ↵
                            "Unexpected format.")))

                return
            }

            completionHandler(deserializedDictionary, nil)
        }
        //There was an error with JSON deserialization
        catch {
            completionHandler(nil, self.getNSError( ↵
                        fromCode: ErrorCode.jsonParsingError(50, ↵
                        "There was an error with JSON deserialization.")))
        }
    }

    // Add the task to the tasks list
    dataTasks.append(task)

    //Start the task
    task.resume()
}
```

## Populating the Data Model

We will complete the WeatherForecastService class with the implementation of the getForecast(:forCity:) method (Listing 14-8). The method is responsible for connecting to the server and populating the forecast model with the data that comes back.

*Listing 14-8.* Implementation of getForecast Method

```
//Get a forecast from OpenWeatherMap service
//and populate the forecast model
public func getForecast( forecastModel forecastModel : ForecastModel, ↵
    forCity city: String, completionHandler: (NSError?) -> Void) {

    //Clean all previeously entered items from the model
    forecastModel.removeAll()

    //Set the forecast API entry point
    let urlString = ↵
        "\(apiBasePath)forecast?q=\(city)&units=metric&APPID=\(apiKey)"
```

```
//Encrypt the URL string to use percent characters instead of blank spaces
let encodedUrlString = ↵
    urlString.stringByAddingPercentEncodingWithAllowedCharacters( ↵
        NSCharacterSet.URLQueryAllowedCharacterSet())

//Try to create a NSURL instance from the encoded URL string
guard let url = NSURL( string:encodedUrlString! ) else {
    completionHandler( self.getNSError( ↵
            fromCode: ErrorCode.urlFormatError(50) ) )
    return
}

//Connect to the web service and get data as dictionary
requestToServer(apiEndpoint: url) { ↵
    (json:NSDictionary?, error:NSError?) -> Void in

    guard error==nil else {
        //Signal that the operation has finished with an error
        completionHandler(error)
        return
    }

    //Check if there is a list of forecast data
    guard let forecastList = json!["list"] as? NSArray else {

        //Check if the server responded with a
        //valid JSON but with error code inside
        if let errorCode = json!["cod"] as? String {

            //Get the server's error message
            let errorMesage : String? = json!["message"] as? String

            //Construct en error message
            let serverError = self.getNSError( ↵
                fromCode: ErrorCode.serverError(Int(errorCode) ?? 50, ↵
                errorMesage ?? "unknown error") )

            //Signal with server error
            completionHandler(serverError)
            return
        }
        else {
            //Signal with error: there is no valid forecast data
            completionHandler( self.getNSError( ↵
                        fromCode: ErrorCode.noForecastData(50) ))
            return
        }
    }
```

```
        for entry in forecastList
        {
            //Check if all needed forecast properties
            //are present in the dictionary
            guard let forecastTempDegrees = ↵
                        entry["main"]!!["temp"] as? Double,
                rawDateTime = entry["dt_txt"] as? String,
                forecastIcon = entry["weather"]!![0]!["icon"] as? String

            else {
                //Signal with error that there is no forecast data
                completionHandler( self.getNSError( ↵
                        fromCode: ErrorCode.noForecastData(50) ) )
                return
            }

            //Hydrate the forecast model with data
            forecastModel.appendItem(
                newItem: ForecastItem(temperature: "\(forecastTempDegrees)",
                    dayAndTime: "\(rawDateTime)",
                    imageID: forecastIcon)
            )
        }
        //Signal that the operation has finished
        completionHandler(nil)
    }
}
```

To retrieve data from the server, this method calls requestToServer(apiEndpoint: completionHandler), which requests a JSON-formatted forecast. Note that before constructing an NSURL instance for the desired endpoint we first encode the endpoint string to ensure it is in a valid URL format. We use the stringByAddingPercentEncodingWithAllowedCharacters method of the String class to convert any blank spaces and Unicode characters into a valid URL.

After the data is received and converted to NSDictionary it is getForecast's responsibility to be aware of the forecast data format and its conversion to match the forecast model. In other words, it needs to check if all of the values we require are present and have corresponding keys in the dictionary.

We will use them to create a new instance of ForecastItem and add it to the forecast model. If there are any errors from a previous operation or not all the data can be found, we signal the caller with an error.

Note that there is a case when the server can return a valid JSON response that contains an error message. At the end of the function you will find a code block, which performs a check if the response contains an error message.

## Creating Error Messages

We will complete the WeatherForecastService class with the implementation of the getNSError:FromCode method (Listing 14-9). Inside we use a switch to determine the type of error and to create a NSError instance with a corresponding error message that will mean something to the user.

*Listing 14-9.* getNSError Method Implementation

```
//Transforms ErrorCode to NSError
func getNSError( fromCode errorCode:ErrorCode ) -> NSError {
    switch errorCode {
    case .noForecastData(let code):
        return NSError(domain:errorDomain, code:code, userInfo: ↵
                [NSLocalizedDescriptionKey:"There is no forecast data."])
    case .urlFormatError(let code):
        return NSError(domain:errorDomain, code:code, userInfo: ↵
                [NSLocalizedDescriptionKey:"URL format error."])
    case .serverError(let code, let message):
        return NSError(domain:errorDomain, code:code, userInfo: ↵
                [NSLocalizedDescriptionKey:"Server error: \(message)"])
    case .jsonParsingError(let code, let message):
        return NSError(domain:errorDomain, code:code, userInfo: ↵
                [NSLocalizedDescriptionKey:"JSON parsing error: \(message)"])
    }
}
```

# Showing the Forecast in a Table View

Finally, we are ready to show the forecast to the user. We will display every forecast item on a separate row of the table view we added in the beginning of the chapter. Open ViewController.swift file and get ready to code.

As we saw in **Chapter 6**, the table view needs to get its data from an object, which conforms to the UITableViewDataSource protocol. We will modify the ViewController class to work as a data source and conform to the protocol by first adding the protocol name to ViewController's inheritance list:

```
class ViewController: UIViewController, UITableViewDataSource
```

Then we will add two of the protocol's methods: tableView(_:numberOfRowsInSection:) and tableView (_:cellForRowAtIndexPath). For now let us just stub them out as shown in Listing 14-10.

*Listing 14-10.* Implement UITableViewDataSource Protocol's Methods

```
class ViewController: UIViewController, UITableViewDataSource {

    //The rest of the code goes here

    func tableView(tableView: UITableView, ↵
        numberOfRowsInSection section: Int) -> Int {
        return 0
    }

    func tableView(tableView: UITableView, ↵
        cellForRowAtIndexPath indexPath: NSIndexPath) -> UITableViewCell {
        return UITableViewCell()
    }

}
```

Let us override UIViewController's viewDidLoad method and set up ViewController as the data source for the table view in it (Listing 14-11).

*Listing 14-11.* Set Up the Data Source for the Table View

```
class ViewController: UIViewController, UITableViewDataSource {
    override func viewDidLoad() {
        super.viewDidLoad()
        tableView.dataSource = self
    }

    //The rest of the code goes here
}
```

Next, we will add two properties to ViewController to work with data: an instance of ForecastModel to keep the data and an instance of WeatherForecastService to fetch it from the server (Listing 14-12).

*Listing 14-12.* Instantiate the WeatherForecastService and ForecastModel Classes

```
class ViewController: UIViewController, UITableViewDataSource {
    //The rest of the code goes here

    let weatherService = WeatherForecastService()
    let forecastModel = ForecastModel()

    //The rest of the code goes here
}
```

Let us now add implementation to the two methods we stubbed out earlier, so that the forecast items can appear in the table view. First we will have tableView(_:numberOfRowsInSection:) work out and return the number of items in the forecast model, which corresponds to the number of rows we need in the table (Listing 14-13).

*Listing 14-13.* Work Out the Number of Rows in the Table

```
func tableView(tableView: UITableView, ↵
        numberOfRowsInSection section: Int) -> Int {
    //Return forecast items number
    return self.forecastModel.getItemCount()
}
```

The tableView(_:cellForRowAtIndexPath:) method is called when the table view needs to populate a given cell with data and this is what we will implement it to do (Listing 14-14).

*Listing 14-14.* Populate a Cell in the Table with Data

```
func tableView(tableView: UITableView, ↵
cellForRowAtIndexPath indexPath: NSIndexPath) -> UITableViewCell {

    //Create new table cell for the row
    let cell = UITableViewCell()

    //Get a forecast item corresponding to the row number
    let forecastItem = self.forecastModel.getItem( atIndex: indexPath.row )
```

```
//Set the cell's text label to the forecast item's
//temperature, date and time
cell.textLabel?.text = ↵
        "\(forecastItem.temparature)° C | \(forecastItem.dayAndTime)"

if forecastItem.uiImageCache == nil {
    weatherService.downloadForecastImage( forecastItem ) { (error) in

        dispatch_async(dispatch_get_main_queue(), {[weak self] in
            if let error = error {
                //If there is an error message print it
                print(error)
            }
            else {
                //Assign the cached image to the cell's image view
                cell.imageView?.image = forecastItem.uiImageCache

                //Refresh data in the row
                self!.tableView.reloadRowsAtIndexPaths([indexPath], ↵
                                            withRowAnimation: .None)
            }
        })
    }
}
else {
    //Assign the cached image to the cell's image view
    cell.imageView?.image = forecastItem.uiImageCache
}

return cell
}
```

In the code in Listing 14-14 we first get a forecast item from the model that matches the row of the cell that has been requested. Then we set the cell's textLabel property to display the temperature and the date. The interesting part is how we load a weather image in the cell.

The UITableViewCell class comes with a property called imageView, which we use to display a weather image. If the uiImageCache property of the forecast item is not empty, we can assign its value directly to the cell.imageView.image property. Otherwise we have to download the image first and do the assignment once the download is complete. Thus we call the downloadForecastImage method with a closure completion handler, in which the cell's image view can be updated.

Note the dispatch_async(dispatch_get_main_queue(),{() -> Void}) call in the completion handler. It ensures that the image view update happens on the main thread, as this is the only thread that is allowed to access the user interface in iOS, while our completion handler is most likely to be called on the thread where the download happened.

---

■ **Note**    To keep things simple and the focus on network operation, we have taken the approach of creating a new cell every time we provide cell data in Listing 14-14. Apple strongly discourages this practice. Instead, UITableView offers a memory-efficient mechanism for cell reusing. See Chapter 6 for details.

---

The last bit of code in the app will be the implementation of the Search button action that queries the server and populates the model with forecast items. Do you remember the @IBAction searchForCity stub we created earlier? This is where we will add the implementation (Listing 14-15).

To populate the model we just need to call weatherService.getForecast and hand a model reference to it. It takes a completion handler, which we will implement as a closure. In it we ask the table view to reload its data if there were no errors while fetching the forecast. Again, we make sure that any UI update happens on the main thread.

*Listing 14-15.* Implementation of the searchForCity Action

```
@IBAction func searchForCity(sender: AnyObject) {
    weatherService.getForecast( forecastModel:forecastModel, ↩
            forCity: cityTextField.text!){ ( error : NSError? ) -> Void in

        if let error = error {
            //If there is an error message print it
            print(error)
        }
        else {
            dispatch_async(dispatch_get_main_queue() , {[weak self] in
                //Refresh data in the table view
                self!.tableView.reloadData();
                })
        }
    }
}
```

---

■ **Note** The format of the code in Listing 14-15 may already look familiar from the iCloud tutorial we did in Chapter 13. In case you are not doing the tutorials in order, however (why should you?!), here is a quick note on some of the syntax that may look unfamiliar. When a response has come from the server and there is no error, we update the user interface to load the new data by calling self!.tableView.reloadData(). This call is made in a closure—a block of code that can be passed around. You can see the closure using the self keyword to reference the current instance of our ViewController class. Closures are independent objects (i.e., although this closure can access ViewController via self, it is not itself part of the ViewController class). In order for it not to retain the reference that will count toward the ViewController instance's reference count, we use the weak keyword. For more details on weak and strong references see Chapter 21.

---

And this is it. Run the app and type the name of the place you live in to see if the weather service can find it. If it does, you will get the weather forecast for the next five days (Figure 14-5).

*Figure 14-5.* *Our weather forecast app running in a simulator*

Let us see what the weather in London, UK, will be like. Hard to believe! There are some sunny days ahead.

# Summary

In this chapter you saw how to create a network session to a remote web service, download images, and work with JSON-formatted data. You built a weather forecast application that retrieves data from the OpenWeatherMap service using the HTTP API the service provides.

In the next chapter we will explore the power of push notifications and Apple's advertisement channel as a way to monetize your apps.

# CHAPTER 15

■ ■ ■

# Adverts and Push Notifications

Let's be frank: making apps is fun, but it is also a business undertaking. And with the App Store flooded with beautifully crafted and free apps, a professional app developer faces the dilemma of how to balance providing value for users and keeping app prices competitive. In this chapter we address two aspects of the business of making apps: monetization and keeping in touch with users.

Using advertisements in your app is a popular business model: it allows you to get paid for your work while keeping your app free for end users. Apple has provided an integrated ad platform to help implement this, and over the next few pages you will see how to include it in your app in a matter of minutes.

Next comes keeping in touch with your customers: after all, the business transaction does not stop with the user downloading your app. Push notifications give you a way of keeping your users up to date with news, updates, and other relevant information.

In this chapter you will do the following:

- Explore the most popular ways to monetize your app and to stay connected with your users.

- Learn how to use the iAd framework to show adverts in your app.

- Build an app that exploits different ad formats, such as banner and interstitial ads.

- Learn about remote notifications and how to use them to keep your users up to date.

- Build an app that receives push notifications and a server-side script that sends them.

When you are done, you will have two apps: one that uses Apple's iAd adverts channel and another one that incorporates push notifications for keeping in touch with your users.

---

■ **Note**    Provisioning your app to handle push notifications requires that you enroll in Apple's iOS Development Program. This is a paid membership program, which you can add to your account on Apple's web site.

---

© Radoslava Leseva Adams and Hristo Lesev 2016
R. L. Adams and H. Lesev, *Migrating to Swift from Flash and ActionScript*,
DOI 10.1007/978-1-4842-1666-8_15

# Adverts

There are a few ways to get revenue from your app: sell the app, offer in-app purchases, or show advertisements.[1] Apple's mobile advertisement platform iAd provides help with the last one. It is quite powerful and gives iOS developers an easy way to embed advertisements in their applications. iAd has been around for a while now and has had a chance to mature enough to let you turn your app into an ad-eating monster in less than ten minutes. Don't believe me? Grab a timer and let's get on with the tutorial.

## Setting Up the App

Let us start by creating a *Single View Application* project in Xcode. Name the project DemoSwiftiAds.

To start with, we need to import the iAd framework. Find ViewController.swift in Project navigator and add the line shown in Listing 15-1 to the import section of the file (where import UIKit is).

***Listing 15-1.*** Import the iAd Framework in ViewController.swift

```
import iAd
```

There are a couple of different ad formats that your application can integrate, depending on how they are shown on the screen: banner ads use a strip of your app's screen space to display an advert, whereas interstitial ads take the whole screen. We will have a go at both kinds.

## Banner Ads

As a next step we will add a banner ad view to our view controller. In the ViewController.swift file add a member of type ADBannerView! to the ViewController class, as shown in Listing 15-2.

***Listing 15-2.*** Add a Banner View Member to the ViewController Class

```
class ViewController: UIViewController {
    // Add this line:
    var rectAdView: ADBannerView!

    // Leave the rest of the code as it is
    // ...

}
```

---

■ **Note**    According to Apple's guidelines, you should create only one instance of ADBannerView and share it across multiple views. Another must from Apple is that you should hide the banner view if no ads are showing at the moment.

---

We will initialize the rectAdView member inside the viewDidLoad method of the ViewController class. Find the method in the ViewController.swift file and change it as shown in Listing 15-3.

---

[1]Another common case for developers is to release a free app with ads and to offer an in-app purchase option to turn off ads.

***Listing 15-3.*** Change viewDidLoad to Start Using Ads

```
override func viewDidLoad() {
    super.viewDidLoad()

    // This line is enough for a banner to appear
    // at the bottom of the view:
    canDisplayBannerAds = true;

    // Initialize the rectangle ad view:
    rectAdView = ADBannerView(adType: .MediumRectangle)

    // Set ViewController as the delegate of the rectangle ad,
    // so it receives notifications from it:
    rectAdView.delegate = self
}
```

Instances of UIViewController, which is what our ViewController class is, have a property named canDisplayBannerAds. Setting it to true is enough for a banner to automatically appear at the bottom of our view. We do not need to worry about whether the banner is loading or when it should appear; the iAd will create the required subview and will populate it with the right content.

We will use the rectAdView to demonstrate how to control ads' showing and siding. The next line in the code above takes control of how ads will be shown: rectAdView is instantiated and initialized with ad type ADAdType.MediumRectangle, which would occupy a rectangle area of the view.

We will receive communication from the banner ad via a delegate, which will be notified when an ad is ready to be shown or when there is an error in the ad delivery process. To make our ViewController instance a delegate for rectAdView, we need to do two things: first, assign it to the banner view's delegate property and, second, make ViewController conform to the ADBannerViewDelegate protocol by adding it to the class definition as shown in Listing 15-4.

***Listing 15-4.*** Change ViewController to Conform to the ADBannerViewDelegate Protocol

```
// Add ADBannerViewDelegate to the list of superclasses and protocols
// that ViewController inherits and conforms to:
class ViewController: UIViewController, ADBannerViewDelegate {
    ...
}
```

If you hit the *Run* button at this point, the app should compile and run on your device or in the iOS simulator, but you should not see any ads yet. For the rectangle ad to appear, ViewController needs to provide implementations for two methods of the ADBannerViewDelegate protocol. The first one is named bannerViewDidLoad and is called when we receive an advert. The second one, rectAdView, gets called if there has been an error with the delivery of the ad content. Listing 15-5 shows the implementations you need to add to the ViewController class in ViewController.swift.

***Listing 15-5.*** Add Implementations of ADBannerViewDelegate's Methods to ViewController

```
func bannerViewDidLoadAd(banner: ADBannerView!) {
    // Add the rectangle ad view to the screen when an Ad is loaded:
    self.view.addSubview(banner)
    self.view.layoutIfNeeded()
}
```

```
func bannerView( ↵
    banner: ADBannerView!, didFailToReceiveAdWithError error: NSError!) {
    // There was an error with the ad content, so remove the banner:
    banner.removeFromSuperview()
    self.view.layoutIfNeeded()
}
```

What these two functions do is to add the banner view as a child to the controller's view if there is an ad ready to be shown and remove the banner if something went wrong.

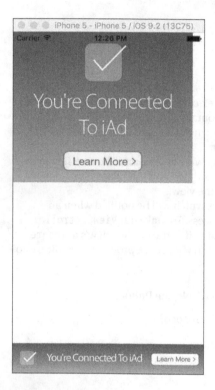

***Figure 15-1.*** *Showing a banner and rectangular ads*

If you run the app now, you will see the banner view at the bottom of the screen as shown on Figure 15-1. Next we will have a look at another important type of advertisement.

## Interstitial Ads

Interstitial ads cover the entire user interface (UI) of an application. They are typically used at transition points in the app (e.g., when moving between screens). To demonstrate this we will add a second screen to the app and implement a transition to it.

In *Project navigator* find the Main.storyboard file and click to open it. Drag a new *View Controller* instance from the *Object library* and place it to the right of the view controller that is already there, as shown in Figure 15-2.

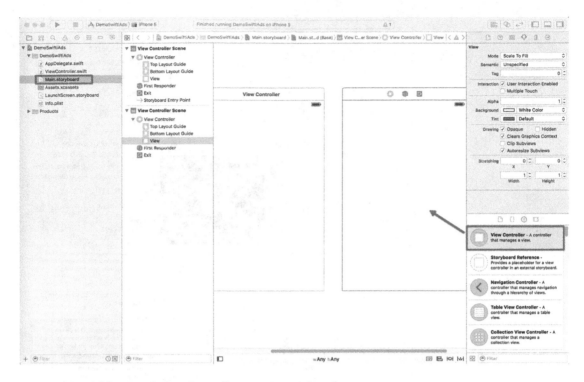

***Figure 15-2.*** *Add a second View Controller to Main.storyboard*

Now let's add a button to our main view controller (the one on the left), which will trigger a transition from it to the second view controller. Find a *Button* view in the *Object Library* panel and drag it into the upper left corner of the main view controller. *Ctrl-click* the button and drag the line that appears toward the second view controller. Release the mouse button and select **ActionSegue ➤ Show** from the pop-up menu as shown in Figure 15-3.

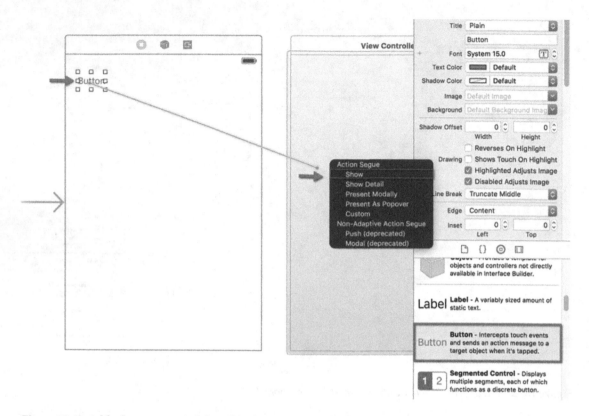

**Figure 15-3.** *Add a button to switch between the two view controllers*

Next, we will override a method that handles the transition between the views, called `prepareForSegue`, to enable automatic interstitial ads for the transition between the two views of the app. Add the implementation in Listing 15-6 to the `ViewController` class.

**Listing 15-6.** Override the prepareForSegue Method in ViewController to Display an Interstitial Ad

```
override func prepareForSegue(segue: UIStoryboardSegue, sender: AnyObject?)
{
    let destination = segue.destinationViewController as UIViewController
    destination.interstitialPresentationPolicy = &#x00E5;
        ADInterstitialPresentationPolicy.Automatic
}
```

Interstitial ads are not part of the segue, but they are injected automatically during the segue and before the view transition begins. And one last thing about the interstitial ads: if you are building an app with more than one screen to transition to, you might want to control in which transitions to show an interstitial ad. To do that you should check the value of the `destinationViewController` property of the segue first before setting the interstitial ad policy.

Displaying an ad involves downloading assets from the iAds server, so there can be a significant delay between the start of the view transition and when the ad content is delivered. To avoid this, we can ask the `ViewController` class to request iAds earlier than when they are needed. `UIViewController` has a method, called `prepareInterstitialAds`, which will prefetch assets from the server. Let's add that at the end of `ViewController`'s `viewDidLoad` method (see Listing 15-7).

*Listing 15-7.* Prefetch Interstitial Ad Content

```
override func viewDidLoad()
{
    // Leave the rest of the code as it is
    // ...

    // Add this line to the end of the viewDidLoad method:
    UIViewController.prepareInterstitialAds()
}
```

Run the app and when it starts, press the button you added to start transitioning to the second view. At that point an interstitial ad should appear like that in Figure 15-4.

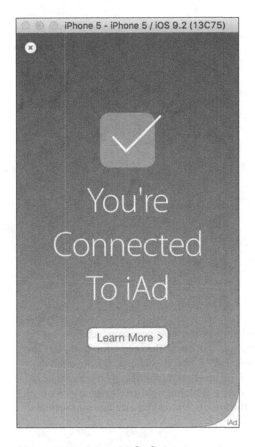

*Figure 15-4. Interstitial ad view*

## Configuring iAds Test Settings

So far so good: our app works and displays different kinds of ads. But what happens if there is a problem like a missing Internet connection or Apple could not provide the type of ad you requested? It is important for an app to be able to handle such issues. Fortunately Apple has provided a mechanism for simulating situations like that during development.

Open *Settings* on your device or in the iOS simulator, scroll down, tap on *Developer* settings to open them, and find the *IAD DEVELOPER APP TESTING* group —it should look like the one in Figure 15-5.

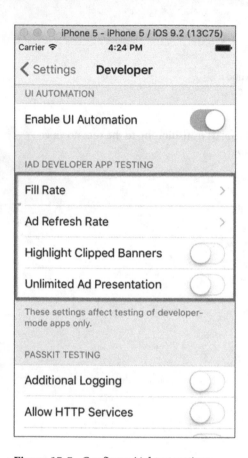

***Figure 15-5.*** *Configure iAd test settings*

This is where you can simulate different situations, in order to stress-test how your app handles advertisements. Use *Fill Rate* to simulate what percent of the time ads will be available to your app: you can set this from *0%—Always Error* to *100%—Always Provide Ad*. *Ad Refresh Rate* lets you specify how often the ads should change. *Highlight Clipped Banners* shows you areas of the ads that might be covered by other UI and thus be invisible or not available for tapping on: if the banner view is highlighted green, the banner is all in view, a red highlight means that there are dodgy areas. When turned on, *Unlimited Ad Presentation* lets you set the gaps between ads to zero during development.

---

■ **Note**    The advertisements that you see during development are fake test ones. In order to enable live adverts and start monetizing their use in your app, you will need to enable iAd in your Apple account.

---

And this is it! Did you manage to go through this tutorial in less than ten minutes? Nice job!

Now take a quick break and roll up your sleeves for the second part of this chapter: keeping in touch with your customers via remote notifications.

# Remote Notifications

Remote notifications are an excellent way to keep your users informed about what is new in your app. These notifications come in the form of text messages displayed on the home screen of the device any time you decide to send them. You can use them to announce updates, news, sale offers, and so on. They are also a great way to bring users back to your app and increase engagement. You can target specific groups of users with push notifications. Just don't be too "pushy," as this may backfire: choose carefully how often you send messages to users and what you say in them.

---

■ **Note**    There are two types of notifications on iOS: local and remote. They share the same purpose: to enable an app to notify its users when there is something new. The difference between them is where they come from: local notifications are scheduled and delivered by an app on the same device it is installed on, while remote notifications are sent by a server to the Apple Push Notification service, which then routes or pushes the notifications to selected devices. Remote notifications are also known as push notifications.

---

## Remote Notifications Overview

There are three participants in the process of sending and receiving a push notification:

- a *notification provider*, which generates and sends out notifications for a specific device or a group of devices;

- the *Apple Push Notification service (APNs)*, which routes the notifications to the correct devices; and

- your app, which sits on the device that receives the notification and processes it on receipt.

APNs uses device tokens to identify the devices that are registered to receive notifications from a specific provider. A device token is a long unique list of numbers. It is usually requested by your app and generated by APNs when the app launches. Figure 15-6 illustrates the process.

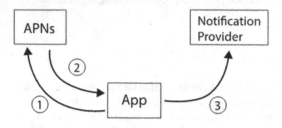

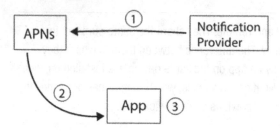

***Figure 15-6.*** *The steps involved in registering for and receiving push notifications*

On application launch,

1.  The app registers itself with APNs for notifications by requesting a device token.

2.  APNs generates a device token and send it back to the app.

3.  The app informs the notification provider that it is now registered to receive notifications by giving it its device token.

When a notification is sent,

1.  The notification provider sends the notification message to APNs and gives it a list of devices (identified with their device tokens) that it should be sent to.

2.  APNs routes the notification to the chosen devices.

3.  The notification arrives on the device and the app processes it.

Your app is responsible for obtaining a device token and for processing notifications when it receives them. APNs handles the generation of unique device tokens and routes them to the correct devices, based on these tokens. The notification provider's responsibility is to generate notifications and to tell APNs which devices to route them to. This notification provider is usually a program that sits on a server and is your responsibility: you can develop one yourself or you can use a third-party service instead. Don't worry, though, a provider can be as simple as a few lines of PHP code, and this is what we will use in this tutorial.

---

■ **Caution**  Apple warns that delivery of remote notifications is not guaranteed. So you should not use the notification payload to deliver critical data that cannot be retrieved by other means.

---

# Setting Up the App

Start by creating an empty *Single View Application* Swift project. Name the project DemoSwiftPushNotifications. We will use this name later, when we set up the application bundle, so if you choose a different name for your project, make sure to replace DemoSwiftPushNotifications with it wherever it appears in the rest of the tutorial.

Select your project in Project navigator and then select the app target to modify its settings. On the *Capabilities* tab scroll down to find *Push Notifications* and turn the switch on to enable them, as shown on Figure 15-7. Xcode might ask you which developer profile to use for enabling the notifications.

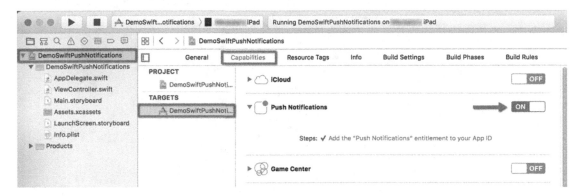

***Figure 15-7.*** *Enable push notifications for the project*

---

■ **Note** The Push Notifications feature cannot be tested in the simulator, so before you continue, make sure you have an iOS device handy and plugged in your computer.

---

At this point Xcode should create a provisioning profile for your app, but it may also need a bit of help to do that. With your app target still selected, go to the *General* tab in the editor and have a look at the **Identity ➤ Team** setting. You may need to select an Apple account as the *Team* setting if it's empty. If a warning appears under *Team*, telling you "No matching provisioning files found," let Xcode sort this out by clicking *Fix Issue (*Figure 15-8*)*.

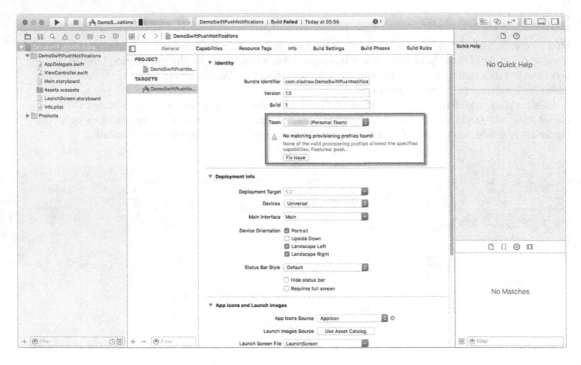

**Figure 15-8.** *Fixing the "No mathing provisioning files found" issue*

# Requesting a Device Token

Now it's time to get the app to ask permission and register itself for push notifications. In Project navigator find and open the AppDelegate.swift file and replace the default application(_:didFinishLaunchingWith Options:) method with the methods from Listing 15-8.

**Listing 15-8.** Implement Callbacks in the App for Handling Remote Notifications

```
func application(↵
    application: UIApplication, ↵
    didFinishLaunchingWithOptions launchOptions: [NSObject: AnyObject]?)↵
-> Bool {
    // Request a device token from APNs
    application.registerForRemoteNotifications()

    // Ask the user permission to send notifications
    application.registerUserNotificationSettings(↵
            UIUserNotificationSettings(forTypes: .Alert, categories: nil))

    return true
}

func application(application: UIApplication, ↵
    didRegisterForRemoteNotificationsWithDeviceToken deviceToken: NSData) {
    // This method is called if the device token request succeeds.
```

```
    //Get a pointer to the deviceToken data as if it is an array of characters
    let tokenChars = UnsafePointer<CChar>(deviceToken.bytes)
    //The token string will be buld in here
    var tokenString = ""

    for i in 0..<deviceToken.length {
        //Convert each character to a hex string equivalent
        tokenString += String(format: "%02.2hhx", arguments: [tokenChars[i]])
    }

    // Copy the device token from Xcode's terminal –
    // we will need to give that to the notification provider.
    print( "Registered for remote notifications. Device token: \(tokenString)" )

func application(↵
    application: UIApplication, ↵
    didFailToRegisterForRemoteNotificationsWithError error: NSError) {
    // This method is called if the device token request fails.
    print( "Could not register for remote notifications: \(error)" )
}

func application(application: UIApplication, ↵
    didReceiveRemoteNotification userInfo: [NSObject : AnyObject]) {
    // This method is called when a notification arrives.
    // For now just print out the notification content in Xcode's console:
    print( "Received remote notification: \(userInfo)" )
}
```

Let us take a minute to dissect the code in Listing 15-8.

- application(_:didFinishLaunchingWithOptions:) is called when the application starts. This is the moment to do the preparation steps:

  - Request a device token from APNs; application(_:registerForRemoteNotif ications:) initiates the registration process with APNs. According to Apple's manual, the device token can change at any time, so you need to call this method every time the app is launched.

  - Ask the user permission for sending notifications by calling application(_:re gisterUserNotificationSettings:). This method shows a dialog, which asks the user if he or she wants to receive notifications from your app. When the user gives permission for that, the choice is remembered by iOS, so next time this method is called the remembered response is used to determine the types of notifications the app may or may not use.

The next three methods are in effect callbacks. The first two listen for a response to the device token request from APNs. The last one is called when a notification arrives. For now let's have all three callbacks print out their information in Xcode's console. We will see how to show an arriving notification in an alert box at the end of the chapter.

- application(_:didFailToRegisterForRemoteNotificationsWithError:) is called if there is a problem with the registration process. The NSError object contains information about why registration failed.

- application(_:didRegisterForRemoteNotificationsWithDeviceToken:) if the registration succeeds, this method is called back and its parameter, deviceToken, contains the obtained device token.

- application(_:didReceiveRemoteNotification:) is called when the app receives a notification from APNs. The userInfo parameter contains the notification information in the form of a dictionary. This may include an allert message, alert sound, badge number, identifier, and custom data.

Now run the app on your device in debug mode. After the app has started, a modal dialog like the one in Figure 15-9 will pop up asking if you would like to accept notifications from the app. Tap *OK*.

*Figure 15-9.* *When the app is first run, it asks the user for permission to use notifications*

---

■ **Note**   Notifications can also be enabled or disabled for your app from the device's settings.

---

If the app managed to register itself with APNs successfully, you should see the device token printed out in the Xcode's console, as shown in Figure 15-10.

*Figure 15-10.* *The device token, printed out in Xcode's console*

Make a note of the token somewhere, as we will need to use it when we set up the notification provider: copy and paste it, but get rid of the brackets and the whitespaces. The code we wrote so far should be enough for the app to be able to handle remote notifications. In order to do a test, however, we have a bit more work to do.

## Creating Certificates for Push Notifications

Sending and receiving remote notifications will require communication with APNs via a Secure Socket Layer (SSL)-encrypted connection. For that to work, we will need a certificate that is linked to our App ID and which we will use when we set up a notification provider. The following sections will guide you through the process.

## Create a Certificate Signing Request

Launch the *Keychain Access* app on your computer. From the main menu select **Keychain Access ➤ Certificate Assistant ➤ Request a Certificate from a Certificate Authority** to show the Certificate Assistant dialog (Figure 15-11).

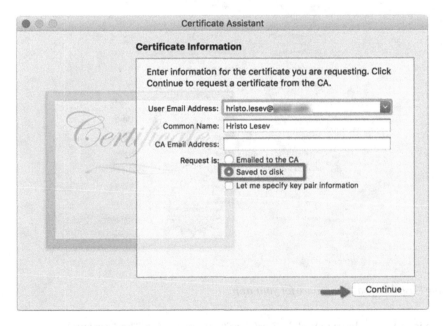

***Figure 15-11.*** *Certificate Signing Request (CSR) dialog*

In the dialog enter your e-mail address and a name for your private key and tick the *Save to disk* radio button. Click *Continue* and save the CSR file on your machine. We will use this file in the next step of the process.

## Create a Certificate for Push Notifications for Your App

Open a browser and navigate to Apple's *Developer Member Center*. Log in with your iOS development account and go to **Certificates, Identifiers & Profiles ➤ iOS Apps Identifiers**. In the list of app IDs find the one that Xcode has created for you: it should contain DemoSwiftPushNotifications, unless you gave a different name to your project (Figure 15-12).

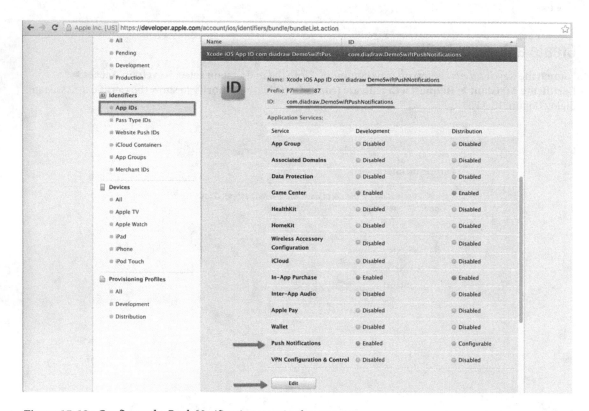

***Figure 15-12.*** *Configure the Push Notifications service for your app*

Click the app id to open it and scroll down to find the *Push Notifications* service. The *Development* column next to it should say *Configurable*. Click *Edit* button to open the settings for Push Notifications as in Figure 15-13.

***Figure 15-13.*** *Create an SSL Certificate for Push Notifications*

Make sure the checkbox next to *Push Notifications* is ticked and click *Create Certificate* in the *Development SSL Certificate* panel. A dialog will appear that will prompt you to upload the CSR file you created on your machine in the previous step. Click *Generate*: this will create a certificate, named aps_development.cer, which you can then download.

## Create a .p12 Certificate

Double-click the aps_development.cer, which was generated for you in the last step. This should import it in your computer's *Keychain Access* app. Inside *Keychain Access* find the imported certificate under **login ➤ My Certificates** and right-click it. You should see a pop-up menu like the one shown on Figure 15-14.

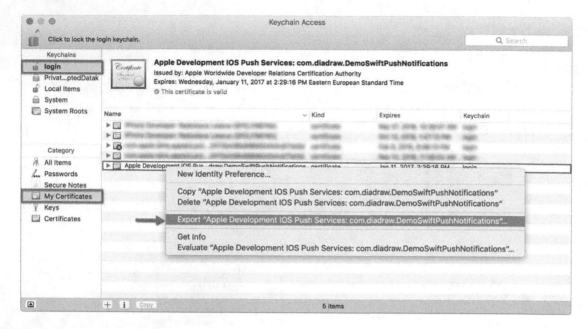

**Figure 15-14.** *Export the .cer file into .p12*

Select the *Export* option and export the certificate into .p12 format: the .p12 file contains the certificate and the private key together. Name the exported file PNKey.p12 and choose a password for it (the password I will be using for the rest of this tutorial is *PassKey*) as shown on Figure 15-15.

**Figure 15-15.** *Enter a password for the .p12 file*

Now you should have two certificate files on your machine: aps_development.cer and PNKey.p12.

## Generate a Certificate for the Notification Provider

The PHP script we will use as our notification provider needs a TLS certificate to be able to send requests to APNs. We will use the certificates we obtained so far to generate one. Open the Terminal on your Mac and navigate to the folder where you saved aps_development.cer and PNKey.p12.

Run the following command to generate a certificate for the provider:

```
openssl x509 -in aps_development.cer -inform der -out PNCertificate.pem
```

This should make a file named PNCertificate.pem appear in the same folder.
Next, run the following command, which will generate a .pem key:

```
openssl pkcs12 -nocerts -in PNKey.p12 -out PNKey.pem
```

When you are asked to *Enter Import Password*, type the password you set for the .p12 file earlier (*PassKey* if you used the same one as I did). You should see *MAC verified OK* in the console (Figure 15-16).

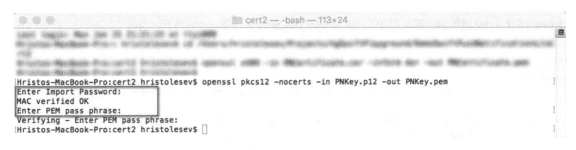

*Figure 15-16.* *Generating PNKey.pem result*

You will then be asked to enter a PEM pass phrase—this is a new password that you need to make up. Make a note of it—we will need it when we set up the PHP script later on. The password I will use is *PEMPassKey*.

The next command (Listing 15-11) will test if the certificate and the key file we just generated work for connecting to APNs's sandbox:

```
openssl s_client -connect gateway.sandbox.push.apple.com:2195 -cert ↵
    PNCertificate.pem -key PNKey.pem
```

You can see the result of the execution of this command in Figure 15-17.

```
● ● ●                              ServerTest — -bash — 113×22
Hristos-MacBook-Pro:cert2 hristolesev$ openssl s_client -connect gateway.sandbox.push.apple.com:2195 -cert PNCert
ificate.pem -key PNKey.pem
[Enter pass phrase for PNKey.pem:
CONNECTED(00000003)
depth=1 /C=US/O=Entrust, Inc./OU=www.entrust.net/rpa is incorporated by reference/OU=(c) 2009 Entrust, Inc./CN=En
trust Certification Authority - L1C
verify error:num=20:unable to get local issuer certificate
verify return:0
---
Certificate chain
 0 s:/C=US/ST=California/L=Cupertino/O=Apple Inc./CN=gateway.sandbox.push.apple.com
   i:/C=US/O=Entrust, Inc./OU=www.entrust.net/rpa is incorporated by reference/OU=(c) 2009 Entrust, Inc./CN=Entru
st Certification Authority - L1C
 1 s:/C=US/O=Entrust, Inc./OU=www.entrust.net/rpa is incorporated by reference/OU=(c) 2009 Entrust, Inc./CN=Entru
st Certification Authority - L1C
   i:/O=Entrust.net/OU=www.entrust.net/CPS_2048 incorp. by ref. (limits liab.)/OU=(c) 1999 Entrust.net Limited/CN
=Entrust.net Certification Authority (2048)
---
Server certificate
-----BEGIN CERTIFICATE-----
MIIFMzCCBBugAwIBAgIETCMmsDANBgkqhkiG9w0BAQUFADCBsTELMAkGA1UEBhMC
VVMxFjAUBgNVBAoTDUVudHJ1c3QsIETuYy4x0TA3BgNVBAsTMHd3dy5lbnRRydXN0
```

*Figure 15-17.* *Test connection result*

The PHP script we are about to write will need the .pem certificate and key to be in the same file. The final command will do this for us and combine the two files into PNCertificateAndKey.pem:

```
cat PNCertificate.pem PNKey.pem > PNCertificateAndKey.pem
```

## Setting Up the Provider

Below is a PHP script (Listing 15-9), which will act as a notification provider and send messages to the APNs's sandbox. Create a file, named testAPNS.php in the same folder as PNCertificateAndKey.pem and copy the following code into it.

*Listing 15-9.* testAPNS.php: The PHP Script, Which Will Send Notifications to Our App

```php
<?php
//Replace the device token with the one you copied from Xcode's console:
$deviceToken = ↵
        '8cccee83f03a788686bda17793441c8ce279ebf519b890de8b6b41a2e9b42d6e';

//Replace this with the PEM pass phrase you set when creating PNKey.pem
$keyPassword = 'PEMPassKey';

//Replace this with the name and path
//to the file you combined the .pem certificate and key in:
$pemCertFile = 'PNCertificateAndKey.pem';

//Put your push notification message here:
$message = "Hello, app! I am a PHP script.";

//APNs sandbox url
$sandboxAddress = 'ssl://gateway.sandbox.push.apple.com:2195';
//Set up the connection
$stream = stream_context_create();
stream_context_set_option($stream,'ssl','passphrase',$keyPassword);
stream_context_set_option($stream,'ssl','local_cert',$pemCertFile);
$connectionTimeout = 30;
$connectionType = STREAM_CLIENT_CONNECT | STREAM_CLIENT_PERSISTENT;
$connection = ↵
        stream_socket_client($sandboxAddress, ↵
                             $errorNumber, ↵
                             $errorString, ↵
                             $connectionTimeout, ↵
                             $connectionType, ↵
                             $stream);

//Quit if we can't connect to the APNs service
if (!$connection)
{
    echo "Connection failed. Error = $errorString <br/>";
    exit;
}
```

```
else
{
    echo "Connection succeeded. <br/>";
}

//Create the remote notification and send it
$messageData['aps'] = ↵
    array('alert' => $message, 'sound' => 'default','badge' => 1);

$payloadData = json_encode($messageData);
$notification = chr(0) . pack('n', 32) . pack('H*', $deviceToken) . ↵
    pack('n', strlen($payloadData)) . $payloadData;
$sendResult = fwrite($connection, $notification, strlen($notification));

if (!$sendResult)
{
    echo "Could not send push notification.<br/>";
}
else
{
    echo "Successfully sent a push notification to device with token ↵
        $deviceToken<br/>";
}

fclose($connection);
?>
```

Let us take a moment and examine the internals of the script. Even if you don't have any previous experience with PHP it will be easy to read and understand the basic idea behind it.

The first four lines declare a few variables, the values of which you will need to replace with your own:

- $deviceToken: assign it the device token APNs sends to your app. If you haven't run your app yet, run it: the device token will be printed out in Xcode's console when ap plication(_:didRegisterForRemoteNotificationsWithDeviceToken:)gets called. Delete the brackets and the whitespaces from the token string.

- $keyPassword: this should contain the PEM pass phrase you chose when you created PMKey.pem.

- $pemCertFile should have the path to the file in which you combined the PEM certificate and key.

- $message contains the message you would like your notification to display.

The script initiates a secure socket connection to the APNs server and prepares a notification message. A $messageData array is created with a single item in it, named aps. This item contains the notification properties. Notifications are transported as a JSON-formatted string. The final notification message is packed in the $notification variable, which is then sent to the APNs.

## Sending a Notification

With the PHP script from the previous step customized, it is time to test it and send a notification to your app. To execute the PHP script, you need a server and a PHP interpreter. If you are using OSX Mavericks or newer, you will have your PHP environment already set up for you and nothing extra to do. If you are on an older OSX version, you can download a MAMP solution stack, which comes with all the tools you need to run a PHP server on your machine.

To start the PHP server, in the Mac Terminal navigate to the folder where you saved testAPNS.php and run the following command:

```
php -S localhost:8000
```

You can now test the sending and receiving of push notifications. To make sure your app receives the notification, run it on your device through the Xcode debugger. Then, on your Mac, open your favorite web browser and execute the PHP script by navigating to http://localhost:8000/testAPNS.php. If all goes according to plan, you should see the notification message printed out in Xcode's console (Figure 15-18).

```
DemoSwiftPushNotifications

Received remote notification: [aps: {
    alert = "Hello, app! I am a PHP script.";
    badge = 2;
    sound = default;
}]


All Output ◇
```

*Figure 15-18. Notification message received—watch Xcode's console*

## Bonus Step: Display the Notification on the Device

The setup and code you have so far is enough as a proof of concept and covers the basics you need in order to send and receive push notifications. It would be nice, however, to know how to display the notifications on the device, rather than look for them in Xcode's console. In your project in Xcode open the AppDelegate.swift file and modify the implementation of the application(_:didReceiveRemoteNotification:) method as shown in Listing 15-10.

*Listing 15-10.* Add an Alert Dialog to Display the Notification

```
func application( ↵
    application: UIApplication, ↵
    didReceiveRemoteNotification userInfo: [NSObject : AnyObject]) {
    print( "Received remote notification: \(userInfo)" )

    // Check if the message is in the expected format:
    if let notification = userInfo["aps"] as? NSDictionary,
    let alert = notification["alert"] as? String {
        // Create an alert controller to display the received message:
        let alertCtrl = ↵
```

```
        UIAlertController(title: "Notification", ↵
        message: alert as String, preferredStyle: UIAlertControllerStyle.Alert)

    // Add an OK button, which will close the alert:
    alertCtrl.addAction(
        UIAlertAction(title: "OK", ↵
        style: UIAlertActionStyle.Default, handler: nil))

    // Find the root view controller of the app:
    var presentedVC = self.window?.rootViewController

    // Walk the view controller's hierarchy
    // until a presented view controller is found:
    while let presented = presentedVC?.presentedViewController {
        presentedVC = presented
    }

    // Show the alert's view controller in the currently presented VC:
    presentedVC?.presentViewController( ↵
        alertCtrl, animated: true, completion: nil)
    }
}
```

Recompile and run the app on your device. Then refresh the browser where you loaded the path to the PHP script to execute it again. When the notification is received, you should see this alert box (Figure 15-19):

***Figure 15-19.*** *Notification alert*

And that's it! You have a fully working app that can receive push notifications and a provider, which is set up to send them.

# Summary

You are now familiar with two of the most used tools for mobile app monetization and user retention. Using iAd makes you a part of Apple's mobile advertisement network and gives you a share from a rapidly expanding market. You have set up and used two different kinds of ads and know how to test them: banner and interstitial ads. To keep the users of your app in the loop we have also implemented the full circle of push notification services, from the notification provider to the app itself.

And if you are still hungry to learn new frameworks, put on your seatbelt and get ready for the next chapter, where we will play with graphics APIs.

# CHAPTER 16

■ ■ ■

# Using the High-End Graphics APIs

The ability to play games was an amazing addition to the world of mobile devices. It unleashed developers' imaginations and allowed users to solve puzzles, create and defend kingdoms, or relieve stress by throwing some really angry birds around.

When developing a game, it is always more fun to focus on the gameplay and the game mechanics, rather than worry about things like rendering speed, user interface (UI) elements, or layout. In recognition of that, Apple introduced two frameworks: SpriteKit, which focuses on building 2D games, and SceneKit, which helps create and manage 3D content.

In this chapter you will do the following:

- Learn about the SpriteKit and the SceneKit frameworks.

- Learn how to create a game scene, animate objects on the screen, and work with cameras, geometry, materials, and lights.

- See how to use Xcode as a game scene editor.

- Build a 2D app with SpriteKit in which a spaceship chases your finger on the screen.

- Build an app with SceneKit and learn how to let the user move objects in 3D.

When you are done, you will have two mobile app projects with basic elements of iOS game development in 2D and 3D.

## Creating 2D Games with SpriteKit

SpriteKit is Apple's framework, which helps developers create 2D games. You can think of it as a fully equipped game engine, as it comes with

- a built-in scene hierarchy manager;

- an animation engine;

- a sound engine;

- a physics engine;

- a collision detector; and

- graphics support for lighting and *shader* effects.[1]

---

[1]A shader is a small program which is executed by the GPU. Shaders are used mainly for color calculation, geometry altering, and tessellation. For example, we can define a new material by writing a shader that computes how light is reflected from a given point on a surface and thus defines what color it should be.

© Radoslava Lescva Adams and Hristo Lesev 2016
R. L. Adams and H. Lesev, *Migrating to Swift from Flash and ActionScript*,
DOI 10.1007/978-1-4842-1666-8_16

Not only that, but Xcode also has a dedicated SpriteKit editor, which helps you visually build your game.

The framework makes use of the graphics processing unit (GPU), in order to achieve fast scene rendering. As you could guess by its name, the SpriteKit framework is intended to render sprites on the screen. As a Flash developer, you are already familiar with sprites—they are textured images. Before we set up a SpriteKit app, let us briefly go over the framework's architecture.

## Learning the Structure of the SpriteKit

SpriteKit provides a custom view component of type SKView, in which the game content is rendered. SKView is a subclass of UIView—the base class for every UI element on iOS. This means that we can transparently include an SKView and any other element from SpriteKit in the UI of any application for iOS.

Game scenes are presented inside SKView. Every game in SpriteKit is composed of one or more scenes of type SKScene. A scene is the canvas, where all graphic elements of your game are hosted and rendered. You can have multiple scenes for different areas of the game. For example, you could use one scene for the main menu, another scene for the game levels, and a third scene for the scores and ranking. Dividing a game into scenes helps you manage your code and assets by providing a scene container for the different functional areas in your game.

The building blocks of a scene are called *nodes*. A node is represented by the SKNode base class and serves as a container for the game objects and their properties. Nodes can be composed in a parent-child hierarchy.[2] Instead of directly with SKNode we work with its subclasses. For example, to show an image we need an instance of the SKSpriteNode class; to show text we use the SKLabelNode class. There are nodes for displaying shapes, playing audio, simulating a camera, emitting particles, and many more. Nodes are responsible for storing the visual representation, position, and rotation of the game objects in the scene. You can further define a node by attaching objects to it.

One of the objects you can attach to a node is a physics body. It is represented by the SKPhysycsBody class and describes a node's physical characteristics like mass, shape, and friction. SpriteKit's physics simulator, SKPhysicsWorld, uses physics bodies to calculate the position and rotation of nodes. This simulator is quite powerful and lets you define gravity fields, apply forces to nodes, calculate collision, and connect bodies with joints.

We use actions to manipulate the state of a node. An action is represented by the SKAction class: it modifies the properties of the game objects, in order to create an animation. Each action has a duration interval, measured in seconds. The most common use for an action is to change a node's position. Several actions can be composed in sequences or groups to create complex animations.

To display a scene on the screen SpriteKit uses a rendering loop very similar to the one used by the ActionScript virtual machine. It iterates through all nodes in a scene at the beginning of each frame, evaluates any actions associated with them, simulates physics, and then renders the scene on the screen.

This is how SpriteKit works in a nutshell. Now we will explore the framework by making our first SpriteKit application.

## Setting Up a SpriteKit App

The app we are about to develop will display a spaceship sprite on the screen. The spaceship will follow the user's finger—we will animate it to move to the coordinates of each screen touch.

Instead of starting with an empty project we will create the app using Xcode's SpriteKit project template and modify its code.

In Xcode create a Game application project (**File ➤ New ➤ Project...**, then **iOS ➤ Application ➤ Game**) as shown in Figure 16-1.

---

[2]In fact, SKScene is a subclass of SKNode, so any SKNode instance you add directly to it becomes a child of this root node.

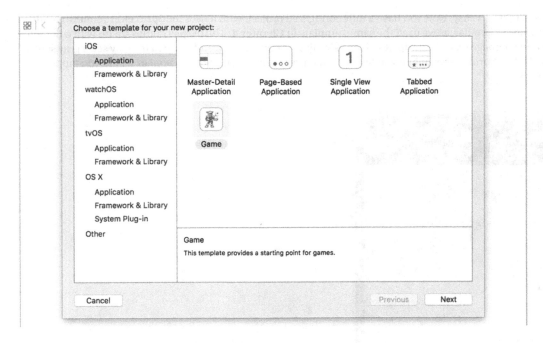

***Figure 16-1.*** *Creating a Game project in Xcode*

Set the project's name to SpriteKitDemo and set **Game Technology** to SpriteKit (Figure 16-2).

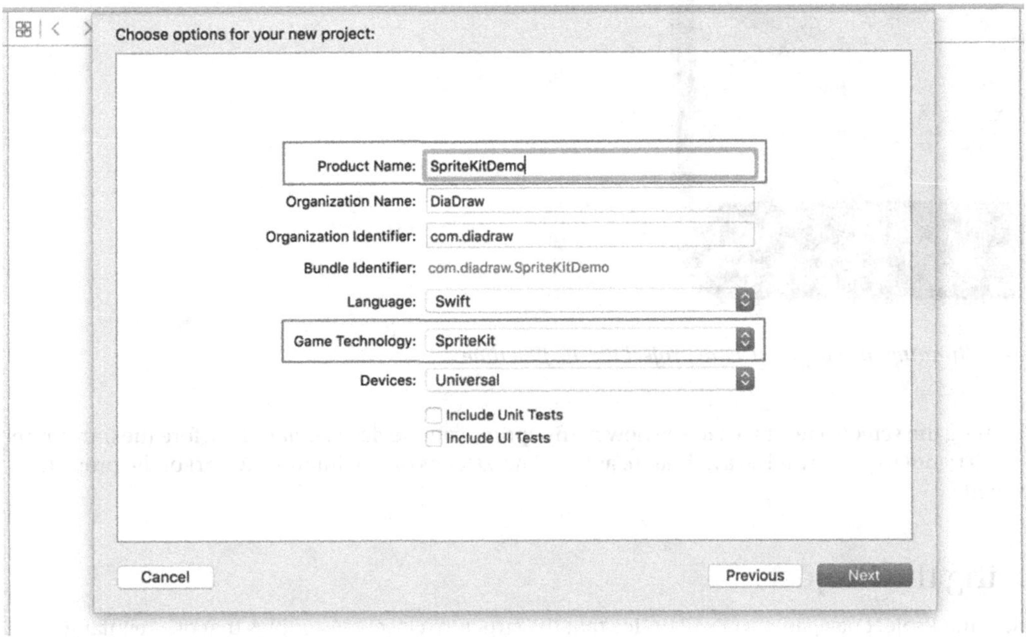

***Figure 16-2.*** *Setting up the project to use the SpriteKit*

Well, that was easy. Now you have a fully configured project, which uses the SpriteKit framework and probably looks familiar, as we used the same template in **Chapter 4**. The project comes set up with a default scene and an image of a spaceship. Run it in a simulator or on a device and you will initially see a gray screen with a "Hello, World!" label. When you tap the screen, a rotating spaceship will appear where you tapped (Figure 16-3).

***Figure 16-3.*** *Running the SpriteKitDemo project for the first time*

Try tapping the screen a few times to see how many sprites your device can handle before the frame rate deteriorates. Try not to get carried away, though, as it is time to focus on the interesting part of the project: the source code.

## Dissecting the Project

If you look at the Project navigator, you will notice that the structure closely resembles that of a regular iOS project. However, there are some new additions.

Let us have a look at the new files in the project tree:

- GameViewController.swift. This file contains the definition of GameViewController—a UIViewController subclass, which is responsible for creating a scene and presenting it on an SKView. The view itself can be found and configured in the Main.storyboard file.

- GameScene.swift. This file defines the game loop logic for the scene. It does gesture handling and takes care of the creation of *nodes* and scene updates. Nodes are the building blocks of a scene.

- GameScene.sks. This is SpriteKit's equivalent of a storyboard. When you open this file, you will see a visual editor, which helps you build a scene by dragging and dropping game nodes on it. This is the scene's resource archive.

Now we are going to look inside these files and see how the game is built.

Open GameViewController.swift and locate the viewDidLoad method (Listing 16-1). Inside it, first an instance of the GameScene class is initialized using the GameScene resource archive. Then a constant is created, named skView, to keep a reference to the view controller's view (SKView). Setting the showsFPS and showsNodeCount properties to true instructs the SpriteKit to display the corresponding debug information.

The scene is shown on the screen by calling SKView's presentScene method. When you have more than one scene in your game, you could use animation for the transition between scenes.

***Listing 16-1.*** Scene-Creating Routines

```
override func viewDidLoad() {
    super.viewDidLoad()

    if let scene = GameScene(fileNamed:"GameScene") {
        // Configure the view.
        let skView = self.view as! SKView
        skView.showsFPS = true
        skView.showsNodeCount = true

        /* Sprite Kit applies additional optimizations to improve rendering performance */
        skView.ignoresSiblingOrder = true

        /* Set the scale mode to scale to fit the window */
        scene.scaleMode = .AspectFill

        skView.presentScene(scene)
    }
}
```

Let us now open the GameScene.swift file. It contains the implementation of the GameScene class, which is responsible for controlling the objects in the current scene. The class inherits SKScene and overrides three of its methods:

- The didMoveToView method is called after the scene is presented on the screen by a SKView instance. This method is used to create the scene's contents.

- The touchesBegan method is called when the user taps inside the view. Here we will add the logic that will make the spaceship follow users' taps on the screen.

- The third method, update, is called by the game loop in the beginning of every frame and is used as an entry point for any necessary updates to the scene.

We will replace the default implementation of these methods with our own, so delete the bodies of all three. The GameScene class should now look like that in Listing 16-2.

*Listing 16-2.* Removing the Default Implementation of the GameScene Class

```
class GameScene: SKScene {

    override func didMoveToView(view: SKView) {
    }

    override func touchesBegan(touches: Set<UITouch>, withEvent event: UIEvent?) {
    }

    override func update(currentTime: CFTimeInterval) {
    }
}
```

In the next section we will add a spaceship sprite to the scene and make it move as we tap the screen.

# Moving the Sprite Around

Start by adding a constant called playerSprite of type SKSpriteNode as a member of the GameScene class. Initialize it with the default Spaceship image resource created by Xcode:

```
let playerSprite = SKSpriteNode(imageNamed:"Spaceship")
```

This line creates a node and assigns an image to it. The node, however, is not part of the scene yet. To show a node on the screen we need to add it to the scene's tree by calling addChild. We want this to happen before the scene becomes visible, so we will put the code inside the didMoveToView function.

Let us do a small adjustment before showing the node on the screen. The original spaceship image is too large, so we will scale it down to a third of its original size by changing its xScale and yScale properties. You can see the code in Listing 16-3.

*Listing 16-3.* Adding a Sprite Node to the Scene

```
override func didMoveToView(view: SKView) {

    //Scale down the sprite to 30%
    playerSprite.xScale = 0.3
    playerSprite.yScale = 0.3

    //Add the playerSprite to the scene
    self.addChild(playerSprite)
}
```

Now that we have added the sprite, let us make it move. When the user touches the screen we want the spaceship to move from its current position to the coordinates of the touch event. First we will get the location of the touch event in scene coordinates and then we will create an action to animate the movement of the sprite towards its new position. We will implement the logic inside touchesBegan (Listing 16-4).

The touchesBegan function supports multitouch (i.e., the user tapping the screen with more than one finger). In our case we will take only one of these touch sites into account and ignore the others. To get the touch location in scene coordinates we call SKNode's helper function named locationInNode.

For the spaceship animation to look realistic we need not only to move the sprite but also to rotate it, so that it faces the direction of the movement. To calculate the angle of rotation we use simple trigonometry: first we construct a vector, which starts at the player's current position and ends at the destination point by subtracting the two points. Then we compute the angle between the vector and the positive x-axis with the help of the atan2 function. atan2 returns the angle in radians, which is a good thing, because SpriteKit prefers angles in radians too. One last thing: the rotation angle is calculated relative to the x axis, but the spaceship's nose is facing the y axis. For that we need to offset the angle by ninety degrees, that is, add $\frac{\pi}{2}$ (approximately 1.56) radians to it.

We create an action for moving and an action for rotating the sprite in order to animate it. To play the actions one after another we create an action sequence in the form of an array. Calling runAction and passing it that array at the end of touchesBegan runs the sequence and creates the animation.

*Listing 16-4.* Animating the Player Node to Follow Touch Coordinates

```
override func touchesBegan(touches: Set<UITouch>, withEvent event: UIEvent?) {

    //Get the scene coordinates of the touch event
    let location = touches.first!.locationInNode(self)

    //Calculate the angle, at which we need to rotate the sprite,
    // in order to face the direction of movement:
    let angle = atan2(location.y - playerSprite.position.y, ↵
        location.x - playerSprite.position.x ) - 1.56

    //Create an action to move the sprite to the touch location coordinates
    let moveAction = SKAction.moveTo(location, duration: 0.5)
    //Create an action to rotate the sprite to face the direction of movement
    let rotateAction = SKAction.rotateToAngle(angle, duration: 0.1)

    //Animate the sprite executing actions sequentially
    playerSprite.runAction(SKAction.sequence([rotateAction, moveAction]))
}
```

Run the application, tap the screen, and you will see the spaceship sprite fly toward the point where you tapped. Touch the screen again and the spaceship will rotate itself and chase your finger (Figure 16-4).

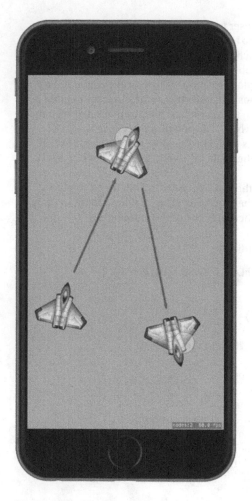

***Figure 16-4.*** *Running the game*

## Using the SpriteKit Scene Editor

Xcode comes with an integrated SpriteKit scene editor, which helps you visually compose scenes for your game. It allows you to drag and drop and arrange and edit nodes inside the integrated development environment (IDE) instead of doing it programmatically.

To open the editor select the GameScene.sks file in the Project navigator. You should see an empty scene like the one in Figure 16-5.

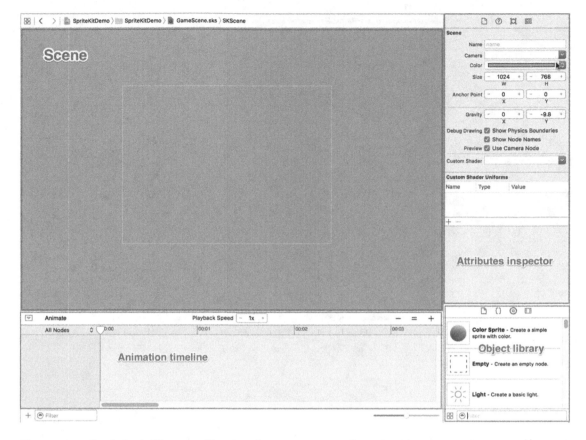

***Figure 16-5.*** *Xcode SpriteKit scene editor interface*

Xcode's Scene editor looks a lot like its Storyboard editor. On the left there is the Attributes inspector, where you set nodes' parameters and the Object library with nodes you can drag and drop on the scene.

Let us add a label node to the scene. Find a label in the Object library and drag it toward the yellow rectangle shown in Figure 16-6. With the label node selected go to the Attributes inspector and set **Text** to `This game is awesome!`

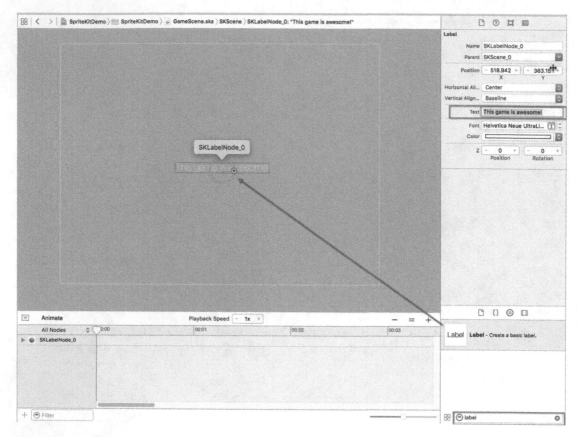

***Figure 16-6.*** *Adding a label node to the scene*

Run the game and you will see the label in the middle of the screen (Figure 16-7).

***Figure 16-7.*** *The scene with the newly added label*

Note that, although the scene editor can save us a lot of time composing content, we still need to initialize sprite instances and program the gameplay by hand.

# Developing 3D Apps with SceneKit

The SceneKit framework is similar to SpriteKit but deals with three-dimensional space. SceneKit is a bit more general and can be used not just for games but also for business-oriented apps that need to show 3D content. For example, you could use it to build an e-book reader, which shows an embedded 3D view alongside the text.

Before SceneKit was released, iOS developers had to use low-level graphic application programming interfaces (APIs) like OpenGL to render 3D objects in their apps. OpenGL is a powerful graphic library, but it forces you to think in terms of triangles, vertex buffers, and color buffers, in order to show something on the screen. SceneKit hides these technical details behind a higher-level framework and allows you to work with objects like geometry, lights, materials, shaders, and cameras.

## Learning the Structure of SceneKit

SceneKit renders its content in a SCNView, which is a standard UI element. All content that will be rendered in SCNView is stored in a scene, represented by the SCNScene class.

A scene is structured as a hierarchical tree of nodes, much like a scene in SpriteKit. All nodes in the tree are linked together with parent-child relationships. This tree of nodes is also known as a *scene graph*. A node is represented by the SCNNode class and has properties describing its position, rotation, and scale relative to its parent node. Basically, nodes are used as placeholders for objects to keep the scene structured. To visualize an object we need to attach it to a node. We can use the following types of objects:

- **Geometry.** Represents a 3D object. SceneKit comes with built-in geometry objects like boxes, spheres, cones, and planes. You can also create geometry programmatically or load it from a file. SceneKit supports COLLADA files, an industry-standard file format, which can be exported from many 3D modeling programs.

- **Camera.** Represents the viewer of the scene.

- **Light.** Represents objects that can cast light onto the scene. Lights are parameterized and can simulate a variety of light sources from a light bulb to the sun.

- **Physics body.** You can simulate physical effects such as gravity or collisions by creating a physical body and attaching it to a node.

- **Material.** Defines how geometry will be visualized. You can specify how a surface reacts to light and what texture or color to be used to imitate a real-world material.

You can animate all objects on the screen by either changing their properties or manipulating their geometry. SpriteKit allows you to import a *rigged*[3] model with skeletal animation that can be used to change a model's geometry. Skeletal animation is commonly used for animating characters. The rigged objects have a *skinner object,*[4] which is used to control individual bones in the skeletal hierarchy.

Another way to create animation is to use actions like we did in the SpriteKit framework tutorial.

---

[3]Rigging is the process of adding a skeleton to a 3D model, which helps with the animation of movement.
[4]A skinner object helps with animating 3D objects by providing access to their skeleton.

Speaking of SpriteKit, there is another similarity between the two frameworks: the game loop. SceneKit goes through the same steps in the game loop to prepare and render the scene graph on the screen. First the scene graph is updated, next all actions and animations are applied, then physics is simulated, and finally the scene is rendered on the screen.

This is the end of our brief overview of SceneKit's structure. Now is time to use it in an app.

## Setting Up the App

Let us create a project using Xcode's SceneKit project template. We will go through the project's code and see how a 3D scene is created and populated with objects first.

In Xcode create a Game application project (**File ➤ New ➤ Project...**, then **iOS ➤ Application ➤ Game**), name it SceneKitDemo and set **Game Technology** to SceneKit (Figure 16-8).

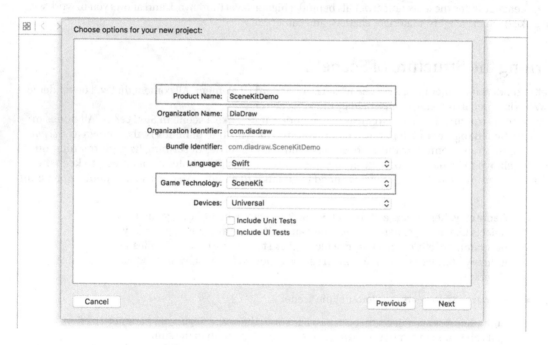

***Figure 16-8.*** *Creating a SceneKit project*

When you click **Next**, Xcode will generate a simple project with one view and a SCNView inside. The default scene has one geometry node, which contains a 3D model of a spaceship, two light nodes, and a camera node. If you run the project, you will see a rotating spaceship on a black background (Figure 16-9).

*Figure 16-9. Running the SceneKitDemo project*

Let us examine the source files that Xcode has generated for us.

## Examining the SceneKit Project's Structure

The project strongly resembles a typical iOS app project structure. There is a storyboard with one view inside, a view controller, and an assets group.

The only difference with the iOS app templates we have been using so far in the book is that here the root view element in the storyboard is of type SCNView. This makes the game cover the whole available screen space. If your application only needs to render 3D scenes in a smaller portion of the screen, SCNView can be used in a layout with other UI elements and be put in a container, for example. You can easily show a scene view in a table or in another container.

In the Project navigator there is a group called art.scnassets. Inside you will find a file called ship.scn and an image: texture.png. The PNG image is used as a texture that will cover the spaceship geometry model. Here textures are used as skins on top of 3D models. This allows us to show visual detail without necessarily creating complex 3D geometry. For example, instead of constructing every element of the spaceship's cockpit in 3D and thus adding more triangles to its geometry, we show these elements in a 2D texture.

The ship.scn file contains a ready-made scene graph. Click it to open Xcode's visual 3D scene editor. In it you can compose scenes by dragging and dropping nodes, geometry, lights, cameras, and many more scene elements.

And now let us look at the most interesting part of this project: the GameViewController.swift file. Inside is the source code responsible for scene creation, animation, and the rest of the game's logic. Open the file and search for the viewDidLoad() function; it contains the code for setting up the scene.

## Adding a Scene

The default SceneKit workflow starts with creating a scene, configuring it, and assigning it to a SceneKit View to be rendered on the screen (Listing 16-5).

You can create an empty scene or to load one from an .scn file by calling the SCNScene(named:) class initializer. To visualize a scene, you need to assign it to the scene property of a SceneKit view instance. You can create multiple scenes and choose which one is visible at any given time by assigning it to the SceneKit view.

***Listing 16-5.*** Adding a Scene

```
// create a new scene
let scene = SCNScene(named: "art.scnassets/ship.scn")!

// retrieve the SCNView
let scnView = self.view as! SCNView

// assign the scene to the view
scnView.scene = scene
```

## Adding a Camera

As a next step we will add a camera to the scene. You can think of the camera as the eye of the observer of the scene. What the camera sees is what the user will see. To move the user's view point in the scene we change camera's position, angle, field of view, and other parameters. Listing 16-6 shows you how to create and configure a camera.

First we create an SCNNode instance, which will "host" the camera in the node tree. Next, we initialize a SCNCamera instance and attach it to the node by assigning it to its camera property. Then we add the camera node as a child node of the scene graph. The final step is to set the camera's position in 3D space with the help of a class, which represents three-dimensional vectors: SCNVector3. With this we move the camera by 15 units[5] backward from the center of the scene.

***Listing 16-6.*** Adding a Camera

```
// create and add a camera to the scene
let cameraNode = SCNNode()
cameraNode.camera = SCNCamera()
scene.rootNode.addChildNode(cameraNode)

// position the camera
cameraNode.position = SCNVector3(x: 0, y: 0, z: 15)
```

---

[5]SceneKit uses meters as a default unit measurement.

# Adding Light

If you go inside the `viewDidLoad()` function, comment these two lines of code,

```
scene.rootNode.addChildNode(lightNode)
scene.rootNode.addChildNode( ambientLightNode)
```

and run the app, you will notice that the spaceship does not look very three-dimensional but, rather, like a collection of flat-colored objects. To add depth to the scene, we need light.

We can choose between four types of light sources in SceneKit:

- **Omni.** Also known as *point light*, it emits light equally in all directions. It can be used to simulate a light bulb.

- **Ambient.** Ambient light illuminates all objects in the scene from all directions. It is used to approximate the light bouncing between objects the way it happens in nature, and prevent our scene from getting too dark.

- **Directional**. Directional light simulates a distant light source, which emits light in a given direction. It is often used to simulate the sun.

- **Spot.** This one represents a cone-shaped light source like the floodlights used in stadiums and theaters.

You can see how an omni light source is added to the scene in Listing 16-7. First a container node for the light object is created. Then an instance of the SCNLight class is assigned to the `light` property of the node. The SCNLight class represents a general light object; setting its `type` property to `SNLightTypeOmni` makes it an omni light. We set the position of the light as a SCNVector3.

**Listing 16-7.** Adding an Omni Light

```
// create and add a light to the scene
let lightNode = SCNNode()
lightNode.light = SCNLight()
lightNode.light!.type = SCNLightTypeOmni
lightNode.position = SCNVector3(x: 0, y: 10, z: 10)
scene.rootNode.addChildNode(lightNode)
```

This omni light will be the main light source in the scene, but if we use it as the only light source, most of the scene will appear dark. A directional light source illuminates only surfaces that face it and leaves the rest of the surfaces in shadow.

In order to fill the scene with light, we will add an ambient light source too—you can see this done in Listing 16-8. This looks similar to how we created the omni light, but without setting a position for it. Ambient sources cast light from all directions in the scene.

**Listing 16-8.** Adding an Ambient Light

```
// create and add an ambient light to the scene
let ambientLightNode = SCNNode()
ambientLightNode.light = SCNLight()
ambientLightNode.light!.type = SCNLightTypeAmbient
ambientLightNode.light!.color = UIColor.darkGrayColor()
scene.rootNode.addChildNode(ambientLightNode)
```

## Animating the Spaceship

Next, we will animate the spaceship model to rotate infinitely around the y axis, as if on a turntable.

In order to assign animation to the spaceship node, we will locate it by its name in the scene graph by calling `childNodeWithName(name:recursively:)`. This function iterates through all child nodes of a given node and looks for a name match. Setting the `recursively` parameter to `true` will make it iterate through the subtrees coming out of the node's children too.

Once we have located the spaceship node, we will attach an `SCNAction` instance to it to do the rotation and repeat it forever (Listing 16-9).

*Listing 16-9.* Animating the Spaceship

```
// retrieve the ship node
let ship = scene.rootNode.childNodeWithName("ship", recursively: true)!

// animate the 3d object
ship.runAction(SCNAction.repeatActionForever(SCNAction.rotateByX(0, y: 2, z: 0, duration: 1)))
```

## Selecting an Object

Making the 3D scene interactive involves letting the user select an object by tapping it. In general this requires quite a lot of calculations, in order to determine which of the objects in the scene lies underneath a certain point in the 2D space, which is available to the user for tapping. SceneKit makes our job easier by handling a lot of these calculations. With the next few listings we will implement object selection (picking) in our demo project.

We start by adding a tap gesture recognizer handler to the SceneKit view (Listing 16-10).

*Listing 16-10.* Add a Handler for the Tap Gesture

```
// add a tap gesture recognizer
let tapGesture = UITapGestureRecognizer(target: self, action: "handleTap:")
scnView.addGestureRecognizer(tapGesture)
```

The actual object picking happens in the `handleTap(:)` function, shown in Listing 16-11.

*Listing 16-11.* Implementing Object Picking and Highlighting

```
func handleTap(gestureRecognize: UIGestureRecognizer) {
    // retrieve the SCNView
    let scnView = self.view as! SCNView

    // check what nodes are tapped
    let p = gestureRecognize.locationInView(scnView)
    let hitResults = scnView.hitTest(p, options: nil)
    // check that we clicked on at least one object
    if hitResults.count > 0 {
        // retrieved the first clicked object
        let result: AnyObject! = hitResults[0]

        // get its material
        let material = result.node!.geometry!.firstMaterial!
```

```
    // highlight it
    SCNTransaction.begin()
    SCNTransaction.setAnimationDuration(0.5)

    // on completion - unhighlight
    SCNTransaction.setCompletionBlock {
        SCNTransaction.begin()
        SCNTransaction.setAnimationDuration(0.5)

        material.emission.contents = UIColor.blackColor()

        SCNTransaction.commit()
    }

    material.emission.contents = UIColor.redColor()

    SCNTransaction.commit()
    }
}
```

On the first line of code in this function we get a reference to the scene view that generated the touch event. Then we use it to get the coordinates of the point of the touch event with the `locationInView` function. Calling the view's `hitTest` method gives us the objects, which fall under the finger. `hitTest` returns an array of `SCNHitTestResult` objects that match the hit test. An instance of `SCNHitTestResult` contains the scene graph node of a matching object, as well as the 3D coordinates (in world space) of the touch event's projection onto the object.

When we get the array of matching objects, we first check if it contains anything (i.e., if there were objects the tap gesture managed to hit). If there were any, we take the first one and highlight it with red by modifying the `emission` property of its material and creating a little animation that will make it glow in red. Note the line where the material of the object is obtained:

```
let material = result.node!.geometry!.firstMaterial!
```

This line relies on several assumptions to be true:

- We have hit a node in the scene tree.

- The node has a geometry mesh attached.

- The geometry has at least one material.

This line of code can be dangerous and can cause a runtime error if we execute it on an arbitrary scene. We know it will work in our current project, because the spaceship model satisfies all of these assumptions.

To animate the glow effect an `SCNTransaction` is used. This class controls in a transactional manner all properties of the scene that can be animated. We first create a transaction to be executed for half a second and slowly change the emission color of the object's material to red. When the first transaction is over, inside the `setCompletionBlock` closure we create another transaction to unhighlight the object by changing the emission color to black. If you run the project and tap the spaceship, you will see how the model flashes in red for a fraction of a second (Figure 16-10).

***Figure 16-10.*** *Picking a 3D model from the scene*

The SCNTransaction class can also be used as a mechanism to wrap multiple modifications of the scene in one atomic transaction.

We touched on using materials in this section. In the next one we will add a bit more detail about how SceneKit represent materials.

## Applying Materials

The material of an object defines what this object will look like when rendered on the screen. In physics an object's material describes how the object surface reflects incoming light. In programming terms a material is usually a function, which computes the color of every visible point of the object.

Materials in SceneKit have many properties. You can imitate plastic, wood, aluminum, and many other real-world materials by combining and configuring these properties. The most important ones are

- **Diffuse.** This property defines the base color of the object. A texture is often used as a diffuse color source. To simulate a wood surface, for example, you could use a brownish diffuse texture with rings and knots.

- **Specular.** This property defines the specular reflection of light for the material. If we added a finishing layer to the wood surface material, we would use its specular property to set how shiny it would be.

- **Emission.** This property defines how much light is emitted from an object's surface. Note that this does not make the object a light source, however, and the emitted light will only be visible to the observer (i.e., it will not illuminate and be reflected by other objects in the scene).

- **Normal.** A *normal* is a line or a vector, which is perpendicular to a given surface and thus defines the surface's orientation. Normals are used for lighting calculations both for diffuse and specular light. When we add a material to a surface, we can define different normals in various points of the surface (using a normal map[6]) and thus cause light to be reflected differently at each point, even if the whole surface is flat. This trick allows imitating unevenness and adding detail without having to change and complicate the geometry of the surface.

- **Ambient.** Defines how this material should appear in the presence of an ambient light.

Materials in SceneKit are represented by the SCNMaterial class and their properties—by the SCNMaterialProperty class. SCNMaterialProperty has a property named contents, which can contain information of different types: color, texture, a SCNScene instance, and so on.

To apply a material to an object you add it to the object's geometry. The SCNGeometry class has a property named materials, which is an array of SCNMaterial elements. The fact that the materials property is an array means that a geometry object can have multiple materials applied. If a geometry is composed of multiple elements, traditionally triangles, you can assign a separate material to each element. In other words, we could have a cube geometry, each side of it rendered using a different material.

The SCNMaterial class is designed to help you imitate the appearance of a vast majority of real-world materials. In addition, SceneKit allows you to write your own shaders. For that you can use the OpenGL Shading Language (GLSL).

The SceneKit and SpriteKit frameworks are so powerful that they would each merit a separate book. The scope of a single chapter is too narrow to cover topics like adding physics, enhancing the built-in renderer, using external assets, scene-lighting techniques, and many more. As you are reaching the end of this chapter, however, ideally you have the foundation, on which you can build your 2D and 3D programming techniques for iOS with Swift.

# Summary

In this chapter you saw how to use the SpriteKit framework to build 2D games and the SceneKit framework to present 3D scenes in your app.

This chapter marks the end of **Part III**. In **Part IV** we go deeper with Swift and look at the language in detail.

---

[6]A normal map is a texture. Instead of color information, each of its pixels contains data about the normal at a given point.

**PART IV**

■ ■ ■

# Language Migration

# CHAPTER 17

■ ■ ■

# Swift Language Basics

The first impression Flash developers usually share with us about Swift is "Oh, it's almost ActionScript, isn't it!" What they refer to is how readable syntax-wise a piece of Swift code is, compared to Objective-C, which used to be the typical choice when switching to native iOS programming. And they have a point: in contrast to transitioning to Objective-C, moving to Swift from ActionScript has a much lower entry point. Swift offers a lot more than that and in this chapter we will start unpacking its bag of goodies.

We will start with why you might want to move on to Swift in the first place and how your ActionScript experience can soften the learning curve. Then we will set up a playground, where you can quickly run code snippets, and will cover a few basic points, which you will need before moving on to the next chapters. You will see how to declare variables, constants, and functions and how to control access to your code, and you will become familiar with basic error handling.

## What Swift encourages You to Do

You will discover that a lot of concepts you have been using in ActionScript are not only present in Swift but with added power. This adds richness and expressiveness to the language.

What I personally most like about Swift, however, is the fact that it encourages good programming habits. Or enforces them, as may be the case. It gives you the option and the incentive to be concise with your code, but at the same time it forces you to state your intentions clearly. Swift's compiler is complicit in this: it will guide your hand and occasionally slap it, making it hard for you to write bad code unintentionally.

### Be Concise

The first thing I noticed about Swift was the lack of semicolons. I must admit that at that point I wrinkled my nose at it and thought "But, but, but . . . Why?!"

The thing is, Swift doesn't stop you from using semicolons. But it doesn't require you to use them either, unless you put separate statements on the same line. This underpins part of Swift's philosophy: you can write code as verbose as you need it, but you also have the option to be as concise as humanly possible.

I say "humanly possible," because the trouble with conciseness is not a compiler's problem: if a shortcut is legal, the compiler will understand it. However, both writing code that is too verbose and writing code that is too brief can interfere with human readability, so exercise your judgment.

Here is an example: the two pieces of code in Listing 17-1 and Listing 17-2 are both valid Swift and both do exactly the same: they define an array of integers and obtain a sorted copy of it.

© Radoslava Leseva Adams and Hristo Lesev 2016
R. L. Adams and H. Lesev, *Migrating to Swift from Flash and ActionScript*,
DOI 10.1007/978-1-4842-1666-8_17

*Listing 17-1.* Sorting an Integer Array: Verbose

```
let arrayOfInts: Array<Int> = [6, 3, 4];
let sortedArray: Array<Int> = arrayOfInts.sort(↵
    { (item1: Int, item2: Int) -> Bool in return item1 < item2 } );
```

*Listing 17-2.* Sorting an Integer Array: Concise

```
let arrayOfInts = [6, 3, 4]
let sortedArray = arrayOfInts.sort(<)
```

The rest of the chapters in **Part IV** will explain what is going on with the code in Listings 17-1 and 17-2. For the missing type declarations in Listing 17-2 see the section "Type safety and Type Inference" in **Chapter 19**. For the syntax in the function within the brackets in the first example and how it got reduced to a single operator in the second example see the section "Closures" in **Chapter 22**. To find out what the let keyword means see the section "Declaring Variables and Constants," later in this chapter. As for the missing semicolons . . . get over it. That's how it is in Swift.

# Be Explicit

One of the dangers of getting carried away with conciseness is ambiguity: you may end up writing code that is syntactically valid but doesn't actually do what you meant it to do. For example, in most other languages it is too easy to swap two arguments of the same type by mistake: the code will compile, it will look convincing to the human eye and the mistake will only come to bite you as a bug later on, maybe even after you have shipped the code. (To see how Swift can help with this issue, see the section "Defining and Calling Functions" later in this chapter.)

To say that Swift *encourages* you to be explicit would be an understatement. It's more like your grandmother who lovingly, but with some force, nudged you to say "please" and "thank you" to her neighbors. The Swift compiler nudges you in a similar way to state your intentions with every line of code you write.

For example, the ActionScript equivalent of the code in Listing 17-3 would result in all three print calls being executed, because I didn't put a break statement after each case. In Swift this is not the default behavior: to get execution to continue to the next case statement whether there is a break or not, even if a match has been found, I would need to use the fallthrough keyword.

In fact, the code in Listing 17-3 will not compile. While in other languages you may not even get a warning if you omit the default clause in a switch statement, in Swift this causes a compilation error. For details on what else switch statements can do for you (there is a lot!) see **Chapter 20**.

*Listing 17-3.* Spot the Missing Statement. Hint: It Is Not a break

```
let direction = 3

switch direction {
    case 1: print("Go South")
    case 2: print("Go North")
    case 3: print("Go East")
}
```

The effect of having to be explicit is twofold:

- You are less likely to suffer from bugs caused by accident and which, unfortunately, make for lexically valid code. For example, in Swift you can't unintentionally put the assignment operator (=) where you meant to use the equality operator (==) (more on this in **Chapter 18**).

- By writing code that explicitly states what you mean, you end up with self-documented code and less need for comments that are (a) never read and (b) by definition out of date with the code they explain.

## Take Advantage of the Compiler

In his invaluable work,[1] Steve Maguire talks about a hypothetical compiler, which would catch bugs for you. His book helps C developers get as close possible to this dream by teaching techniques that help the compiler help you (among other things) by adopting certain coding habits—for example, putting the (more) constant value on the left of the equals operator (==), so that the compiler can shout at you if you accidentally used the assignment operator (=).

Although a lot of bugs you will encounter are not possible to catch at compile time, Swift's compiler comes close to Steve Maguire's dream[2] and makes it almost impossible to default to bad habits.

A lot of what would be compiler warnings show up as errors in Swift. As likely as this is to irritate you initially,[3] you will probably be grateful in the long run, as you will have adopted good coding habits and the maintenance of your apps costs you a lot less for lack of easily preventable bugs.

# Coming from ActionScript: Advantages and Surprises

Having experience with ActionScript, you will find yourself at an advantage when you transition to native development with Swift. This section provides a brief overview of the main areas where your prior knowledge will come in handy: syntax, programming concepts, and memory management. I have also included a few differences in Swift, which you may want to be aware of.

## Syntax

If you grew up speaking Objective-C, you were probably used to its bulky syntax and it didn't bother you very much. Transitioning to it from a language like ActionScript, however, was initially an exercise in learning how to read. In contrast, Swift does read a lot like ActionScript in how you define or access things.

With that said, Swift is not ActionScript and there are a couple of things that might seem obscure at first:

- **The Optional type:** you have likely noticed a lot of exclamation and question marks in Swift tutorials and in the examples in the other parts of this book. **Chapter 19** demystifies their use and shows you how optionals can make your life easier.

- **Conciseness,** whose praises we sang earlier, can be a double-edged sword. It is a wonderful thing to be able to keep your statements short and clutter-free, but for a newcomer the second line, shown in Listing 17-2, may seem like a syntax error at first. Practice will help you with this: as Swift doesn't force you to be brief, you can initially opt for the long syntax and gradually transition to omitting bits of code that the compiler can infer and that you can too.

---

[1]Steve Maguire, *Writing Solid Code* (Microsoft Press, 1993).
[2]Or this is my take on it. Mr. Maguire might, in fact, be running away in disgust.
[3]Try to leave an uninitialized class member, for example . . . . More on that in **Chapter 21.**

## Programming Concepts

Swift uses most of the programming concepts with which you are already familiar, including the object-oriented programming paradigm. A big part of your transition from ActionScript will be in the spirit of "Right. How do I bend a spoon in Swift?," rather than having to first bend your mind around the thought that "There is no spoon,"[4] as you might do if you were migrating to, say, a functional language.

If Swift were exactly the same as ActionScript, though, it would probably have been called ActionScript and not Swift, so be prepared for corners where we will need to shed light. Some of these are explained in context:

- **Operator overloading** in **Chapter 18**

- **Optionals** and **tuples** in **Chapter 19**

- **Using labels** in **Chapter 20**

- **Deinitialization** for classes in **Chapter 21**

- **Structures** in **Chapter 21**

To a few ideas, which might need a deeper looking into, we have dedicated a separate chapter (**Chapter 22**).

## Memory Management

ActionScript uses both garbage collection (GC) and automatic reference counting (ARC) to manage memory, though the latter is not spoken of very much. A garbage collector may do a good job of finding cyclic references and freeing up memory that otherwise may have leaked, but you are not in control of when it kicks in and this can hurt performance. Over time, ActionScript developers have come up with hacks and workarounds to get some control over when GC is performed.

Swift classes use ARC, so you should be on familiar ground there. Moreover, as this is not a garbage-collected language, you will have control over when instances are deallocated. And, unlike moving to Objective-C, you will not have to get your head around pointers.

Swift also helps you be more mindful about how you use memory, as it distinguishes between *reference types* and *value types* (more on that in Chapter 21).

# How to Use the Code Examples: Playgrounds

This part of the book presents the Swift language with the help of a lot of little snippets of code. To try them out, you don't need to set up and deploy a big project. Instead, you can take advantage of another goodie that the Xcode has: *Playgrounds*.

A playground allows you to experiment with code and even create prototypes very quickly. Instead of having to build and install your code on a device or on one of the iOS simulators, you can see it being evaluated and run as you type. Ah, I am so excited about what you can do in a playground: animations, interactive UI, sleek-looking documentation in line with your code. Too bad that for our purposes we will only need the more mundane features: typing code and seeing it run will do.

Apart from being able to run examples unburdened by a big project, using a playground also means that you can dip in and out of the following chapters when you need to understand a specific bit of the language while doing the tutorials in the rest of the book.

---

[4]In case you were too young to see *The Matrix* movie when it first came out, type "there is no spoon" in YouTube—the scene is worth a thousand words.

Let us set up your first playground. You can use the same playground for all of the examples in this part of the book or you can create a new one as you start each chapter. When you accumulate a lot of lines of code in the same playground you may find Xcode getting slower, as it runs and evaluates all of the code on each keystroke, so you might find keeping separate playgrounds more practical.

From Xcode's main menu select **File ➤ New ➤ Playground**, give your playground a name (I named mine **Swift Test Playground**) and let the wizard create it for you. Upon first opening you will see an Editor displaying the code in Listing 17-4.

***Listing 17-4.*** Code in a Fresh Playground

```
//: Playground - noun: a place where people can play

import UIKit

var str = "Hello, playground"
```

To dip your toe in, add a call to print out the value of str and let us have a brief exploration of the workspace (Listing 17-5).

***Listing 17-5.*** Add a Line to the Playground Code

```
print(str)
```

The playground looks a lot like what you are used to when creating iOS projects, only trimmed down (Figure 17-1). You have the Editor in the middle: here it has an inspection area on the right, where you can see your expressions evaluated at runtime. There is also a Debug area, where you can output information with print. This is also where you can see compilation and runtime error messages. On the left is the familiar Navigation area, which you can toggle to see the structure of your playground (you can add source and resource files to it), inspect symbols, do textual searches, or explore issues found by the compiler.

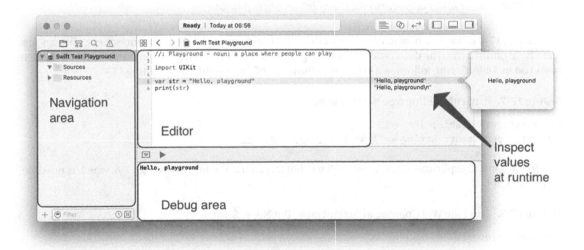

***Figure 17-1.*** *Set up a playground in Xcode*

With your first playground set up, let our journey through Swift begin. We will start with a few basic things before we go deeper in the next chapters.

# First Things About Swift

The rest of this chapter will lay some groundwork and housekeeping rules. You can use the playground we set up in the previous section to try out some of the snippets of code.

## Declaring Variables and Constants

The first thing you are likely to ask when faced with the blank page, all right, screen, is: how do I declare a variable? Use the var keyword to declare a variable and the let keyword to declare a constant (Listing 17-6).

*Listing 17-6.* Declaring Variables and Constants

```
var anIntegerVariable = 10
let aStringConstant = "I am a string. And I am constant."
```

A nice thing about the Swift compiler is that it encourages you to use constants instead of variables wherever possible: if you declare a variable, but never change its value, you will get a warning like the one in Figure 17-2 suggesting that you change it to a constant by replacing var with let.

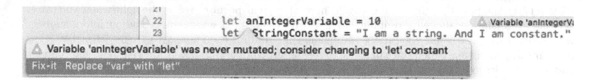

*Figure 17-2.* The compiler encourages the use of let wherever possible

Listing 17-6 shows you how to declare variables and constants in the spirit of conciseness: you can see that I have omitted the type declarations of anIntegerVariable and aStringContant. You can include them as you do in ActionScript, following a colon after the name of the variable, as in Listing 17-7.

*Listing 17-7.* Explicitly adding type declarations

```
var anIntegerVariable: Int = 10
let aStringConstant: String = "I am a string. And I am constant."
```

In the spirit of explicitness, however, Swift will not let you use the line in Listing 17-8, which is possible in ActionScript.

*Listing 17-8.* This Line Will Compile in ActionScript, But Not in Swift

```
var aVariable;
```

The Swift compiler is clever, but it will not tolerate not knowing the type of aVariable. For it to work it out you need to either state it explicitly or assign a value, from which the type can be inferred.

# Making Comments

You add comments in Swift the same way you do in ActionScript. Use two forward slashes to prefix single-line comments:

```
// This is a single-line comment.
```

Put multiline comments inside the familiar forward-slash-plus-asterisk and asterisk-plus-forward-slash combination:

```
/* This is a comment,
which spans multiple lines. */
```

# Printing in the Console

In Swift you can print diagnostic information in Xcode's console with the `print` function, much like you do with `trace` in ActionScript. You can use `print` with any expression: to print it out as part of a string literal, put the expression in parentheses inside the string quotes and prefix it with a backslash (\) as shown in Listing 17-9:

***Listing 17-9.*** Printing Out a Value in the Console

```
print(anIntegerVariable)
// output: 10

print("The value of anIntegerVariable is \(anIntegerVariable).")
// output: The value of anIntegerVariable is 10.
```

For more details on inserting values in string literals and using escape sequences see the section "Strings" in **Chapter 19**.

# Defining and Calling Functions

To define a function, use the `func` keyword, followed by the name of the function, followed by a comma-separated argument list in parentheses and, if the function returns a result, add a return arrow (->), followed by the type of the result (Listing 17-10). If your function does not return a result, you don't need to add anything after the closing parenthesis of the argument list. For functions that don't take arguments you still need the parentheses after the function name, though their argument list will be empty.

***Listing 17-10.*** Defining Functions in Swift

```
func divide(a: Double, b: Double) -> Double {
    return a / b
}

func printAQuote(quote: String, byAuthor: String) {
    print("'\(quote)' \n\(byAuthor)")
}
```

# Naming Arguments

The code in Listing 17-10 could almost be ActionScript, couldn't it? You will notice a difference when making a call to a function, however. The difference is not big, but it is important: in Swift function arguments have what is known as *local* and *external names*. A *local name* is the name that will be used to refer to the argument inside the function body and an *external name* is what the caller of a function will use to label the argument. There are a few rules about local and external names:

- To provide external names for your arguments explicitly, put them before the internal names (Listing 17-11).

**Listing 17-11.** Providing External Argument Names

```
// Add explicit external argument names
func divide(dividend a: Double, divisor b: Double) -> Double {
    return a / b
}

// Label your arguments with their external names when making a call:
divide(dividend: 1, divisor: 0)
```

Now a and b are the names, which the divide function can use locally, but when you call divide you need to label its arguments dividend and divisor, respectively.

Remember what we said earlier about accidentally swapping arguments of the same type? The external argument names (which are actually an Objective-C legacy) help avoid that: they will not make the compiler complain if you swapped 1 and 0 in the example above,[5] but having to label your arguments makes it harder for you to swap them without noticing.

- Local and external names can be the same. If you don't explicitly provide an external name for one of your parameters, its name will serve both as a local and as an external name. The first argument in the list is an exception, which will be explained in the next rule.

For example, calling the second function we defined in Listing 17-10 would look like this (Listing 17-12):

**Listing 17-12.** Calling a Function with External Argument Name

```
printAQuote("Life is too short to remove USB safely.",↵
            fromAuthor: "Anonymous")
```

Notice how the second argument has a label, although we did not explicitly set an external name for it in the function definition.

All arguments of a function, but the first one, get both a local and an external name by default. If you want the first argument to be referred to by an external name too, you need to provide it explicitly. Apple encourages a naming convention, in which the external name of the first argument is implied by the name of the function. For example in printAQuote you would expect to provide a quote as an argument.

There is an exception to this rule too: if the function is an *initializer method*, all of its arguments get external names by default (see **Chapter 21** on initializers).

---

[5] If you call this function with the divisor set to zero, you will see another Swift feature demonstrated. Instead of throwing a "division by zero" error, it returns infinity (inf).

> ■ **Note** Swift 3 introduces a change, in order to establish consistent label behavior across all parameters, including first labels. This means that the first argument too will get a default external name if you do not provide one explicitly. When you call the `printAQuote` function, you will need to provide both labels: `printAQuote(quote: "...", fromAuthor: "...")`.

- You can opt out of external names for your arguments. Once again, you need to state this explicitly by putting an underscore where the external name would be (Listing 17-13):

*Listing 17-13.* Ignoring External Argument Names

```
// Put an underscore in place of the external name:
func printAQuote(quote: String, _ fromAuthor: String) {
    print("'\(quote)' \n\(fromAuthor)")
}

// Now you don't have to label the arguments when making a call:
printAQuote("Programs must be written for people to read, ↵
            and only incidentally for machines to execute.",  "Hal Abelson")
```

# Function Parameters

Let us have a look at how function parameters are treated in Swift and what your options are.

## Parameters Are Constant by Default

By default all parameters of a function are constants and you can't make changes to them inside the body of the function.

## In-Out and Variable Parameters

You can opt for non-constant behavior by prepending a parameter name with the `inout` keyword. An in-out parameter is *passed by reference*. In other words, a function that takes an in-out parameter will access the original variable that you passed in, rather than a copy of it and any changes you make to that variable inside the function will persist after the function returns. Listing 17-14 shows an example of a function, which takes a string and modifies it. Note that at the point of calling the function we need to prepend the in-out parameter with an ampersand (&).

*Listing 17-14.* Using In-Out Parameters

```
func modifyMyString(inout str: String) {
    str = "Ha! I can override you!"
    print(str)
}

var myStr = "I am the boss."
modifyMyString(&myStr)
// Output: "Ha! I can override you!"

print(myStr)
// Output: "Ha! I can override you!"
```

■ **Note**    Swift 3 comes with a different syntax for using the `inout` keyword: it needs to be on the right side of the colon: `func modifyMyString(str: inout String)`.

If you do not need a modified parameter value to persist after the return of the function you passed it in, you can use the var keyword. Note that making changes a var argument will create a copy of it, which serves as a local variable inside the function (Listing 17-15).

***Listing 17-15.***  Using Variable Parameters

```
func modifyMyString(var str: String) {
    str = "Ha! I can override you!"
    print(str)
}

var myStr = "I am the boss."
modifyMyString(myStr)
// Output: "Ha! I can override you!"

print(myStr)
// Output: "I am the boss."
```

■ **Note**    In Swift 3 the `var` keyword is deprecated. Instead of using a var parameter you can declare a local variable and assign the value of the parameter to it. This achieves the exact same behavior but makes it a lot more obvious: a copy of the value is made, which you can modify, but you cannot access the modified value once the function returns.

## Variadic Parameters

A function can be defined to take parameters that vary in number by using a *variadic parameter*. This parameter takes one or more values of the same type and is defined by adding three dots at the end of its declaration. Inside the function you can iterate through the values of the parameter and query their number by calling `parameterName.count`. Something to keep in mind is that you can define only one variadic parameter per function.

The example in Listing 17-16 uses a variadic parameter, called `numbers`, to find the maximum in a list of integer numbers:

***Listing 17-16.***  Iterating Through a Variadic Parameter

```
func findMaximum(numbers: Int...) -> Int {
    var maxNum = Int.min
    for number in numbers {
        if number > maxNum {
            maxNum = number
        }
    }
```

```
        return maxNum
}

findMaximum(300, 4, 99) // returns 300
```

## Providing Default Values

As in ActionScript, you can provide default values for function arguments. You can do this for constant and for variable parameters but not for in-out parameters.

Listing 17-17 shows the printAQuote function, which we used earlier, this time defined to set the byAuthor parameter to "Anonymous" by default. Note that now the call to the function does not have to include a second parameter.

***Listing 17-17.*** Providing Default Parameter Values

```
func printAQuote(quote: String, byAuthor: String = "Anonymous") {
    print("'\(quote)' \n\(byAuthor)")
}

// You can skip the byAuthor argument, as it has a default value:
printAQuote("Sm;)e")
```

# Function Overloading

Here is something that ActionScript does not let you do. You can define several functions with the same name and the same scope: as long as they have a different number or different types of parameters, the compiler will make sure that the correct one is selected when you make a call.

The example in Listing 17-18 illustrates that: we have defined three functions called printInfo, all of which print out their parameters into the console.

***Listing 17-18.*** Overloading Functions

```
func printInfo(i: Int) {
    print("Here is an integer: \(i)")
}

func printInfo(s: String) {
    print("Here is a string: '\(s)'")
}

func printInfo(i: Int, s: String) {
    print("Here is an integer: \(i) and a string: '\(s)'")
}

printInfo(3) // Calls the first function
printInfo("Ta-da!") // Calls the second function
printInfo(40, s: "Ali Baba's thieves") // Calls the third function
```

You can also overload methods (see **Chapter 21**) and subscripts (see **Chapter 22**).

## Access Control Rules

You have already seen from the tutorials in this book how you can structure your projects and that Swift code goes into `.swift` files. These files and the *modules* they form are the basis of defining how code is accessed. Here *module* is meant as a bunch of files you build and ship together as an application or as a framework.

There are three levels of access, which determine the visibility of a piece of code:

- `private` *entities* are only visible to code in the same file where they were defined.

- `internal` bits of code are accessible from source files inside the same module.

- `public` *entities* are accessible everywhere within the same module, as well as to code that uses it. They define the interface to the module.

In the previous definitions I use *entities* as a substitute for "almost anything you can define": global variables, constants, and functions; classes, structures, and enumerations, as well as their members; and also protocols. The access modifiers can be applied to all these. The members of a protocol are an exception: you can define a `private` protocol but you cannot define its members as `private`.

The default access level is `internal` and is applied if you don't explicitly provide an access modifier when you declare an entity.

If you are wondering "How about `protected`?," the answer is that it doesn't exist in Swift. To find out why see **Chapter 21**. This is also where we you can find information on *structures* and *protocols*, which were mentioned previously. For *enumerations*, see **Chapter 22**.

# Handling Errors

To handle error conditions in ActionScript we have the `Error` class at our disposal. We can return `Error` instances as function results or *throw* them in cases, which requires interrupting the flow of execution, when it doesn't make sense to continue an operation if a certain error condition arises, for example. We can also subclass `Error`, in order to customize it and add information.

The situation in Swift is similar, but with some subtle differences. Instead of an error base class, there is a *protocol*, called `ErrorType`. To use an error type, you need to define it yourself and have it conform to the `ErrorType` *protocol*: using an *enumeration* for that is usually quite a good idea. You can read more on protocols and conforming to them in **Chapter 21** and on enumerations—in **Chapter 22**.

If you write a function that throws an error, you need to put the `throws` keyword in its definition: it goes after the argument list and before the return type of the function: `func iMayThrowAnError() throws -> String`.

To catch an error that may be thrown by a function you call, use a `do-try-catch` statement.

In some cases you will want a certain piece of code to be executed at the end of a function (to clean up resources, for example) irrespective of whether the function's execution was interrupted by a thrown error. Such code you can put inside a `defer` statement: this is similar to using `finally` in ActionScript.

Table 17-1 provides a comparison between the skeleton of a `try-catch-finally` statement in ActionScript and a `do-try-catch` statement with a `defer` clause in Swift.

**Table 17-1.** *Comparison Between Try-Catch Statements in ActionScript and in Swift*

| ActionScript | Swift |
|---|---|
| ```
try {
statements;
} catch (e:Error) {
statements;
} finally {
statements;
}
``` | ```
do {
try expression
statement
} catch ErrorType {
statements
}
defer {
statements
}
``` |

A quick note on `defer`: you are not limited to using it only in situations in which you need to handle errors. For example, you can put a block of code inside `defer` to ensure that it is always executed in a function with multiple returns (and save on code repetition before every `return` statement). You can also use it inside loops or do statements. Note that when you have multiple `defer` statements within the same scope, they get executed in reverse order of how they appear in the code.

Let us see all of this in action with an example. Say we are creating an app that allows users to watch TV online and choose a TV channel by typing its name. We will define a couple of functions: `channelNameEntered` will take a channel name as an argument and will be called when the user types it in. A second function, `switchToChannel`, will be called by `channelNameEntered` to do the actual work for finding and switching to the selected channel. `switchToChannel` will alert its caller about possible error conditions that make it impossible to activate the given channel: the channel doesn't exist, it's under parental control, or subscription to it has expired.

The enumeration in Listing 17-19 will represent the error conditions. For the moment you can think of an *enumeration* as a way of keeping a set of names together: in this case it will help us define a set of names for the different errors we may encounter. (See **Chapter 22** for an in-depth introduction to enumerations.)

**Listing 17-19.** Defining an Error Type

```
enum ChannelChangeError: ErrorType {
    case InvalidChannelName
    case ParentalControlOn
    case SubscriptionExpired
}
```

The function that changes the channels checks if there is any reason not to proceed with the change and if it finds one, it throws one of the error names defined in `ChanelChangeError`. Note that `throw` takes the code execution out of the function, much like a `return`[6]— (see the example in Listing 17-20).

**Listing 17-20.** Throwing an Error

```
func switchToChannel(name: String) throws {
    if !channelExists(name) {
        throw ChannelChangeError.InvalidChannelName
    }
```

---

[6]Apple's manual says that a `throw` in Swift is like a `return` when it comes to performance too, as no stack unwinding is done when an error is thrown, in contrast to what typically happens in other languages.

```
    if isParentalControlOn(name) {
        throw ChannelChangeError.ParentalControlOn
    }

    if !inSubscriptionList(name) {
        throw ChannelChangeError.SubscriptionExpired
    }

    // Proceed to change the channel
}
```

Finally, the function that calls switchToChannel needs to handle the different types of errors that may be thrown at it. For that purpose we put the call to switchToChannel inside a do-try statement as shown on Listing 17-21, followed by two catch statements to catch two of the error conditions: ChannelChangeError. InvalidChannelName and ChannelChangeError.ParentalControlOn. The third catch statement is a blanket one: it will catch any other error that is thrown and was not caught by the catch statements above it. Note how one of the catch statements *rethrows* the error, instead of handling it: this way the error is propagated up the call stack to be handled by the caller of channelNameEntered.

The code in the defer statement will be called before the execution of channelNameEntered finishes. This code will run whether an error was caught inside the function or not.

***Listing 17-21.*** Catching, Handling, and Rethrowing Errors

```
func channelNameEntered(name: String) throws {
    do {
        try switchToChannel("Cartoons 24/7")
    } catch ChannelChangeError.InvalidChannelName {
        // Rethrow the error to be handled
        // by the caller of channelNameEntered:
        throw ChannelChangeError.InvalidChannelName
    } catch ChannelChangeError.ParentalControlOn {
        // Handle the error here and don't propagate it up:
        // Update the screen to show a cheeky picture of a parent.
    } catch {
        // This is a blanket error handler for any errors
        // that were not caught by the previous catch statements.
    }
    defer {
        // The code after the defer statement
        // will be executed before the execution leaves this function,
        // no matter whether any error was thrown.

        // Save the chanel name in the browsing history,
        // even if switching to it was not possible.
        // ... possibly to alert parents.
    }
}
```

You can find even more subtle ways of using and catching errors in Apple's online book *The Swift Programming Language.*

# Summary

This chapter paved the way to learning Swift by covering a few essential points: how to declare variables, constants, and functions; how to print out diagnostic information; and the basics of error handling. You are set up with a playground, where you can quickly test code snippets and explore Swift's features.

I hope it also made you excited about learning a new language, which, among other things is designed in a way to encourage good programming habits. The main thing to keep in mind about Swift, however, is that it will not stop you from shooting yourself in the foot: you have all the means and tools to do it. But you really need to mean to shoot yourself in the foot. And explicitly tell the Swift compiler that you do mean it.[7]

With this disclaimer out of the way we can move on to having a closer look at Swift. The next chapter introduces Swift's operators and what surprises they may have for an ActionScript developer.

---

[7]Or, as my husband put it: using Swift is like taking legal advice from a lawyer. He can make it hard for you to do the wrong thing, but he will not stop you from doing it. And in the end, the one person you cannot blame if things go wrong is the lawyer.

# CHAPTER 18

■ ■ ■

# Operators

We start our exploration of the Swift language with a look at the operators it offers. You will find that your ActionScript experience has prepared you for most of what's to come in this chapter. The majority of operators look the same and follow the same syntax and rules for associativity and precedence you would expect.

The first part of the chapter lists operators that both Swift and ActionScript share. We then move on to a few operators that will be new to an ActionScript developer. At the end of the chapter we will see how you can define your own operator implementations or even create custom operators using *operator overloading*.

## Operators You (Almost) Know from ActionScript

In all fairness, even among the operators you are familiar with you will find the occasional subtle difference between Swift and ActionScript. The list points these out in order to minimize surprises when you code.

### Comparison Operators

Most of the comparison operators look and behave the way you would expect them to.

- **Equal to operator:** `(a == b)`
- **Not equal to operator:** `(a != b)`
- **Greater than:** `(a > b)`
- **Less than:** `(a < b)`
- **Greater than or equal to:** `(a >= b)`
- **Less than or equal to:** `(a <= b)`

The following two operators however have a slight difference, although they look the same in both languages:

- **Identity operators:** `(a === b)` and `(a !=== b)`

The ActionScript counterparts of the identity operators are called *strict equality/inequality* and let you compare object references as well as primitive values. In Swift, however, they only serve to compare references: you can check if two constants or variables refer to the same object, but not if two integers or strings have the same value.

© Radoslava Leseva Adams and Hristo Lesev 2016
R. L. Adams and H. Lesev, *Migrating to Swift from Flash and ActionScript*,
DOI 10.1007/978-1-4842-1666-8_18

# Assignment Operator (a = b)

Just like in ActionScript, the assignment operator, well, assigns a value to a variable. And there is a subtle nuance in its behavior: unlike in ActionScript, the operator does not return a Boolean result. It does not return a result at all.

In other words, the code in Listing 18-1 will have different consequences in each language: in ActionScript, the `if (a = 3)` check will return `true`, causing the code after the `if` statement to always be run; in Swift this expression will simply not compile.[1]

***Listing 18-1.*** In Swift the Assignment Operator Does Not Return a Result

```
if (a = 3) {
    // The code after the if statement will always execute in ActionScript,
    // but won't even compile in Swift.
}
```

# Compound Assignment Operators

These look and feel the same in both languages:

- **Addition assignment:** (a += b)
- **Subtraction assignment:** (a -= b)
- **Multiplication assignment:** (a *= b)
- **Division assignment:** (a /= b)
- **Remainder assignment:** (a %= b)
- **Left shift assignment:** (a <<= b)
- **Right shift assignment:** (a >>= b)
- **Bitwise AND assignment:** (a &= b)
- **Bitwise XOR assignment:** (a ^= b)
- **Bitwise OR assignment:** (a |= b)
- **Logical AND assignment:** (a &&= b)
- **Logical OR assignment:** (a ||= b)

# Arithmetic Operators

A new thing here is that the arithmetic operators will not allow overflow or underflow in their result. If either of these occurs, you get a runtime exception `EXC_BAD_INSTRUCTION` thrown. A bit disturbing at first, but quite handy for catching overflow or underflow errors as close to the crime scene as possible, instead of wasting ages debugging weird behavior down the line.

---

[1]Why is it significant that the assignment operator does not return a result in Swift? More often than not statements like `if (a = 3)` are a result of a typo, where the intention was to write `if (a == 3)`. So in languages like ActionScript it's a good habit to put the constant, or the more constant of the two operands, to the left of the comparison operator: `if (3 == a)`. That is, if one of your operands is nice enough to be constant. Why? The ActionScript compiler will let you know that you have made a typo if you mistakenly wrote `if (3 = a)`. The Swift compiler spares you the need to trick it and will instead issue a compiler error if you ever tried to check the result of an assignment operation by mistake or intentionally.

If you want to enable overflow behavior, you need to explicitly use the overflow versions of the addition, subtraction, and multiplication operators: the section "Overflow Operators," later in this chapter, shows you what they look like.

- **Addition:** (a + b). Adds expressions. Note that you can use it to concatenate strings and arrays, as well as numbers.

- **Subtraction:** (a - b). Subtracts numeric expressions.

- **Multiplication:** (a * b). Multiplies numeric expressions.

- **Division:** (a / b). Subtracts numeric expressions.

- **Remainder:** (a % b). The remainder operator has the same specifics both in ActionScript and in Swift, including support for floating-point operations and how it handles signed operands.

- **Unary minus and plus operators:** (-a) **and** (+a). These are fancy names for the minus and plus sign you put in front of numeric values and variables and do exactly what you would expect them to: the minus sign toggles the sign of the operand and the plus sign returns its operand as it is without changing it. No difference between Swift and ActionScript.

A word about two pairs of operators that you may (or may not) miss in Swift: the increment and decrement operators: (a++), (++a), (a --) and (--a). Despite being initially part of the language, they have been voted out of Swift 3, in order to keep code simple and easy to read. As you know from ActionScript, when you use these operators you need to keep in mind the difference between their prefix (++a) and postfix (a++) versions: the prefix version increments/decrements its operand and returns the modified value, while the postfix version returns the operand and then modifies it. The relative conciseness that you get from using these operators was deemed not worth this complexity when reading and maintaining code or when learning how to program from scratch with Swift as the first language.

# Logical Operators

Following are the three logical operators you can use in Swift:

- **Logical NOT:** (!a)

- **Logical AND:** (a && b)

- **Logical OR:** (a || b)

There are no surprises here if you are used to how these work in ActionScript. This includes how logical operators are combined in compound expressions and the use of *lazy evaluation.*

# What Is Lazy Evaluation?

Here is a brief reminder of how it works. If the first operand in a logical OR statement evaluates to true, the rest of the expression after the OR will not be evaluated, as the result will always be true. The same thing happens if the first operand of a logical AND statement evaluates to false: the result of the whole expression is then assumed to be false and no further evaluation is done.

This makes code like that in Listing 18-2 and Listing 18-3, if not a good habit, at least safe to write.

***Listing 18-2.*** Lazy Evaluation in ActionScript

```
// ActionScript code
var s : String = null;
if ( null != s && 0 != s.length )
```

***Listing 18-3.*** Lazy Evaluation in Swift

```
// Swift code
var s : String? // s is nil
if nil != s && 0 != s!.characters.count
```

Without lazy evaluation we would expect to get a runtime exception from both if statements, as the operands to the right of the logical AND (&&) try to access properties of null/nil objects. The rules of lazy evaluation, however, mean that both the ActionScript and the Swift compilers will stop after evaluating the first operand: null != s and nil != s, respectively. Because this results in false, the rest of the logical AND expression will be discarded, its final result will be assumed to be false, and the problematic code will not be run, thereby sidestepping the potential exception.

## Bitwise Operators

Bitwise operators let you deal with data on the level of individual bits.

- **Bitwise NOT:** (~a)
- **Bitwise: AND** (a & b)
- **Bitwise OR:** (a | b)
- **Bitwise XOR:** (a ^ b)
- **Bitwise left and right shift:** (a << b) and (a >> b)

Although all of these look the same in both languages, there are a couple of differences worth noting. First, unlike ActionScript, Swift doesn't convert the operands of the bitwise operators to 32-bit signed integers before performing the operation. And second, where ActionScript has a separate operator to deal with right shift for unsigned integers (>>> and its compound version >>>=), Swift does not. Instead it changes behavior depending on the type of operands you pass to the shift operators.

## Ternary Conditional Operator

The name of this operator probably sounds new, but it's just another name for your old friend, known simply as *conditional* in ActionScript. It looks like this:

```
condition ? result1 : result 2
```

This is shorthand for

```
if condition { result1 } else { result2 }
```

# New Operators in Swift

Here we leave the common ground and explore a handful of operators without parallels in ActionScript.

# Nil Coalescing Operator

The nil coalescing operator is the epitome of conciseness in Swift. This is what it looks like:

```
var c = a ?? b
```

It is shorthand for: `c = ( a != nil ) ? a : b`.

Or, in English: unwrap a; if a is not `nil`, assign its value to c, otherwise assign the value of b to c. This has implications on the types of the two operands: a needs to be optional, but b cannot be. Instead, b needs to match the type that the optional a operand stores.

---

■ **Tip**    For details on value unwrapping have a look at the section "Optionals" in Chapter 19.

---

# Range Operators

Range operators let you define an interval or a range of values and thus are useful tools for `for` loops, pattern-matching `if` and `case` statements (more on these in **Chapter 20**), and working with subsets of strings and arrays. You can choose between two range operators, depending on whether you need to include one or both boundaries of the range:

- **Closed range operator:** (a..b)

- **Half-open range operator:** (a..<b)

The closed range operator defines an interval from a to b, including both a and b. As the example in Listing 18-6 shows, the value of the lower end of the interval is expected to be no greater than the upper value, otherwise you get a runtime error (Listing 18-4).

***Listing 18-4.*** Closed Range Operator Syntax

```
// this prints out the numbers from 1 to 3:
for i in 1...3 { print ( "i = \(i)" ) }

// this results in a runtime error:
for i in 3...1 { print ( "i = \(i)" ) }
```

In contrast, the half-open range operator defines an interval from a to b, including a, but not b. The same rule applies here, as we saw with the closed range operator: the value of a should be no greater than the value of b (Listing 18-5). Writing (a..<a) defines an empty range.

***Listing 18-5.*** Half-Open Range Operator

```
// this prints out the numbers from 1 to 2:
for i in 1..<3 { print ( "i = \(i)" ) }
```

# Pattern-Matching Operator (~=)

The pattern-matching operator works with ranges and tells you if a value is in a given range. The following line evaluates to `true` if row has a value between 0 and 2, including 0 and 2:

```
0...2 ~= row
```

## Overflow Operators

The overflow operators behave just like normal arithmetic operators, which allow value overflow or underflow. As you saw earlier in the section "Arithmetic Operators," the default versions of the addition, subtraction and multiplication operators in Swift will throw an exception if their result over- or underflows. To opt out of this behavior you need to explicitly use these versions of the operators:

- **Overflow addition:** (a &+ b)
- **Overflow subtraction:** (a &- b)
- **Overflow multiplication:** (a &* b)

Like in ActionScript, when a value is too big for the number of bits that its type can hold, the extra bits get truncated, causing the value to wrap around from the minimum value to the maximum or vice versa.

# Operator Overloading

Function or operator overloading is not part of ActionScript. In many other languages, including Swift, you can have multiple functions with the same name but different signatures: the functions may differ in the number or types of arguments they take and/or in the type of the result they return. These namesake functions are called *overloads*. The compiler decides which overload should be executed based on how you call it.

In the context of operators, it is convenient to be able to apply an operator to any type, including your custom types that the operator in question may not support. Providing your implementation (overload) of the subtraction operator, for example, lets you use the more concise and expressive a – b, instead of an equivalent function call: myCustomSubtractionFunction(a, b), where a and b are instances of a type you have defined.

Like using salt in cooking, operator overloading is helpful in carefully considered amounts. Just because you can make + or == do whatever you want, it doesn't mean you should. Providing a dramatically different behavior for an operator would be at best confusing for your fellow programmers and at worst might break its relationships with other operators and lead to strange results in your code.

Operators differ in how many operands they take and how operands are positioned with respect to the operator: on its left, on its right, on both sides, and so on. This leads to difference in the syntax for overloading each sort of operator.

To demonstrate this, we will go through a simple example. Let us declare an enumeration, called WeekDay, which represents the days of the week (Listing 18-9). Each member of the enumeration has a raw value assigned to it, starting with 0 for Monday.

*Listing 18-6.* An Enumeration, Which Represents the Days of the Week

```
enum WeekDay : UInt {
    case Monday = 0, Tuesday, Wednesday, Thursday, Friday, Saturday, Sunday
}
```

▓ **Note**  Chapter 22 covers enumerations in detail.

## Overloading an Infix Operator

Infix operators are put in between their operands (e.g., the addition operator: a + b).

If you tried to use the addition operator to add a number to a WeekDay instance at this point, the compiler would issue an error. You need to define a version of *the global addition operator* that will make sense to the Swift compiler (Listing 18-7).

*Listing 18-7.* Overloading the Global Addition Operator to Work with WeekDay Instances

```
func + (left: WeekDay, right: UInt) -> WeekDay {
    // This ensures that we don't go over the values allowed by WeekDay, so:
    // Tueday + 6 should return Monday
    let dayNumber = (left.rawValue + right) % (WeekDay.Sunday.rawValue + 1)
    assert( WeekDay.Monday.rawValue ... WeekDay.Sunday.rawValue ~= dayNumber )

    return WeekDay(rawValue: dayNumber)!
}

// This allows you to do the following:
let weekDay = WeekDay.Tuesday
let newWeekDay = weekDay + 6 // newWeekDay is WeekDay.Monday
```

## Overloading a Compound Assignment Operator

The operator overload in Listing 18-8 allows you to do this: weekDay += 4. The operand on the left of the operator—in this case the first argument of the operator function—is the one that will be modified. This is why it's declared inout.

*Listing 18-8.* Overloading the Compound Assignment Operator

```
func += (inout left: WeekDay, right: UInt) {
    // We sneakily take advantage of the addition operator
    // that was overloaded in the previous example:
    left = left + right
}
```

---

■ **Note**   The Swift 3 syntax for this function declaration is func += (left: inout WeekDay, right: UInt) {/*...*/}. See Chapter 17 for details on inout parameters.

---

## Overloading a Prefix or a Postfix Operator

Building on the same example, let us have a look at how you can make this work: ++weekDay. The syntax for defining an overload to a prefix operator is similar to what you saw with infix operators, but it includes the keyword prefix (Listing 18-9).

*Listing 18-9.* Overloading the Prefix Increment Operator

```
prefix func ++ (inout weekDay: WeekDay) -> WeekDay {
    weekDay += 1 // Making use of the += overload
    return weekDay
}
```

This function is global too, instead of being a method of WeekDay, as it provides an overload to the global prefix increment operator.

Note the inout keyword in front of the argument in the function signature. As its name suggests, it means that the weekDay argument is to be treated both as an input and an output parameter: its value is taken by the function, modified, and, when the function exits, replaces the original value of flight.

Overloading a postfix operator has the same syntax, except that it uses the postfix keyword instead. Also, when overloading a postfix operator you must remember to return the value that the operand has *before* it gets modified.

---

■ **Caution**    The increment (++) and decrement (--) operators are no longer part of the language since Swift 3.

---

## Providing a Custom Operator

Finally, in Swift you can define your own custom operators. The rules are as follows:

- You are allowed to use some ASCII characters that are employed for conventional operators (/, =, -, +, !, *, %, <, >, &, |, ^, ?, ~) and some Unicode characters.

- There are certain characters and tokens that are reserved and you can't use, for example: =, ->, //, /*, */, ., the prefix operators <, &, and ?, the infix operator ?, and the postfix operators >, !, and ?

- You must first provide a declaration of your custom operator, using the operator keyword and then define an overload for that operator.

---

■ **Tip**    For a complete list of the symbols you can use in a custom operator, as well as how to ensure consistent precedence and associativity for your custom operators, see the "Basic Operators" and "Advanced Operators" chapters in Apple's *The Swift Programming Language* (https://goo.gl/Xj8aef).

---

This last example declares and overloads a custom operator that will reset a WeekDay instance to 0 (Monday). Let us say that we want the operator to be postfix and to be used like this: weekDay^^ (Listing 18-10).

*Listing 18-10.*  Defining a Custom Operator

```
// First, declare the operator
postfix operator ^^ {}

// Then overload it to handle WeekDay
postfix func ^^(inout weekDay: WeekDay) -> WeekDay {
    // Store the original value of the operand:
    let originalWeekDay = weekDay

    // Then modify the operand:
    weekDay = WeekDay(rawValue: 0)!
```

```
    // Finally, return the original value,
    // as we are defining a postfix operator:
    return originalWeekDay
}
```

---

■ **Note**    The Swift 3 syntax for this function declaration is `postfix func ^^(weekDay: inout WeekDay) -> WeekDay {/*...*/}`. See Chapter 17 for details on `inout` parameters.

---

Again, excercise your judgment when you define custom operators. Keeping code readable and easy to grasp at first glance is often worth more than making it short.

# Summary

This chapter showed you how similar operators in ActionScript and Swift are and highlighted the subtle differences that Swift has here and there. It also introduced you to operators that are new in Swift and showed you ways of defining operators for your own custom types.

The next chapter will focus specifically on types and type safety in Swift.

# CHAPTER 19

# Types

Prepare for a relatively fast pace in this chapter. We will speed through topics related to types in Swift and delve in more detail into those that are likely to be less familiar to an ActionScript developer. The chapter starts with an overview of Swift's type policy and goes briefly over some of its primitive types. Then we go a little deeper and explore optional types. Expect weird syntax there. Moving on, we see how to query an object's type and how to type cast. We finish with a few useful references to container types, tuples, and function types. Seatbelt ready?

## Type Safety and Type Inference

Swift is a type-safe language: its compiler performs type checks and lets you know if there are any mismatched types. Making sure to provide a type for everything you declare has two advantages: your code and intentions become self-documented and you have more confidence at compile time that your code will do what you intend it to. It, however, has a couple of disadvantages too: having to add types everywhere can become a chore, and if you have complicated types the result is rather verbose code.

In order to help with this, the Swift compiler can infer types from values assigned to variables and constants. This applies to literal values, as well as values that result from expressions. Thus you have a choice regarding when to explicitly add types to your declarations and can afford conciseness.

A good guideline for when to rely on the compiler and when to be explicit is to write code for humans[1]: omit the type declarations when they are obvious and add them when they provide useful information to the reader.

In order to understand what the compiler will do when a literal is assigned to a type-inferred variable, it is good to know the types of literals. For example, literal integer values are inferred to be Int, rather than UInt, and floating-point values are inferred to be Double by default, rather than Float (Listing 19-1).

*Listing 19-1.* Inferring Types from Literal Values: The Compiler Defaults to Int and Double

```
var age = 64 // age is inferred to be Int, rather than UInt
var height = 1.75 // height is inferred to be Double, rather than Float
```

## Primitive Types

As you come from an ActionScript programming background, primitive types in Swift will be familiar in how they behave for the most part. And, as with most things in Swift, the devil is in the detail: you will find some subtle, but in some cases quite important, differences. Curious? Read on.

---

[1]To quote Martin Fowler, author of books on refactoring and UML (Unified Modeling Language) among other valuable topics: "Any fool can write code that a computer can understand. Good programmers write code that humans can understand."

© Radoslava Leseva Adams and Hristo Lesev 2016
R. L. Adams and H. Lesev, *Migrating to Swift from Flash and ActionScript*,
DOI 10.1007/978-1-4842-1666-8_19

# Integers

You have at your disposal various flavors of signed and unsigned integer types, each conveniently having a self-explanatory name: Uint8 stands for "unsigned 8-bit integer," Int32 for "signed 32-bit integer," for example. Unless you need a specific size for your integer data, most of the time it is prudent to use the Int and UInt type aliases, which have the same size as the platform's native word. You can find the valid range for any integer type by calling its min and max properties—for example, let maxInt = Int.max.

When you work with integer literals you can use decimal, binary, octal, or hexadecimal notation, as Listing 19-2 demonstrates. All notations, except the decimal one, require a prefix: 0b for binary, 0o for octal, and 0x for hexadecimal.

***Listing 19-2.*** Integer Literals in Different Notations

```
// Representations of the number 42 in different notations:
let decimalInt = 42              // no prefix required
let binaryInt = 0b101010         // uses the 0b prefix
let octalInt = 0o52              // uses the 0o prefix
let hexadecimalInt = 0x2A        // uses the 0x prefix
```

# Floating-Point Types

With floating-point values you have a choice between Double, which takes 64 bits, and Float, which takes 32 bits. It is worth noting that as with a lot of things in Swift, you are expected to be explicit:

- A floating-point literal will be inferred to be of type Double, unless you explicitly cast it to Float.

- You can't omit the zero in a floating-point literal. If you do, the compiler issues an error: .5 is not a valid floating point literal; it must be written '0.5'.

- You can't mix numbers of different types in mathematical operations: Swift doesn't do type coercion behind the scenes. This applies to all numeric types.

Listing 19-3 illustrates these points with a few examples.

***Listing 19-3.*** You Need to Be Explicit with Swift Types

```
// Using .5 instead of 0.5 generates a compiler error:
let doubleNumber = 0.5

// floatNumber is inferred to be of type Double by default,
// unless you explicitly cast it to Float:
let floatNumber = 0.2 as Float

// This line does not compile,
// unless you explicitly convert floatNumber to Double:
let difference = doubleNumber - Double(floatNumber)
```

# Booleans

The Boolean type in Swift is named Bool and the constant values it takes are true and false, just as in ActionScript. Unlike in ActionScript, however, other types can't masquerade as Booleans—all in the name of being explicit, as we saw with the numeric types above. For example, the if statement in Listing 19-4 will not compile: the literal Int value provided in place of the condition will not be automatically coerced to Bool.

***Listing 19-4.*** If Statements Take Only Bool Conditions

```
if 1 {
    print("Gotcha!")
}
// error: type 'Int' does not conform to protocol 'BooleanType'
```

# Characters

Swift has a special type, called `Character`, which represents a single human-readable symbol. You can initialize a `Character` with a literal symbol in double quotes. Note, however, that such literals are of type `String`. So, in order to create a `Character` instance, you need to either provide a type explicitly or type cast the literal, as the example in Listing 19-5 shows.

***Listing 19-5.*** Creating and Initializing a Character

```
// Use double quotes around literals and provide type explicitly:
let letterA : Character = "A"

// You can also typecast the String literal,
// in order to initialize a Character:
let letterB = "B" as Character

// Note that the compiler will infer letterC's type as String:
let letterC = "C"

// You can use emoji as literals too:
let smileyFace : Character = "😃"
```

There are a couple of details worth noting about `Character` instances in Swift:

- They don't always take the same amount of memory.

- The same symbol can be represented in more than one way behind the scenes.

Why is that? Characters in Swift are Unicode-compliant and are represented by *Extended Grapheme Clusters*. These are clusters of Unicode codes, called *Unicode Scalars*, each of which stands for a character or for a character modifier. When you want to output a letter with the umlaut modifier, for example ä, you have a couple of options for how it will be stored in memory: it can be represented by a single Unicode Scalar that stands for *a with umlaut* (U+E4) or by a combination of the code for *a* (U+61) and the code for *umlaut* (U+308). Listing 19-6 shows how you can explicitly initialize a `Character` with an Extended Grapheme Cluster.

***Listing 19-6.*** Initializing Characters with Extended Grapheme Clusters

```
let aWithUmlaut : Character = "\u{E4}"
print(aWithUmlaut)
// output: ä

let aWithUmlautModifier : Character = "\u{61}\u{308}"
print(aWithUmlautModifier)
// output: ä
```

These two facts (characters' sizes in memory can vary, and there can be more than one way of encoding the same symbol) *are very important and have the following implications*:

- When you compare two characters for equality, using the == or the != operator, the comparison is not done on the Unicode Scalars that they store but on the symbols that the Unicode Scalars result in. In other words, the two constants in Listing 19-6, aWithUmlaut and aWithUmlautModifier, will be considered equal, although they look different in memory.

- Finding out the length of a character array or a string is not a matter of dividing the number of bytes in the array or string by the size of a character. Instead an iteration is done over the whole array or string to find out and add up the variable sizes of its characters.

- The characters in a string can't be indexed using numbers. That is, you can't do myString[0] or myString.charAt(0) to get to the first character of the string. Instead, you need to iterate over the characters from the start or from the end of the string to get to the one you need to access.

# Strings

Strings in Swift consist of zero or more Unicode-compliant characters. In the next subsection we will see how strings are instantiated, initialized, and modified and will mention some pitfalls it is a good idea to be aware of.

# Initializing Strings

You can use a string literal enclosed in double quotes, or you can provide an array of Character instances, in order to initialize a String (see Listing 19-7).

*Listing 19-7.* Ways of Creating and Initializing a String

```
// Create two empty string constants:
let emptyString = ""
let anotherEmptyString = String()

// Create a string an initialize it with a string literal:
let helloSwift = "Hello, Swift!"

// Initialize a string with an array of characters:
let helloBackArray: [Character] = ↵
    ["H", "e", "l", "l", "o", " ", "b", "a", "c", "k", "!"]
let helloBack = String(helloBackArray)

let smileyFace : Character = "😃"

// Concatenate a String and a Character to get "Hello, Swift! 😃":
var stringWithEmoji = helloSwift + String(smileyFace)
```

You can also use combinations of other String and Character variables or constants to create a new String. Listing 19-8 uses the String and Character constants from the previous example to show you a couple of different ways of concatenating strings and characters: using the + or the += operators and the append method of the String class.

*Listing 19-8.* Concatenating Strings

```
let smileyFace = "😃" // Character
let helloSwift = "Hello, Swift!" // String

var helloDialog = helloSwift + String(smileyFace)
helloDialog += "\n"
helloDialog += helloBack
helloDialog.append(smileyFace)

print(helloDialog)

// output:
//Hello, Swift! 😃
//Hello back! 😃
```

Note that helloDialog in the listing is declared as a variable, rather than a constant. This allows you to modify both its length and its contents.

You can compare strings with the equality (==) and the inequality (!=) operator or by using one of the flavors of the String class compare method. Bear in mind that string comparison is a potentially resource-heavy operation, as we discussed earlier in the section "Characters."

The characters method of the String class gives you access to the characters of the String as an array. Listing 19-9 shows a situation you might find a bit surprising: you can call methods even on literals.

*Listing 19-9.* Enumerating the Characters in a String

```
for ch in "Strange syntax or what?!".characters {
    print(ch)
}

// output:
//S
//t
//r
//a
//n
//g
//e
//
//s
//y
//n
//t
//a
//x
//
//o
//r
//
//w
//h
```

```
//a
//t
//?
//!
```

## Inserting Values into Strings

Something that you will probably find yourself doing a lot is *string interpolation*: inserting values of constants or variables into strings, also known as *string templating*. To insert a value into a string, wrap it with parentheses and prefix it with a backslash: \(value). Listing 19-10 demonstrates how to insert string and numeric values into a string literal. It also shows how you can convert an integer to its hexadecimal string representation and uses an escape sequence to insert a new line (\n) in the middle of the printed sentence. In Swift you can use all escape sequences you are familiar with from ActionScript; the only exception is the sequence for escaping a Unicode Scalar, which has a slightly different syntax, as you saw earlier in Listing 19-6, when we discussed characters.

***Listing 19-10.*** Interpolating Values in Strings

```
// Get the UnicodeScalar for the symbol ä:
let aWithUmlautCode = UnicodeScalar("ä")

// Next, get the UnicodeScalar integer value
// and store its hexadecimal representation into a String:
let hexCode = String(aWithUmlautCode.value, radix: 16)

// Last, print it out, inserting a new line (\n) in the middle of the sentence:
print("The Unicode Scalar for \(aWithUmlautCode) is \(hexCode), \n ↵
        or \(aWithUmlautCode.value) in decimal notation.")

// output:
// The Unicode Scalar for ä is e4,
//   or 228 in decimal notation.
```

## Inadvertently Copying Strings

Let us close the topic on strings with a word of caution. Unlike in ActionScript, where String instances are passed by reference[2] when assigned to other strings or passed to functions, in Swift their default behavior is to be passed by value. In other words, a String instance that is assigned to another variable or passed as an argument to a function might[3] end up being copied multiple times, which can be costly.

# Optionals

If you have tried pretty much any Swift tutorial, you may have wondered what all those question marks and exclamation marks are all about. At first glance it almost reads like the script of a five o'clock soap opera! See what we did there with the exclamation mark? This part of the Swift syntax is potentially the most confusing to a newcomer, so if you want it demystified, you have come to the right place.

---

[2]Not 100% true, actually. . . . In ActionScript strings are *made to behave as if they are passed by value* and copies of them are created only if you modify the String instance via one of its references.

[3]Swift does copy-on-write for value types, so actual copying will happen only if you modify the instance you have assigned or passed as an argument to a function (inout function arguments are an exception—see **Chapter 21**).

# What Is an Optional Type?

Let us start revealing what optionals are by looking at how Swift deals with "normal" types. Consider the example in Listing 19-11, which declares an integer and attempts to print it out.

***Listing 19-11.*** Declaring a Variable of Non-optional Type

```
var age: Int
print("Person's age = \(age)")

// This generates a compiler error:
// variable 'age' used before being initialized
```

These two lines generate a compiler error: `error: variable 'age' used before being initialized`. ActionScript defaults to automatically setting to null or to zero variables that you don't explicitly initialize. Other languages are less merciful and will leave whatever junk is in the memory the variable in question happens to point at. If we had a penny for every hour we have spent in the past chasing a mysterious crash only to trace it down to an uninitialized variable. . . .[4] This bitter experience makes us grateful that the Swift compiler can be of some help: catching situations like this at compile time is invaluable.

Next, let us see what happens if you try to initialize the age variable by assigning `nil` to it like we can do by assigning `null` in ActionScript (see Listing 19-12).

***Listing 19-12.*** Initializing a Non-optional Type of Variable with Nil

```
var age: Int = nil
print("Person's age = \(age)")
// error: nil cannot initialize specified type 'Int'
```

This change begets a different compiler error: `error: nil cannot initialize specified type 'Int'`. In Swift you can't assign `nil` to just any variable. You need to explicitly tell the Swift compiler that this variable can take `nil` as a value. This could be useful if age was assigned the result of a third-party function, which may return `nil`, for example. Listing 19-13 shows you how to let the compiler know that the age variable can take `nil`.

***Listing 19-13.*** Declaring a Variable of Optional Type and Initializing It with Nil

```
var age: Int? // the question mark tells the compiler that age can be nil
// This declaration also automatically initializes age with nil.
```

The question mark after the type signals to the Swift compiler that age can accept the `nil` value. In other words, having an actual integer value is optional: age can contain an integer or it can contain `nil`.

Note that the declaration above also initializes age with nil (i.e., it is shorthand for `var age: Int? = nil`). In other words, if you don't provide a value for your optional variable, it is automatically set to `nil`.

# Why Use Optionals?

Let us have another look at the age variable from the last two examples. Suppose you have a database query, which takes a person's name and tells you how old they are (see Listing 19-14).

---

[4] A crime always committed by another colleague, never by us. Honest!

***Listing 19-14.*** Assigning a Function Result to a Non-optional Variable

```
func getAgeFromName(name: String) -> Int {
    // query a database and return a result
}

var age: Int = getAgeFromName("John Smith")
```

An important question is: how do you deal with results for names that are not found in the database? Return 0? Return -1? Zero is less suitable of the two, as it is a valid age, but it may be your only choice if you were forced to use UInt, instead of Int. In either case you would need to add comments to document your intentions about which value should be interpreted as "no information about this person's age."

How about returning something that is neither Int nor UInt? Having getAgeFromName return nil to indicate missing information has two merits: it's consistent and self-documented.[5] Listing 19-15 shows this subtle change.

***Listing 19-15.*** Assigning a Function Result to an Optional Variable

```
func getAgeFromName(name: String) -> Int? {
    // Query a database and return a result.
    // The result can now be nil.
}

let age: Int? = getAgeFromName("John Smith")
// If age contains any integer value, you know that "John Smith"
// was found in the database. A nil result on the other hand tells you
// that either the name was not found or age information was missing for it.
```

Note that in both listings you can omit the type from the declaration of age, as the compiler will infer it from the function result you assign to it:

```
let age = getAgeFromName("John Smith").
```

# Unwrapping an Optional

*Unwrapping* is fancy speak for accessing the value of an optional variable or constant. For this to make complete sense it might be a good idea to peek behind the scenes first. In Swift Optional is actually a separate type, which looks like Listing 19-16.

***Listing 19-16.*** The Optional Type in Swift

```
public enum Optional<Wrapped> : _Reflectable, NilLiteralConvertible {
    case None
    case Some(Wrapped)

    // Initializers and methods follow...
}
```

---

[5]Plus, it requires that the caller unwrap the result, so your colleagues can't claim they didn't know nil was a possibility. We will see what unwrapping is in the next section.

Unless you skip to **Chapter 22**, some of the syntax above, namely, enum and <Wrapped>, may look unfamiliar. For the moment you can think of the code in Listing 19-16 like this: it declares a type, named Optional, which can have two states: None, which means "no value" and Some, which means "some value of type Wrapped." Here Wrapped is not an actual type but a type placeholder. You can declare an Optional variable that can hold an Int value: Optional<Int> or a String value: Optional<String> or whatever value type you decide to plug in place of Wrapped.

The ? suffix after an optional-type declaration is syntactic shortcut for Optional<YourTypeHere>, so the following two declarations in Listing 19-17 are the same.

*Listing 19-17.* Two Different Ways of Declaring an Optional Variable

```
// These two lines declare the same thing:
var age: Int?
var age: Optional<Int>
```

■ **Tip**  Optional<Wrapped> is a generic enumerated type. You can find information and examples on enumerations and generics in Chapter 22.

So when you declare an optional Int variable, this effectively means you are not declaring an Int that might be nil but an Optional that may or may not contain an Int value. Getting this value out of the Optional variable is called *unwrapping*.

You can access the value of an Optional in one of two ways:

- by assigning its value to a temporary constant or variable, called *optional binding*; and

- by using *forced unwrapping*.

You can also use a third way, which requires a slightly different kind of optional, called *implicitly unwrapped optional*. We will have a brief look at each of these choices in the next few subsections.

## Optional Binding

You bind an optional's value by assigning it to a temporary constant or a variable. This allows you to perform a check for whether a value is available or whether the optional contains nil.

Listing 19-18 shows an example that extracts the value of the optional age variable into the constant tempAge. The code following the if statement will only be run if a non-nil value is assigned to tempAge.

*Listing 19-18.* Optional Binding

```
var age: Int? = 64
if let tempAge = age {
    // Use tempAge
}
```

## Forced Unwrapping

Force-unwrapping an optional is a bit dramatic. First, you need to be confident that what you unwrap has a non-nil value. Second, you use the exclamation mark suffix to do the unwrapping (see Listing 19-19). What could declare confidence better than that?

*Listing 19-19.* Forced Unwrapping of an Optional

```
var sureAge = age! // The exclamation mark unwraps age's value
```

This line effectively says "I am sure that there is a non-nil value inside this variable and am not afraid to use it." The consequence of overconfidence is a runtime error:

```
fatal error: unexpectedly found nil while unwrapping an Optional value.
```

## Implicitly Unwrapped Optionals

Instead of using the exclamation mark to unwrap an optional every time you need its value, you can declare an optional variable in a way that makes sure its value is unwrapped when you access it. Such a variable is called *implicitly unwrapped* and you can create one by adding an exclamation mark after its type (see Listing 19-20).

*Listing 19-20.* Declaring an Implicitly Unwrapped Optional

```
var implicitlyUnwrappedAge: Int! = 64
```

---

■ **Note** Here is some behind-the-scenes information. In Swift 2 implicitly unwrapped optionals have a type of their own: ImplicitlyUnwrappedOptional<Wrapped>. In other words, the declaration in Listing 19-20 is a shortcut for

```
var implicitlyUnwrappedAge: ImplicitlyUnwrappedOptional<Int> = 64
```

Swift 3 keeps the syntax for declaring implicitly unwrapped optionals but treats the exclamation mark as a type attribute. So, implicitlyUnwrappedAge from the last example would no longer be of type ImplicitlyUnwrapped Optional<Int>, but of type Optional<Int> with a value that may be implicitly forced.

---

As is the case with optionals, if you do not provide an initial value when you declare an implicitly unwrapped optional, it is automatically initialized with nil. You can think of an implicitly unwrapped optional as a hybrid between an optional and a non-optional variable or constant: it has the option of containing nil, but can also be used as your usual variable or constant without the need to unwrap its value every time (Listing 19-21).

*Listing 19-21.* Accessing the Value of an Implicitly Unwrapped Optional

```
let sureAge = implicitlyUnwrappedAge // no need for an exclamation mark
```

Using implicitly unwrapped optionals has its pros and cons. On the one hand, it unclutters your code from exclamation marks. On the other hand, a variable which contains nil when it shouldn't makes your code more likely to break and, at the same time, makes it less obvious why it broke. For instance, if we did not initialize implicitlyUnwrappedAge and then tried to print it out, this would result in a runtime error (Listing 19-22).

*Listing 19-22.* Accessing an Implicitly Unwrapped Optional, Which Has Been Initialized with Nil

```
var implicitlyUnwrappedAge: Int! // The variable is is initialized with nil.
print(implicitlyUnwrappedAge) // This results in a runtime error.
```

## ACTIONSCRIPT ANALOGY

The behavior of implicitly unwrapped optionals is pretty much how typical ActionScript variables and constants behave:

- They can contain a value or `null`;

- They don't require a special syntax for accessing that value;

- They are initialized with `null` by default unless you provide a value explicitly; and

- Accessing a variable or a constant that contains `null` results in a runtime error.

## Optional Chaining

Optional chaining saves you the need to check if an optional variable or constant is `nil` before you access its properties or call one of its methods. What you get as a result of that access, instead of a slap on the wrist, is another optional value.

Let us illustrate this with an example. The code in Listing 19-23 declares two classes: `Person` and `PersonalInformation`. `PersonalInformation` contains a single property: age of type `Int`. `Person` contains a single property too, `personalInfo`, of type `PersonalInformation?`, which may optionally contain an instance of `PersonalInformation` or may contain `nil`.

*Listing 19-23.* Declaring a Class with an Optional Property

```
class PersonalInformation {
    var age = 20
}

class Person {
    var personalInfo: PersonalInformation?
}
```

In Listing 19-24 the first line instantiates `cookieMonster` of type `Person`. Because no initial value is given to its property `personalInfo`, it is automatically assigned `nil`. So what's going on on the second line, where `cookieMonster.personalInfo?` is accessed and why doesn't it result in an exception?

*Listing 19-24.* Accessing a Property Through Optional Chaining

```
var cookieMonster = Person()
var monstersAge = cookieMonster.personalInfo?.age
print(monstersAge)

// output: nil
```

Accessing a property (or calling a method or subscript) on an optional variable that may be nil and getting away with it is what *optional chaining* affords you. The way the compiler does it is: if cookieMonster. personalInfo? is nil, then the result of cookieMonster.personalInfo?.age is inferred to be an optional, which contains nil. The compiler then infers the same type for monstersAge, which gets assigned that result.

# What's Your Type?

When coding, you can have situations where you either need to check if an object is of a certain type or to find out what type it is. In this section we see how you can do these checks.

## Using the is Operator

You check if an object is of a certain type with the is operator (see Listing 19-25). It takes an instance and a type and returns true if the instance is of that type or descends from it, false otherwise.

*Listing 19-25.* Using the is Operator for Type Checking

```
var randomInt = 42
var amIString = randomInt is String // returns false
var amIInt = randomInt is Int // returns true
```

---

### ACTIONSCRIPT ANALOGY

If this looks familiar, it's because it is. ActionScript has an is operator, which functions in the same way.

---

## Type Queries

You can query an instance's runtime type with obj.dynamicType, as in Listing 19-26.

*Listing 19-26.* Querying an Object's Type

```
var instanceOfInt = 66
print("\(instanceOfInt.dynamicType)") // prints Int
```

---

▪ **Note**    In Swift 3 dynamicType is no longer a property of the type but an operator. In other words, instead of calling obj.dynamicType, you will need to call dynamicType(obj).

---

You can obtain the type of a class or a protocol as a value with the postfix expression self. Listing 19-27 shows you a couple of examples.

*Listing 19-27.* Querying the Type of a Class and a Protocol

```
print("\(MyClass.self)") // prints MyClass
print("\(MyProtocol.self)") // prints MyProtocol
```

---

**ACTIONSCRIPT ANALOGY**

In ActionScript you have a few ways of getting dynamic type information, which work differently than `dynamicType` in Swift:

- `getQualifiedClassName` and `getQualifiedSuperclassName` give you type information as a string.

- `describeType` returns a very detailed report about an object's type and its characteristics in XML format.

- `typeof` distinguishes between six compile-time types: `String`, `MovieClip`, `Object`, `Function`, `Number`, and `Boolean` and gives you type information in string format.

---

# Type Casting

Like ActionScript, Swift offers you the as operator for type casting. Unlike the ActionScript version, it comes in two flavors: as? and as! If you have read the previous section on optionals, this syntax will look familiar.

The as? version of the operator returns an optional value, which is set to `nil` if the cast is unsuccessful. The as!, otherwise known as *the forced form* of the operator, does not give you the option of checking but throws a runtime error when the type casting is not possible. Use it when you feel confident in your type casting. Or not at all.

The examples that follow illustrate the two scenarios. Listing 19-28 declares an Int instance, tries to cast it as a String, and, if the cast succeeds, assigns the result to a temporary constant, named `stringVersion`. Note how the declaration of `stringVersion` uses optional binding, which we covered earlier in the section "Optionals."

*Listing 19-28.* Using the as? Operator for Type Casting

```
var instanceOfInt = 42

if let stringVersion = instanceOfInt as? String {
    print("Casting an Int to a String succeeded: \(stringVersion)")
}
else {
    print("The cast did not succeed.")
}

// output: "The cast did not succeed."
```

Using the same integer instance, `instanceOfInt`, Listing 19-29 casts it to a String and force-unwraps the result, which leads to a runtime error.

*Listing 19-29.* Using the as! Operator for Type Casting

```
print("Casting an Int to a String: \(instanceOfInt as! String)")
// throws a runtime error
```

If you try these examples at home, you will notice that the compiler very gracefully issues a warning at the line of type casting, telling you that `Cast from 'Int' to unrelated type 'String' always fails`.

---

### ACTIONSCRIPT ANALOGY

The as operator will be familiar to you from ActionScript, where it behaves like Swift's optional form: as? and returns null if the cast is unsuccessful.

---

# Nested Types

In Swift a type can be defined within the context of another type. The example in Listing 19-30 defines the class HostClass, which contains two levels of hosted classes: FirstNestedClass and SecondNestedClass. This demonstrates the syntax for nested types: the definition of the nested type must be put within the curly brackets of its host. It also shows you that you can use more than one level of nesting.

*Listing 19-30.* Defining Nested Types

```
class HostClass {
    class FirstNestedClass {
        class SecondNestedClass {
            let secondNestedClassField = "I am three levels deep."
        }
    }
}
```

The purpose of nesting types within one another usually is to keep a type within the context in which it is needed: for example, if HostClass is the only class that uses FirstNestedClass, it would make sense to keep FirstNestedClass's definition within the scope of HostClass. However, if you need to access a nested type outside its host, you can do that by prefixing its name with the name of its enclosing type(s) as shown in Listing 19-31.

*Listing 19-31.* Accessing a Nested Type Outside Its Containing Type

```
let secondNestedInstance = HostClass.FirstNestedClass.SecondNestedClass()
print("\(secondNestedInstance.secondNestedClassField)")
```

# Some Types Worth Getting to Know

We will now have a look at a few types you are likely to use quite a lot when you program with Swift: containers, tuples, and function types.

## Container Types: Array, Set, Dictionary

The container types in Swift are implemented as generic classes. We will go over generics in **Chapter 22** in detail. For now, you can think of a generic class like this: Array<String> stands for "an array of String items and nothing else" and Array<Int> stands for "an array of Int items and nothing else." By "nothing else" here we mean that an Array, or a Set in Swift contain items of the same type: you can have an array of Strings or an array of Ints, but you can't have an array that contains a String and an Int.

```
┌─────────────────────────────────────────────────────────────────┐
│                     ACTIONSCRIPT ANALOGY                          │
└─────────────────────────────────────────────────────────────────┘
```

You will find the Swift container classes: `Array`, `Set` (a set being a special kind of array) and `Dictionary` very close to how their ActionScript counterparts operate, but there is a subtle difference. With the exception of `vector<T>`, in ActionScript you can have items of various types in the same container, while in a Swift container items are always of the same type.

# Array

Let us see how we can manipulate arrays in Swift: from creating and initializing them to iterating through their items and making modifications.

## Ways of Creating and Initializing an Array

Following are some typical ways you may use to create an `Array` and give it initial values. The first example (Listing 19-32) shows you how to create an empty array of `String` items. The square brackets tell the Swift compiler that you are declaring an array and the type between them is the type of the items it will contain.

***Listing 19-32.*** Creating an Empty Array

```
var theThreeMusketeers = [String]()
```

Note that this is shorthand for writing `var theThreeMusketeers : Array<String> = []`.

---

■ **Tip**    If `Array<String>` looks strange, have a look at the section on generics in Chapter 22.

---

Listing 19-33 shows you how to declare an array with an initial size and an initial value for its items.

***Listing 19-33.*** Creating Array of a Given Size and Initializing Its Members with a Certain Value

```
var theThreeMusketeers = [String](count: 3, repeatedValue: "")
```

You can also create an array using an array literal: the syntax in the Listing 19-34 will look familiar from ActionScript. Note how once you provide literal values the compiler is able to infer their type, so you can be concise in your declaration and omit the type declaration part.

***Listing 19-34.*** Initializing an Array with an Array Literal

```
var theThreeMusketeers = ["Athos", "Porthos", "Aramis"]
var extraMusketeers = ["D'Artagnan"]
```

Finally, you can combine the arrays you declared previously and create a third one, as in Listing 19-35, using the + operator.

***Listing 19-35.*** Creating an Array by Combining Two Other Arrays

```
var theFourMusketeers = theThreeMusketeers + extraMusketeers
```

413

## How to Iterate over an Array

You can use a for-in loop to iterate over the items in an array. For example, see Listing 19-36.

**Listing 19-36.** Iterating over an Array Using a for-in Loop

```
for musketeer in theFourMusketeers {
    print("Musketeer's name: \(musketeer)")
}
```

Here is a neat trick, shown in Listing 19-37: the Array class has a method, called enumerate, which allows you to iterate not only over the items in the array but also over their indices. Neat, huh?

**Listing 19-37.** Iterating over an Array by Calling Its Enumerate Method

```
for (index, value) in theFourMusketeers.enumerate() {
    print("\(index + 1). Musketeer's name: \(value)")
}
```

---

■ **Tip** We will go over the specifics of the for-in loops in Swift in Chapter 20.

---

## Working with the Items of an Array

You can query the number of items in an array by calling its count method. The isEmpty method lets you check whether the array has any items in it. The next couple of examples in Listing 19-38 and Listing 19-39 show you how to add items to an array and how to modify them. Some of the ways will look familiar to you from ActionScript. Others may be new (e.g., replacing a range of array items with a new array), as shown on the third line of code of Listing 19-39.

**Listing 19-38.** Adding Items at the End of an Array

```
var theThreeMusketeers = [String]()

// adds "Athos" to the end of the array:
theThreeMusketeers.append("Athos")
// the array contains ["Athos"]

// concatenates theThreeMusketeers with the array ["Porthos", "Aramis"]
theThreeMusketeers += ["Porthos", "Aramis"]
// the array now contains ["Athos", "Porthos", "Aramis"]
```

**Listing 19-39.** Modifying the Values of Array Items

```
// creates an array of four Strings and initializes them with an empty string:
var theFourMusketeers = [String](count: 4, repeatedValue: "")
// the array contains ["", "", "", ""]

// replaces the first string in the array with "D'Artagnan":
theFourMusketeers[0] = "D'Artagnan"
// the array now contains ["D'Artagnan", "", "", ""]
```

```
// replaces the range of items 1, 2 and 3 with new values:
theFourMusketeers[1...3] = ["Athos", "Porthos", "Aramis"]
// the array now contains ["D'Artagnan", "Athos", "Porthos", "Aramis"]
```

Inserting and removing an item at a specific index is done with the insert(_:atIndex:) and the removeAtIndex(_:) methods—very similar to the insertAt and removeAt methods of the ActionScript Array.

# Set

A Set in Swift represents a collection of unique items. You can think of it as an Array, which can only contain the same value once. Like an Array, a Set collection is unordered. All of the functionality for working with arrays applies to sets too, except that there is no shorthand form for declaring a Set (Listing 19-40).

***Listing 19-40.*** Creating a Set and Initializing It with an Array Literal

```
var fireflyCharacters: Set<String> = ["Mal", "Inara"]
```

You can perform logical set operations, using the union(_:), subtract(_:), intersect(_:), and exclusiveOr(_:) methods of the Set class. All of these create a new set and return it as a result. For example, the code in Listing 19-41 finds the intersection between two sets.

***Listing 19-41.*** Finding the Intersection Between Two Sets

```
var fireflyCharacters: Set<String> = ["Mal", "Inara"]
var serenityCharacters: Set<String> = ["Mal", "Inara", "Kaylee", "Simon"]

var commonCharacters = fireflyCharacters.intersect(serenityCharacters)
// commonCharacters contains ["Mal", "Inara"]
```

Swift gives you the ability to compare sets and determine if they are equal by using the equals operator (==). You can also check if one set contains another set by using the isSubsetOf(_:)/isStrictSubsetOf(_:) and isSupersetOf(_:)/isStrictSupersetOf(_:) methods. The isDisjointWith(_:) method returns true if two sets have no items in common.

# Dictionary

If you use dictionaries in ActionScript, you won't have much of a learning curve with the Swift Dictionary type. Like its ActionScript cousin, it stores a collection of associated *key-value* pairs. The next few subsections show ways of creating and initializing a Swift Dictionary.

## Ways of Creating and Initializing a Dictionary

The example in Listing 19-42 creates an empty dictionary, in this case with keys of type String and values of type Double.

***Listing 19-42.*** Creating an Empty Dictionary

```
// creates an empty dictionary with keys of type String and Double values:
var macOsXVersions = [String: Double]()
```

The line in Listing 19-42 creates an empty dictionary with keys of type Double and values of type String. Note that this is the shorthand notation for

```
var macOsXVersions : Dictionary<String, Double> = [:].
```

---

■ **Tip**    For a detailed explanation of the angle brackets syntax go to the section on generics in Chapter 22.

---

Listing 19-43 shows you how to create a dictionary and initialize it with a dictionary literal. You can see the Swift type inference in action here: you don't need to explicitly specify the key-value types: the compiler guesses them from the literals you provide.

***Listing 19-43.*** Initializing a Dictionary with a Dictionary Literal

```
// creates a dictionary with keys of type String and values of type Double:
var macOsXVersions = ["Cheetah" : 10.0, "Puma" : 10.1, "Jaguar" : 10.2]
```

## Iterating over a Dictionary

The for-in loop is your friend here too. With dictionaries you have an option to iterate over keys and values together (Listing 19-44) or separately (Listing 19-45).

***Listing 19-44.*** Iterating over a Dictionary's Keys and Values

```
for (versionName, versionCode) in macOsXVersions {
    print("\(versionName) \(versionCode)")
}
```

***Listing 19-45.*** Iterating over a Dictionary's Keys and Values Separately

```
// Iterating through the keys only
for versionName in macOsXVersions.keys {
    print("Mac OS X version name: \(versionName)")
}

// Iterating through the values only
for versionCode in macOsXVersions.values {
    print("Mac OS X version code: \(versionCode)")
}
```

## Accessing and Modifying Keys and Values

The next few examples in Listing 19-46, Listing 19-47, and Listing 19-48 show you how to add, modify, and remove items from a dictionary.

***Listing 19-46.*** Adding a New Key-Value Pair to a Dictionary

```
macOsXVersions["Panther"] = 0.0
// macOsXVersions now contains
// ["Cheetah" : 10.0, "Puma" : 10.1, "Jaguar" : 10.2, "Panther" : 0.0]
```

When you need to modify an existing value for a given key, you can do that by accesing the value directly, using a *subscript*, represented by the square brackets surrounding the key (more on *subscripts* in **Chapter 22**). You can also call the updateValue method of the Dictionary class, which gives you a chance to retain the old value of the key after you have replaced it with a new one (Listing 19-47).

***Listing 19-47.*** Modifying the Value for a Given Key

```
// You can update a value using subscript
macOsXVersions["Panther"] = 0.3
// macOsXVersions now contains
// ["Cheetah" : 10.0, "Puma" : 10.1, "Jaguar" : 10.2, "Panther" : 0.3]

// ... or you can call the updateValue(_:forKey:) method
if let oldValue = macOsXVersions.updateValue(10.3, forKey: "Panther") {
    print("The old value for Mac OS X 10.3 was \(oldValue).")
}
// macOsXVersions now contains
// ["Cheetah" : 10.0, "Puma" : 10.1, "Jaguar" : 10.2, "Panther" : 10.3]
```

To remove a key-value pair from a Dictionary you simply replace the value with nil, as shown in Listing 19-48.

***Listing 19-48.*** Removing a Key-Value Pair from a Dictionary

```
macOsXVersions["Panther"] = nil
// macOsXVersions now contains
// ["Cheetah" : 10.0, "Puma" : 10.1, "Jaguar" : 10.2]
```

# Tuples

Tuples are useful for temporarily keeping a group of values together. "Temporarily" here means as a way of returning multiple values from a function, for example. To keep values together that will have a longer lifespan than that, you would normally be better off keeping them in a class or a structure.

You define a tuple as a comma-separated list of types, enclosed in parentheses. Listing 19-49 declares a tuple, weatherStats, which contains two values: wind speed in miles per hour and wind direction. This means that the tuple's type is (Int, String).

***Listing 19-49.*** Defining a Tuple

```
let weatherStats = (7, "North") // Tuple of type (Int, String)
```

You can read the values in a tuple by assigning them to a temporary constant. The next few examples show you how to do that and how to read or ignore values selectively.

The code in Listing 19-50 assigns the values of the tuple we just declared to two temporary constants: windSpeed and windDirection.

***Listing 19-50.*** Accessing Individual Values in a Tuple

```
let (windSpeedMph, windDirection) = weatherStats
print("wind speed: \(windSpeedMph) mph, direction: \(windDirection)")
```

You don't have to define constants for all of the tuple's values if you are not interested in all of them. Use underscore to ignore values that you don't need to access (Listing 19-51).

*Listing 19-51.* Selectively Accessing Individual Values in a Tuple

```
let (_, windDirection) = weatherStats
print("wind direction: \(windDirection)")
```

Each of the tuple's values has an index which you can access by putting a dot, followed by the index's number after the name of the tuple. Calling weatherStats.0 gives you access to the first member of the tuple, weatherStats.1—to the second, and so on, as shown in Listing 19-52.

*Listing 19-52.* Using an Index to Access a Tuple's Member

```
print("wind speed: \(weatherStats.0) mph, direction: \(weatherStats.1)")
```

As an alternative to using indices, you can name each tuple member and use its name to access it. Listing 19-53 defines the tuple weatherStats with two named elements—windSpeed and windDirection— and then accesses their values as weatherStats.windSpeed and weatherStats.windDirection.

---

■ **Note**    To use names, a tuple must have at least two elements.

---

*Listing 19-53.* Using Names for Tuple Elements

```
let weatherStats = (windSpeed: 7, windDirection: "North")
print("wind speed: \(weatherStats.windSpeed) mph,↵
direction: \(weatherStats.windDirection)")
```

The example in Listing 19-54 shows you a function, which returns a tuple.

*Listing 19-54.* A Function, Which Returns a Tuple as a Result

```
func getWeatherStats() -> (Int, String) {
    return (7, "North")
}
```

## ACTIONSCRIPT ANALOGY

Tuples are similar to using dynamic objects in ActionScript—see if the code in Listing 19-55 looks familiar.

---

The code in Listing 19-55 shows the ActionScript analogue of the tuple we defined in Listing 19-53.

*Listing 19-55.* Using Dynamic Objects in ActionScript Is Close in Syntax to Swift's Tuples

```
// ActionScript code:
var weatherStats : Object = {windSpeed: 7, windDirection: "North"};
trace("wind speed: " + weatherStats.windSpeed + "mph, ↵
direction: " + weatherStats.windDirection);
```

# Function Types

In Swift the type of a function is its signature. Listing 19-56, for example, declares a function of type (String) -> String. This means that the function takes one argument of type String and returns a String result.

**Listing 19-56.** Declaring a Function of Type (String) -> String

```
func capitalize(str: String) -> String {
    return str.uppercaseString
}
```

When you know a function's type, you can assign it to a variable, as shown in Listing 19-57. You define the type of the variable as (**functionArguments**) -> **functionReturnType.**

**Listing 19-57.** Assigning a Function to a Variable

```
// the next line declares a variable
// and assigns a function of type (String)->String to it:
let capitalizeFunction: (String) -> String = capitalize

// accessing the variable and giving it an argument
// results in the function being called:
print("capitalization: \(capitalizeFunction("fallaciloquence"))")
```

You can also pass a function type as an argument to another function. Again, you use the function's signature as the type of the argument, so capitalizationFunction's type in Listing 19-58 is (String) -> String.

**Listing 19-58.** Using a Function Type as a Parameter to Another Function

```
// This function takes another function as an argument:
func printCapitalizedString(capitalizationFunction: (String) -> String, ↩
                            str: String) {
    let capitalizeFunction: (String) -> String = capitalize
    print("capitalization: \(capitalizeFunction("fallaciloquence"))")
}
```

Or, you can have a function that returns another function as a result. A bit weird, but only syntax-wise. The first arrow in Listing 19-59 is put before the return type of getCapitalizationFunction. The second arrow is part of its return type: (String) -> String.

**Listing 19-59.** Returning a Function Type as a Result of Another Function

```
func getCapitalizationFunction() -> (String) -> String {
    return capitalizeFunction
}
```

## ACTIONSCRIPT ANALOGY

Swift's function types are very similar to ActionScript's Function type.

## Type Aliases

Finally, you can name any existing type on a whim using the `typealias` keyword. Say you are writing an app that takes payments and want a more meaningful name for the type you would use to store prices. Using `Price` as an alias to `UInt` makes it obvious not only that it allows only non-negative values but also why (Listing 19-60).

*Listing 19-60.* Defining a Type Alias

```
public typealias Price = UInt
```

# Summary

You are now familiar with the basics of the types in Swift and know how to take advantage of the compiler's type inference, how to query an instance's type, and how to type cast it. This chapter has also, it is hoped, demystified Swift's syntax weirdness around optional types and now you are comfortable with all of the question marks and exclamation marks in the code. Add to that some essential information on a bunch of important types and you are set to go!

## CHAPTER 20

■ ■ ■

# Control Flow

We have so far covered types and operators in Swift and you know how to declare variables and constants. Now is time to go over how you can control the execution of your code. It's all about loops, conditional statements, keywords for changing the course of action, and Christmas carols . . .

## Loops

It is Christmas as I am writing this and the shops and cafés around me are playing the obligatory Christmas carols in a loop. One in particular strikes me as an example I could steal to play with and show you how loops work in Swift. It's called *The Twelve Days of Christmas* and goes like this:

*On the first day of Christmas my true love sent to me*

*a partridge in a pear tree.*

*On the second day of Christmas my true love sent to me*

*two turtle doves*

*and a partridge in a pear tree.*

*On the third day of Christmas my true love sent to me*

*three French hens,*

*two turtle doves*

*and a partridge in a pear tree.*

. . . and so on until we collect a whole menagerie on day 12.[1] The song has a simple structure, which iterates through a set of days, 12 to be precise. Each iteration follows the same pattern: a day is enumerated, a gift is associated with it, and then another iteration is done, this time backward, through all of the accumulated gifts thus far.

The examples I am going to run you through will try to build the lyrics of the song, using for or while loops. For that purpose, let us declare all the Christmas gifts in an array first. We will then iterate over that array in various different ways. Listing 20-1 declares a constant array, called christmasGifts, which contains the description of the gifts for each day. We will also declare another constant: christmasDays to keep the number of days to iterate through, which equals the number of items in the christmasGifts array.

---

[1]Speaking of menagerie, you might like Frank Kelly's version of the text. Go on, look it up on YouTube, you know you want to.

© Radoslava Leseva Adams and Hristo Lesev 2016
R. L. Adams and H. Lesev, *Migrating to Swift from Flash and ActionScript*,
DOI 10.1007/978-1-4842-1666-8_20

**Listing 20-1.** Declaring an Array of Christmas Gifts, Which We Will Use in the Next Examples

```
// An array of Christmas gifts
let christmasGifts = ["a partridge in a pear tree",
                      "two turtle doves",
                      "three french hens",
                      "four calling birds",
                      "five gold rings",
                      "six geese a-laying",
                      "seven swans a-swimming",
                      "eight maids a-milking",
                      "nine ladies dancing",
                      "ten lords a-leaping",
                      "eleven pipers piping",
                      "twelve drummers drumming"]

let christmasDays = christmasGifts.count
```

# for

We will introduce loops with something that will look familiar from ActionScript but is on its way out in Swift: the straightforward for loop. It works and almost looks like its ActionScript counterpart, except that you do not need to enclose the definitions after the if statement, the so-called *initialization, condition,* and *afterthought,* in parentheses. Listing 20-2 demonstrates the syntax. This example declares a variable, called day, which is initialized with a value of 1 and keeps incrementing after each execution of the loop until it reaches the value of christmasDays. In the body of the loop day is used to print out the day and what gift was received on it. The corresponding gift is effectively the value of christmasGifts[day - 1], as Swift arrays, like their ActionScript cousins, have indices starting at 0.

**Listing 20-2.** A for loop with a Counter

```
// Define a counter, named day
// and use it to iterate over the christmasGifts array:
for var day = 1; day <= christmasDays; day += 1 {
    print("On the \(day) day of Christmas my true love sent to me")

    // Like in ActionScript, arrays in Swift are indexed from zero.
    print("\(christmasGifts[day - 1])\n")
}

// output:

//On the 1 day of Christmas my true love sent to me
//a partridge in a pear tree

//On the 2 day of Christmas my true love sent to me
//two turtle doves

//On the 3 day of Christmas my true love sent to me
//three french hens

// ...
```

The output of this loop leaves a few things to be desired. First, the verses are not quite right: we are missing the iteration through the accumulated gifts. Second, it would be nice if we had "1ˢᵗ" instead of "1", "2ⁿᵈ" instead of "2," and "3ʳᵈ," instead of "3" when we enumerate the days of Christmas. We will tackle both of these shortcomings in the course of the chapter.

---

■ **Caution**    This form of the `for` loop is deprecated in Swift 2.2 and will not be part of Swift 3. Its substitute, the `for-in` loop is better suited for most situations where you will need to loop through items: iterating through collections or going through a range of values. More on that in the next section.

---

## for-in

The `for-in` flavor of the `for` loop is a bit more versatile than its ActionScript `for..in` and `for each .. in` counterparts and offers you more ways of counting or iterating through items.

Let us start with an exact equivalent of the loop in the last example, but using more concise syntax. Instead of for **initialization; condition; afterthought** the code in Listing 20-3 declares a loop with the following anatomy: for **counter** in **range**, where **range** goes from 1 to the value of `christmasDays` and **counter** loops through that range. Note that the bounds of the range don't have to be constants. Both this loop and the `for` loop in Listing 20-2 produce the same result.

---

■ **Note**    The range declaration in the example below uses the *closed range operator*, which we covered in Chapter 18.

---

*Listing 20-3.* A for-in Loop, Which Counts Within a Range

```
for day in 1...christmasDays {
    print("On the \(day) day of Christmas my true love sent to me")
    print("\(christmasGifts[day - 1]) \n")
}

// output:

//On the 1 day of Christmas my true love sent to me
//a partridge in a pear tree

//On the 2 day of Christmas my true love sent to me
//two turtle doves

//On the 3 day of Christmas my true love sent to me
//three french hens

// ...
```

## Ignoring the Counter

Instead of the full version of the syntax, for **counter** in **range**, you can use for _ in **range**. The underscore tells the compiler that you don't care for the values of the **counter** variable and want to ignore them. The next example illustrates that, if not in the most efficient way. It ignores the values that the for-in loop provides and instead uses a variable outside the loop, named day, which gets incremented with each iteration. The numberOfGifts variable accumulates the values that day goes through and in the end contains the total number of Christmas gifts in the song (Listing 20-4).

***Listing 20-4.*** You Can Ignore the Counter in a for-in Loop

```
var numberOfGifts = 0
var day = 1

// Ignore the counter
for _ in 1...christmasDays {
    day += 1
    numberOfGifts += day
}
print("I received \(numberOfGifts) gifts for Christmas.")

// output: I received 78 gifts for Christmas.
```

## Iterating Through Items in an Array

Straying from our mission to build that Christmas carol for a just bit longer (don't worry, we'll get there), let me show you how you can enumerate the items in an array, using a for-in loop. The code in Listing 20-5 prints out a bullet list of the items in the christmasGifts array. Does that look familiar? It should: bar a couple of extra parentheses, you would do exactly the same thing in ActionScript, using a for each ... in loop.

***Listing 20-5.*** A for-in Loop That Enumerates the Items in an Array

```
print("I received a whole menagery for Christmas:")
for gift in christmasGifts {
    print("• \(gift)")
}

// output:

//I received a whole menagery for Christmas:
//• a partridge in a pear tree
//• two turtle doves
//• three french hens
//• four calling birds
//• five gold rings
//• six geese a-laying
//• seven swans a-swimming
//• eight maids a-milking
//• nine ladies dancing
//• ten lords a-leaping
//• eleven pipers piping
//• twelve drummers drumming
```

# Looping Backward Through a Range

Let us go back to what we set out to do in the beginning of this chapter, which was to have the lyrics of *The Twelve Days of Christmas* printed out by a loop in Swift. What we achieved so far in Listing 20-2 and Listing 20-3 was to have the beginning of each verse printed out by a for or a for-in loop. The next step is to add the missing lines to the verses: every verse will be a line longer than the previous one and will enumerate backward the gifts received so far.

To build a backward-iterating loop, we will take advantage of a method that you can call on integer types in Swift.[2] The method is called stride(to: end_value, by: step) and produces a sequence of values ranging from the value of the number you call the method on to end_value, spaced by step (Listing 20-6).

**Listing 20-6.** Producing a Backward-Counting for-in Loop

```
// The stride(to:_, by:_) method
// lets you count backwards from the current value of day
for dayBackwards in day.stride(to: 0, by: -1) {
    // compose verse here
}
```

To get the verses of the song composed properly, we need to nest this loop inside the loop, which enumerates each day from 1 to the value of christmasDays: the outer loop will go through the days and the inner loop through the gifts that have been accumulated on each day.

Before we do that, however, let us take care of some extra business: when gifts are enumerated, each line describing a gift requires different punctuation, depending on which verse it appears in and what gift is being described. For example, we want to add a full stop to the last line of each verse: "a partridge in a pear tree." On the days after day one this last line will also have an extra "and" at the start and will appear as "and a partridge in a pear tree." In addition, we want the lines about the gifts to be separated by commas, except the last two because of that extra "and" between them. Listing 20-8 takes care of all this in a function that we will call composeVerseLine. It takes the index of the day the verse is about (day), a gift description (gift), and a Boolean parameter (needsPrefix), whose job is to help us decide whether the line being composed needs an "and" prepended to it (Listing 20-7).

**Listing 20-7.** Taking Care of the Punctuation in the Verse Lines

```
// This function composes a song line, which describes a gift.
func composeVerseLine ↵
        (day: Int, gift: String, needsPrefix : Bool = true) -> String {
    // From the second day onwards, we want to prepend "and"
    // at the start of the last verse, in order to get
    // "and a partridge in a pear tree".
    let versePrefix = (1 == day && needsPrefix) ? "and " : ""

    // We want every line that describes a gift,
    // but the last two, to end with a comma.
    // The penultimate line doesn't need punctuation
    // and the last one needs a fullstop.
    let versePostfix = 1 == day ? "." : (2 == day ? "" : ",")

    // Finally, ready to assemble the line:
    return "\(versePrefix)\(gift)\(versePostfix)"
}
```

---

[2]Integers, as well as all the other primitive types in Swift, are implemented as *structures* behind the scenes and thus can have properties and methods. You can read about structures in **Chapter 21**.

■ **Tip** The assignments to versePrefix and versePostfix use the ternary conditional operator (a ? b : c). For details on it and how it compares to its ActionScript counterpart see Chapter 18.

We can now put the two loops together and have them output the lyrics of the song (Listing 20-8).

*Listing 20-8.* Two Nested for-in Loops

```
for day in 1...christmasDays {
    print("\nOn the \(day) day of Christmas my true love sent to me")

    // Enumerate the days backwards, starting with the current day:
    for dayBackwards in day.stride(to: 0, by: -1) {
        // Call the function we defined that adds punctuation to each line:
        let verseLine = ←
          composeVerseLine(dayBackwards, ←
            gift: christmasGifts[dayBackwards - 1], needsPrefix: day > 1)
        print("\(verseLine)")
    }
}

// output:

//On the 1 day of Christmas my true love sent to me
//a partridge in a pear tree.

//On the 2 of day Christmas my true love sent to me
//two turtle doves
//and a partridge in a pear tree.

//On the 3 of day Christmas my true love sent to me
//three french hens,
//two turtle doves
//and a partridge in a pear tree.

// ...
```

Now that's more like it: the song lyrics look almost exactly as we would expect to see them. Except for the annoying "On the 1 day," "On the 2 day,"... We will take care of these in due course.

---

## ACTIONSCRIPT ANALOGY

The ActionScript for..in and for each .. in loops both let you iterate through the elements of an array: one gives you access to the arrays' indices and the other to the values of the items in the array. This just about covers their similarities with the for-in loop in Swift. They don't let you define ranges but can loop through the dynamic properties of an object.

# while

The while loop in Swift will be like an old friend to you if you are used to while loops in ActionScript. And if you have avoided them altogether, I can't blame you: it is usually easier to go into an infinite loop with while than with for, although with perseverance you can achieve anything. The syntax you use in Swift looks like this: while **condition** {**statements**}. The loop will repeat the statements in the curly brackets as long as **condition** evaluates to true.

Listing 20-9 continues the Christmas theme we started when we went over for loops. This time we will be printing the verses backward, starting from the twelfth day of Christmas and going down to the first.

*Listing 20-9.* Printing Out Verses with a while Loop

```
// Redefine christmasGifts as a variable, so we can change its size:
var christmasGifts = ["a partridge in a pear tree",
                      "two turtle doves",
                      "three french hens",
                      "four calling birds",
                      "five gold rings",
                      "six geese a-laying",
                      "seven swans a-swimming",
                      "eight maids a-milking",
                      "nine ladies dancing",
                      "ten lords a-leaping",
                      "eleven pipers piping",
                      "twelve drummers drumming"]

while 0 < christmasGifts.count {
    // The number of gifts left in christmasGifts
    // will tell us which day we are singing about:
    let day = christmasGifts.count

    // The last gift in the array gets extracted:
    let lastGift = christmasGifts.popLast()

    print("\nOn the \(day) day of Christmas my true love sent to me")
    print("\(lastGift!)")
}

// output:

//On the 12 of day Christmas my true love sent to me
//twelve drummers drumming

//On the 11 of day Christmas my true love sent to me
//eleven pipers piping

//On the 10 of day Christmas my true love sent to me
//ten lords a-leaping

// ...
```

Each iteration of the loop extracts a gift description from the end of the christmasGifts array and prints out the start of the verse that introduces that gift. The loop runs while there are items in the array. In order to be able to modify the size of the christmasGifts array, we need to make it *mutable* (i.e., define it as a variable rather than a constant). **Chapter 19** introduced arrays: have a look if you need more details on how to work with them.

---

## ACTIONSCRIPT ANALOGY

ActionScript's while loop only differs in syntax from its Swift cousin in that in ActionScript you must put *condition* in brackets: while (**condition**) {**statements**}, whereas in Swift the parentheses are optional.

---

## repeat-while

A repeat-while loop has the following syntax in Swift: repeat {**statements**} while **condition**. It first runs the statements inside the curly brackets and then checks if **condition** is true or false. If it is true, the **statements** are run again and again until **condition** evaluates to false. This way the statements in the body of the loop are guaranteed to run at least once, whatever **condition** evaluates to initially.

Let us rewrite the while loop from the previous example into a repeat-while loop. As you can see in Listing 20-10, the two loops are almost identical. With the repeat-while version it becomes necessary to ensure that there is a string in the array to extract before we use it, because the loop will run once before we get a chance to check if the array had items in it. The if let lastGift = christmasGifts.popLast() statement does that.

*Listing 20-10.* Printing Out Verses with a repeat-while Loop

```
repeat {
    // The loop will execute at least once
    // The number of gifts left in christmasGifts
    // will tell us which day we are singing about:
    var day = christmasGifts.count

    // An attempt to extract the last item from the christmasGifts array.
    // If we have already run out of items,
    // the code in the if statement's body won't execute.
    if let lastGift = christmasGifts.popLast(){
        print("\nOn the \(day) of Christmas my true love sent to me")
        let verseLine =
                composeVerseLine(day, gift: lastGift, needsPrefix: false)
        print("\(verseLine)")
    }

// the loop repeats until there are no items left in the array
} while christmasGifts.count > 0

// output:
//On the 12 of Christmas my true love sent to me
//twelve drummers drumming,

//On the 11 of Christmas my true love sent to me
//eleven pipers piping,
```

```
//On the 10 of Christmas my true love sent to me
//ten lords a-leaping,

//...
```

Now, just for fun, we could combine a repeat-while and a while loop to print out the complete verses of the song. Listing 20-11 uses the repeat-while loop we just put together and nests inside it a while loop, which counts down the remaining items in the array (without removing them) and prints out the gifts for the days preceding the current one. As a result, the song gets printed out, but starting from the last verse and continuing to the first one.

***Listing 20-11.*** A Nested Pair of repeat-while and while Loops, Which Print the Song Verses Backward

```
repeat // The loop will execute at least once {
    // The number of gifts left in christmasGifts
    // will tell us which day we are singing about:
    var day = christmasGifts.count

    // An attempt to extract the last item from the christmasGifts array.
    // If we have already run out of items,
    // the code in the if statement's body won't execute.
    if let lastGift = christmasGifts.popLast()
    {
        print("\nOn the \(day) day of Christmas my true love sent to me")
        let verseLine = ↵
                composeVerseLine(day, gift: lastGift, needsPrefix: false)
        print("\(verseLine)")

        // Now count down the previous days
        // and list the accumulated gifts.
        // Note that the prefix - operator
        // decrements day before its value is checked.
        while --day > 0
        {
            let verseLine = ↵
                    composeVerseLine(day, gift: christmasGifts[day - 1])
            print("\(verseLine)")
        }
    }

// The loop repeats until there are no items left in the array.
} while christmasGifts.count > 0

// output:

//On the 12 day of Christmas my true love sent to me
//twelve drummers drumming,
//eleven pipers piping,
//ten lords a-leaping,
//nine ladies dancing,
//eight maids a-milking,
//seven swans a-swimming,
```

```
//six geese a-laying,
//five gold rings,
//four calling birds,
//three french hens,
//two turtle doves
//and a partridge in a pear tree.

//On the 11 day of Christmas my true love sent to me
//eleven pipers piping,
//ten lords a-leaping,
//...

//...

//On the 1 of Christmas my true love sent to me
//a partridge in a pear tree.
```

---

## ACTIONSCRIPT ANALOGY

In ActionScript the the do..while loop provides `repeat-while` functionality.

---

# Conditional Statements

Time to talk about choice. You have several conditional statements at your disposal: `if`, which helps you make a choice based on a condition of type `Bool`, guard to ensure certain conditions are met before execution can proceed, and `switch`, which takes care of the more complicated decisions.

## if

You have already met with the `if` statement on many occasions in Swift. The last one was in Listing 20-11 where we checked whether an item could be extracted from the array of Christmas gift descriptions. Here it is again in Listing 20-12:

*Listing 20-12.* An if Statement, Which Does Optional Binding

```
// The last gift in the array gets extracted:
if let lastGift = christmasGifts.popLast() {
    // ...
}
```

---

## ACTIONSCRIPT ANALOGY

The `if` statement in Swift is very similar to what you are used to in ActionScript: it does what it says on the tin and you can branch out with `else` and `if-else` statements. In terms of syntax in Swift you have the option to put parentheses around the statement's condition or not.

---

Following are a few more differences between `if` statements in ActionScript and in Swift, which are worth noting:

- You can't use anything else but a `Bool` literal or an expression that evaluates to `Bool` as the condition of an `if` statement. Numbers, for example, will not be automatically cast to `Bool`, so a line like this will not compile: `if 1 {}`. Similarly, checking if a variable contains `nil` needs to be explicit. Listing 20-13 demonstrates that the first if statement in it generates a compiler error: `optional type 'Int?' cannot be used as a boolean; test for '!= nil' instead`.

***Listing 20-13.*** Checking If a Variable or a Constant Is Nil in an if Statement Needs to Be Explicit

```
var intVar: Int?

// This line will not compile:
if intVar { /*...*/ }

// But this line will:
if nil != intVar { /*...*/ }

// And so will this line, which uses optional binding:
if let _ = intVar { /*...*/ }
```

> ■ **Tip**  `intVar` in the example above has been declared as an optional. You can check if an optional instance contains a value or `nil` by doing `if let _ = intVar`—this will evaluate to `true` if `intVar` is not `nil`. More on optionals in Chapter 19.

- The condition after the `if` statement you see in Listing 20-12 does what is called *optional binding*: `let lastGift = christmasGifts.popLast()`.

  This simple one-liner does quite a lot of work: it declares the temporary constant `lastGift`, extracts the last element of the `christmasGifts` array and assigns it to `lastGift`. This temporary constant is inferred to be of type `Optional` with two possible values: an instance of whatever type the `christmasGifts` array holds (`String` in this case) or `nil`. The whole line evaluates to `false` if `lastGift` contains `nil` and to `true` if it holds a `String` instance. Put simpler: the body of the `if` statement will be executed only if `lastGift` is not `nil` and indeed contains the last element of the `christmasGifts` array.

  The last line in Listing 20-13, `if let _ = intVar`, also uses optional binding but omits the assignment step by providing an undeerscore instead of declaring a temporary constant: you can use this when you only care whether an optional instance contains a value but do not need to know what the value is.

- *Optional binding* is the only case, in which you can use the assignment operator (=) as part of the condition in an `if` statement. An `if` statement's condition is expected to evaluate to `Bool` and, as we saw in **Chapter 18**, the assignment operator (=) in Swift does not return a `Bool` result.

> ■ **Tip**  You can read more on optional binding in Chapter 19.

## guard

The guard statement makes sure that a given condition is met before execution can proceed. Its syntax is as follows:

```
guard booleanCondition else { /* Transfer control elsewhere */ }
```

Functionally guard works the same way as an if-else statement. It is however more concise than if-else and documents your intentions better in cases where control flow should be transferred elsewhere—out of a loop or back to the caller of a function—unless a condition is met. Note that, unlike if, guard always requires an else clause.

Let us see how we could use guard. In Listing 20-10 we used an if statement with conditional binding in order to extract the last item from the christmasGifts array and use it to compose a song line like this:

```
if let lastGift = christmasGifts.popLast(){/* Compose and print song line... */}
```

In Listing 20-14 we replace this with a guard statement. It checks if there are items in the array and if the array is empty, breaks out of the repeat-while loop.

***Listing 20-14.*** Using a guard Statement to Check Conditions

```
guard christmasGifts.count > 0 else {
    break
}

// The next lines will only be executed if christmasGifts.count is not zero:
let lastGift = christmasGifts.popLast()
// Compose and print song line...
```

## The Mightier Switch

You are already familiar with the concept of a switch statement from ActionScript: it lets you check an expression against a number of discreet values and choose a course of action, depending on whether the expression matches one of these values. The switch statement in Swift uses the same principle but might also surprise you with how much more powerful and foolproof it is. We will go through its superpowers one by one.

## Superpower 1: It Won't Let You Miss a Case

The clauses in a switch statement in Swift must cover all possible scenarios. Depending on the type you are switching on, you have two choices for how to achieve this. You can provide case clauses that cover every value the type might take: this may make sense for types that have a finite set of values, like *enums*, for example (more on *enums* in **Chapter 22**). Or, if the type doesn't allow that, you must provide a default clause, which would handle any value not explicitly covered by a case clause.

The example in Listing 20-15 uses a switch statement to print the name of the month, given a number. Its case statements cover the numbers from 1 to 12 and its default statement deals with any other input.

***Listing 20-15.*** A switch Statement in Swift Must Be Exhaustive

```
let month = 3
```

```
switch month {
    case 1: print("January")
    case 2: print("February")
    case 3: print("March")
    case 4: print("April")
    case 5: print("May")
    case 6: print("June")
    case 7: print("July")
    case 8: print("August")
    case 9: print("September")
    case 10: print("October")
    case 11: print("November")
    case 12: print("December")

    default: print("Can't match month name to \(month)")
}

// output: March
```

The last example shows you the syntax of a basic `switch` statement. What you might notice as a contrast to ActionScript syntax is:

- If you don't add the `default` clause at the end, this code won't compile. The compiler issues an error: `Switch must be exhaustive, consider adding a default clause`. Brilliantly foolproof.

- An example of making a `switch` statement exhaustive without the need for a `default` clause would be using *enumerations*. An enumeration defines a finite set of what you can think of as named constants, so when you use them in the `case` clauses of a `switch` statement, the compiler will make sure that you either have a `case` for every possible value of the enumeration or that you include a `default` clause instead. You can see examples of that in **Chapter 22**, where we delve into enumerations in detail.

- You don't need parentheses around the expression after the `switch` statement. By now you are probably not surprised by this typical Swift syntax.

- There are no break clauses—more on that in the next section.

## Superpower 2: It Won't Let You Fall Through by Mistake

So, why are those breaks missing? We will explain by contrasting `case` clauses in ActionScript and in Swift.

---

### ACTIONSCRIPT ANALOGY

If you don't put a `break` at the end of a `case` clause in ActionScript and it matches the expression you are switching on, the body of that `case` will be executed, as well as the body of whatever comes next: another `case` or a `default` clause. This is called *fallthrough*. Fallthrough is sometimes a desired behavior, but more often than not, a missing `break` is missing by mistake. Moreover, for someone reading your code it's not likely to be obvious which one it is: whether you omitted the `break` on purpose or forgot to add it. Write code for humans, remember?

---

In Swift a case clause will not implicitly fall through to the next clause whether you provide a break or not. In fact, you need to explicitly state it if you want fallthrough behavior by using the keyword fallthrough. In addition, you can provide multiple matches in a case clause: you do that by separating them with commas.

Listing 20-16 uses a switch statement, which takes a month and prints out the seasons it spans in some parts of the Northern hemisphere. You can see how several of its case statements use multiple matches: for example, input of either 1 (January) or 2 (February) will result in "winter" being printed out. You can also see the use of the fallthrough keyword, which causes an input of 3 (March) to result in "spans winter and spring".

*Listing 20-16.* Special Syntax for Providing Multiple Matches

```
let month = 3

switch month {
    case 1, 2:      print("winter")
    case 3:         print("spans winter and")
                    fallthrough

    case 4, 5:      print("spring")
    case 6, 7, 8:   print("summer")
    case 9:         print("spans summer and")
                    fallthrough

    case 10, 11:    print("autumn")
    case 12:        print("spans autumn and winter")

    default: print("Hmm, not sure about month \(month)... ↵
                    Which calendar did you have in mind?")
}

// output:

//spans winter and
//spring
```

## Superpower 3: You Can Switch Between Ranges of Values

The previous example can be made even more concise with another superpower of Swift's switch statement: matching ranges. In place of case 6, 7, 8: it is perfectly acceptable to put case 6...8:, using the *closed range operator* (Listing 20-17).

*Listing 20-17.* Range Matching

```
let month = 7

switch month {
    case 1...2:    print("winter")
    case 3:        print("spans winter and"); fallthrough
    case 4...5:    print("spring")
    case 6...8:    print("summer")
```

```
case 9:      print("spans summer and"); fallthrough
case 10...11: print("autumn")
case 12:     print("spans autumn and winter")

default: print("Hmm, not sure about month \(month)... ↵
                    Which calendar did you have in mind?")
}

// output: summer
```

Note how this time we put the `fallthrough` keyword on the same line as the `print` statement and separated the two with a semicolon. As we mentioned in **Chapter 17**, you can use semicolons at the end of statements in Swift but are not required to, unless you need to separate statements on the same line.

---

■ **Tip** The closed range operator a...b defines a range of values between a and b, including a and b. You can read about it in more detail in Chapter 18.

---

## Superpower 4: You Can Have Overlapping Case Statements

Swift will also let your `case` statements overlap. Admittedly it's debatable whether this is more of an Achilles's heel or a superpower in earnest, as you can easily shoot yourself in the foot: when you provide overlapping values or ranges of values in your case statements, the first one found to be a match is the one that is executed.

Listing 20-18 modifies the last example by allowing the ranges to overlap, so for an input of 3 or 9 you have two matching `case` statements each. It's important to note that we still need the `fallthrough` keyword, in order to have an input of 3 print out "spans winter and spring," otherwise only the body of the first matching `case` will be executed resulting in "spans winter and."

*Listing 20-18.* Overlapping Case Statements

```
let month = 3

switch month {
    case 1...2:   print("winter")

    // Note that we still need the fallthrough keyword,
    // inspite of the overlapping cases:
    case 3:       print("spans winter and"); fallthrough
    case 3...5:   print("spring")
    case 6...8:   print("summer")

    // Note that we still need the fallthrough keyword,
    // inspite of the overlapping cases:
    case 9:       print("spans summer and"); fallthrough
    case 9...11:  print("autumn")
    case 12:      print("spans autumn and winter")
```

```
    default: print("Hmm, not sure about month \(month)... ↵
                        Which calendar did you have in mind?")
}

// output:

//spans winter and
//spring
```

## Superpower 5: You Can Switch Between Different Types of Values

Swift doesn't limit you to only matching integer values in your switch statements. The next three examples showcase switch statements that use Double, String and Tuple values.

The first example in Listing 20-19 defines a range, which helps round a double number up or down to its nearest integer. Note that the range this time is defined by the *open range operator* a..<b.

***Listing 20-19.*** Matching Double Values

```
let doubleNumber = 17.5
let fraction = doubleNumber - Double(Int(doubleNumber))

switch fraction {
    case 0.0..<0.5: print("The nearest integer is \(Int(doubleNumber))")
    default:        print("The nearest integer is \(Int(doubleNumber) + 1)")
}

// output: The nearest integer is 18
```

---

■ **Tip**   The open range operator a..<b defines a range of values between a and b, including a, but not b. You can find out more in Chapter 18.

---

Listing 20-20 uses a string as criteria for switching:

***Listing 20-20.*** String Matching

```
let monthName = "April"

switch monthName {
    case "December", "January", "February":    print("winter")
    case "March", "April", "May":              print("spring")
    case "June", "July", "August":             print("summer")
    case "September", "October", "November":   print("autumn")

    default: print("Can't mstch a season to \(monthName)")
}

// output: spring
```

The next example in Listing 20-21 is a bit more elaborate. It starts with defining an *enumeration* for the days of the week (see **Chapter 22** for details on enumerations). For the purposes of this example you can think of an enum as providing a set of named values, where WeekDay.Monday has a value of 1, WeekDay. Tuesday has a value of 2, and so on. The timeAndDay constant is a *tuple* (a type, which holds two or more values together), which has a time and a day for shopping. The switch statement that follows checks the time and the day and decides whether these fall inside the local stores' opening times: 9 a.m. to 5 p.m. Monday to Saturday. Each case statement checks two values: the time and the day.

*Listing 20-21.* Tuples

```
// An enumeration of week days (see Chapter 22 for details on enums)
enum WeekDay : Int {
    case Monday = 1, Tuesday, Wednesday, Thursday, Friday, Saturday, Sunday
}

let timeAndDay = (13, WeekDay.Saturday)

// Check if the stores are open at the given time
switch timeAndDay {
    case (_, WeekDay.Sunday): print("The stores are closed all day on Sunday.")
    case (9...17, _): print("The stores are open.")

    default: print("The stores are closed.")
}

// output: The stores are open.
```

---

■ **Tip**    Enumerations are shown off in their glory in Chapter 22 and you can read more on tuples in Chapter 19.

---

You have probably noticed some weirdness in the syntax of the case statements above in the lurking underscores. This leads us to another superpower . . .

## Superpower 6: Using Any Value

Putting an underscore in place of one of the values inside a case clause, as shown in Listing 20-21, is construed as "any value." So, for example, case (_, WeekDay.Sunday) should be read as "any time on Sunday" and case (9...17, _) as "Between 9 a.m. and 5 p.m. on any day of the week." The switch statement in the Listing 20-21 first checks if the day in the time tuple is Sunday. If it is, then it ignores the time and prints out "The stores are closed all day on Sunday." If time is on a different day, then the switch doesn't care which day it is: as long as the time is between 9 a.m. and 5 p.m., the stores are opened. The default clause takes care of the values not covered by the two case clauses: when the day is between Monday and Saturday and the time—outside the 9 a.m.- 5 p.m. interval.

## Superpower 7: Value Binding

Value binding allows you to assign values to temporary variables or constants in the case clauses, in order to access these values. Listing 20-22 shows a modification of the switch statement in Listing 20-21. The first case clause in it defines a temporary constant called time and assigns the first element of the timeAndDay tuple to it. The value of time is then passed to the print function.

*Listing 20-22.* Value Binding

```
switch timeAndDay {
    // Create a temporary constant, called time
    // and assign the first element of the tuple to it:
    case (let time, WeekDay.Sunday):
        print("The stores are closed on Sunday at \(time).")

    case (9...17, _): print("The stores are open.")

    default: print("The stores are closed")
}

// output: The stores are open.
```

## Superpower 8: You Can Provide Nuance with where Clauses

We are getting to the end of the list of superpowers. This last one, however, is extra special. You can make the checks in the case clauses even more elaborate by adding conditions to them, using a where clause. In this last modification of the store opening times example, shown in Listing 20-23, the last case clause is a different way of expressing "any day of the week between 9 a.m. and 5 p.m." with a where clause (given we have already filtered Sunday out). It also defines two temporary constants and binds timeAndDay's two values to them.

*Listing 20-23.* Where Clauses

```
switch timeAndDay {
    // Create a temporary constant, called time
    // and assign the first element of the tuple to it:
    case (let time, WeekDay.Sunday):
        print("The store is closed on Sunday at \(time)")

    case let (time, dayOfWeek) where time >= 9 && time <= 17:
        print("The store is open on \(dayOfWeek) at \(time)")

    default: print("The store is closed")
}
```

# Jumping Around: Control Transfer

We will finish this chapter with a few words on control transfer statements, all of which you have encountered so far either by using their ActionScript counterparts or when you did the previous examples in this chapter.

## continue

As in ActionScript, you use continue to interrupt the current iteration of a loop and to start the next one.

## break

You can use break to stop the execution of a loop or to exit out of a case in a switch statement. As we saw earlier when we were delving into the superpowers of switch, break statements are optional.

# fallthrough

This is your new friend when you work with `switch` statements. Instead of making sure you don't forget to put break at the end of each `case`, omit all the breaks, and use `fallthrough` when you intend execution to continue into the next `case` or `default` clause. See Listing 20-16 in the section "Superpower 2" for an example implementation.

# return

As you would expect, `return` transfers the control out of the current function or method. Nothing to add to what you already know from your ActionScript experience. I, however, have a little something for you: just as you thought I had forgotten my promise to polish *The Twelve Days of Christmas* example . . . Listing 20-24 shows a function that will help us print out the day names with their proper suffixes: it uses a simple `switch` statement, which abruptly interrupts the execution of the function and returns a result as soon as it finds a match.

***Listing 20-24.*** Using return

```
func getNumberSuffix(number : Int) -> String {
    switch number {
        case 11...13: return "th"

        default:
            switch number % 10 {
                case 1: return "st"
                case 2: return "nd"
                case 3: return "rd"

                default: return "th"
            }
    }
}
```

# Labels

When you have nested loops or `switch` statements, you can use labels in order to distinguish them. A label is a name that you come up with, followed by a colon that you put at the start of your loop or `switch` statement. Then, when you use the `break` and `continue` statements, you can be explicit about which loop or `switch` you want to continue or break out of.

The final example in this chapter completes the mission of printing out the lyrics of *The Twelve Days of Christmas*. It uses the function `getNumberSuffix` we defined in Listing 20-24 and prints out the names of the days as ordinal numbers.

In order to demonstrate the use of labels, I have allowed myself a perversion. See if you can spot it in Listing 20-25.

***Listing 20-25.*** Using Labels in Loops

```
// Label the outer loop:
outerLoop: for day in 1...christmasDays {
    print("\nOn the \(day)\(getNumberSuffix(day)) ↵
        day of Christmas my true love sent to me")
```

```
    var previousDay = day

    // Label the inner loop:
    innerLoop: while true // Don't do this at home! {
        if --previousDay < 0
        {
            // Transfer control back to the for loop
            // and continue with its next iteration:
            continue outerLoop
        }

        let verseLine = ↵
                composeVerseLine(previousDay, ↵
                        gift: christmasGifts[previousDay], ↵
                        needsPrefix: day > 1)
        print("\(verseLine)")
    }
}
```

Did you see my misdemeanor? I made the inner while loop infinite, in order to show you how to use labels. When the loop's condition (--previousDay < 0) evaluates to true, we call continue outerLoop, which transfers control to the next iteration of the outer for loop. At last, this code outputs the song lyrics almost as we would expect to see them:

```
On the 1st day of Christmas my true love sent to me
a partridge in a pear tree,

On the 2nd day of Christmas my true love sent to me
and two turtle doves.
a partridge in a pear tree,

On the 3rd day of Christmas my true love sent to me
three french hens
and two turtle doves.
a partridge in a pear tree,

On the 4th day of Christmas...
```

. . . almost, as you would normally expect to see the days of Christmas spelled out as "first," "second," and so on, instead of "1st," "2nd," and so on. Let me guess . . . You are reading this in June, aren't you?

# Summary

This chapter gave you the tools for understanding and controlling the flow of execution in your code. We saw how loops work and especially how they might surprise you if you are coming from an ActionScript background. The different flavors of the for and while loops almost look and feel the same as their ActionScript counterparts, but they hide some subtle differences. We also uncovered the superpowers of Swift's switch statement: from its safety mechanisms to its versatility with different types and ways of defining conditions.

With this much ground covered, we are ready to move on to object-oriented programming topics. I'll meet you at the next chapter.

# CHAPTER 21

■ ■ ■

# Object-Oriented Programming Topics

In this chapter we will go over the object-oriented side of Swift. Having experience with ActionScript, you are already familiar with the object-oriented programming (OOP) paradigm. It treats a piece of software as a system, which is broken down into *objects*. Each object is responsible for a part of the system and looks after its own state.

Swift uses four main OOP entities:

- Classes

- Structures

- Enumerations

- Protocols

Each of these entities defines a type (classes, structures, and enumerations) or part of a type (protocols). *Classes* in Swift are very similar to classes in ActionScript. A lot of the techniques that you will need to know when you define and use classes apply to *structures* and *enumerations* too. *Protocols* serve similar purpose as *interfaces* do in ActionScript: they define a way of communicating with a set of types by requiring each of those types to conform to a set of requirements. Implementing these requirements is called *conforming* and is typically left to the types that adopt the protocol.

We will have a detailed look at how classes work first. Then we will highlight what makes *structures* different from classes and when it is preferable to use one or the other. We will also see how *protocols* are defined and adopted.

*Enumerations* only get a mention in this chapter. As they may be new to an ActionScript developer, enumerations have a dedicated in-depth section in **Chapter 22**, which deals with new and different concepts.

## Classes

A class provides a mold, from which objects (class instances) are made. This is true for structures and enumerations too: each of these entities defines placeholders for data (properties) and logic for working with data (methods and subscripts). Most of the ideas and techniques that will help you define and use classes in Swift are valid for structures and enumerations. To avoid duplicating information, we will present classes in detail and will point out the similarities and the differences that you need to be aware of when using structures and enumerations. Where something applies to all three entities, we will refer to them as *types* for conciseness.

© Radoslava Leseva Adams and Hristo Lesev 2016
R. L. Adams and H. Lesev, *Migrating to Swift from Flash and ActionScript*,
DOI 10.1007/978-1-4842-1666-8_21

## Syntax for Defining a Class

The way you define a class in Swift is very similar to how it is done in ActionScript: you use the `class` keyword, followed by the name of the class, followed by the definitions of the class's members in curly brackets: properties, methods, and subscripts. Let us define a class, called `File`, which we will add to later to make a very simplistic representation of an iOS file (Listing 21-1).

*Listing 21-1.* Class Declaration Syntax

```
class File {
    // add class members here
}
```

## Access and Visibility

In ActionScript we are used to putting each class in its own file with a matching name and to defining packages for accessing classes. For example, to access a class called `MyClass`, which has been defined as `public` or `internal` in the `com.diadraw` package, you need either to import `com.diadraw` in the files where you want to use `MyClass` or to access it as `com.diadraw.MyClass`.

In Swift you don't have to define classes in separate files and you are not forced to name source files after your classes. As we saw in the section "Access Control" in **Chapter 17**, visibility is defined in terms of source files and *modules*, where a module is a collection of source files that you build and ship together either as an application or as a framework. The control modifiers we introduced—`public`, `internal`, and `private`—can be used to control access to whole classes, structures, enumerations, and protocols, as well as to their individual members:

- An entity marked as `private` is only visible to code in the same source file.

- The default level is `internal` and makes an entity visible within the same module. You don't have to use the `internal` modifier explicitly: unless you put another modifier, `internal` is assumed.

- Mark your entities as `public` to make them visible to external code that may use your module.

Access modifiers go before the class definition, as shown in Listing 21-2.

*Listing 21-2.* Declaring a Private Class

```
private class MyPrivateClass {
    // add class members here
}
```

Note that to make a class or a structure `public`, you need to define at least one public *initializer* for it or, in ActionScript words, it needs to have a public *constructor*. More on initializers later.

## Adding Properties

Properties are defined in the body of the type (i.e., inside the curly brackets), a syntax that should look familiar from ActionScript.

Like ActionScript, Swift lets you define *type properties*, marked with the `static` keyword and *instance properties*. A member marked `static` is part of the type, rather than of an instance of the type, and there will be only one copy of it, no matter how many instances you create.

For class members there is another keyword, `class`, which is used to declare type properties in a very specific situation: when you want a *computed property* to be overridden in subclasses, you need to mark it with the `class` keyword, instead of with `static`. We will see what computed properties are later.

In terms of how property values are retrieved, Swift distinguishes between three kinds of properties: *stored, computed,* and *lazy.* We will look at each of these in detail.

## Stored Properties

*Stored properties* have their values kept for immediate retrieval in variables or constants: you declare a variable property with the `var` keyword and a constant property with the `let` keyword, like we saw in **Chapter 17**. You can provide an initial value for a stored property as part of its declaration: this is its *default value.*

Let us add a couple of stored properties to the class `File` we declared earlier: we will have a Boolean property, called `isOpen` to indicate whether the file is currently open and a type property: `numberOfOpenFiles`, of type `Int`, which will keep track of how many files are currently open in the file system. It will have the same value for every instance of `File` (see Listing 21-3).

*Listing 21-3.* Adding Stored Properties

```
class File {
    // The instance property isOpen
    // has a different value for every instance of File:
    var isOpen = false

    // The type property numberOfOpenFiles
    // has the same value for every instance of File:
    private static var numberOfOpenFiles = 0
}
```

Note that the type inference we talked about in **Chapter 19** applies here too: if you provide *default values* for your stored properties, the property types will be inferred from these values. Thus, instead of defining `var isOpen: Boolean = false`, we do just `var isOpen = false`.

## Computed Properties

*Computed properties* are not necessarily backed up with a constant or a variable, but provide *getter functions*, which work out the property's value at runtime. They can also have optional *setter functions*. Because you don't supply default values for computed properties, their types are not automatically inferred and you need to explicitly state the type in the property declaration.

To see what this looks like, we will first add another stored property to the `File` class: let us call this `location` and have it store the full path to the file as an `NSURL` object. The `NSURL` class is part of the iOS SDK. It stores locations of resources or paths to local files and is handy for parsing these paths. It has similarities with the `URLRequest` and `File` classes in ActionScript.

Next we will define a property `name`, which will be computed at runtime, using the value of `location` and will let us read or change only the file name. A computed property is declared as a variable followed by curly brackets: inside the curly brackets we define a getter and an optional setter. Because the getter and the setter functions are defined within the definition of the property, they don't need elaborate signatures: the type of the value they return or receive is inferred from the type of `name`.

I will confess in advance that the code in Listing 21-4 will not compile at this stage: the Swift compiler comes with the wonderful[1] feature of not letting you leave anything uninitialized, and if you look at the location property, you will notice that we have not provided an initial value for it. More on *initialization* later.

***Listing 21-4.*** Adding Computed Properties

```
class File {
    // The rest of the class definition stays the same

    // This property stores the full path and file name:
    var location: NSURL

    // The file name is computed at runtime
    var name: String {
        get {
            return (location.lastPathComponent)!
        }

        set (newFileName) {
            let newUrl = location.URLByDeletingLastPathComponent
            location = newUrl!.URLByAppendingPathComponent(newFileName)
        }
    }
}
```

We can make the setter function even more concise: if we omit its parameter name, the parameter will not disappear but will be available to us with the implied name of newValue. So we can rewrite the setter like the example in Listing 21-5 shows.

***Listing 21-5.*** Using the Implied Parameter newValue from a Setter Function

```
set {
    let newUrl = location.URLByDeletingLastPathComponent
    location = newUrl!.URLByAppendingPathComponent(newValue)
}
```

## Lazy Properties

*Lazy properties* are variable properties, which are marked with the lazy keyword. They are similar to stored properties in that they store their values. The initial value of a lazy property is usually the result of a function call, which is only made when the property is accessed for the first time.

Declaring a property as lazy can save unnecessary overhead, if the property's initial value requires heavy computation and there is a chance that it will never be needed, for example. The flipside of this is that you are not in control of when initialization happens and it can potentially hurt performance at an inopportune time. This also leads to a couple of formalities that the compiler will remind you of, if you forget.

- A lazy property can only be a variable and not a constant, so you must declare it with the var keyword.

- You must provide a *default value*: this will typically be a call to a function or an initializer that will provide an initial value for the property.

---

[1] . . . also mildly irritating—but mostly wonderful, trust me.

Let us add a property to the File class that will give us access to its contents. As this might require loading of a lot of data and may never be needed in the lifespan of a File instance, it is a good candidate for a lazy property. We will also add a function, called loadContent that will load a file's contents, given its path (Listing 21-6).

***Listing 21-6.*** Adding Computed Properties

```
func loadContent(fromPath path: NSURL?) -> String? {
    // Potentially lenghty operation
    // ...
}

class File {
    // The rest of the class definition stays the same

    lazy var contentAsString: String? = self.loadContent(fromPath: self.location)
}
```

# Getting Notified About Changes: Property Observers

When a property is set, it is useful to be able to react to the potential change. In Swift you have a couple of options for how and when to do that: you can declare a property setter, like we saw with computed properties earlier, or you can add *property observers*, which will fire just before and just after the property value is set. The observers are functions, called willSet and didSet, which you define in curly brackets after the declaration of the property you need to observe.

---

### ACTIONSCRIPT ANALOGY

The idea of property observers is similar to using the [Bindable] metadata keyword in Flex. When you mark a property as [Bindable], an event is dispatched whenever the property value changes.

The similarities, however, stop here. Following are some differences, which emphasize the main ideas behind property observers in Swift:

- [Bindable] only dispatches an event if the observed value has changed. willSet and didSet get called when a property is set, even if the new value and the old value are the same. They are in a way alarms that scream "Someone is about to touch your property!" and "Someone just touched your property!"

- [Bindable] dispatches an event only after the fact, whereas Swift's property observers give you a chance to react at two different moments: willSet is called just before the property is set and didSet just after; both give you access to the old and to the new value of the property.

- [Bindable] binds properties, which live in different classes or packages: one is considered to be the source and the other the destination. Whenever the source changes, the changes are copied over to the destination. In contrast, property observers in Swift are not accessible outside the type they are defined in. Instead, they give that type the option to control its internal state.

---

Here is something to keep in mind: you can't define property observers for just any property in Swift. The observed property needs to be stored, non-lazy and variable, rather than constant. Following are the reasons:

- Constant properties do not allow their values to be set, except inside an initializer method (constructor) or at the point where they are defined: at both points the containing type has full control over how the value is set, so firing observers would be unnecessary.

- Lazy properties behave as if their initial values are set at the moment you request them to be set, but the actual setting may happen at a later point or not at all (see the start of the section "Properties," on how lazy properties work).

- You can define setter methods on computed properties: these give you control over the value of a property at the same points when willSet and didSet would fire.

Let us add observers to the isOpen property of our File class in order to see how they are defined. Listing 21-7 defines willSet and didSet functions inside curly brackets following the declaration of isOpen. In the willSet observer we will simply print what isOpen is about to be set to and in didSet we will increment or decrement the total number of open files.

Both willSet and didSet have implied parameters, called newValue and oldValue, respectively, which give you access to the value the property is about to be set to or the value it had before it was set. Instead of using newValue and oldValue, you can give the parameters custom names, which you put in brackets after the name of the observer (e.g., willSet(toValue)); the type of the parameter is inferred.

*Listing 21-7.* Adding Property Observers

```
class File {
    // The rest of the class definition stays the same

    var isOpen = false {
        willSet {
            print("About to set isOpen to \(newValue)")
        }

        didSet {
            // If the value hasn't changed, we don't want to do anything:
            if oldValue == isOpen
            {
                return
            }

            // If the file was just open,
            // increment the total number of open files.
            // If the file was closed, decrement the total number.
            if isOpen {
                File.numberOfOpenFiles += 1
            }
            else {
                File.numberOfOpenFiles -= 1
            }
        }
    }
}
```

# Accessing Properties

You access properties using the familiar dot syntax, prefixing a property with a name of an instance for instance properties (file.isOpen = true), or with the name of a type for static properties (File.numberOfOpenFiles = 12).

The rules for access control we saw in **Chapter 17** apply to properties too: unless you specify an access modifier explicitly (public, internal, or private), properties are declared internal by default.

# The Self Property

Every class, structure, or enumeration has a property, called self. It is implicit and you don't have to declare it yourself. You can only access the self property of a type from inside one of its methods:

- When accessed from an instance method, self gives you access to the instance. In value types like structures and enumerations you can make assignments to self—we will see how that works when we look at structures later on.

- When accessed from a type method (marked as static), self refers to the type and can give you access to the type's other properties and methods.

---

## ACTIONSCRIPT ANALOGY

Swift's self property corresponds to the implied property this in ActionScript: self and this help disambiguate names. For example, we could rewrite the didSet observer of the isOpen property of File like this:

```
class File {
    // The rest of the class definition stays the same

    var isOpen = false {
        didSet (isOpen) {
            // self.isOpen is the property, while isOpen is the parameter:
            if isOpen == self.isOpen {
                return
            }

            // ...
        }
    }
}
```

In the example above the didSet observer receives a parameter, called isOpen, which has the same name as the property we observe. Using self.isOpen inside the observer to refer to the property avoids the ambiguity and shows the compiler which variable we mean in which case.

---

# Adding Methods

In Swift you can add methods to classes, structures, and enumerations in a similar way you do in ActionScript: you define the method within the curly brackets of the type definition.

Differentiating between instance and type methods will also be familiar to you: to define a type method, you mark it with the `static` keyword. A method marked `static` will only have access to properties of the type marked as `static` or `class` and not to instance properties.

Let us add a few methods to the `File` class to demonstrate the syntax for method definition. Listing 21-8 defines two instance methods: these simply mark a file as open or closed. There is also a type method, which resets the total number of open files.

*Listing 21-8.* Adding Methods to a Class

```
class File {
    func open() {
        isOpen = true;
    }

    func close() {
        isOpen = false;
    }

    static func resetNumberOfOpenFiles() {
        numberOfOpenFiles = 0;
    }

    // The rest of the class definition comes here.
}
```

# Overloading Methods

You can overload methods (i.e., provide several methods with the same name), but with different types or number of parameters, the way you can overload any function. Flip back to the introductory **Chapter 17** to see examples.

# Initializer and Deinitializer Methods

*Initializer methods* in Swift are the equivalent of what you know as *constructors* in ActionScript. Instead of being named after the type they initialize, however, the syntax for defining an initializer is as follows: you use the keyword `init`, followed by zero or more arguments wrapped in parentheses, followed by curly brackets where the body of the method goes. Initializers can be overloaded: you can define several initializer methods, which have a different number or different types of parameters.

*Deinitializer methods* only apply to classes in Swift and do not have an ActionScript analogue. Although they are technically methods, you can't call them directly. Instead, they are called automatically just before an instance of a class gets deallocated. This gives you a chance to clean up any resources that the instance might be using: close an open file, for example. To define a deinitializer, use the keyword `deinit`, followed by curly brackets, between which you write the logic of the method. Note that you don't need parentheses after `deinit`.

Listing 21-9 adds an initializer and a deinitializer to the `File` class we defined at the start of this chapter. The initializer takes a single parameter, `location`, which provides an initial value for the `location` property of the class. Remember how we could not compile the code before? This initializer will make the compiler happy: now we do not have any uninitialized properties.

The deinitializer makes sure that a file we might have opened is closed before the instance of `File` gets deallocated.

***Listing 21-9.*** Defining Initializers and a Deinitializer

```
class File {
    init(location: NSURL) {
        self.location = location
    }

    deinit {
        close()
    }

    // The rest of the class definition comes here.
}
```

## Invoking Initializers

An initializer will be called at the point where you create an instance of a type. You have two options: you can call an initializer directly by prefixing it with the type name and a dot, like you would call any other method, for example:

```
File.init("Documents\\textFile.txt")
```

You can also just use the type name, followed by parentheses, and pass in any arguments your chosen initializer takes, for example:

```
File ("Documents\\textFile.txt")
```

## Rules for Initialization

As we pointed out in the opening **Chapter of 17** and have seen time and time again, Swift is all about being explicit but concise at the same time, and about taking maximum advantage of the compiler to protect you from unintentionally omitting or defining things badly. This is especially true for initialization.

There are rules you need to follow when you initialize your types, which we will mention in passing here. You can find the complete set of rules in *The Swift Programming Language* manual on Apple's web site. You do not have to worry about remembering all of them: keeping in mind the goal behind the rules and letting the compiler guide you through what is allowed and what isn't should stand you in good stead.

Initialization in Swift is designed so that no part of an instance is left in an undefined state. This means that all of the stored properties of that instance need to have an initial value by the time the instance has finished initializing. For class instances this includes stored properties that are inherited from base classes.

As in ActionScript you have two options for when a stored property is initialized. You can provide a default value at the point where you declare the property, as we saw in the section "Properties": this is phase one of the initialization. You can also assign it an initial value in an initializer function: this is phase two of the initialization. Or you can do both.

Phase one and phase two of the initialization process are the only times when you are allowed to set the value of a constant stored property.

Following are a few main points to keep in mind:

- All stored properties must have an initial value when an instance of a class, structure, or enumeration is created.

- You can assign default values to stored properties where you declare them, but you don't have to: any property without a default value must be assigned an initial value in an initializer function.

- If all of the stored properties of an instance have default values, you don't need to declare an initializer explicitly: a default initializer without parameters will be defined for you by the compiler behind the scenes.

- You can define multiple initializers.

- Initializers can call other initializers.

- You can call a base class initializer from within a child class initializer by using `super.init(/*parameters go here*/)`.

- If you define an initializer that has the same signature as a superclass initializer, you are effectively overriding the superclass initializer, so you must prefix the child class one with the `override` keyword.

- The Swift compiler distinguishes between two types of initializers, depending on whether they fully initialize an instance:

  - *Designated initializers* make sure that every stored property has an initial value.

  - *Convenience initializers* do not need to fully initialize an instance. Being able to write a convenience initializer means that you need not duplicate initialization code. However, in the spirit of making sure that the instance is fully initialized, a convenience initializer needs to call other initializers that will fill in the gaps. The rule is: in the chain of initializer calls there should be at least one designated initializer. You mark convenience initializers with the `convenience` keyword.

Listing 21-10 defines a class `Directory` with two stored properties—name, which is a `String` without a default value, and `parentDirectory,` which is an optional `Directory` with a default value of `nil`. Any initialization path we define will need to make sure that name receives an initial value.

Let us add two initializers: the first one takes no parameters and sets a new directory's name to "unnamed directory." The second one takes a reference to another `Directory` instance, with which it initializes the `parentDirectory` property. Since it does not assign a value to the name property, we need to mark this initializer with the `convenience` keyword and make it call the designated initializer method to make sure that all properties have initial values.

***Listing 21-10.*** Designated and Convenience Intializers

```
class Directory {
    var name: String
    var parentDirectory: Directory?

    init() {
        name = "unnamed directory"
    }
```

```
    convenience init(parentDirectory: Directory) {
        self.init()
        self.parentDirectory = parentDirectory
    }
}
```

## When Things Fail

You may remember from the section "Optionals" section in **Chapter 19** that you need to tell the Swift compiler explicitly if a variable is allowed to have a value of nil by declaring it as an *optional type*. Similarly, when you have an initializer, which may fail to initialize an instance for any reason, you need to signal the compiler by declaring it as *failable*. You do this by adding a question mark after the init keyword: this will make the initializer create an *optional type* and return nil to fail.

When can initialization fail? Say one of the properties of your type needs to get its initial value from data, which you request over a network connection. The network connection falling apart, for example, would be a scenario you need to provide for.

To demonstrate this, let us modify the example from Listing 21-10 and make the second initializer in Directory check if the directory we are about to assign to parentDirectory exists and fail the initialization if it doesn't. The modified initializer is marked as fallible by adding a question mark after init and by returning nil when conditions for initialization are not met (Listing 21-11).

***Listing 21-11.*** Designated and Convenience Intializers

```
class Directory {
    var name: String
    var parentDirectory: Directory?

    func exists() -> Bool {
        // check if the directory exists
    }

    init() {
        name = "unnamed directory"
    }

    convenience init?(parentDirectory: Directory) {
        guard parentDirectory.exists() else {
            return nil
        }

        self.init()
        self.parentDirectory = parentDirectory
    }
}
```

---

■ **Note**    Listing 21-11 uses a guard statement to ensure that conditions are met (a parent directory exists) before execution can proceed. We covered guard in Chapter 20.

---

## Adding Subscripts

Subscripts are the third kind of member you can add to Swift types. A subscript lets you access a type's data with an index, a key, or even a list of keys in square brackets, much like you would query an array or a dictionary. For example, file[10..100] could be made to retrieve a range of bytes from a file. Subscripts get their own detailed section: for how to define and use them see **Chapter 22**.

## Memory Management for Classes: ARC

Unlike in ActionScript, where all types are passed by reference, in Swift there are different memory management rules for classes, structures, and enumerations. In this section we will go over the rules that apply to classes and later, when we introduce structures and enumerations, we will see the differences in memory management for these types.

## Reference types

Classes in Swift are *reference types*. In other words, if you create an instance of an object, assign it to a variable (or a constant) and then assign that variable to a second variable, instead of two copies of the same instance, you end up with one instance and two references to it: one in each variable. When you make changes to the object using one reference, the same changes will be accessible via the second reference.

Listing 21-12 shows this in practice: it has a definition of a class with a single property name of type String. We create an instance of this class and assign it to a variable named originalReference, after which we assign originalReference to a variable of the same type, named secondReference. Now, if we change the name property of one of the references, we would expect to see the name property of the other reference change too.

***Listing 21-12.*** Assigning Reference Type Instances

```
class SitcomCharacter {
    var name: String

    init (name: String) {
        self.name = name
    }
}

// We create a new instance of SitcomCharacter,
// which originalReference refers to:
var originalReference = SitcomCharacter(name: "Lister")

// secondReference refers tot he same instance as originalReference:
var secondReference = originalReference

// Changing a property via one of the references changes the instance:
secondReference.name = "David Lister"

// We can see the change reflected in the gamePlayerB reference:
print(originalReference.name) // prints out "David Lister"
```

The same thing happens when you pass a class instance as an argument to a function: the function argument creates another reference to the same instance, instead of another copy of it.

■ **Note**    This only applies to classes in Swift. Structures and enumerations obey different rules—read on to find out.

To manage the memory taken by class instances, Swift uses *Automatic Reference Counting* (ARC). This means keeping track of the number of references a given instance has and automatically deallocating the memory it occupies once that count goes down to zero. For you as a developer, this means that you do not need to worry about manually freeing memory. Instead, what you need to pay attention to is the scope of each reference you declare and make sure references live long enough to serve their purpose, but no longer, so that they do not hog valuable memory.

## Memory Leaks from Strong Reference Cycles

If you think that hogging memory for too long is hard to achieve with ARC, think again. Let us look at an example of two classes: Country and Capital, defined in Listing 21-13. Country has a property of type Capital? and Capital has a property of type Country?. The question marks in the declarations make both of these properties *optional* and also causes them to be initialized to nil, as we have not provided default values for them. We learned how optionals work in Swift in **Chapter 19**; flip back to it if you need a reminder.

*Listing 21-13.* Defining Types That Hold References to One Another

```
class Country {
    var name: String?

    // Country holds a reference to Capital:
    var capital: Capital?

    init(name: String) {
        self.name = name
    }

    deinit {
        print("Instance of Country is being deallocated.")
    }
}

class Capital {
    var name: String?

    // Capital holds a reference to Country:
    var country: Country?

    init(name: String) {
        self.name = name
    }

    deinit {
        print("Instance of Capital is being deallocated.")
    }
}
```

Next, let us create an instance of each class and assign the Country instance to the Capital's country property and vice versa, as shown in Listing 21-14.

**Listing 21-14.** Creating a Strong Reference Cycle

```
var bulgaria: Country? = Country(name: "Bulgaria")
var sofia: Capital? = Capital(name: "Sofia")

bulgaria!.capital = sofia
sofia!.country = bulgaria
```

Now bulgaria.capital holds a reference to sofia and sofia.country holds a reference to bulgaria. As diligent programmers we want each of these instances to be deallocated when we are done with it, so we assign nil to each of the original references we declared (Listing 21-15).

**Listing 21-15.** Setting the Original References to Nil to Decrease the Reference Count

```
bulgaria = nil
sofia = nil
```

This is where we get into a chicken-and-egg situation. Each of our instances has two variables referencing it (i.e., two references): the variable we declared when creating the instance (bulgaria and sofia) and a property in the other class's instance (sofia.country and bulgaria.capital) (see Figure 21-1). The line bulgaria = nil removes one reference from the reference count of the Country instance and we are left with one reference, held by sofia.country. The same thing happens to the Capital instance when we do sofia = nil. After these two lines we are left with an instance of Country and an instance of Capital and no way of accessing them in order to have the memory deallocated, hence a memory leak. You can verify this by executing the lines above and checking if anything gets printed in the console: if the Capital instance gets deallocated, for example, we would expect the print call we put in its deinitializer to get executed.

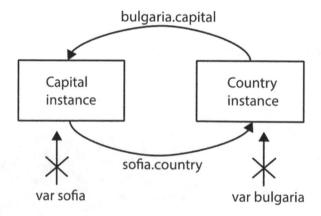

**Figure 21-1.** A strong reference cycle

The problem we just saw is known as a *strong reference cycle* and Swift offers a couple of options for avoiding it. In order for a reference not to affect the reference count of an instance, you can mark it as weak or unowned. Following is a summary of the types of references you can use:

- **Strong.** This is the default type of reference that you create. It doesn't need any keywords and causes a reference to be counted toward the reference count of an instance. The instance will be deallocated when its strong reference count goes down to zero.

- **Weak.** A weak reference is marked with the weak keyword and doesn't count toward the references that ARC keeps track of. Weak references must be declared as *optional types*, as they are allowed to have no value (i.e., they can contain nil). ARC will automatically set a weak reference to nil when the instance it refers to gets deallocated. Because a week reference is allowed to change value (it will when it is automatically set to nil), you can't use it with constants.

- **Unowned.** An unowned reference is marked with the unowned keyword and it too will not keep an instance alive when its strong reference count goes to zero. Unlike weak references, unowned ones cannot be optional types. This means that they can't contain nil and will not automatically be set to nil when the instance they refer to gets deallocated.

Listing 21-16 shows the Capital class, now redefined to keep a weak reference to Country. This is enough to avoid the strong reference cycle we created earlier and to have both instances deallocated when you execute the lines from Listing 21-15.

***Listing 21-16.*** Declaring a Weak Reference

```
class Capital {
    var name: String?

    // Capital holds a reference to Country:
    weak var country: Country?

    init(name: String) {
        self.name = name
    }

    deinit {
        print("Instance of Capital is being deallocated.")
    }
}
```

# Comparing References

Swift distinguishes between comparison of class instances and comparison of references to class instances.

To be able to compare instances of the same class, the equality (==) and the inequality operator (!=) must be defined for that class: for example, they could do member-wise comparison of the two instances and declare them equal if all properties in both instances have the same value.

Comparing references is a different matter: when two variables refer to the same instance of a class, they are said to be *identical*. You can check if two references are identical with the identity operators: === and !==.

# Extending Functionality

One of the principles of OOP is that entities should be "open for extension, but closed for modification." In most other OOP languages this means that you can only extend a class or another entity's functionality by inheriting it. Swift seemingly breaks the open-closed principle, though in a clever way: it allows you to add to existing entities, including SDK or third-party classes, structures, and so on, by writing *extensions*.[2] We will see how this is done later in this section.

## Subclassing and Inheritance

Most of what you are used to when inheriting classes in ActionScript is true in Swift. Here we will point out a few things that are worth paying attention to, because they either work differently in Swift or build on ideas that ActionScript does not have.

---

■ **Note**    Subclassing only applies to classes. Structures and enumerations can't inherit other structures or enumerations.

---

Following are the main guidelines for using inheritance in Swift:

- To declare a subclass, put a colon after the class name and then add the name of the base class. What comes after the colon is called *inheritance list*. Note that Swift does not support multiple inheritance. Instead, the inheritance list can contain one base class name and one or more *protocol* names, which the class conforms to. More on protocols at the end of this chapter.

- To override a method in a subclass, use the override keyword.

- To access a parent entity's method, property or subscript, use the super keyword, followed by a dot and the name of the member.

- A subclass can access properties of superclasses in the hierarchy but has no way of knowing which properties are stored and which ones are computed. As a consequence, you can define property observers for any base class property in a subclass. The only condition is that the property you need to observe is accessible for modification (i.e., it's not a stored constant or a computed read-only property).

- In a subclass you can define custom getters and setters for properties of a base class either by overriding existing ones or by writing them from scratch for a stored property. You can even provide a setter for a read-only base class property and thus make it read-write. You can't do the opposite and make a read-write property read-only, though.

- Overriding a property setter and providing a property observer for a base class property are mutually exclusive: you can do one or the other, but not both at the same time.

- You can prevent members of a class from being overridden in descendant classes by marking them with the final keyword.

- You can use the final keyword to stop a whole class from being inherited.

---

[2]*Extensions* are not a new concept that appeared with Swift. You will find the same idea in Objective-C, where it is called *categories*.

Let us illustrate how subclassing works with an example. Listing 21-17 redefines the File class we have been working with throughout this chapter and defines another class, which inherits from it: TextClass. TextClass adds custom observers for the name property of the File class. It also overrides File's default initializer to customize the value of name.

***Listing 21-17.*** Inheriting a Base Class

```
// File is a base class:
class File {
    var name: String

    init() {
        name = "unnamed file"
    }
}

// TextFile is a subclass of File:
class TextFile: File {
    // Declare property observers
    // for a base class property:
    override var name: String {
        willSet {
            print("About to change the file name to \(newValue)")
        }

        didSet {
            print("The file name was changed from \(oldValue) to ↵
                    \(super.name)")
        }
    }

    // Override the default initializer:
    override init() {
        // Call the superclass initializer:
        super.init()

        // Override the
        name = String("\(name).txt")
    }
}
```

---

## ACTIONSCRIPT ANALOGY

There are a couple of nuances in how inheritance works in Swift that you need to be aware of if you come from an ActionScript background:

- **Common base classes**. This is more of an ActionScript contrast, rather than an analogy. While in ActionScript all types inherit from the SDK's Object class, classes in Swift do not have a common base class. As a consequence, whereas in ActionScript you can call toString() on any type, for example, a Swift class does not automatically inherit functionality, unless you explicitly derive it from another class.

- **Access control and inheritance**. In addition to marking instances and types as `public`, `internal`, and `private` ActionScript offers another level of access, which is missing from Swift: `protected`. In ActionScript, as well as other languages, this modifier links access control with inheritance: a `protected` property of a class, for example, is accessible only to that class and its descendants. When Swift was designed, it was decided that access control should be kept simpler and consistent throughout the language, without having to consider whether we are in a class hierarchy situation or not; hence, you will not find `protected` members here.

## Extensions

Instead of inheriting an existing type in order to add functionality to it, you can extend it and add properties or methods to it after it has been defined. This applies to types you have written, as well as to SDK or other third-party types, whose implementation source code you can't access.

To provide an extension for an existing entity, you use the `extension` keyword, followed by the name of the entity, followed by curly brackets in which you add the extending functionality. There are two things out of bounds to extensions:

- You can only provide new functionality and can't override existing methods, properties, or subscripts. This is in line with the open-closed principle we saw earlier.

- You can add stored type properties but not stored instance properties. Anything you add to an extension is available to all instances of it, even if they were defined before the extension. Adding a stored property would change the memory footprint of an instance, which in Swift can't be done at runtime.

We will see how this works by writing an extension to Swift's `String` type (see Listing 21-18). To get the reverse of a String instance in Swift you need to call the `reverse` method on its `characters` property, which returns a new copy of the string's character view. We will provide a method as a shortcut for that, which makes it look as if the string's contents were reversed in place.

*Listing 21-18.* Adding a Method to the String Type

```
extension String {
    public mutating func reverse() {
        self = String(self.characters.reverse())
    }
}
```

A quick note: see the `mutating` keyword and the assignment to `self` inside the method we added? These aren't relevant to providing an extension, but they are an important parts of Swift: we will see why later when we talk about *structures*.

You can now call the `reverse` method on an instance of `String`, as if the method was always part of the type (see Listing 21-19).

*Listing 21-19.* Calling an Extension Method

```
var palindrome = "Rats at a bar grab at a star."
print("Palindrome: \(palindrome)")
palindrome.reverse()
print("Reversed palindrome: \(palindrome)")
```

```
// output:
// Palindrome: Rats at a bar grab at a star.
// Reversed palindrome: .rats a ta barg rab a ta staR
```

See **Chapter 22** for another example of extending the String type by adding a subscript to it, which lets us access individual characters in a string using a numeric index (e.g., `myStr[2]`).

# Structures

Structures are a concept that doesn't have a direct parallel in ActionScript, so let us introduce them by comparing and contrasting them with classes.

Like classes, structures keep together data in the form of properties and provide functionality in the form of methods and subscripts. You access a structure's properties, methods, and subscripts using the same dot syntax you use with classes. A structure can also conform to protocols, which translated to ActionScript roughly means "to implement interfaces." The syntax for declaring a structure looks very much like declaring a class, except that you use the `struct` keyword, instead of the `class` keyword.

Now, onto the differences between classes and structures.

- Structures have a completely different way of managing memory —more on this below.

- There is no subclassing: structures can't inherit classes or other structures.

- Structures don't have deinitializer methods.

- Structure methods are not allowed to make changes to the structure, unless you mark them as `mutating`.

- You get an additional initializer automatically generated for you if you don't provide initializers explicitly and ensure all stored properties of the structure have initial values. Read on to find out what these automatically generated initalizers look like.

The example in Listing 21-20 shows a structure definition, which holds the x and y coordinate of a point and has a Boolean method, which checks whether the point is at the origin of the coordinate system.

***Listing 21-20.*** Defining a Structure

```
struct Position2D {
    var x: Int = 0
    var y: Int = 0

    func isAtOrigin() -> Bool {
        return 0 == x && 0 == y
    }
}
```

## Instantiating a Structure

The rules for instantiating classes and defining initializers apply to structures too. For classes that provide default values for all of their stored properties, the compiler defines a default initializer without parameters behind the scenes. Structures get the same treatment and more: they also get a member-wise initializer automatically, which takes parameter values for every stored property.

This means that without adding any more code to the Position2D structure from the last example, we can create instances of it using one of the two automatically generated initializers, as shown in Listing 21-21.

***Listing 21-21.*** Instantiating a Structure

```
// Uses the default initializer:
let origin = Position2D()

// Uses the memberwise initializer:
let randomPoint = Position2D(x: 10, y: 10)
```

# Memory Management for Structures and Enumerations

Unlike classes, which use references, structures and enumerations are *value types*. In other words, when you instantiate a structure and assign it to a variable and then assign this variable to another variable and try to modify it, the second variable gets a copy of the structure and you end up with two structure instances. This is known as *copy on write*. The same thing happens when you pass a structure or an enumeration as an argument to a function: the value of the structure or enumeration gets copied over if there is an attempt to write to it.

Here is an example to illustrate that: we will try the same experiment we did with classes in Listing 21-12 to see the difference. The example in Listing 21-22 declares a variable pointA and initializes it with an instance of the Position2D structure we defined in Listing 21-20. It then declares a second variable, pointB, and assigns pointA to it. Now, if we change one of the properties of Position2D via pointB, we will see that the changes do not appear in pointA: pointA and pointB each has separate instances of Position2D.

***Listing 21-22.*** Structures as Value Types

```
// pointA contains an instance of Position2D:
var pointA = Position2D(x: 5, y: 10)

// pointB gets a copy of this instance:
var pointB = pointA

// If pointB changes, this doesn't affect pointA:
pointB.x = 0
print(pointA.x) // prints out 5
print(pointB.x) // prints out 0
```

It's worth being aware that most of the primitive types in Swift are implemented as structures behind the scenes: this includes all numeric types, the String type, and also the collection types Array and Dictionary.

Working with value types on the one hand means that you need to be careful when passing them around or doing assignments and to be aware of both the memory and performance overhead this might have. Having copies created every time there is an assignment takes additional memory and also takes time for initialization. On the other hand, Apple's manual points out that things are optimized behind the scenes, so that actual value copying only takes place "when it is absolutely necessary" and that a programmer doesn't necessarily need to go out of her way to avoid assignment of value types.

---

## ACTIONSCRIPT ANALOGY

All ActionScript types are *reference types*. Basic types like String and Number, however, are made to behave as if they are *value types* and create instance copies when you try to modify an instance via multiple references.

---

## Mutating Methods

One of the rules for working with value types is that you cannot modify their properties from within instance methods. In order to enable a method to change the properties of a structure or an enumeration, you need to mark it as mutating.

Listing 21-23 adds two mutating methods to the Position2D structure: one of them changes the x and y properties; the second changes the whole structure by making an assignment to its implied self property.

***Listing 21-23.*** Changing the Properties of a Structure Instance from Within a Mutating Method

```
struct Position2D {
    var x: Int = 0
    var y: Int = 0

    func isAtOrigin() -> Bool {
        return 0 == x && 0 == y
    }

    mutating func moveTo(x x: Int, y y: Int) {
        self.x = x
        self.y = y
    }

    mutating func moveTo(position newPosition: Position2D {
        self = newPosition
    }
}
```

## When to Prefer Structures

Structures don't use inheritance and are always passed by value. In other words, you can't take advantage of a structure hierarchy to create sophisticated logic and you need to be careful with the memory footprint of your structures and the price you pay when new instances are automatically created. This makes structures best suited for encapsulating and keeping pieces of data together: the fewer, the better. Use classes when you require more complicated logic and need to take advantage of inheritance.

# Enumerations

An *enumeration* or enum is a type that you declare to define a set of names. Like classes and structures, enumerations can have properties and methods and conform to protocols. Like structures, they are *value types*. **Chapter 22** spends time delving into the subtleties of enumerations.

# Protocols

A *protocol* defines how an entity should be interacted with: what properties and methods other entities can use to access it. We will start by comparing and contrasting protocols with their ActionScript analogue: *interfaces*. Then we will depart as far away from ActionScript as we can.

```
┌─────────────────────────────────────────────────────────────┐
│                    ACTIONSCRIPT ANALOGY                        │
└─────────────────────────────────────────────────────────────┘
```

Protocols in Swift are related to ActionScript interfaces: they define a way of interacting with types by setting requirements that a conforming type must implement.

Now, let us see how protocols and interfaces are different:

- Interfaces only set requirements for what methods a type needs to implement. Protocols can set requirements for methods, properties, subscripts, and even initializers.

- Interfaces leave the implementation entirely to the types that adopt them. Protocols also typically leave the implementation to the conforming types but can also provide a default implementation.

- An interface can only be marked as `public` or `internal`. A protocol can be `public`, `internal`, or `private`.

## Defining a Protocol

You define a protocol with the `protocol` keyword, followed by curly brackets. Inside the curly brackets is where the definition of the protocol's requirement goes. This is much like defining a class or a structure, except that method, subscript, and property definitions have a slightly different syntax in a protocol.

Following is a protocol we will define as an example. It is called `Countable` and offers a way for a type, which contains a collection, to report the number of items in the collection and the unit for that number (Listing 21-24).

*Listing 21-24.* Defining a Protocol

```
protocol Countable {
    static var unit: String { get }
    func count() -> Int
}
```

Let us look at the requirements set by `Countable`.

The first one is that any conforming type should have a readable *type property*, called `unit`, which is of type `String`. The fact that the property is readable is expressed by the get keyword inside curly brackets after the property definition. Note that this requirement can be satisfied by a stored property, as well as a computed property with a getter. For a property that's required to be readable and writeable, the definition would contain `{ get set }`.

The second requirement defined by the protocol is that conforming types should implement a method, called `count`, which returns an integer. The protocol defines only the signature of the method, without an implementation, hence the lack of curly brackets.

## Conforming to a Protocol

Now let us see how a type might conform to this protocol. We will redefine the `Directory` class that we used earlier in the chapter for that purpose (see Listing 21-25).

***Listing 21-25.*** Conforming to a Protocol

```
class Directory: Countable {
    // Property, required by the Countable protocol:
    static var unit = "Files and folders"

    var files: [File] = []
    var directories: [Directory] = []

    // Method, required by the Countable protocol:
    func count() -> Int {
        return files.count + directories.count
    }
}
```

You can see that the protocol name appears in the declaration the same way you would put the name of a base class: after the type name, separated by a colon. The rule is: a type can conform to multiple protocols, which you list, separated by commas. If there is a base class the type inherits apart from the protocols, it should appear first in the list.

The definition of the property and the method, required by the Countable protocol, comes inside the definition of the Directory class like any other property or method. In this case an instance of Directory will return the number of files and directories it contains.

## Facts About Protocols

We could easily dedicate a whole chapter to the power of protocols. However, for the scope of this book it is more important that you are aware of the things protocols can do for you and explore them in depth when you need to. Apple's *The Swift Programming Language* online manual is a very good source.

- Protocols can be adopted by classes, structures, and enumerations.

- A protocol can set a restriction that it is only adoptable by classes by putting the keyword class in its *inheritance list*, for example:

    ```
    protocol Countable: class /*Any inherited protocols come after 'class'.*/ {}
    ```

- Protocol methods that may need to change the internals of a type instance must be marked as mutating, in case the protocol is adopted by a structure or an enumeration.

- Protocols can inherit each other and form hierarchies.

- They can set requirements for initializers. When such an initializer is implemented in a conforming class, it is marked with the required modifier, unless the class has been defined as final. The required modifier signals to any subclasses that may inherit the conforming class that they need to provide an implementation for the initializer in order to conform to the protocol. This is illustrated with the example in Listing 21-26. It declares a protocol, named MyProtocol and a class that conforms to it, called MyBaseClass. The protocol defines an initializer (a default initializer without parameters in this case), which any conforming class needs to implement. When we define this initializer in MyBaseClass, we need to include the required keyword: this makes the initializer compulsory in MyDerivedClass, which we have declared as a subclass of MyBaseClass.

***Listing 21-26.*** Making a Type Conform to a Protocol Through an Extension

```
protocol MyProtocol {
    init()
}

class MyBaseClass: MyProtocol {
    // The keyword required makes sure
    // that any subclasses of MyBaseClass
    // will also implement this initializer:
    required init() {
        // The body of the initializer
    }
}

class MyDerivedClass: MyBaseClass {
    // MyDerivedClass needs to implement this initializer
    // and include the keyword required, in case it has subclasses:
    required init() {
        super.init()
    }
}
```

- You can define extensions to protocols like you do for other types.

- You can make a type conform to a protocol via an extension. As an example let's play with Swift's String type again to make it conform to the Countable protocol we defined earlier and have it report the number of characters it contains (Listing 21-27).

***Listing 21-27.*** Making a Type Conform to a Protocol Through an Extension

```
extension String: Countable {
    static var unit: String {
        get {
            return String(Character.self)
        }
    }

    func count() -> Int {
        return self.characters.count
    }
}
```

You will see that String implements the required unit property differently. Instead of a stored property, unit is defined as a calculated property and returns the type name of Character as a String.

Let's test the extension by calling count on a String instance, as shown in Listing 21-28.

***Listing 21-28.*** Testing Protocol Conformance

```
let s = "Ready, fire, aim!"
print("'\(s)' has \(s.count()) instances of \(String.unit).")

// output:
// 'Ready, fire, aim!' has 17 instances of Character.
```

## The Merit of Protocols

Protocols can be used as types in their own right. For example, if you declare a function that takes a parameter of type `Countable`, you can then call that function and pass it a `String` instance or a `Directory` instance. This way protocols let structures and enumerations take advantage of polymorphism, even if they can't use inheritance.

The main advantage of protocols, however, will be revealed when we look at *generics* in **Chapter 22**. Generic programming allows you to write code that can be applied to many different types of data. Protocols help add constraints to that and make *generic types* really powerful.

# Summary

In this chapter we covered the tools and techniques that Swift provides for Object-Oriented Programing. In particular we saw the differences between classes and structures, the variety of ways that Swift can handle properties, and how we can extend types without modifying them. Finally we covered the basis of protocols, the power of which we will see in the next chapter, as we cover Swift's support for generics. Stay tuned . . .

## The Merit of Protocols

## Summary

# CHAPTER 22

■ ■ ■

# New and Different Concepts

In this chapter we open the door to four topics that either have no counterpart in ActionScript or that Swift redefines in a way that can make them seem new to an ActionScript developer. *Enumerations* and *generics* fall under the first category. *Subscripts* and *closures*, although present in ActionScript, are taken to a whole new level in terms of functionality and expressiveness. Curious? I was . . .

## Enumerations

An enumeration or enum is a type that you declare to define a set of names, which can also have values attached to them.

| ACTIONSCRIPT ANALOGY |
|---|
| Although there is no equivalent to enumerations in ActionScript, online forums abound in clever ways of "faking" them: from using named constants to writing sophisticated classes that simulate an enumerated type and maintain its consistency. |

### Why Use Enumerations?

Let us consider the alternative. Suppose one part of your app sends images to a server and generates a code that tells you whether the upload succeeded. You may want to write a function that processes this code and returns something more meaningful that you can either show on the screen or add to a log file. Let us say that you have three codes to consider:

- 0 means that the upload was successful;
- 1 means that the upload failed because of a server error;
- 2 means that the upload failed because the user canceled it.

Listing 22-1 shows what your processing function might look like.

*Listing 22-1.* Making a Choice Without Using Enumerations

```
func getMessageFromCode(resultCode : Int) -> String {
    switch errCode {
    case 0: // Success
        return "The file was sent successfully."
```

© Radoslava Leseva Adams and Hristo Lesev 2016
R. L. Adams and H. Lesev, *Migrating to Swift from Flash and ActionScript*,
DOI 10.1007/978-1-4842-1666-8_22

```
    case 1: // Server error
        return "The server responded with an error."

    case 2: // The user cancelled sending
        return "The user aborted the operation."

    default:
        return "Unknown error code"
    }
}
```

This function does the job, but there are a couple of things that can be improved upon.

- You need to keep track of an arbitrary mapping between result codes and their meaning. If you add new codes to the part of your app that deals with the uploads, you must remember to add them to geMessageFromCode too.

- The function doesn't give you the flexibility for additional information: for example, finding out the reason for the server failure based on an error code that might have come from the server.

## Using an enum with Raw Values to Handle Value Mapping

Using named constants instead of 0, 1, and 2 would partially solve the problem with the arbitrary mapping between return codes and their meaning. Using an enumeration can give you that and more: it lets you define a set of names and (optionally) attach constant values to them. It also keeps the set's integrity: unlike with named constants, in an enumeration you don't have to worry about two constants having the same value by accident.

To declare an enumeration you use the keyword enum, the name of the enumeration and list the set of names in curly brackets (see Listing 22-2).

*Listing 22-2.* Declaring an enum of Integers

```
enum FileUploadResult : Int {
    case Success = 0
    case ServerError = 1
    case UserCancelled = 2
}
```

Having declared this, you can use FileUploadResult.Success (or simply .Success) where you need 0, .ServerError where you need 1, and so on. Let us rewrite getMessageFromCode to take advantage of this, as shown in Listing 22-3.

*Listing 22-3.* Replacing Hard-Coded Integers with Names from an enum

```
func getMessageFromCode(resultCode: FileUploadResult) -> String {
    switch errCode {
    case .Success:          return "The file was sent successfully."
    case .ServerError:      return "The server responded with an error."
    case .UserCancelled:    return "The user aborted operation."
    }
}
```

There are a few things that are worth noting in this improved version of getMessageFromCode:

- The integers we assigned to the enum members are called *raw values* in Swift.

- The code is now self-documented and does not need comments.

- FileUploadResult is a new type, which defines a closed set of integers. As a result the resultCode argument can now make use of this type and have its possible values limited to the only three that have meaning in this context.

- You don't need a default statement any more. As you saw in **Chapter 20**, the Swift compiler insists that a switch statement be exhaustive: it either needs to provide a case statement for every possible value of the type it handles or have a default clause to cover values that do not have case statements. The case statements here cover every possible value of the FileUploadResult type.

- A side effect of omitting the default clause is that you don't have to remember to add new case statements if you create new return codes: the compiler will let you know if you fall short on case statements.

- The .Success, .ServerError, etc. syntax is short for FileUploadResult.Success, FileUploadResult.ServerError, and so on.

## More Facts About Raw Values

Here are a few more things that are good to know about raw values in enumerations:

- **Raw values are optional.** You can define an enum of names without values attached to them. The code in Listing 22-4 shows you an enum without raw values and another valid syntax, where you list names on the same line:

***Listing 22-4.*** Enum Without Raw Values

```
enum FileUploadResult {
    case Success, ServerError, UserCancelled
}
```

- **Integer raw values can auto increment.** If you define an enum with integer raw values but only assign a value to one of its members, all members that come after it will assume raw values that autoincrement from the assigned one. For example, in Listing 22-5 the declaration of FileUploadResult .ServerError automatically assumes a raw value of 1 and .UserCancelled a raw value of 2.

***Listing 22-5.*** Autoincremented Raw Values

```
enum FileUploadResult: Int {
    case Success = 0, ServerError, UserCancelled
}
```

- **Raw values can be strings, characters, and integer or floating-point numbers.**

- **Raw values are constant and have the same type for all members of an enum.**
  Once assigned, raw values cannot be changed and are a characteristic of the enum
  type you have declared: each instance of the enum will have the same raw values
  assigned to its members. When you want to use raw values, you need to tell the
  compiler what type they will be by declaring your enum to be of that type (an Int or a
  String, for example). Each member of the enum is then considered to be of the same
  type, whether it has a raw value assigned to it or not.

- **To read a raw value, use the** rawValue **property:**

*Listing 22-6.* Accessing a Raw Value

```
let returnCode = FileUploadResult.Success.rawValue
```

# Adding Associated Values to Handle Variable Information

When it comes to enumerations most programming languages stop at what you saw in the last example: an
enum allows you to use named integers. And this is usually good enough.

Swift, on the other hand, offers more. Instead of a *raw value*, a member of an enum type can have
another kind of value mapped to it, called *associated value*. You can think of an *associated value* as an
additional property of the enum member. It can be of any type, it can store custom information, and you can
change the value of that information from one line of code to the next.

In the file upload result example the enum passed to getMessageFromCode could have more detailed
information attached to its members. For example, FileUploadResult.ServerError could have an Int and
a String that indicate an error code and a message from the server; FileUploadResult.UserCancelled
could have an additional String that explains how the user canceled the upload. In Swift you express that by
providing a list of associated value types in brackets after an enum member's name (see Listing 22-7).

*Listing 22-7.* Syntax for Associated Values in enums

```
enum FileUploadResult {
    case Success                  // doesn't need an associated value
    case ServerError (Int, String) // (server error code, server message)
    case UserCancelled (String)   // (how the user cancelled the upload)
}
```

Note how this declaration specifies only types associated with two of the members without assigning
values to them. This is like declaring variables that can be attached to .ServerError and .UserCancelled
that you populate once you create an instance of FileUploadResult, as shown in Listing 22-8.

*Listing 22-8.* Assigning Associated Values

```
var returnCode = FileUploadResult.ServerError(400, "Bad request")

// You can later change the associated values in returnCode
// by doing another assignment:
returnCode = FileUploadResult.ServerError(404, "Not found")
```

Listing 22-9 shows a version of getMessageFromCode, which makes use of the enum's associated values.

*Listing 22-9.* Using associated values

```
func getMessageFromCode(resultCode : FileUploadResult) -> String {
    switch resultCode {
    case .Success:
        return "The file was sent successfully."

    case .ServerError (let serverErrorCode, let serverMessage):
        return "The server responded with error:↵
                \(serverErrorCode), \(serverMessage)."

    case .UserCancelled (let additionalInfo):
        return "The user aborted operation. ↵
                Additional information: \(additionalInfo)"
    }
}
```

Well, this looks like a handful. For the sake of simplicity let us dissect just one of those case statements (see Listing 22-10).

*Listing 22-10.* Reading Associated Values

```
case .UserCancelled (let additionalInfo):
        return "The user aborted operation.↵
                Additional information: \(additionalInfo)"
```

The code in the brackets inside the case statement declares a local constant called additionalInfo and assigns the associated value of .UserCancelled to it. The next line then uses that variable to build a string and return it as the function's result. This solves the second issue we had with the very first version of getMessageFromCode: its argument can now carry additional information.

It is worth noting that the values you read in the code in Listing 22-10 are part of the resultCode *instance* of FileUploadResult, not part of the FileUploadResult type or .UserCancelled. In other words, if you declare another FileUploadResult instance and add associated values to it, they can be different from those in resultCode.

## More Facts About Enumerations

Some of the rules that apply to enumerations might surprise you, for example:

- **Raw and associated values are mutually exclusive.** Currently the Swift compiler will not let you declare an enum that has both raw and associated values attached to its members.

- **An enum is like a class.** It can be extended, can conform to protocols, and can have instance methods and initializers defined for it.

# Subscripts

Subscripts do have a counterpart in ActionScript. Swift, however, puts a new spin on this concept, which we will focus on here.

```
ACTIONSCRIPT ANALOGY
```

Whenever you access an element of a container by its index or an Object's property by its name in square brackets, you use a subscript. In ActionScript a subscript is called the *array access operator []*.

```
// ActionScript code
var dictionaryElement : String = dictionary[3];
var objProperty : Number = object["propertyName"];
```

## Defining a Subscript

In Swift you can use subscripts in similar situations and, unlike in ActionScript, you can also define them. In other words, you can decide what happens when `dictionary[3]` is called.

I will illustrate this with an example. In Swift you can access the individual characters in a `String` by providing an instance of a class called `Index`, but you can't simply ask for `str[3]`. Let us extend the `String` class and define a subscript that takes integers to make this possible.

You declare a subscript like you would a method, but use the `subscript` keyword, instead of `func`, as in Listing 22-11.

*Listing 22-11.* Defining a Subscript in Swift

```
extension String
{
    public subscript (i: Int) -> Character
    {
        let index = self.startIndex.advancedBy(i)
        return self[index]
    }
}
```

Now you can access the characters of a given `String` with an integer literal in square brackets (see Listing 22-12).

*Listing 22-12.* Using a Subscript

```
let str: String = "I swear by my pretty floral bonnet..."
let ch: Character = str[3] // returns 'w'
```

## Subscript Overloading

You were acquainted with the concept of overloading operators in **Chapter 18** and saw how to overload methods in **Chapter 21**. Subscripts, being just another type of function, can be overloaded too. The only condition is that the subscript methods defined for a given type all have different signatures.

In fact, what we provided in the last example was a subscript overload to the already existing `String` subscript that takes an `Index` instance and returns a character.

## Subscript Varieties

In Swift you can define subscripts that take ranges, multiple dimensions, or indices that are not numbers.

# Using a Range

The example in Listing 22-13 defines another subscript for the String type, which takes a range, a lower index and an upper index, and returns the substring of characters that fall between (and including) these indices.

*Listing 22-13.* Defining a Subscript That Uses a Range

```
extension String {
    subscript(characterRange: Range<Int>) -> String {
        let start = self.startIndex.advancedBy(characterRange.startIndex)
        let end = self.startIndex.advancedBy(characterRange.endIndex)
        let range = start..<end
        return self[range]
    }
}

// You can now get a subset of the string's characters like this:
let str: String = "I swear by my pretty floral bonnet..."
let chSubset = str[3...6] // returns 'wear'
```

# Using Multiple Dimensions

Subscripts can be multidimensional too. The code in Listing 22-14 defines a structure that represents a Tic-tac-toe board and can tell you what's in a given cell of the board, defined by a row and a column.

*Listing 22-14.* Defining and using a multidimensional subscript

```
struct TicTacToeBoard {
    // Create the tic-tac-toe grid and initialize it with spaces:
    var mGrid: [[Character]] = ↩
        [[" ", " ", " "], [" ", " ", " "], [" ", " ", " "]]

    func areIndicesValid(row: Int, column: Int) -> Bool {
        return 0...2 ~= row && 0...2 ~= column
    }

    subscript (row: Int, column: Int) -> Character {
        // Ensure that we are operating with valid indices:
        assert(areIndicesValid(row, column: column))
        return mGrid[row][column]
    }
}

// Call the two-dimensional subscript like this:
var ticTacToe: TicTacToeBoard = TicTacToeBoard()
let centreCell = ticTacToe[1, 1] // Returns " "
```

# Using Non-numeric Indices

The indices you use in a subscript don't have to be integers. For example, the two lines of code in Listing 22-15 initialize a Dictionary of String-Int key-value pairs and then use a String as the subscript index to access a value in the Dictionary:

*Listing 22-15.* Using String as the Subscript Index

```
let starWarsFilms = ↵
        [ "Star Wars": 1977, "The Empire Strikes Back": 1980, ↵
          "Return of the Jedi": 1983 ]
let firstStarWarsFilmRelease = starWarsFilms[ "Star Wars" ]! // returns 1977
```

# Closures

Closures are not an entirely new concept for an ActionScript 3 developer. As with a lot of old tricks, however, you will find that Swift has reinvented this one too to offer more expressiveness. And this is what merits including closures in this chapter.

---

### ACTIONSCRIPT ANALOGY

Whenever you use a nested function or a `Function` object in ActionScript, you use a closure.

---

## Closures in Swift Can Be Very Concise

Very. So concise indeed that some of the closure syntax can be baffling at first. We will ease into it with an example, which will first show you a familiar ActionScript closure and then its Swift counterparts, each of which will optimize some part of the syntax.

## An ActionScript Example

Let us start with something familiar. In ActionScript 3 you can filter an array by calling the Array class's `filter` function, which is defined thus:

```
function filter(callback: Function, thisObject:* = null): Array
```

Here the `callback` parameter is a *closure*: a function that you supply and that will be run on each element of the array. The manual page for `filter` tells us that `callback` is expected to have the following signature:

```
function filter(callback: Function, thisObject:* = null): Array
```

If you want to filter an array of integers and leave only the ones that are larger than three, this is what you might do. First, implement a filter callback function, then use it as an argument in the Array's `filter` function (see Listing 22-16).

*Listing 22-16.* Closure Implementation and Use in ActionScript

```
// ActionScript code
// First, implement a callback function for filtering array elements:
function filterCallback(item : Object, index : int, array : Array) : Boolean {
    return item > 3;
}
```

```
// Then use the callback to filter an array:
var initialArray : Array = [1, 2, 5];
var filteredArray: Array = initialArray.filter( filterCallback );
```

After this is run, `filteredArray` should contain just [5].

## Literal Translation to Swift

The `Array` container type in Swift happens to have the same method, called `filter`. How convenient. It takes a closure, which applies criteria to an element of the array and returns `true` if the element passes the criteria and `false` otherwise (Listing 22-17).

*Listing 22-17.* Defining a Closure and Using It in Swift

```
// Implement the closure function, which is run on each array element:
func includeElement(item : Int) -> Bool {
    return item > 3
}

// Then use the closure to filter an array:
let initialArray = [1, 2, 5]
let filteredArray = initialArray.filter(includeElement)
```

## Optimization 1: Inlining a Closure Expression

Instead of defining a closure as a separate function, you can inline it where it is needed, as shown in Listing 22-18.

*Listing 22-18.* An Inline a Closure in Swift

```
let filteredArray = initialArray.filter( ↵
    {(item: Int) -> Bool in return item > 3})
```

Note the following:

- The closure is now anonymous (i.e., doesn't have a name). The Swift SDK calls 'unnamed closures written in a lightweight syntax that can capture values from their surrounding context' *closure expressions*.

- The full syntax for a *closure expression* looks like this: the whole expression is put in curly brackets and starts with the closure parameters in parentheses, followed by the closure return type, the keyword in, and the closure body:

  ```
  { (parameters) -> return type in closure body }
  ```

It is also worth noting that with this optimization we haven't waded in deep Swift waters yet, as ActionScript allows you to define inline closures too.

## Optimization 2: Letting the Compiler Infer Types from Context

The *closure expression* in **Optimization 1** can be made even shorter by omitting the types of the argument and the result, as the Swift compiler will infer them from the context (Listing 22-19).

***Listing 22-19.*** Closure Expression with Argument and Return Type Inferred

```
let filteredArray = initialArray.filter({item in return item > 3})
```

# Optimization 3: Using an Implicit Return

If you look at the body of our *closure expression*: `item > 3`, you will notice a couple of things about it:

- It's a single expression.
- Its result matches the return type of the closure, `Bool`.

The Swift compiler is quite happy for you to omit the return statement in cases of *single-expression closures*, which shortens code even further, as you can see in Listing 22-20.[1]

***Listing 22-20.*** Using Implicit Return in Single-Closure Expressions

```
let filteredArray = initialArray.filter({item in item > 3})
```

# Optimization 4: Using Shorthand Names for Parameters

Arguments passed to a closure can be referred to with what is called *shorthand names* in Swift. A *shorthand name* is a symbol that represents an argument, based on where in the list of arguments it is. The convention is: $0 refers to the first argument in the list, $1 refers to the second argument in the list, and so on.

If you apply this convention the inline closure will look like Listing 22-21.

***Listing 22-21.*** Using Shorthand Names in Closures

```
let filteredArray = initialArray.filter({$0 > 3})
```

Note that this also spares you the need to provide the list of arguments before the body of the closure and gets rid of the `in` keyword.

# Optimization 5: Using an Operator Function

Think `{$0 > 3}` is short? How about getting rid of the curly brackets altogether and cutting this down to a single symbol?

To illustrate how this works, let us take a different example. Calling an `Array`'s `sort` function in Swift takes a closure with two arguments. The two arguments are elements of the array and the closure returns `true` if the first argument should be placed closer to the top of the array and `false` if the second argument should be placed closer to the top. Listing 22-22 is the long inline version of that closure, which helps sort the array in ascending order.

---

[1]All this cutting down on syntax because of the cleverness of the compiler reminds me of an old, old joke from Gabrovo (Bulgaria), whose citizens are known to be a bit financially conservative…

A merchant goes to a distant town to sell wheat. Before heading back he walks into a post office and writes the following telegram to send to his wife: "Dear Ana, I sold the wheat profitably. Coming back tomorrow. Yours, Ivan." He counts the words and decides to lower the cost of the telegram by skipping the first part, as his wife is obviously dear to him. So he shortens the telegram to: "Sold the wheat profitably. Coming back tomorrow. Yours, Ivan." He looks at the text and thinks "But she knows I always sell with profit . . ." and shortens the telegram further: "Coming back tomorrow. Yours, Ivan." Eager to lower his expenses, he reasons that of course his wife knows he is coming back shortly, why wouldn't he?! And the text becomes: "Yours, Ivan." The merchant looks at this final version, scratches his head, and says to himself, "Well, I am hers and she knows that." Then he tears the telegram form and walks out of the post office.

*Listing 22-22.* Using a Closure to Sort an Array

```
let sortedArray = initialArray.sort( ↵
    { (item1: Int, item2: Int) -> Bool in return item1 < item2 } )
```

If you apply **Optimization 4** to this, the closure will simply read {$0 < $1}. Turns out that in this case you can again rely on the ingenuity of the compiler to infer what you are trying to do and simply leave the *less than operator* to stand for the whole closure (see Listing 22-23).

*Listing 22-23.* The Sorting Closure Reduced to a Single Operator

```
let sortedArray = initialArray.sort(<)
```

Neat? Weird? Definitely.

## More Facts About Closures

There are a couple more things to mention about closures. The first one provides an addition to our "strange syntax" collection:

- **Trailing closures.** When you don't have the luxury of a *single-expression closure* and instead have more work to do in the closure body, you can use what Swift calls a *trailing closure*. The only condition: the closure needs to be the last argument that is passed to a function. This is a call to the filter function we have been playing with, this time with a *trailing closure*. Note in Listing 22-24 how the closure comes in curly brackets after the argument list of the function. The parentheses after filter are optional if the closure is the only argument that you need to pass.

*Listing 22-24.* Using a Trailing Closure

```
let filteredArray = initialArray.filter() {
    $0 > 3
}
```

```
//You can even omit the parentheses after the function name in this case:
filteredArray = initialArray.filter{$0 > 3}
```

- **Closures have access to constants and variables defined outside them.** Like a nested function in ActionScript, a Swift closure can access and modify the values of variables and constants in its surrounding context. For example, take a look at Listing 22-25.

*Listing 22-25.* Accessing Variables and Constants from the Surrounding Context

```
func sumArrayElements( arr: Array< Int > ) -> Int {
    var arrayTotal: Int = 0;

    func addArrayElement( item: Int ) {
        arrayTotal += item
    }

    for ( element ) in arr { addArrayElement( element ) }

    return arrayTotal
}
```

The function in this snippet takes an array of integers and returns the sum of the array's elements. The *nested closure* defined inside it, addArrayElement, can read and modify arrayTotal, which lives in the context of the enclosing function, sumArrayElements.

# Generics

*Generic programming*, also known as *template metaprogramming* in other parts of the programming world, allows you to write code that can be parameterized not just on the values it handles but also on the types it can work with. Sound too abstract? Read on.

## A Generic Function in Swift

What would a function look like that takes types, as well as values, as parameters?[2]

Let us begin by declaring a function, called isContained, that takes an array and an object and returns true if the object is contained in the array, false otherwise.[3] If you were to write the body of this function, it would probably do the following: iterate through the array elements until it finds a match with the given object or until it runs out of array elements. The function's insides would be the same if you wanted it to look for a string in an array of strings, a number in an array of numbers, and so on. You can imagine the amount of duplicated code you would end up with if you were to provide an implementation of this function for every single type you need it to handle.

Swift spares you that need and instead delegates the job of providing type-specific implementations to the compiler, when you declare your function as in Listing 22-26.

**Listing 22-26.** Generic Function Syntax

```
func isContained<T>( arr : Array<T>, obj : T ) -> Bool
```

Translated into English, this reads: isContained is a function that takes an array of any type and an object of the same type. In the declaration of the function that type will be called T. In order to stop the compiler from complaining it doesn't know what T is, we need to tell it that T is a type parameter (alias): this is what <T> after the name of the function stands for. It is conventional to use one-letter aliases such as T, but you can use any name you like, as long as it's not an existing type or a reserved keyword.

## Calling a Generic Function

How would you make a call to isContained? In many other languages you would need to explicitly provide the type you want to use in place of T at the time of the call. Due to the powers of the Swift compiler to infer types from context, however, you wouldn't know you were calling a generic function (Listing 22-27).

**Listing 22-27.** Calling a Generic Function

```
let intArray = [45, 2, 6]
let objFound = isContained(intArray, obj: 2) // returns true
```

---

[2]It would be fair to say that the parameter analogy only goes so far: a conventional parameter to a function gets it value at runtime, while a type parameter must be resolved at compile time.
[3]And let us pretend for a moment that array.indexOf() does not exist in Swift.

# The Compiler Does the Dirty Work

What happens when you call a generic function is that the compiler creates code for you behind the scenes, which is compiled with the rest of your code. So, if you called isContained once with Int and once with String, the compiler would generate two implementations of isContained: one for handling each type. The code will only be generated at compile time and will not appear in your source files.

---

## ACTIONSCRIPT ANALOGY

There is no direct analogue to generics in ActionScript. A similar effect, at least from the point of view of writing code that works with arbitrary types, is achieved by using polymorphism: you can declare a function to take parameters of type Object or the star type (*).

```
// ActionScript code
function isContained(arr : Array, obj : Object) : Boolean
```

This allows you to use any ActionScript type for the elements of arr and for obj, which looks very similar to how we made a call to the same function in Swift in the previous example. There are some significant differences between the two approaches, however. I will take a bit of a detour to outline them in the next section.

---

# Generic Programming and Polymorphism

Both generic programming and polymorphism are tools and each tool has its time and place where it is a better choice than others. It is like having a flat-head and a cross-head screwdriver in your toolbox: none of them is better than the other in general, but you would prefer one or the other depending on what you want to achieve. Following are some of the situations in which you might prefer generics to polymorphism. And hope that polymorphism doesn't take it personally.

- **When you need to be able to plug in unrelated types.** <T> can be used as an alias for any type, while requiring an Object as a parameter means that what you pass in a function needs to descend from Object.[4]

- **When you need to enforce type safety across unrelated types.** The ActionScript function declared in the last example can take an array of strings and look for an integer in it. No errors will be thrown, but using isContained like this would be somewhat wasteful. The generic declaration of isContained in Swift makes it clear that both the array and the object will need to be of the same type, whatever that type may be and the compiler will enforce that. This has the added benefit of documenting your intentions.

- **When you want to take advantage of compile-time error checking for unrelated types.** A compiler or a linker error is worth about a hundred runtime errors. If inside the body of your generic function you tried to use a type-aliased argument in a way that its type doesn't allow, the Swift compiler will let you know about it. Using an Object in ActionScript, on the other hand, allows you to do all sorts of things that may only turn out to be a problem at runtime.

---

[4]This is, admittedly, the case for all types in ActionScript.

- **When speed is important.** With polymorphism, you can resolve which override method to call at runtime. And that's one of the great things about polymorphism. When you don't need polymorphic behavior, however, and just code that will run with types that are totally unrelated to one another, you are better off with generics speed-wise. As we saw earlier, the compiler expands generic functions for you, so a specific version of your function will be called without the need to work it out at runtime.

## A Generic Type in Swift

In Swift, in addition to generic functions, you can define and use generic structures, classes, or enumerations. Listing 22-28 shows an example of a generic structure, called SimpleCollection. It has a member, mCollectables, which is an Array that can hold any type.

***Listing 22-28.*** Declaring a Generic Type

```
struct SimpleCollection<T> {
    var mCollectables = [T]()

    mutating func collect(item: T) {
        mCollectables.append(item)
    }
}
```

## You Use Generics in Swift Whether You Know It or Not

The container types in Swift, Array, Dictionary and Set, which you saw in **Chapter 19**, are all generic types. This allows you to create collections of any type you need to.

In addition, the first version of Swift offered a number of global generic functions, such as sorted, which would sort the elements of a container. Most of these have been moved to methods of the container classes in Swift

## Setting Constraints

Writing generic code for any type is quite flexible. Often, however, you want to restrict the types that a generic function or type allows because of what you need to do with them.

We will go back to our generic function example to illustrate this. This time let us add the function body (see Listing 22-29).

***Listing 22-29.*** Generic Function Body

```
func isContained<T>( arr : Array<T>, obj : T ) -> Bool {
    for arrElement in arr {
        if arrElement == obj { return true }
    }

    return false
}
```

This line—if `arrElement == obj`—looks simple enough, but it has a glitch: not every type is guaranteed to have the *equals operator* (`==`) defined for it. Indeed, if you try to compile this code, the compiler will helpfully tell you that *"Binary operator '==' cannot be applied to two T operands."*

The way to ensure that only types that support the *equals operator* can be used with this function is to put a constraint on the type placeholder T and force it to conform to the `Equatable` protocol. This changes the signature of the function as shown in Listing 22-30.

***Listing 22-30.*** Generic Function with a Constraint

```
func isContained<T: Equatable>( arr : Array<T>, obj : T ) -> Bool
```

# More facts About Generics

We will close the section on generics with a brief list of points that are worth knowing:

- **You can have more than one type alias or placeholder (e.g.,** see Listing 22-31).

***Listing 22-31.*** Using More Than One Type Alias

```
func mapTwoTypes<T, U>( instanceOfT: T, instanceOfU: U )
```

- **Type placeholders can be used in protocols too.** In that case they are called *associated types* and are specified with the keyword `typealias`. This is what a protocol for our `SimpleCollection` structure might look like Listing 22-32.

***Listing 22-32.*** Using an Associated Type with a Protocol

```
protocol SimpleCollectionProtocol {
    typealias T
    mutating func collect(item: T)
}
```

- **Generic types (classes, structures, protocols, enumerations) can be extended.**
- **There are even more elaborate ways of constraining type placeholders.** You can constrain a type placeholder to conform to protocols or inherit certain classes, as in Listing 22-33.

***Listing 22-33.*** Constraining Type Placeholders

```
func mapTwoTypes<T: CertainClass, U: CertainProtocol> ↵
    ( instanceOfT: T, instanceOfU: U )
```

You can define even more specific constraints by using the `where` clause. Here is an example of that: let us define a protocol to use for collections and define an *associated type* in it, called `ItemType`. A generic function that compares two collections can then impose the following constraints on its arguments:

- The two collections can be of different types (an `Array` and a `Set`, for example), but the items they contain must be of the same type.
- The items in the collections must conform to the `Equatable` protocol, so that they can be compared.

The code in Listing 22-34 shows all this expressed in Swift

***Listing 22-34.*** Constraining Type Aliases with the where Clause

```
protocol Collection { typealias ItemType }

func compareCollections ↵
    <T: Collection, U: Collection ↵
        where T.ItemType == U.ItemType, T.ItemType : Equatable>() ↵
            ( collection1: T, collection2: U ) -> Int {
            // implementation goes here }
```

# Summary

The new and different concepts presented in this chapter included the following:

- **Enumerations.** A concept that ActionScript doesn't have, but which comes in handy when you prefer to use sets of names, instead of hard-coded values.

- **Subscripts.** You have been using subscripts (the *array access operator []*) your whole ActionScript life, but did you know you could define them too? You can in Swift.

- **Closures.** Closures probably also looked familiar at the start. That is, until their syntax got weirder and weirder when we started taking advantage of the compiler's ability to infer things from context.

- **Generics.** Generics help you write code that takes not only different values as parameters but also different types. Not entirely possible in ActionScript.

This concludes our overview of the Swift programming language. Our hope is that it has offered you enough to not only kick-start your transition to it but also to give you the confidence that you know what happens behind the scenes of your code. In moments of doubt you can always return to this part of the book and use it as a reference or delve even deeper with Apple's comprehensive manual, *The Swift Programming Language*.

In the last chapter we will talk business and cover Apple's process for enrolling in a developer program and submitting apps to the App Store.

# CHAPTER 23

■ ■ ■

# Releasing Your App in the App Store

A book on iOS development would not be complete without an overview of the process of releasing your app. Being able to share it with users is the main goal of developing a mobile app, after all. Apple's release process evolves and changes all the time, so it is important to keep in mind that by the time you read this some of the screens we show may have changed. The main ideas behind this multistep process come from the desire to ensure quality and security for the apps that make it into the App Store and this is what we would like you to take away.

In this chapter you will do the following:

- Learn about the App Store submission process.

- Create a distribution provisioning profile.

- Archive your app for submission.

- Learn how to manage your apps via iTunes Connect.

- Submit your app for review by Apple.

When you are done you will have an understanding of the application submission process and the tools that can help you with it.

## Understanding the App Store Submission Process

It is a great feeling when you declare a piece of code ready for release. You rub your hands together and prepare to show your creation to the world. But wait, where is the Upload button? If only things were as simple as that. . . . Publishing your app in Apple's App Store involves several steps and some work on your part. Here is why.

Apple is known for its obsession with quality and security. This extends to third-party apps that run on Apple hardware and operating systems. Before an app can reach its end users it goes through a rigorous review process. We will briefly list the stages a typical app release goes through, so you can arm yourself with patience and stay calm to the very end.

1.  **Enrolling in the iOS Development program.** This is a prerequisite step. We have mentioned this program a few times already in previous chapters. This is a paid subscription program, which gives you access to early releases and lets you use advanced SDK features and distribute your apps worldwide.

2.  **Obtaining a distribution provisioning profile.** You will need one for each app you want to release. We saw what provisioning an app means in **Chapter 2**.

© Radoslava Leseva Adams and Hristo Lesev 2016
R. L. Adams and H. Lesev, *Migrating to Swift from Flash and ActionScript*,
DOI 10.1007/978-1-4842-1666-8_23

3. **Creating an app archive.** You need to make a release build of your app and *archive* it for submission. An archive is a container for the app's binaries, symbol information, and metadata.

4. **Creating a record for your app via iTunes Connect.** iTunes Connect is Apple's web-based tool for managing your apps in the App Store, including updating binaries, dealing with banking and tax information, generating promo codes, reviewing sales reports, and so on. Creating a record for your app involves providing a description, screenshots, a price tag, and keywords and other information that applies to the app.

5. **Uploading your app archive to iTunes Connect.** Note that although you use iTunes Connect to manage your apps in the App Store, you cannot use it to upload an app archive. Instead, either you do the upload directly from Xcode or you can use the Application Loader tool. Both of them perform automated checks to ensure that your app archive meets certain criteria like not containing malicious code or making calls into private frameworks, for example.

6. **Waiting for your app to be reviewed.** After an app has been uploaded, it is reviewed by Apple's staff. A reviewer typically runs your app to see what it looks like, to see whether it runs smoothly, and to ensure that it does not crash. The reviewer also makes sure that the app is appropriate for the App Store audience. For example, an app containing offensive or pornographic content will be rejected. Apple has published guidelines that you must follow for your app to pass the review. You can find them at `https://developer.apple.com/app-store/review/guidelines/`. This part of the process may take days; this is where your daily meditation practice can come in handy.[1] Also bear in mind that any change you make to your app's archive, even if it is a typo in the comments to its code, means that the app needs to be submitted for another review and that sends it to the back of the queue.

7. **Promoting and maintaining your app.** When your app has been accepted, it is your responsibility to let the world know that it exists, communicate with its users, fix bugs, update its content, and so forth. iTunes Connect can help at the maintenance stage: it has a dashboard, where you can manage updates and monitor your earnings.

# Submitting an App: A Step-by-Step Guide

On the following pages we will go through the whole process of preparing and submitting your app for review. First, here are the steps in a nutshell:

1. Registering an App ID.
2. Creating a distribution provisioning profile.
3. Archiving the app.
4. Creating a record for the app in iTunes Connect.
5. Uploading the app's archive with Xcode or Application Loader.
6. Monitoring the progress of the submission while waiting for Apple's verdict.

---

[1] I know . . . who in the world has time for that before a release?! Well, waiting for Apple's verdict on your app can be a good excuse to start.

Let us start with the first step on our list, registering an App ID.

# Registering an App ID

To demonstrate the submission process we will use the SpriteKitDemo project from **Chapter 16**. If you have not done that tutorial yet, you can go through it really quickly. It is fun too, as it demonstrates one of Xcode's game project templates. When you are done, open SpriteKitDemo.xcodeproj in Xcode.

In order to be published in the App Store, an app needs to have a unique identifier, also known as *App ID. Unique* here implies that the app cannot have an identifier that has already been registered either by you or by any other iOS developer. This includes IDs of apps still in development that have not been released yet.

We will create an App ID in Apple's Developer portal. Before that let us make a note of the app's *bundle identifier*: this is the identifier you specified when you created the project. To find it, select the SpriteKitDemo project in the Project navigator and then select the SpriteKitDemo target in the Editor. Open the **General** tab and locate **Identity ➤ Bundle Identifier** (Figure 23-1).

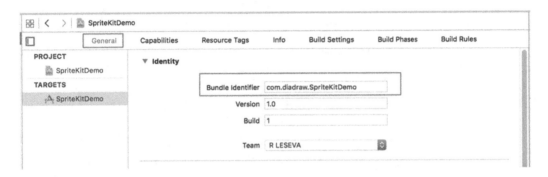

***Figure 23-1.*** *Finding the app's bundle identifier*

---

■ **Note**    The App ID and bundle identifier we use in this tutorial are for demonstration purposes only. When you submit an app to the App Store, you will need to use your own unique identifiers.

---

Next, in a browser navigate to http://developer.apple.com and log in with your Apple ID. After you log in, click on **Certificates, Identifiers & Profiles** to go to the provisioning portal (Figure 23-2).

***Figure 23-2.*** *Click Certificates, Identifiers & Profiles to go to the provisioning portal*

Once you are in the provisioning portal, go to **Identifiers ➤ App IDs** and click the plus button to add a new App ID (Figure 23-3).

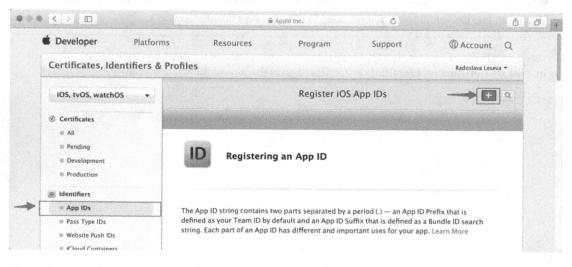

***Figure 23-3.*** *Registering a new App ID*

Give your app a name. The name can be any string that does not contain special characters. Make sure that the **Explicit App ID** radio button is selected and set **Bundle ID** to the bundle identifier you gave your app in Xcode (Figure 23-4).

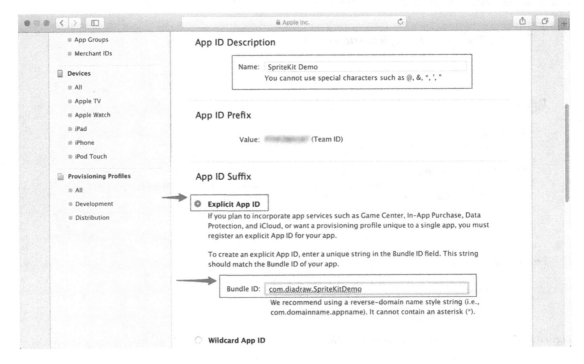

*Figure 23-4.* *Filling in the Bundle ID*

Leave the **App Services** section on the **Registration** page as it is; normally here you need to specify any services your app uses, such as Push Notifications or iCloud. Click **Continue** and then **Register** to proceed with creating the App ID.

## Generating a Distribution Certificate

Back in **Chapter 1** we helped Xcode create a *signing identity* for you, which is used to sign your apps to ascertain that they were developed and built by you. In **Chapter 2** we saw what *app provisioning* is and used your development signing identity to provision an app for running on physical devices. Provisioning an app for distribution requires a distribution certificate and signing identity, which you need to create in the provisioning portal. This is what we will do in this section.

On the **Certificates, Identifiers & Profiles** page, select **Certificates ➤ Production.** Unless you have packaged apps for distribution before, there will be no certificates listed in this section. If this is the case, click the + sign to create a new certificate. Select **Production ➤ App Store and Ad Hoc** for the type of certificate as shown in Figure 23-5 and click **Continue** at the bottom of the page.

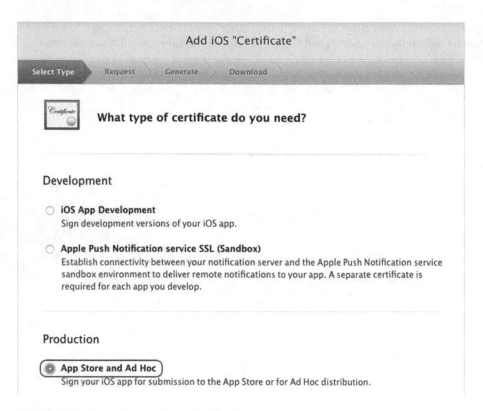

***Figure 23-5.*** *Creating a certificate for distribution*

The next step will guide you through creating and uploading a Certificate Signing Request (CSR): a file that is generated by the Keychain Access app on your Mac. This file is used to generate the distribution certificate. Once you have supplied the CSR, your distribution certificate should be ready for download (Figure 23-6).

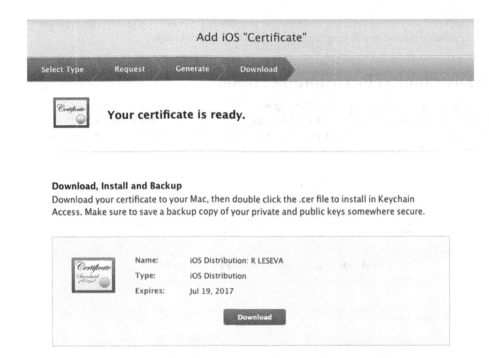

*Figure 23-6.* *Downloading the new distribution certificate*

Download the file and double-click to install it on your Mac. This should make it appear under **login ➤ My Certificates** in your Keychain Assistant app as shown in Figure 23-7.

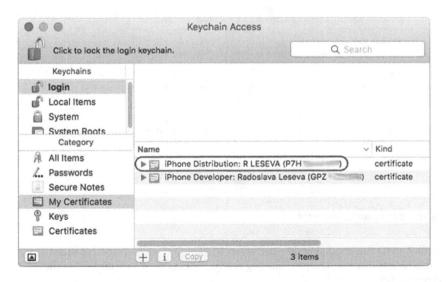

*Figure 23-7.* *The distribution certificate after installation in Keychain Assistant*

Note that you do not need to create a separate distribution certificate for every app you want to release in the app store. This certificate is used to put your signature on an app as a developer.

## Generating a Distribution Provisioning Profile

Next comes the distribution provisioning profile that the app will need. Back in the provisioning portal in your browser, on the **Certificates, Identifiers and Profiles** page, select **Provisioning Profiles ➤ Distribution** and click the + button to create a new profile. Set the profile type to **Distribution ➤ App Store** and click **Continue** (Figure 23-8).

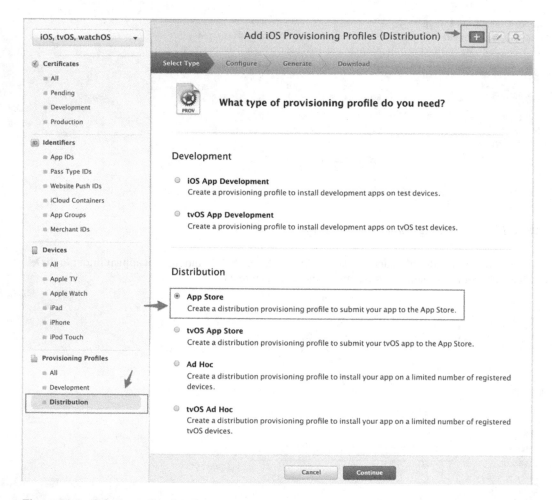

***Figure 23-8.*** *Creating a distribution provisioning profile*

At the next step locate the App ID you created earlier and select it. After that you will need to select a distribution certificate with which to link the new provisioning profile. Select the one we created in the previous step as shown in Figure 23-9.

*Figure 23-9.* *Linking the provisioning profile with a certificate*

Finally, name your provisioning profile. Its name will be useful for locating it among all the other profiles that you or Xcode have created, so it is best to name it after the app with which you will use it. Click **Continue**: here you may need to wait a few minutes for the profile to be generated. When the profile is ready, download it and double-click the downloaded file to install it on your development machine (Figure 23-10).

*Figure 23-10.* *Downloading the provisioning profile*

## Configuring the App and Building an Archive

Let us set up our app to use the distribution provisioning profile we just created. Open the SpriteKitDemo project in Xcode. Select the project file in the Project navigator to load its settings in the Editor.

Apple recommends letting Xcode choose the appropriate signing identity and provisioning profile for you by opting for automatic code signing. Let us configure our project to take advantage of that:

1.  First, we will set the project's code signing build settings to their defaults. In the Editor select the SpriteKitDemo project and go to the **Build Settings** tab. Locate the **Code Signing** section and set **Code Signing Identity** to iOS Developer for all build configurations. Then set **Provisioning Profile** to Automatic (Figure 23-11).

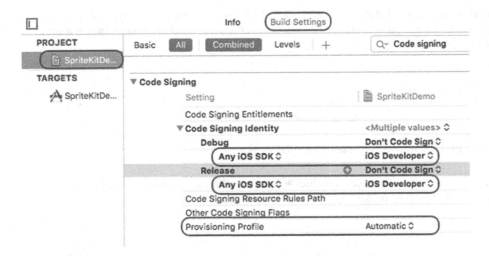

***Figure 23-11.*** *Configuring the project to use automatic code signing*

2. Next, select the app target and on the **General** tab set **Team** to None. This is a temporary change that will allow us to modify the target's code signing settings.

3. On the **Build Settings** tab replicate the settings we applied to the project's Code Signing section. Set **Code Signing Identity** to iOS Developer for all build configurations and **Provisioning Profile** to Automatic.

4. Back on the **General** tab set **Team** to your development team (or your Apple ID).

5. Restart Xcode.

---

■ **Note**    You can also manually configure the app target's code signing settings by setting `Code Signing Identity > Release` to iOS Distribution and `Provisioning Profile` to the profile we created earlier.

---

We need to ensure that our app has a full set of icons before we build it for release. In the Project navigator select the `Assets.xcassets` file and let Xcode guide you through setting up the required icon sizes, as shown in Figure 23-12.

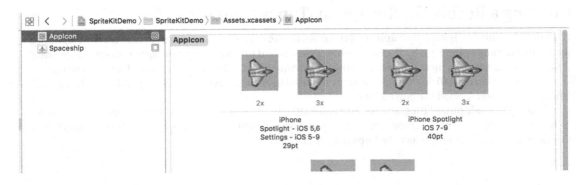

***Figure 23-12.*** *Add an icon set to your app project*

Now let us create a release build of the app, which we will later submit to the App Store. This process is called *archiving.* To archive an app, we first need to ensure that the project's **Deployment Target** is set to Generic iOS Device (Figure 23-13).

*Figure 23-13.* *Setting the Deployment Target to Generic iOS Device*

Then, from Xcode's the main menu select **Product ➤ Archive**. This starts a build in Xcode. When it finishes, the Organizer window pops up to show you the archive (Figure 23-14).

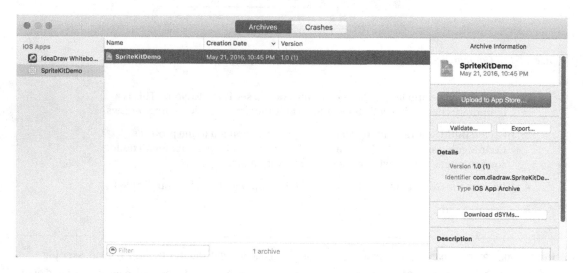

*Figure 23-14.* *The archive in the Organizer window*

This archive is now ready to be uploaded. Before we do that, however, we need to create a record for our app, into which we can upload its archive.

## Creating a Record for the App in iTunes Connect

When you eventually upload your app archive for submission, you will be able to see and manage it through the iTunes Connect platform. It offers a web-based dashboard for managing your applications, monitoring downloads and sales, signing contracts, setting up banking information, and obtaining finance reports.

In this section we will go through the steps required to create a record for our app in iTunes Connect, where we can later upload the app archive.

Your iOS Development Program account automatically gives you access to iTunes Connect. In a web browser navigate to https://itunesconnect.apple.com and login with your Apple ID. Once inside iTunes Connect, on the dashboard select **My Apps** (Figure 23-15).

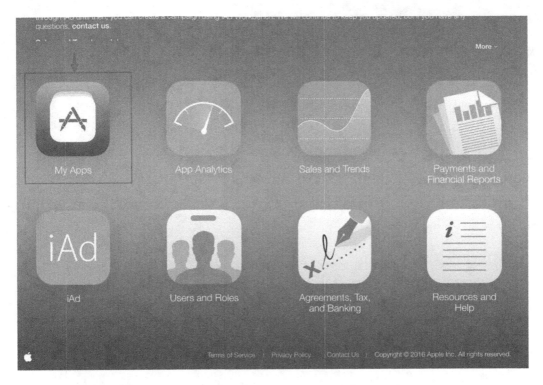

**Figure 23-15.** *The iTunes Connect dashboard*

If you have previously submitted applications for release, you will be able to see them here. Click the + button and select **New App** from the menu, in order to create a record for the app (Figure 23-16).

**Figure 23-16.** *Creating a new app record*

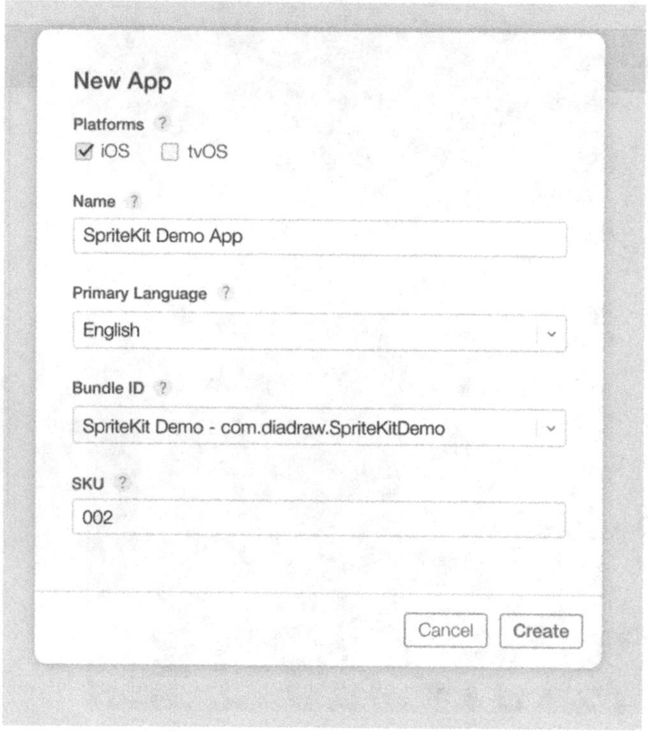

*Figure 23-17. Adding new app information*

In the dialog that appears you will need to fill in the following (Figure 23-17):

- **Platforms**. Specify the platforms, on which the app will run; iOS in our case.

- **Primary Language**. This is the language of the app's user interface, which in our case is English.

- **Bundle ID**. This requires the Bundle ID, of which we made a note earlier, when we provisioned the app.

- **SKU**. If your app corresponds to a physical product, this Stock Keeping Unit (SKU) serves as a link between the two. It is just for your reference and will not show up in the App Store.

After you fill in the required information, you will see the app shown on the applications dashboard. Click it to open the App Information page. Here you will see several tabs.

- **App Store**. On this tab you can edit the information you filled in to create the app record. There is also a bit more information you will be required to fill in: screenshots from the app, contact information, and so on. More on that later.

- **Features**. Allows you to manage features like in-app purchases and encryption. Here you can also generate promotion codes, with which users will be able to download your app for free—a really useful marketing tool.

- **TestFlight**. TestFlight is an Apple service that lets you create and manage a group of beta testers for your app and get useful feedback before you release it in the App Store.

- **Activity**. This is where you will find a log of all submitted versions of your app, see the app's current state in the review process, and read user reviews.

Go to the **App Store** tab, select **App Information** and fill in the required fields, such as the app's category (Figure 23-18).

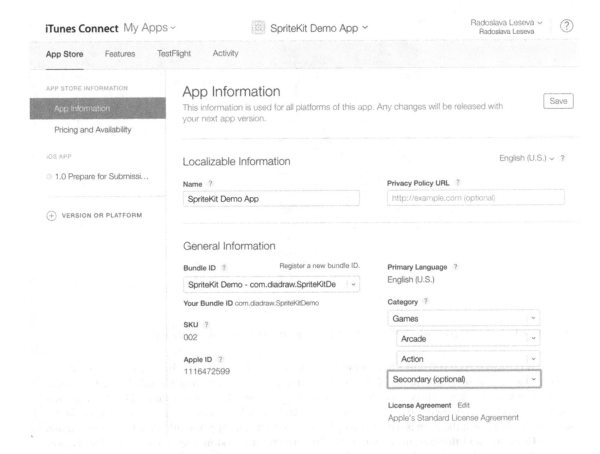

***Figure 23-18.*** *Application information page*

Still on the **App Store** tab, open the **Pricing and Availability** page to set up a price for the app and to select in which parts of the world it will be sold. Note that, unless you decide to distribute your app for free, you will need to sign a distribution contract on the Tax and Banking page in iTunes Connect.

Next, go to the **iOS APP ➤ 1.0 Prepare for Submission** page, in order to set up how your app's record will appear in the App Store. The first thing to notice is the **App Preview and Screenshots** area. Inside you need to add screenshots or videos from your app. Their sizes must match Apple's requirements, which you can find at https://goo.gl/Pv8srF.

iTunes lets you create separate screenshot galleries for each of the devices and screen sizes your app supports. Figure 23-19 shows the gallery of our demo app with a screenshot for the 4.7-inch iPhone 6 in it.

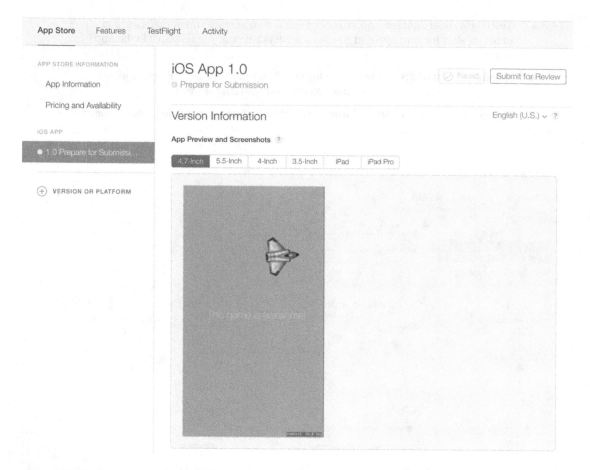

*Figure 23-19. Create a screenshot gallery for every device and screen size the app supports*

Below the gallery you will find a field, where you can put the description of the app as you want it to appear in the App Store. The contents of this description will be checked by Apple's staff during the review process. The same applies to the keywords you provide for your app. Here you are limited to 100 characters, including the comma separator, so focus only on the most relevant keywords that will help the users find your app. Further down the page is where you upload an icon for your app and fill in your seller information.

The **General App Information** section of the **Prepare for Submission** page allows you to leave a note for the app reviewer. Use it to make it easy for Apple's staff to test your app: provide instructions for testing and a demo account if your app requires a login.

The **Version Release** section lets you decide when your app will become visible in the App Store after it gets approved. You can choose to automatically release it once it has passed the review, to schedule a release on a specific date, or to do it manually.

When you have filled in all the required information, click the **Save** button at the top right-hand corner of the page. This completes the app's iTunes record and we can move on to uploading the app archive.

## Uploading the App to iTunes Connect

There are currently two options for uploading the app archive to iTunes Connect: you can do it directly from Xcode or you can use the Application Loader tool. In this section we will walk through the steps involved in uploading an app from Xcode and will add a few words about Application Loader at the end.

## Uploading an App Archive from Xcode

In Xcode select **Window ➤ Organizer** from the main menu. On the **Archives** tab inside Organizer select the app archive that we created earlier and click the **Upload to App Store...** button (Figure 23-20).

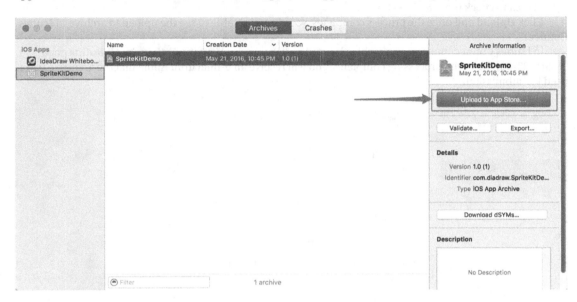

*Figure 23-20.* *Select an archive to upload*

Xcode starts a validation process, in which it checks your app's binary and entitlements. You can monitor its progress in the dialog that appears. On the same dialog there is an Upload button, which becomes enabled if no errors are found (Figure 23-21).

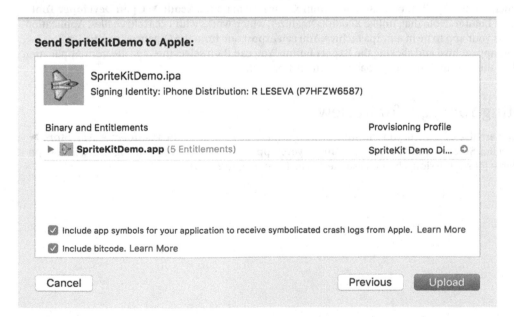

*Figure 23-21.* *App upload validation dialog*

At the bottom of the upload dialog there is a checkbox, titled **Include bitcode**. Selecting it will instruct Xcode to upload not only the binary for your app but also an intermediate LLVM presentation of the code. This can be used by Apple to automatically recompile your app for newly released hardware and save you time manually updating your app if a new iPhone with a better graphics chip comes out, for example, so it is a good idea to check the box.

Click **Upload** and once the process completes, you should be able to see the uploaded archive in iTunes Connect.

In iTunes Connect the new app archive is listed as "(Processing)" on the **Activity ➤ All Builds** page (Figure 23-22). Once the processing completes, you will receive an e-mail from Apple that the archive can be used for submission.

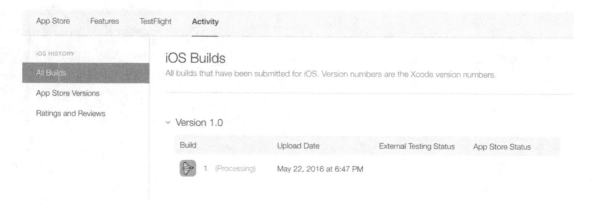

*Figure 23-22.* *The new app archive in iTunes Connect*

## Uploading the App Archive with Application Loader

You can launch Apple's Application Loader tool from Xcode's main menu: **Xcode ➤ Open Developer Tool ➤ Application Loader**. Note that, unlike Xcode's Organizer, which works with .xcarchive files, Application Loader expects your app to be in an .ipa archive. You can export one from the Organizer window by selecting your app archive and clicking the **Export** button. You can then select the .ipa file from Application Loader and let the tool analyze and upload it to iTunes Connect.

## Submitting Your App for Review

With your app archive uploaded, you can submit the app for review. Go to **iTunes Connect ➤ App Store ➤ iOS APP** and click **Select a build before you submit your app**. This will show you a dialog with a list of app builds available for submission—in our case there is just one (Figure 23-23).

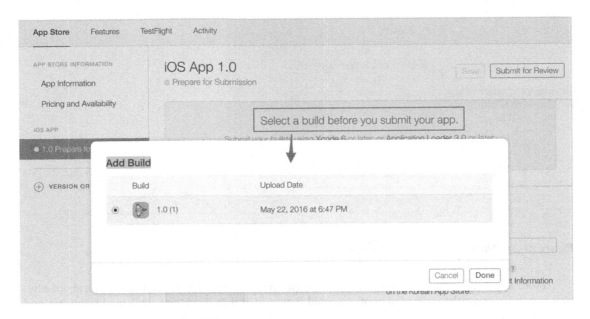

***Figure 23-23.*** *Selecting an app build for submission*

Select the build and click **Done** to dismiss the dialog. Back on the main page click **Save** and then **Submit for Review**. At this point iTunes Connect will let you know if any information about your app is missing and will prompt you to fill it in. When you are done, the label at the top left of the page, next to the yellow dot, should change from "Prepare for Submission" to "Waiting for Review."

---

■ **Note** When you upload your app to the App Store, it goes to an Apple server in the United States. This makes it a US export product, regardless of which part of the world you intend to distribute it, so it needs to be compliant with US export laws. In particular, if your app uses encryption, you will be required to provide documentation for it, such as an Encryption Registration approval. iTunes Connect's submission process has a step that asks you questions about cryptography. It is worth getting familiar with Apple's guidelines on the topic, which can be found in the section "Cryptography and U.S. Export Compliance" at `https://goo.gl/37TLra`.

---

The next step is crossing your fingers and waiting for Apple's verdict on your app.

Once your app is in the queue to be reviewed, the **App Store Versions** page shows you a log of the stages the app goes through during the review process, so you can monitor it (Figure 23-24).

***Figure 23-24.*** *Monitoring the review process*

If your app is rejected, do not worry. You will receive an e-mail from Apple with information about why your app did not pass the review and what you could change to fix that. Read the e-mail, modify the app, and submit it again.

If your app is approved, then congratulations, your first app is ready for publishing in the App Store!

# Summary

This chapter added one of the most important pieces to your iOS development workflow: publishing an app in Apple's App Store. It is a multistep process, which takes some time and is not necessarily intuitive. But you now know how to complete it or where to find out details about each step if any of Apple's requirements change.

With this chapter your training is over, my young Jedi. We look forward to seeing your apps in the App Store. Let us know when you publish your first one or have questions during any stage of the development process. We will be happy to hear from you on radoslava.leseva@diadraw.com and hristo.lesev@diadraw.com.

May the Swift source be with you!

# Index

© Radoslava Leseva Adams and Hristo Lesev 2016
R. L. Adams and H. Lesev, *Migrating to Swift from Flash and ActionScript*,
DOI 10.1007/978-1-4842-1666-8

# Get the eBook for only $5!

Why limit yourself?

Now you can take the weightless companion with you wherever you go and access your content on your PC, phone, tablet, or reader.

Since you've purchased this print book, we're happy to offer you the eBook in all 3 formats for just $5.

Convenient and fully searchable, the PDF version enables you to easily find and copy code—or perform examples by quickly toggling between instructions and applications. The MOBI format is ideal for your Kindle, while the ePUB can be utilized on a variety of mobile devices.

To learn more, go to www.apress.com/companion or contact support@apress.com.